Under Their Own Vine and Fig Tree

Under Their Own Vine and Fig Tree

The African-American

Church in the South

1865–1900

WILLIAM E. MONTGOMERY

Louisiana State University Press

Baton Rouge and London

Copyright © 1993 by Louisiana State University Press
All rights reserved
Manufactured in the United States of America
First printing
02 01 00 99 98 97 96 95 94 93   5 4 3 2 1

Designer: Laura Roubique Gleason
Typeface: Sabon
Typesetter: Graphic Composition, Inc.
Printer and binder: Thomson-Shore, Inc.

Library of Congress Cataloging-in-Publication Data

Montgomery, William E., 1943–
    Under their own vine and fig tree : The African-American church in
the South, 1865–1900 / William E. Montgomery.
      p.   cm.
    Includes index.
    ISBN 0-8071-1745-5
    1. Afro-American churches—Southern States.   2. Afro-Americans—
Southern States—Religion.   I. Title.
BR563.N4M66   1992
277.5'081'08996073—dc20   92-21041
                                                          CIP

But they shall sit every man under his vine and under his fig tree; and none shall make them afraid; for the mouth of the LORD of hosts hath spoken it.

Micah 4:4

Contents

Illustrations

Preface

For many generations, scant data and many misconceptions combined to obscure the view of African-American history. Blacks themselves treasured their own rich experiences, but preserving them for others to appreciate was problematic because of the oppressions of slavery and the effects of white racism. As a consequence, African-American history was largely locked into African-American culture. Around the turn of the twentieth century, black writers such as William E. B. Du Bois, George W. Williams, and Carter G. Woodson made prodigious efforts to unlock that history. They were truly the pioneers of African-American studies. White scholars, with only a few exceptions, were not much interested in the subject. In the last few decades, however, researchers of both races have investigated the history of African Americans, and their work has illuminated many heretofore hidden facets of the African-American experience.

The church has occupied a central position in the community through much of the span of African-American history. That has been true because religion has been a major force in the lives of African Americans, but the church has been far more than a religious institution. It has served many social, political, and economic functions as well. Over the years, scholars in many disciplines have been attracted to it as a field of study. Sociologists have made many valuable contributions to church studies; Du Bois and his Atlanta University students examined it at the turn of the century, Benjamin E. Mays and Joseph W. Nicholson wrote about it in the 1930s, and E. Franklin Frazier looked at it in the 1960s. Historians have been particularly drawn to the slaves' churches, and political scientists have analyzed the church as an element in black political activity. Despite all the attention the church has received, however, few scholars have yet focused on the extremely important role it played in the critical period between emancipation and the urban migration early in the twentieth century. Woodson covered the period in his *History of the Negro Church* (1921), but not adequately and not with the benefit of recent scholarship.

Those years were crucial to African Americans as they advanced from slavery to freedom. With unreliable friends and meager resources, they endeavored to realize the full promise of emancipation against a variety of obstacles and many implacable foes. As the freed people and those who had been unbound before the Civil War worked together to reorganize their society, the church served as a cornerstone. It not only provided instruction in spiritual matters but dealt in worldly business as well. It offered recreation and a measure of social security to its many adherents. Ministers served as political leaders while they acted as teachers and counselors. So vitally important was the church, in fact, that it is difficult to imagine how the black community in the post–Civil War South could have developed as well as it did without it.

The church helped to perpetuate the sense of group identity that had characterized slave and free black culture through the first half of the nineteenth century. The existence of a unique culture, derived from African as well as European sources, set African Americans apart from the whites among whom they lived. In slave religion, one finds many examples of African retentions blended with Christian beliefs and practices. Although the strength of African religious beliefs had weakened considerably by the late nineteenth century, they remained evident in many black churches long after the coming of freedom and continued to contribute to a unique African-American culture. This should not be taken to imply, however, anything like black solidarity or the existence of a homogeneous black society in the postemancipation South. Quite to the contrary, African-American society was complex and factious. Likewise, the church was not uniform; indeed, the concept of a monolithic black church that sometimes slips into our thinking and our discourse grossly oversimplifies historical reality, and one must take great care to avoid overlooking the essential character of this remarkable institution.

This book examines the black church following emancipation. It is based on a variety of primary and secondary sources, but it is, in the final analysis, exploratory rather than definitive. We still have much to learn about African-American life during that period and about the church's place in it. More research is necessary before the final word on the history of the African-American church can be written. The book is more a treatment of the church than of religion, although the two are obviously inseparable. It focuses on the South, although there is no strict definition here of what the South is. Chapter 1 provides some background by tracing the history of the church through slavery. Chapters 2 through 5 deal somewhat chronologically with the church's development and its social functions from emancipation through the end of the nineteenth century. Chapter 6 looks at the church largely as a religious institution. Chapter 7 describes the preachers and their evolving status as the black community matured. The Epilogue provides a recapitulation along with a brief look at some of the changes in African-American society early in the twentieth century that affected the church to such a degree as to make the continuation of the story the subject of a subsequent study.

I have benefited greatly from the aid of teachers, colleagues, librarians, and many other helpful people. I would have been lost without the assistance of the staffs of the Sunday School Publishing Board of the National Baptist Convention, U.S.A., Incorporated, American Baptist Historical Society, Virginia State Library, Georgia Department of Archives and History, New York Public Library, Trevor Arnett Library of Atlanta University, Morris Brown College Library, Union Theological Seminary Library, Howard University Library, University of Texas Library, Paul Quinn College Library, Amistad Research Center, Southwestern Theological Seminary, Baylor University Library, Historical Society of Pennsylvania, Library of Congress, and National Archives and Records Service. I am grateful to Barnes F. Lathrop who first guided me into this subject. And I am indebted to Howard Miller and the anonymous readers who criticized this book at various stages in its preparation and offered me their insight and many useful suggestions.

Under Their Own Vine and Fig Tree

1

The Beginnings

Any attempt to examine the black church in the post-emancipation era by describing it and explaining how it functioned must begin by identifying the cultural and historical framework upon which it rested. The roots of African-American culture branch out in many directions, and tracing them can be frustrating, but some understanding of the evolution of that culture helps in appreciating the value of institutions like the church. Culture gives people, or allows them to develop, a sense of themselves. It is the foundation of community awareness, a reflection of society's past as well as its present. It links the past and present and connects them both with the future. The myths, for example, that are enveloped in a people's culture, especially religious ones, serve that purpose. Churches keep religious myths alive and help maintain a sense of continuity from life through death. The institutions and religious beliefs that make up traditional churches also offer the people an explanation of life that can help them interact with the world around them.

Sometimes, though, the historical path of cultural evolution is broken. The historical record is lost. As a result, the myths and institutions of the present culture become disconnected from the past. People forget the exact origins of their culture, but they do not necessarily lose their distinctive cultural identity or their awareness of it. The historian Lawrence W. Levine has noted an important distinction between the origins of culture and people's consciousness of it: "We have only gradually come to recognize not merely the sheer complexity of the question of origins but also its irrelevancy for an understanding of consciousness." In other words, people can be acutely aware of their peculiar cultural traits even if they do not know their exact origins. They continue to transmit them from one generation to the next and carry them along in their migrations. This to some extent has been the case with African Americans. The manifestations of African-American culture are evident enough to have defined

1

an African-American nationality, but their origins are not so clear. The African slaves who were transported to North America during the seventeenth and eighteenth centuries left their homeland with their cultural—if not their material—possessions intact, but the explanation of what then became of their West African customs remains clouded to this day.[1]

The evolution of African-American culture has been the subject of a long and intriguing controversy among scholars. Some have contended that in the Africans' adjustment to the conditions they encountered in America they lost their cultural heritage. In the torturous passage from their homeland in Africa to the farms and plantations of the New World, the slaves became estranged from the people, places, and thoughts with which they were familiar and from which they drew an understanding of themselves and the world in which they lived. And if African culture somehow managed to survive the ravages of the slave ships, it was beaten out of the men and women who embodied it by their new masters. But others have argued that West African culture survived the hardships endured by its human hosts and established itself in various places in America despite the tremendous pressure on them to abandon their native beliefs and customs and to think and behave like European Americans. Drawn in such simple terms, the issue can never be resolved because both of the arguments are to some extent correct.[2]

1. Lawrence W. Levine, *Black Culture and Black Consciousness: Afro-American Folk Thought from Slavery to Freedom* (New York, 1977), 24.

2. In 1919, the historian-sociologist Robert Park wrote, "The Negro, when he landed in the United States, left behind him almost everything but his dark complexion and his tropical temperament" (Robert E. Park, "The Conflict and Fusion of Cultures with Special Reference to the Negro," *Journal of Negro History,* IV [April, 1919], 116). That statement set the tone for much of the early twentieth-century scholarship on the subject of African-American culture. Guy B. Johnson, *Folk Culture on St. Helena Island, South Carolina* (Chapel Hill, 1930), and E. Franklin Frazier, *The Negro Family in the United States* (Chicago, 1939), both contended that African culture did not survive in North America and that what has been called "African-American culture" is the African adaptation of Anglo-American customs and beliefs. For many years that view was stated or implied by most students of the African-American experience. Among the noteworthy early exceptions to that hypothesis were William E. B. Du Bois and Melville Herskovits. The former in such books as *The Souls of Black Folk: Essays and Sketches* (Chicago, 1909) and *The Negro Church: Report of a Social Study Made Under the Direction of Atlanta University* (Atlanta, 1903) and the latter in *The Myth of the Negro Past* (New York, 1958) and *The New World Negro* (Bloomington, 1966) argued that African culture did survive the disorienting and disintegrative effects of enslavement and that it was successfully transplanted in the Western Hemisphere, including North America. This thesis has found support in studies that have

Making general statements about the effects of enslavement and relocation in North America on African slaves is risky because their experiences varied widely according to the age and gender of the people, when they were transported, where they disembarked, and the condition of their employment at the time of their arrival in America. In at least one respect, however, they shared a common fate: unlike most European immigrants, they lost control over their lives when they were forcibly uprooted from their homeland and transported to the New World. They were compelled to live—and die—in an alien society that cared little for them as human beings or about their ways of life. The physical hardships they faced from their capture in Africa through their coffled march to coastal ports and finally the horrible passage in the cramped, stinking holds of slave ships took them to the limits of human endurance, and beyond, but was compounded by the psychological effects of being isolated from African friends, kinspeople, institutions, and spirits and by the destruction of the social relationships that had defined their lives. Those relationships, especially kinship ties, had served to extend their identity beyond the boundaries of the self and gave special meaning to day-to-day existence. Transportation to America disintegrated their world and made it chaotic. To the extent that they ultimately found alternatives to the people, institutions, and beliefs of Africa, they reintegrated themselves into a larger world of living and spiritual beings and consequently became more American than African.[3]

African slaves who were brought to the plantation islands of the Caribbean and to the Carolinas on the North American mainland in the seventeenth and eighteenth centuries entered societies that were controlled by Europeans but were culturally African. The external conditions of their lives were ruthlessly ordered by their masters, and although the work they were required to perform was similar to the work they had done in Africa, the regulations that governed it along with the circumstances that controlled their households, family relationships, and per-

emphasized Africans' skill in adapting both African and Western traditions to meet their needs. For example, see Eugene D. Genovese, *Roll, Jordan, Roll: The World the Slaves Made* (New York, 1972); Peter H. Wood, *Black Majority: Negroes in Colonial South Carolina from 1670 Through the Stono Rebellion* (New York, 1974); and Levine, *Black Culture and Black Consciousness.* Each of these historians has found numerous examples of "Africanisms" in black culture and even in some aspects of white culture.

3. Ira Berlin, "Time, Space, and the Evolution of Afro-American Society on British Mainland North America," *American Historical Review,* LXXXV (1980), 44–78.

sonal property were foreign to them. As they restructured the more internal or private aspects of their lives they drew heavily upon African beliefs and customs, which was easier to do as the African population grew larger and larger. Midway through the eighteenth century, one Barbados planter noted that African slaves were "very tenaciously addicted to the rites, ceremonies, and superstitions of their own countries, particularly in their plays, dances, music, marriages, and burials. And even such as are born here, cannot be entirely weaned from those customs." [4]

In regions like New England during the late seventeenth and early eighteenth centuries, where the population of West African descent was relatively small and highly diffused among whites, Africans established new relationships and developed a new culture using elements of the larger and dominant European society. That similarities between European-American and African-American cultures existed at some times and in certain places, however, should not be taken to mean that when Africans came to New England they quickly or easily wrapped themselves in a foreign ethos and adopted the worldview that was derived from it. On the contrary, a significant body of evidence suggests that Africans adhered to their traditional beliefs for as long as they could and then adapted some of them to the reality of their changing circumstances. They discarded customs and beliefs only when they became irrelevant or were forbidden by their new masters. Actually, their white masters did not permit them to become fully acculturated. And a steady if small influx of Africans to the region reinforced a variety of African traditions and folkways and kept them alive. [5]

Religious acculturation, as one facet of a more general African assimilation into Western society, began slowly in colonial America. Africans understood that life was governed by supernatural powers exercised by gods and spirits. Bad things happened to them because of the intrusion of spirits into the living world. It seems reasonable to assume that under the extreme stress of enslavement and the "middle passage" from Africa to America, Africans clung to native beliefs from which their lives and experiences had taken order and meaning. They must have searched their religious beliefs for an explanation of what was happening to them.

4. Charles Joyner, *Down by the Riverside: A South Carolina Slave Community* (Urbana, 1984), 143; Griffith Hughes, *The Natural History of Barbados* (London, 1750), 15.
5. Berlin, "Time, Space, and Evolution"; William D. Pierson, *Black Yankees: The Development of an Afro-American Subculture in Eighteenth-Century New England* (Amherst, 1988).

Moreover, Africans were not presented with a coherent alternative to their traditional beliefs that would explain their enslavement. During the seventeenth century slave owners in North America were averse to converting their slaves to Christianity. They were primarily interested in Africans as laborers and held to the belief, echoed by a Christian missionary, that "Baptism makes the Slaves proud and Undutifull." What was more, they feared that their slaves' Christianization might require their release from bondage. Whites had used the Africans' heathenism along with a race ideology to justify their enslavement. Christianity was one of the characteristics of white culture that in whites' eyes differentiated them from and elevated them above African slaves. Thus the Christianization of slaves would weaken the rationale for the slave system.[6]

Toward the end of the seventeenth century and into the eighteenth, whites began to instruct slaves in the tenets of Christianity. The government and the church, however, not the slave owners, assumed the initiative. English authorities instructed colonial governors to encourage the Christianization of slaves. The king's Council for Foreign Plantations undertook to determine how slaves "may be best invited to the Christian Faith." The Anglican church, through its Society for the Propagation of the Gospel in Foreign Parts (SPG), sent missionaries to work among the slaves of the colonies. The church also attempted to overcome planters' resistance to the Christianization of their slaves by assuring them that Christian chattels, as opposed to pagan ones, did not represent a threat to their labor system. Indeed, in 1727 the bishop of London proclaimed that it was the Christian's duty to convert all heathens, including slaves, and maintained that spiritual status had no bearing on the slave's condition as another man's property. In the South, these efforts to Christianize the slaves met continued opposition from slave owners. Francis Le Jau, an SPG missionary in South Carolina, was frustrated by whites who "wou'd not have me urge of Contributing to the Salvation, Instruction and human usage of Slaves and ffre Indians." "I recommend to the Masters that care be taken of their [slaves'] Souls, some submit to my Exhortation (few indeed) and all Generally seem to be more Concerned for loss of their Money." Slave owners claimed that religious instruction pro-

---

6. Geoffrey Parrinder, *West African Religion: A Study of the Beliefs and Practices of Akan, Ewe, Yoruba, Ibo, and Kindred Peoples* (New York, 1969), 13–59; Frank L. Klingberg, ed., *The Carolina Chronicle of Dr. Francis Le Jau* (Berkeley, 1956), 125. For a discussion of the rationale for slavery see David Brion Davis, *The Problem of Slavery in Western Culture* (Ithaca, 1966), 245–47, 345–46.

duced "untoward and haughty behavior" in their slaves, who "became lazy and proud, entertaining too high an opinion of themselves, and neglecting their daily labor." In the worst cases, slave owners believed, Christianity generated "rebellious behavior," and for that reason Le Jau required that adult slaves who wanted to be baptized first sign a statement declaring "in the presence of God and before this Congregation that you do not ask for holy baptism out of any design to free yourself from the Duty and Obedience that you owe to your Master while you live, but merely for the good of Your Soul." [7]

The slaves who did not accept Christianity made it unpleasant for the small number who did by taunting and ridiculing them. One Christian minister noted that when some slaves prepared for baptism "all other slaves do laugh at them." Le Jau commented on converted slaves who "prayd and read some part of their Bibles in the field and in their Quarters in the hearing of those who could not read, and took no notice of some Profanne men who laught at their Devotions." But the taunts of their peers were hard for them to bear and inhibited many from accepting the Christian faith. [8]

Other individuals and organizations also undertook the religious instruction of slaves. The Quakers not only instructed slaves in Christian principles but also questioned the validity of slavery. In New England, Puritan clergymen, including John Eliot and Cotton Mather, began teaching blacks the principles of Calvinist belief. The Puritans failed to convert many African slaves, however, primarily because the intellectual pitch of the church's theology required more education than most slaves possessed. It was not until the revivals of the 1730s and 1740s, known as the Great Awakening, that New England slaves were brought in any significant numbers into the Christian church. Jonathan Edwards noted that several blacks had been "born again" during the revivals he conducted in Northampton, Massachusetts, between 1734 and 1736. Blacks generally did not warm to the gospel of New England Puritanism, but they did

7. Marcus W. Jernigan, "Slavery and Conversion in the American Colonies," *American Historical Review*, XXI (1916), 504–11; Klingberg, ed., *Carolina Chronicle of Dr. Francis Le Jau*, 16, 50, 105. Peter Wood's assessment of the missionaries' efforts in South Carolina through the early eighteenth century is that they did not succeed in propagating the Christian gospel. See Wood, *Black Majority*, 143–44.

8. Frank J. Klingberg, *An Appraisal of the Negro in Colonial South Carolina: A Study in Americanization* (Washington, D.C., 1941), 24n; Klingberg, ed., *Carolina Chronicle of Dr. Francis Le Jau*, 174.

respond enthusiastically to the preaching of Methodist, Presbyterian, and later Baptist ministers who brought the Christian message to the masses of common folk, both black and white.[9]

By the end of the eighteenth century, the culture of at least some African Americans in the North was similar in many respects if not identical to that of Anglo Americans. In language, attitudes, and behavior they resembled neighboring whites. This was largely because of the spatial proximity between blacks and whites in that section of the country, the abolition of slavery and the end of direct importation of Africans, and blacks' learning that by adopting the dominant white culture they stood a better chance of advancing toward higher status and privilege than if they remained isolated by adhering to different customs. Accordingly, the religious practices of acculturated African Americans and European Americans in that region took on many similar forms. Interracial worship was common, and blacks began to subscribe to white religious beliefs and to participate in the rituals of white churches. And occasionally black preachers exhorted white congregations.[10]

Racially integrated worship services in the North, however, did not erase the long-standing prejudice of whites against blacks. Making slaves Christians did not require freeing them, nor did it transform blacks into the equals of whites; thus discrimination in seating, in participation in the various activities of the churches, and even in church membership, although not based solely on race, were attributes of northern churches that reflected the prevailing social relationship between whites and blacks and helped to define the separate and subordinate status assigned to blacks in biracial churches.[11]

Free and self-respecting blacks established separate black churches in the North at the close of the eighteenth century in response to the intolerable discrimination they encountered in biracial churches. Richard Allen, a lay Methodist exhorter and a former slave who converted to Christianity during the Great Awakening revivals of midcentury, led an effort

9. Jernigan, "Slavery and Conversion," 512–14; Pierson, *Black Yankees*, 49–73; Lorenzo J. Greene, *The Negro in Colonial New England* (New York, 1942), 257–89; Albert J. Raboteau, *Slave Religion: The "Invisible Institution" in the Antebellum South* (New York, 1978), 128–29.

10. Pierson, *Black Yankees*, 146–49.

11. Greene, *Negro in Colonial New England*, 257–89; Leon F. Litwack, *North of Slavery: The Negro in the Free States, 1790–1860* (Chicago, 1961), 187–213; Pierson, *Black Yankees*, 65–73.

to organize the first independent black church in the North. In 1786 he was preaching to black members of Philadelphia's St. George's Methodist Church. If being in demand as a preacher was any measure of success, Allen had good reason to take pride in his ministry. As he wrote in his autobiography, "It was not uncommon for me to preach from four to five times a day." As the number of black communicants in St. George's multiplied, though, whites became increasingly antagonistic toward them, first requiring that they sit together on one side of the sanctuary and then that they situate themselves along the walls. When the congregation moved into a new building, the blacks were isolated in a segregated section of the gallery. Allen deeply resented the treatment he and other blacks received. Preferring complete separation to discrimination in biracial gatherings, he sought permission from church officials to form an independent congregation, but they denied his request. The developing crisis in the relationship between blacks and whites in St. George's finally came to a head late in 1787. On a Sunday morning in November, a church official approached Allen and another black parishioner, Absalom Jones, who were seated together with other blacks in the white section of the gallery, and ordered them to move. They were on their knees in prayer at the time and asked to be allowed to finish, but the determined official would not wait and began dragging them from their places. Allen later recalled that when the prayer ended he and the other blacks left the building, adding that "they were no more plagued with us in the church." [12]

The withdrawal of Richard Allen and the other black members of St. George's was the first step toward the creation of an independent black congregation in Philadelphia. Other blacks in the city joined them in a nonsectarian organization called the Free African Society. Although the society had no denominational affiliation, it was a religious group, and most of its members desired some denominational association. The majority joined Jones in forming St. Thomas Protestant Episcopal Church, but Allen, who remained loyal to Methodist doctrine and organization, led the remainder in establishing Bethel African Methodist Episcopal Chapel. Allen thereby reestablished his connection with St. George's. He thought that by remaining organizationally apart from the white congregation, he could avoid the humiliation he and the others had experienced. But racial prejudice and discrimination continued to plague the relation-

---

12. Richard Allen, *The Life Experience and Gospel Labors of the Rt. Rev. Richard Allen* (2nd ed.; Nashville, 1960), 20–25.

ship, and Bethel Chapel and St. George's never grew close. Finally, in 1816, Allen secured legal recognition for Bethel Church as an independent entity. Then he joined with Daniel Coker, who had founded an African Methodist church in Baltimore, and with another congregation in New York to form the African Methodist Episcopal denomination. Coker became the group's first bishop, but he resigned immediately to become a missionary to Africa, and Allen became its official leader.[13]

The creation of Bethel Church in Philadelphia was a defiant act by assertive blacks who also were devoted to regular Methodist theology and polity. The church was African in name, in membership, and to the very significant extent that it promoted a sense of unity and worthiness among African Americans, whom whites typically shunned and degraded. This action, however, contributed little in any direct sense to the development of an African-American theology. Before he began preaching to blacks in Philadelphia, Allen had ministered to the spiritual needs of whites in Delaware and New Jersey. Neither he nor his followers had reason to renounce the religious beliefs that had become the premise for their understanding of life. Allen had discovered great personal comfort and a sense of transcendent purpose in Methodist beliefs. He adopted for use in his church the white Methodists' *Articles of Religion* and *General Rules of the Methodist Episcopal Church*. Methodist theology did not draw invidious distinctions between whites and blacks; on the contrary, it held that God was no respecter of man's earthly condition and that he loved the poor and the despised as much as the rich and privileged. Nor was discrimination intrinsic to the system of Methodist organization. Allen's complaint was with the worldly and ungodly prejudice of white people within the Methodist society.

Blacks responded similarly to racial discrimination in other cities, notably in New York, where black Methodists resented the onerous restrictions that whites placed on their religious activities. In 1800 the New York Conference instructed Francis Asbury to meet with some blacks who had been conducting separate services, to appoint whites as assistants to the black preachers, and to recommend to them that their gatherings not last so long into the evening. The conference allowed black ministers to preach, but only under certain restrictions and not as members of the regular itinerant ministry. At that time there were three black

13. Carol V. R. George, *Segregated Sabbaths: Richard Allen and the Emergence of Independent Black Churches, 1760–1840* (New York, 1973), 3–10.

preachers and one assistant. As the numbers of blacks in the churches increased, tension between the races mounted. Black members of the John Street Church objected most to the racial discrimination directed at them. In 1796 a committee of black members made up of Francis Jacobs, William Brown, Peter Williams, Abraham Thompson, and June Scott had petitioned Asbury asking that they be permitted to meet separately. He assented to such gatherings during regular worship hours. The black congregation, not satisfied with meeting in a converted cabinetmaker's shop and existing only as an adjunct of the John Street Church, then began planning a building of its own and independence from whites. When white church officials realized that the blacks were determined to separate from the rest of the congregation, they proposed that the two groups draft articles of agreement so that the church's affairs might remain under the direction of the general conference. The blacks agreed to these terms, and in 1801 the African Methodist Episcopal Church of New York, also called the African Chapel and later Zion Chapel, came into formal existence. The board of trustees was restricted to African Americans, but the agreement called for whites to manage the chapel's affairs. Specifically, a white elder was to oversee the church's spiritual affairs and administer the ordinances of baptism and holy communion. Blacks would control church property.

Some of the blacks, however, were not happy. Two of the three ministers, Abraham Thompson and June Scott, believed that they should receive more pay for their services than they were getting and criticized the white church. They talked about renouncing the agreement of 1801 and striking out entirely on their own, although neither one actually did so. In 1813 a former trustee of the African Chapel, Thomas Simpkins, whom the church had expelled for rebellious behavior, set out to establish another African Methodist congregation in New York. Several blacks became members of what they referred to as Asbury Chapel. That church's relationship with the white Methodist church was similar to that of the African Chapel.

A schism within the white church finally led to the creation of an African Methodist denomination out of the two African chapels. The issues were largely temporal and nonracial, including resentment on the part of the lay members over increasing clerical control of the church, disagreement over the disbursement of funds by the board of trustees in New York, and dissatisfaction with the presiding elder system. In July, 1820, William Stillwell, a minister and leader of the dissidents, announced that he and several hundred followers were leaving the church. The Stillwell secession affected black Methodists because since 1818 he had supervised the African and Asbury chapels. The blacks now could choose from several options: they could remain in the white-controlled organization, follow Stillwell, align themselves with Richard Allen's African Methodist Episcopal connection, or follow an independent path. Led by Thompson, Christopher Rush, and James Varick, they chose the latter, naming themselves the African Methodist Episcopal Zion Church. Varick, Thompson, and Leven Smith became elders, and Stillwellite ministers formally ordained them. A conference in 1821 brought together several other African churches and elected Varick the African Methodist Episcopal Zion connection's first superintendent.[14]

Meanwhile, slaves in the southern colonies had produced a culture that was far more distinguishable from Anglo-American culture than that of northern blacks. The large proportion of Africans in the southern population explains why that happened. The number of blacks in the South grew appreciably during the eighteenth century, in part because a large number of slaves were imported directly from Africa. Roughly 345,000 Africans came into the colonies during the period. This influx ensured the continued existence of a sizable semiacculturated slave population. The newly arrived Africans clung to their culture for as long as they could or for as long as African traditions were relevant to their living conditions, reinforcing the elements of African culture already present in America. Remnants of African ways endured well into the twentieth century among slaves in coastal South Carolina and Georgia, who were concentrated on large plantations, largely insulated from European cultural influences because there were so many of them and so few whites with whom they were in direct contact, and had little prospect of improving their situation by adopting the culture of the master class. Indeed, the migration of African Americans who escaped, were manumitted, or were sold to new masters elsewhere diffused surviving African traditions throughout the colonies. Africans recognized in their new environment many similarities to their homeland, allowing them to continue familiar ways of living. They thus built bridges between the past and the present over which they transported African traditions to America. They used many African skills and traditions such as methods of treating illness,

14. David H. Bradley, *A History of the A.M.E. Zion Church* (2 vols.; Nashville, 1956–70), I, 42–93; James W. Hood, *One Hundred Years of the African Methodist Episcopal Zion Church* (New York, 1895), 64.

fishing, basket weaving, crop cultivation, home design, and carpentry in their struggle for survival in the New World. They perpetuated familiar parables and trickster tales and continued old patterns for naming their offspring that also maintained continuity with their African past.[15]

Neither the spatial nor the cultural separation of Africans from whites was complete or uniform throughout the colonial South, however, nor was the distance between Africans and Europeans in the South generally as great as it was in the Caribbean basin and in certain other regions of Latin America, where many pure Africanisms were evident in the local culture. Some slaves lived and worked in the households of their masters, and most field hands were under the direction of white overseers. The contact between Africans and Europeans on southern plantations made at least some exchange of ideas, values, and institutions across racial and cultural lines unavoidable. Indeed, their masters sometimes exerted considerable pressure on newly arrived slaves to abandon African ways, particularly in names and language (important elements in personal identity), and the slaves' instinct to survive in an alien society caused them to adapt to that society's culture. But pressure to change their ways was counterbalanced by a natural desire to cling to native traditions and customs that still had meaning for them. The challenge for African slaves, and the crux of a crisis of identity for African-American people both then and later, involved balancing those two imperatives—selecting from both traditions to meet the demands of their masters and the requirements of their physical and psychic survival. The process of melding old and new ideas was a rational one. To suggest, as some scholars have, that African-American culture included meaningless and anachronistic Africanisms would be as simplistic and unwarranted as deducing from blacks' adoption of various aspects of the prevalent white culture that African mores had no permanent influence on their attitudes and behavior. Furthermore, to appreciate fully the character of African-American culture, one must train the eye to see its dynamic quality, to perceive the ongoing interplay between African and European traditions. Slave culture was an aggregation of evolving attitudes and behaviors that originated in West Africa and were then shaped and textured by the people's experience in America, developing ultimately into something neither altogether African

15. Philip D. Curtin, *The Atlantic Slave Trade: A Census* (Madison, 1969), 72–73, 145; Wood, *Black Majority,* 119–24, 167–91; Joyner, *Down by the Riverside,* 41–89, 113, 118–19, 122, 172–95; Sterling Stuckey, *Slave Culture: Nationalist Theory and the Foundations of Black America* (New York, 1987), 3–137.

nor completely Western. Scholars have called attention to the Africans' capacity to assimilate new values and behaviors and adapt to changing external circumstances. Most but not all of the Africanisms that constituted the slaves' cultural baggage either disappeared or lost their original meaning over time. Their influence as formative agents in the evolution of a new African-American culture is clear. European influences, exerted through the slaves' masters, also contributed substantially to the lifeways of slaves. Thus people who came to America from different societies in Africa with distinctive languages incorporated common constructions with the language patterns of their English masters to form a totally new, creole grammar that enabled them to communicate among themselves and forge new communities and social institutions. They took from African as well as European traditions to formulate a new, coherent religion that explained their origins, their present oppression, and their ultimate salvation.[16]

The experience of enslavement and transportation to America shattered the Africans' vision of the world and led eventually to the formulation of a new one. West African religions integrated the spiritual and the living worlds. The sharp divisions between heavenly and worldly domains, between good and evil, that were common in Western religious thought were unknown to West African people. Furthermore, faith systems were inseparable from the homeland and from ancestors. Holy places and holy objects were used to invoke the power of the deities. Gods, spirits, and ancestors exercised the pervasive force of the sacred cosmos, and through prayer or sacrifice deities were induced to act on behalf of living persons. Deceased but remembered ancestors represented a connection between the spiritual and living worlds. These living dead

---

16. For broad developmental analyses that suggest a melding of African and European cultures see Berlin, "Time, Space, and Evolution," 47–78; and Levine, *Black Culture and Black Consciousness*, 3–135. Wood, *Black Majority*, 119–24, 170–73, 189, and Joyner, *Down by the Riverside*, 196–224, contain richly detailed pictures of creole culture among African Americans in South Carolina from the eighteenth century through the early nineteenth century. Pierson, *Black Yankees*, explores the evolution of African-American culture in New England. Mechal Sobel, in *The World They Made Together: Black and White Values in Eighteenth-Century Virginia* (Princeton, 1987), develops the idea that African traditions had a substantial influence on the development of Anglo culture. Geoffrey Parrinder observed among West Africans "little reluctance to accept new gods or cults." See his *West African Religion*, 11. Melville Herskovits fell into the trap of overstating the survival of Africanisms. See his *Myth of the Negro Past* and *New World Negro*. Sterling Stuckey makes a strong and effective argument for the survival of Africanisms in *Slave Culture*.

possessed the attributes of both spirits and living people. They lived in
the memories of those who had known them and were part of the present,
but they were physically dead and buried and inexorably slipped into the
past in the Africans' concept of time. As the living dead passed from the
now into the hereafter, they became transformed into spirits infused with
supernatural powers and in that form returned periodically to influence
the lives of the living. In their metamorphosis, the ancestors not only affirmed each living person's ultimate destiny but symbolized the eternal
circle of life. The effect of the Africans' enslavement and removal from
their native lands caused the sacred cosmos to disintegrate by separating
them from their ancestors and the spirit world. Disassociated from holy
people and sacred places and objects in Africa, they were unable to interact with the spirit world as they used to. Their prayers lost efficacy. The
separation damaged the linkages between them as living persons and divine spirits. The Africans' world became incoherent.[17]

The incongruity between African beliefs that incorporated the homeland, gods, and ancestor spirits on one hand and the reality of life in
North America on the other produced stress and anxiety in newly transported slaves. Olaudah Equiano, an African slave who was transported
to America in the 1750s, at first thought the Englishmen he saw were
spirits who were going to kill and eat him. His only basis for evaluating
his surroundings was his African understanding of the world, and much
of that was irrelevant to the new world he was entering. "As every object
was new to me, every thing I saw filled me with surprise." The degree of
tension and stress produced by such dissonance varies from situation to
situation. It is the natural outcome of living and learning that mature and
well-adjusted individuals usually learn to cope with, but if the conflict
involves primary beliefs, the resulting tension can lead to acute suffering.
Because of the great importance of religious beliefs in providing Africans
with a sense of personal worth and security and the glaring inconsistency
between those beliefs and the Africans' new surroundings, they suffered
acute stress and anxiety. When Equiano found himself alone on a Virginia farm, with no other person he could talk to or understand, he be-

---

17. Parrinder, *West African Religion*, 60–114; John S. Mbiti, *African Religions and Philosophies* (New York, 1969), chap. 3; Melville Herskovits, *Dahomey, an Ancient West African Kingdom* (2 vols.; New York, 1938), II, 194–238; Leonard E. Barrett, *Soul-Force: African Heritage in Afro-American Religion* (Garden City, N.Y., 1974), 15–39.

came depressed. "In this state I was constantly grieving and pining, and wishing for death rather than anything else." [18]

Such tension induces behavior that is intended to restore consistency or harmony between belief and reality. The greater the tension and resulting stress, the greater is the compulsion for compensatory behavior. Among African slaves the drive to restore consonance between belief and reality was compelling because if they succeeded in reestablishing coherence to their belief system they could reintegrate themselves with the sacred world and once again enjoy the status and security that their African religions had accorded them.

Generations of historians have wrestled with the question of how slaves accomplished that reconciliation. It is probably an insoluble problem because of the scarcity of information about Africans' psychological responses to enslavement, but conjecture can do no harm and might provide some insights. The slaves could have responded by maintaining their traditional faith, but to do that would have required either denying the reality of their existence in America or returning to their ancestral homeland. The evidence does not suggest that slaves engaged in denial, and obviously they were not permitted to go back to Africa, although some, believing or hoping that after death they would return to their homes, did attempt suicide. Another response could have been to abandon their beliefs altogether and adopt a new set of understandings that conformed to the concrete circumstances of their lives and to the beliefs of their captors—somewhat the way hostages or concentration camp inmates do. Some scholars have suggested that, and there is evidence to support them. "In America," E. Franklin Frazier wrote, "the Negroes plunged into an alien civilization in which whatever remained of their religious myths and cults had no meaning whatever." Because their native beliefs were irrelevant, they discarded them and adopted the Christian religion of the dominant whites around them. Frazier concluded that "from the available evidence it is impossible to establish any continuity between African religious practices and the Negro church in the United States." Olaudah Equiano eventually learned to communicate in English and lost much of

18. The premise for this hypothesis and the following discussion is the theory of cognitive dissonance posited by Leon Festinger in *A Theory of Cognitive Dissonance* (Palo Alto, 1957). Olaudah Equiano, *The Interesting Narrative of the Life of Olaudah Equiano, or Gustavus Vassa, the African* (4th ed.; Dublin, 1791), 46, 50, 55, 59.

his fear of whites: "I no longer looked upon them as spirits, but as men superior to us; and therefore I had the stronger desire to resemble them; to imbibe their spirit, and imitate their manners." Stanley Elkins, in his examination of the relationship between master and slave, emphasized the absolute power of life and death that masters held over slaves. Those conditions, Elkins claimed, caused slaves to develop a fawning, servile personality. To explain the development of a slave personality type known as "Sambo," he drew an analogy to World War II Nazi concentration camp prisoners. The victims of such extreme repression often adopt the values of their captors as a strategy for survival, drawing as close to them as they can so as to resolve conflicts and lessen the likelihood that their captors will harm them. Elkins likened the slave plantation to a concentration camp.[19]

The suggestion that slaves reconciled the conflict between their African beliefs and an American existence by adopting the religion of their white captors is problematic from the standpoint of motive, and it has crumbled under the weight of a growing body of evidence pointing to a powerful and enduring African influence on their religion. Demoralized hostages or prisoners feel alienated from normal support groups and are totally dependent on their captors; no other individuals or groups can aid in their survival. Consequently, they identify with their captors in order to survive. An analogy involving African slaves must assume the total destruction of African social cohesion and the absence of support groups. Scholars who, like Frazier and Elkins, have argued that hypothesis assumed that the slaves had no common worldview and spoke no common language; therefore, they could not have agreed on values or religious beliefs and without a common language could not have disseminated values or beliefs or given each other strength or comfort. Africans, according to that view, were drawn into the white world in which their masters provided them with a Christian framework for interpreting their lives, redefining the sacred world, and establishing a sense of community. Recent studies, however, clearly demonstrate that although their ties to tra-

19. Jernigan, "Slavery and Conversion," 504–27; William D. Pierson, "White Cannibals, Black Martyrs: Fear, Depression, and Religious Faith as Causes of Suicide Among New Slaves," *Journal of Negro History,* LXII (1977), 147–59; Frazier, *Negro Church in America,* 6; Equiano, *Interesting Narrative,* 86; Stanley M. Elkins, *Slavery: A Problem in American Institutional and Intellectual Life* (3rd ed.; Chicago, 1976), 81–139; Bruno Bettelheim, "Individual and Mass Behavior in Extreme Situations," *Journal of Abnormal and Social Psychology,* XXXVIII (1943), 417–52.

ditional African communities were effectively broken by their forced relocation to America, slaves quickly reestablished social networks among themselves and built new communities on the basis of common African cultural patterns with relatively little borrowing from whites. The slaves' own institutions took the place of African communities and institutions. The various ethnic identities of West, Southwest, and Central Africa steadily gave way to African-American solidarity in the New World. Slaves reshaped native ideas such as kinship, burial rites, the naming of offspring, crop cultivation, diet and food preparation, and language to fit the requirements of their new environment. African culture proved to be so resilient that slaves even transmitted many of their ideas and customs to their white masters. Thus there was no compelling reason for them to abandon their native beliefs and adopt wholesale the culture of their captors.[20]

The argument that Africans simply slipped into the Christian faith of their plantation masters is further weakened by the fact that even in their oppressed condition, they generally did not experience the pressure or persuasive appeal that would draw them to the religious beliefs of an alien and hostile society. Until the late eighteenth century, whites showed scant interest in the slaves' religious activities. Whereas many blacks in the northern colonies could hope for higher status through identification with white society and, with the help of favorable demographic factors, sometimes achieved relatively high status, southern slaves were virtually excluded from the society that bore the foreign religious ideology, valued it, took meaning from it, and rewarded behavior based on it.[21]

A more plausible explanation of how Africans restored consonance to their beliefs and coherence to their world is that in some forms of Protestant Christianity they recognized beliefs that were similar to their own. For example, the Christian belief in an omniscient and omnipotent God had its counterpart in the supreme god of West African religions. Africans, like most Protestant Christians, conceived of God as the origin and the sustenance of being. He was spiritual rather than physical, but a per-

---

20. Frazier, *Negro Church in America*, 1–5; Elkins, *Slavery*, 98–103; Joyner, *Down by the Riverside*, 96, 208; Levine, *Black Culture and Black Consciousness*, 3–135; Wood, *Black Majority*, 167–91; Stuckey, *Slave Culture*, 3–97; and Sobel, *World They Made Together*, 15–168.

21. Donald G. Mathews, *Religion in the Old South* (Chicago, 1977), 188–89, 192; Wood, *Black Majority*, 133–36; John B. Boles, *Black Southerners, 1619–1869* (Lexington, Ky., 1983), 154–55.

son rather than an abstract power. He was loving, merciful, and just. And he was simultaneously separate from the living world (being a deity) and directly involved in it. Not only did Africans who were exposed to Christianity notice the similarities, but whites sometimes saw them from the other side of the cultural gulf as well. An Anglican missionary, Francis Varnod, reported religious ideas among the non-Christian slaves that were very much like his own: "I find that some of our negro-pagans have a notion of God and of a Devil, and dismal apprehensions of apparitions. Of a God that disposes absolutely to all things." Asking a non-Christian woman how she came to be a slave, Varnod learned from her that "God would have it so and she could not help it." They also believed in a Devil, "who leads them to do mischief, and betrays them, whereby they are found out by their masters and punished." Other elements that were common to both West African and European-American Protestant religions were a clergy that mediated between living people and deities and sacred music and singing. Such similarities allowed Africans to ease from one belief system into another, not by abandoning one faith completely and adopting the other but by integrating credible features of Protestant Christianity with their own traditional beliefs and their understanding of reality. This was not difficult for them to do because their religions were remarkably flexible. Geoffrey Parrinder has remarked that in traditional West African religions "there is little reluctance to accept new gods or cults, no narrow doctrinal walls, or jealous gods that forbid the addition of new beliefs, provided that the traditional deities are not attacked." A new religion, then, was formulated by melding African and European-American religious beliefs gradually and creatively into a unique and genuine African-American religious system.[22]

Although the Anglican church catechized slaves during the colonial period, it did not recruit them aggressively. And that was the key to the church's failure to convey Christian beliefs to significant numbers of southern slaves. Even if it had been more energetic in its efforts, however, it may not have been significantly more successful because the atmosphere in Anglican congregations was not very appealing to Africans. Slaves were admitted to Anglican services, but the church in both subtle and direct ways reminded them of their subordinate status. It converted

22. Mechal Sobel, *Trabelin' On: The Slave Journey to an Afro-Baptist Faith* (Westport, 1979), 99–135; Raboteau, *Slave Religion*, 43–92, 126–27; Boles, *Black Southerners*, 155–57; Joyner, *Down by the Riverside*, 141–71; Klingberg, *Appraisal of the Negro in Colonial South Carolina*, 56; Parrinder, *West African Religion*, 11, 13–14, 72–78.

heathens by catechism, that is, by teaching principles by a question-and-answer method, but it offered no great reward for responding correctly. It was never made clear to the slaves how the presence of God's spirit would change their lives in meaningful ways. Thus Anglicanism's hierarchical organization, which gave power and status to the elite, along with its formalized, intellectual, and somnolent service and doctrine left slaves unmoved.[23]

The Great Awakening evangelicalism, however, surging through the South during the late eighteenth and early nineteenth centuries, attracted significant numbers of slaves to Christian theology and profoundly influenced their religious views. Evangelical ministers, much more than their Anglican counterparts, actively sought out Africans as church members along with whites. "O . . . my business is plain," wrote Richard Fuller, a Baptist minister, after preaching to a group of blacks in South Carolina, "a humble preacher among the poor & destitute—for this only have I voice, mind, or heart." The style of evangelical preaching, especially that of the Methodists, as well as the gospel itself, attracted large numbers of slaves, especially in the Upper South. During revivals in Virginia and North Carolina, for instance, the evangelical minister Devereaux Jarratt recorded that hundreds of Africans were in attendance, "with tears streaming down their black cheeks." By 1800, only a few years after the southern revivals began, there were twelve thousand to fifteen thousand black Methodists and perhaps nearly twenty thousand Baptists in the South.[24]

The central concept in evangelical doctrine, which infused Christianity with a relevance to slaves not conveyed through Anglican doctrine, was the idea that a radical, ego-shattering conversion experience was necessary to gain entry into Heaven. Through a process beginning with a humbling awareness of their utter worthlessness and leading to a spiritual rebirth as redeemed Christians people could be made acceptable to God. In presenting that simple precept to audiences, evangelical ministers appealed to people's deepest feelings of guilt, fear, and joy. The main purpose of the sermon was to awaken individuals to their sinfulness and their

---

23. Mathews, *Religion in the Old South,* 188–89, 192.

24. *Ibid.,* 66, 193; Joseph B. Earnest, *The Religious Development of the Negro in Virginia* (Charlottesville, 1914), 48; Du Bois, *Negro Church,* 19–20; William Warren Sweet, *The Story of Religion in America* (New York, 1930), 420–21; Luther P. Jackson, "Religious Development of the Negro in Virginia from 1760 to 1860," *Journal of Negro History,* XVI (1931), 168–239.

helplessness to overcome it. Only through God's love and forgiveness, offered by way of Christ's sacrifice on the cross, could the sinner escape the torments of Hell and be redeemed. And only by accepting one's sinfulness, humbling oneself before God, and being reborn as a Christian dedicated to a life lived according to God's will could one enter the Christian brotherhood, a community of true believers set apart and protected from the wickedness of the world.[25]

Such an exhilarating prospect, tendered in the boisterous tones and animated style that typified evangelical preaching, generated a powerful appeal that had its greatest impact on unlettered audiences like slaves. They responded eagerly to the evangelical message, both to its style and to its assertion that through the conversion experience they would be lifted to the select status of Christian. It fostered a feeling of self-worth that transcended the degradation of their social condition; it elevated them to the same status in the eyes of God as the richest, most powerful and genteel whites. God cared for them as much as he cared for anyone, and they could feel his love. The importance of the concept of conversion to oppressed and degraded blacks, as Donald G. Mathews has written, was that to "be important to God, one did not have to possess wit, learning, wealth, family connections, or even a white skin."[26]

The evangelicals' egalitarian doctrine carried with it revolutionary social implications that slaves as well as many lower-class whites found alluring. The power of the conversion experience pierced all conventional social barriers, rendering privilege irrelevant and elevating all of God's creatures to the same condition. It did not matter what one's station in life was, what rituals one practiced, or the status of one's skills of logical reasoning. Only the experience of being convicted of sin and a complete surrender to God's redeeming power separated God's blessed children from Satan's fodder. Evangelical Christians set about to restructure society so as to make it reflect God's kingdom as much as possible. Underclass believers looked forward to a higher status than they held when the elite dominated earthly society and seemed to be favored by God as well. The social and political ramifications of evangelical doctrine reverberated through the South during the late eighteenth and early nineteenth centuries. The inference that blacks drew from the gospel was their liberation from slavery. As Mathews has written, "No matter how disguised or de-

25. Mathews, *Religion in the Old South*, 1–38.
26. *Ibid.*, 35.

based, Christianity contains a message which liberates those who are bound, frees those who are oppressed, and promises to revolutionize social ranking in God's kingdom: the 'last shall be first, and the first last' (Matt. 20:16)." The meek would inherit the earth if white slave owners lived according to the moral principle of treating everyone with Christian love, kindness, and respect. Slavery was against God's wishes because it was built on brutality and degradation, and though despised and oppressed by whites, slaves, as God's people, would ultimately be vindicated by emancipation. And if liberation did not come in this lifetime, it surely would come on Judgment Day.[27]

The communalism of evangelical Christianity was another powerful attraction to slaves. In congregations, class meetings, and missions, converted Christians bonded together in a community, caring for and helping each other live according to God's will through discipline and prayer. The individual Christian was not expected to stand alone against the temptations of sin. After promoting conversion, the evangelical sermon taught correct behavior. Members of the congregation assisted one another in their attempt to live righteous lives. Interaction with other Christians in congregations and the love and support that existed within the evangelical communities established relationships between people that were comforting in times of stress. Evangelicalism forged bonds between the people and God that elevated all members of the community, regardless of race, status, or any other worldly distinction, above those—including the slaves' white masters—who languished outside. The Christian communities appealed greatly to slaves, who knew nothing but humiliation and physical suffering in the world.[28]

The racial composition of congregations reflected evangelical Christianity's egalitarianism. Whites and blacks worshiped together, testified about their conversion experiences, and enjoyed the communion of Christian brethren. Even within the ministry, blacks enjoyed more privilege and respect than the conventional social order allowed, particularly in Baptist churches, which permitted slaves to preach to white and black audiences. Preaching required a "gift," meaning "popular talents, Great Piety, & a strong voice." It required neither formal education nor mastery

---

27. Rhys Isaac, *The Transformation of Virginia, 1740–1790* (Chapel Hill, 1982); Timothy Smith, "Slavery and Theology: The Emergence of Black Christian Consciousness in Nineteenth Century America," *Church History,* XLI (1972), 497–512; and Mathews, *Religion in the Old South,* 194–95.

28. Mathews, *Religion in the Old South,* 36–37, 41.

of the Scriptures. An untutored black person might just as well mount the pulpit as an educated white person. Blacks appreciated the relative absence of discrimination and were especially responsive to the preaching of other blacks. Great Awakening evangelicalism appealed strongly to African Americans because of its exciting doctrines and emotional preaching, its offer of high status and community identity, and its acceptance of black preachers.[29]

Beyond its intrinsic appeal, evangelical Christianity was malleable, and slaves modified it to accommodate their traditional West African beliefs and practices. The resulting religious forms were superficially Protestant Christian but substantively African in many aspects. For instance, the Protestant concept of spiritual conversion or "rebirth in Christ," the symbolic use of water in baptism, and the emphasis on experiential rather than intellectual routes to salvation were features of European-American evangelical religion through which slaves maintained related African traditions such as initiation rites, water ceremonies, and spirit possession. The slaves grafted onto Protestant Christianity's monotheistic system—but one that still recognized multiple manifestations of God in the forms of Christ and the Holy Spirit—their own pantheon of gods and spirits, including venerated ancestors. They altered Protestantism's dogma of original sin so that it became indistinguishable from the more life-affirming, even secular, notion of justice that characterized the West African moral structure. African religions did not incorporate the concept of original sin that doomed unrepentant man to damnation. Man's transgressions were acts of injustice that were punishable, but not by the condemnation of the immortal soul. African-American slave religion incorporated the idea of original sin, but Christian slaves were less concerned with it than whites were. African-American Christian worship was more notable for its dancing, singing, and hand-clapping, all of which were conspicuous elements in West African religion and were easily fitted into the pattern of Protestant evangelical worship, which was itself often noisy, spontaneous, and exuberant. Eugene Genovese has written of the deep irony in African-American slave religion: "The slaves reshaped the Christianity they had embraced; they conquered the religion of those who had conquered them."[30]

29. Boles, *Black Southerners*, 155–57; Isaac, *Transformation of Virginia*, 171–73; Mathews, *Religion in the Old South*, 58.

30. Raboteau, *Slave Religion*, 10–11, 13, 17, 19, 20, 27–28, 30–31, 35–37, 44–45, 54, 57–58, 63–65, 68–74; Mathews, *Religion in the Old South*, 190–91; Stuckey, *Slave Culture*, 3–97; Genovese, *Roll, Jordan, Roll*, 212.

In the Protestant evangelical culture that slaves entered, the seeds of African beliefs in deities took deep root and bloomed brilliantly. What appeared to be a Christian tenet was in many instances an African belief encased in Christianity. According to Sterling Stuckey, who has written insightfully about the transplantation of African religious traditions in America, "For the slave convert to Christianity there was as much concern about relating to the ancestors as to a Christian God." African-American conversion experience illustrates the interplay between elements from different but remarkably similar religious traditions within the context of slave worship. Spirit possession existed in both Christian and African religions. In the evangelical Christian tradition, sinners became Christians when the spirit of God took possession of their bodies as well as their souls. The experience was dramatic and was often manifested in hand-clapping, shouting praises to God, and feelings of profound ecstasy. Converts heard God's voice and were keenly aware of the presence of his spirit. The effects of the experience were positive and uplifting. Possession held a prominent place in West African religious traditions in which spirits were believed to inhabit the living person's body. Spirits entered the living body and caused the person to fall to the ground in fits or to leap and shout. West African spirit possession was associated with religious ceremonies and often occurred in conjunction with dances in which the people clapped their hands, leaped into the air, and moved together in a circular, tornadolike, counterclockwise motion. The circle symbolized the eternal cycle of birth, death, and reincarnation, and the omnipresent circular movements and configurations of traditional African ceremonies were metaphors for the African understanding of life. The slaves' conversion experience showed similarities to both conventional Protestant Christian conversion and African spirit possession. It occurred within the context of Christian theology, and it was an intense experience, with participants passing into altered states of consciousness, shouting and clapping, and exhibiting convulsive and ecstatic behavior. The European traveler Fredrika Bremer witnessed a conversion experience among black Methodists in New Orleans in the 1850s. The setting was a class meeting, and the words she heard were standard Christianity: "Hold fast by Christ! He is the Lord! He is the mighty one! He will help!" But the physical responses were African. In response to exhorters, the communicants shouted and cried out and began to leap like corks flying out of bottles. "And as they leaped, they twisted their bodies round in a sort of corkscrew fashion, and were evidently in a state of convulsion." Amid the excitement, an exhorter approached one woman and began to preach to her and she to him, "with evident pleasure." She became so agitated that she had to be restrained; then she rose to her feet and walked up and down the church, shouting "Hallelujah!" Eventually, she kneeled down in front of the altar. When Bremer asked someone what had happened to the woman, she was told simply, "converted." "The tornado gradually subsided in the church, shrieking and leaping, admonishing and preaching, all became hushed." Slaves viewed uncontrolled body action as a sign of spirit possession, and the more violent the action the more evident was the presence of the Holy Spirit. Because the rite of spiritual conversion occurred in much the same way among poor, uneducated whites, it might be thought of as a class rather than an ethnic characteristic. But African-American religious traditions were the outgrowth of the people's unique experiences. The behavior of people who were far more uniformly oppressed than were whites, who were denied most other means of expressing great elation and other strong emotions, and who had a tradition of motor responses to emotional stimulation in the excitement of evangelical preaching was a cultural characteristic, a part of the peoplehood of African-American slaves.[31]

Contemporary whites denigrated such behavior, asserting that it was primitive and that it had no place in Christian worship. A white man in the Sea Island district of Georgia told the northern traveler Frederick Law Olmsted that he had attempted to curb the slaves' excitement because "there was not the slightest element of religious sentiment in it." In a letter to Lewis Tappan, William G. Kephart of the American Missionary Association (AMA) described Alabama blacks as having "an excessive effervescence of emotional feelings with very little intelligent understanding of even the most elementary principles of the gospel." It was a comment repeated over and over by whites who regarded those characteristics of slave religion as at best corruptions of standard Christian principles and at worst evidence of the primitiveness, sensuousness, and superstition of black people.[32]

31. Stuckey, *Slave Culture*, 53–57, 254; Mathews, *Religion in the Old South*, 190–92; Adolph B. Benson, ed., *America of the Fifties: Letters of Fredrika Bremer* (New York, 1924), 275–78; Dickson D. Bruce, *And They All Sang Hallelujah: Plain-Folk Camp-Meeting Religion, 1800–1845* (Knoxville, 1974), 73–75, 86, 89; Parrinder, *West African Religion*, 67, 78, 80–81.

32. Frederick Law Olmsted, *Journeys and Explorations in the Cotton Kingdom: A Traveler's Observations on Cotton and Slavery in the American Slave States* (2 vols.; London, 1861), I, 259; W. G. Kephart to Lewis Tappan, May 9, 1864, in American Missionary

It is tempting to dismiss such remarks as the rantings of white racists who did not appreciate the cultural significance of what they witnessed in slave worship. To a large extent such an assessment is justified. Most were racists, and they did not appreciate the nature of slave culture. They believed that slave worship was a mindless mania or the childlike exuberance of an inferior race of people who knew little of Christian faith. But whites saw what many modern scholars have failed to discern—that below its surface slave religion differed significantly from the Christianity with which whites were familiar. Many whites understood it for precisely what it was, a Christian container holding a distinctly African substance. Bremer interpreted the worship service in New Orleans exactly right, as "the element of true African worship" embedded in African-American Christianity. "The result," Olmsted reported of Christianity's influence on African-American religion, "in the majority of cases has been merely to furnish a delusive clothing of Christian forms and phrases, to the original vague superstition of the African savage." Eugene Genovese has found, after examining numerous private letters and memoirs, that many whites "never doubted that their slaves' Christianity contained a good dose of African belief." The slaves' Christianity included African traditions of shouting and dancing as well as the belief that through the mediation of ancestors, or "the spirit," one interacted with God and drew closer to Heaven.[33]

In form as well as content, slave worship varied according to locality; yet the diffusion of African traditions from coastal regions to the interior and the transmission of those traditions from older to younger generations made them virtually universal features of slave church services and helped to define African-American slave worship. Even though many of the characteristics of slave worship were derived from the same sources as white religion, a distinctively African-American religion existed, based on the African religious traditions that slaves carefully nurtured within the environment of Protestant Christianity. Those traditions in conjunction with the slaves' interpretation of Christian doctrine distinguished their worship from that of whites.[34]

Association Archives, Amistad Research Center, Tulane University (hereinafter cited as AMA Archives).

33. Frederick Law Olmsted, *A Journey in the Back Country in the Winter of 1853–4* (2 vols.; New York, 1907), I, 116; Genovese, *Roll, Jordan, Roll*, 216.

34. Stuckey, *Slave Culture*, 3–97.

Mechal Sobel has outlined some of the African beliefs that slaves incorporated into their African-American ideology. One concerns the spiritual death and rebirth of the sinner.

> The white and black visions of death and rebirth share some elements but are nevertheless significantly different. In both, the individual begins in a low state and is saved by a cry for mercy to see God in His Glory and to be reborn. The black visions have four unique aspects; (1) the concept of the two selves, the "little me" in the "big me" permeating the whole vision structure; (2) the detailed journey or travels of the soul from Hell to Heaven; (3) the appearance of a little (white) man as a guide on this journey; and (4) the visual description of Heaven and God, with its emphasis on whiteness. In each case, these differences between white and black visions can be attributed to an African ethos which was an integral part of the black's Christian cosmos.

The conversion experiences described by former slaves indicate not only the commonness of those features that Sobel describes but also that they were largely consistent across denominational lines.[35]

Shouting and dancing were other elements of slave worship that originated in West Africa. This is no better illustrated than in the "ring shouts" and "ring dance." Exhorters led the "shout," and its main elements were singing, prayer, hand-clapping, shouting, and dancing performed by worshipers who formed a circle in the center of a "praise house" and moved in a counterclockwise direction just as West Africans performed it. The ring dance, which was a common activity during shouts, occurred in the heavily black region of the Sea Islands, where African traditions were more deeply rooted and survived intact longer than in most other parts of North America and where Frederick Law Olmsted encountered it. Olmsted noticed places of worship that blacks called "prayer-houses" on most of the large rice plantations around Savannah. One planter there told him that he had provided the slaves on his plantation with a prayer-house and furnished it with seats having a backrest, but the slaves had asked that the chairs be removed because they did not have enough room to pray. "It was explained to me," Olmsted wrote, "that it is their custom, in social worship, to work themselves up to a great pitch of excitement, in which they yell and cry aloud, and finally, shriek and leap up, clapping their hands and dancing, as it is done at heathen festivals." The architecture of American church buildings, espe-

35. Sobel, *Trabelin' On,* 109.

cially the presence of pews or benches, probably forced slaves to modify the ring dance that Africans usually performed outside. But it clearly demonstrates a linkage between African religious traditions and the worship of American slaves. Nor was the ring dance confined to the Sea Islands. It existed throughout the South and was even present among free blacks in the North.[36]

The slave spiritual was another vital part of the black worship service and a catalyst for ecstatic behavior as well as a medium for expressing the feelings that defined their unique experiences. The themes of slave spirituals were generally biblical in nature and contained orthodox Protestant Christian ideas, but the singers used the lyrics to express their own very personal feelings about life and redemption. Slaves improvised by applying secular interpretations to spiritual verses or by adding and subtracting words according to their moods and thoughts. Through song, slaves conveyed emotions that otherwise they would have had to suppress. The flexible structure of the spiritual allowed individuals to vocalize their feelings and then to enjoy the understanding and support of the congregation as the entire group sang along. As an expression of the unique but common experiences of African-American slaves, therefore, the spiritual was an art form that gave definition and resolution to African-American culture.[37]

Many independent black churches, of which the largest number were Baptist, grew out of evangelical revivals and the Baptists' habit of permitting blacks to preach to other blacks. There is evidence of the existence of a black Baptist congregation on the plantation of William Byrd III on the Bluestone River in Virginia in 1758. Black Baptists founded another congregation at Silver Bluff, South Carolina, in 1777. Among the preachers who ministered to that group was a slave named George Leile, whose master, a Tory, fled the United States during the Revolution. Although his master's flight freed Leile, he too ultimately departed the country for Jamaica, where he became a Christian missionary. A member of Leile's congregation, a slave named Andrew Bryan, continued the work in Savannah after Leile's departure. He encountered the hostility of whites who did not approve of slave preachers. On one occasion he endured a severe

---

36. The terms *prayer-houses* and *praise-houses* are interchangeable. Raboteau, *Slave Religion*, 72; Olmsted, *Journeys and Explorations in the Cotton Kingdom*, I, 259; Levine, *Black Culture and Black Consciousness*, 29; Stuckey, *Slave Culture*, 12, 24, 36, 43–63, 79, 93, 96.

37. Raboteau, *Slave Religion*, 246.

beating from an angry mob. His master's intervention saved both him and his congregation from destruction, and in 1788 they designated themselves the First African Baptist Church of Savannah. Other Baptist churches grew up among southern blacks between the Revolution and the Civil War. Many of them were composed of free blacks, some had white ministers, and most were located on the periphery of slavery. For many of the same reasons that black churches in the North were similar in the form and substance of worship to white churches, worship in these southern black churches was very much like that in white churches.[38]

Methodists and Presbyterians were more conservative than Baptists about allowing blacks to preach to congregations. Their attitude emanated from a concern for maintaining an educated clergy, which in turn reflected their wish to ensure denominational discipline and, especially in the case of Presbyterians, doctrinal purity. Educated black preachers were rare, and if the ministry were not adequately controlled, unorthodox views and practices might enter the church through the pulpit. Methodist and Presbyterian authorities, therefore, were reluctant to ordain black ministers, although blacks commonly served as lay preachers and exhorters. Ecclesiastical law prohibited them from administering the sacraments of the eucharist or baptism, but they preached and they converted other blacks. And despite prohibitions, they sometimes functioned as pastors of congregations.[39]

Early in the nineteenth century, the African Methodist Episcopal (AME) church penetrated the South, bringing its orthodox theology and ordained ministry to southern blacks. For political reasons, whites did not welcome it. They were becoming increasingly suspicious of all independent black churches, and they correctly believed that the AME church was actively involved in the antislavery movement. African Methodist congregations existed mostly in the border states and in cities such as Mobile, New Orleans, and Charleston. Like some of the early Baptist congregations, the AME organizations were an elite church among

38. Emanuel K. Love, *A History of the First African Baptist Church of Savannah from Its Organization, January 20th, 1788, to July 1st, 1888* (Savannah, 1888), 1–6; Edgar G. Thomas, *The First African Baptist Church of North America* (Savannah, 1925), 9–32; Walter H. Brooks, "The Evolution of the Negro Baptist Church," *Journal of Negro History,* VII (1922), 11–22; Jackson, "Religious Development of the Negro in Virginia," 170–80; Sobel, *Trabelin' On,* 250–51.

39. Donald G. Mathews, *Slavery and Methodism: A Chapter in American Morality* (Princeton, 1965), 64–65.

southern blacks. For the most part they were congregations of free blacks. Morris Brown, a wealthy free black, who enjoyed the respect of many whites, founded an AME congregation in Charleston in 1817 and remained its pastor until 1822. The slave conspiracy led by Denmark Vesey, an African Methodist, frightened the local white population and resulted in an order that the congregation be disbanded. Beginning in 1841 there was an AME congregation in New Orleans. Jordan W. Early, who had gone there as a missionary, obtained permission from white officials to organize a congregation of free blacks called the St. James AME Church. In 1852 the AME bishops sent John M. Brown to assume the pastorate of St. James. Brown had been educated at Oberlin College. He remained in New Orleans for five years, during which time he organized two other congregations, Morris Brown and Trinity. There were four black Methodist churches in New Orleans in 1860.[40]

Mounting abolitionist pressure on the slave system in the 1830s, coupled with the heightened fear that the religious instruction of slaves would incite them to rebel, caused white southerners to think very carefully about the influence of Christian theology on slaves. Abolitionists maintained that the slave system denied Christian instruction to the slaves and thus prevented them from becoming morally responsible and entering the kingdom of God. Some southern evangelists such as Charles Colcock Jones, a Georgia planter and slave owner who was trained in a northern seminary, were convinced that masters had not accepted responsibility for caring for their slaves' spiritual condition. Since the Great Awakening revivals, blacks had been taught the same religious doctrines as whites, but outside of the church little had been done to teach them about the redeeming power of Christ. Consequently, Jones believed that blacks, both slave and free, had been left "in moral darkness, and destitution of the means of grace." He and other southern evangelicals urged that whites become more active in the Christianization of slaves, arguing that without their guidance blacks would remain an isolated and immoral force that would be a constant threat to the unity and tranquillity

40. Joe G. Taylor, *Negro Slavery in Louisiana* (Baton Rouge, 1963), 48; Charles S. Smith, *A History of the African Methodist Episcopal Church* (1922; rpr. New York, 1968), 34–37; Letitia Woods Brown, *Free Negroes in the District of Columbia, 1790–1846* (New York, 1972), 132–33; Marina Wikramanayake, *A World in Shadow: The Free Black in Antebellum South Carolina* (Columbia, 1973), 113–54; John W. Blassingame, *Black New Orleans, 1860–1888* (Chicago, 1973), 13; Ira Berlin, *Slaves Without Masters: The Free Negro and the Antebellum South* (New York, 1974), 288–97.

of the South. The future security of the South rested on the creation of a biracial community. To Jones, the evangelization of slaves was not only a Christian obligation of the white master class but a necessity for its own survival.[41]

But many whites believed that teaching blacks such Christian principles as spiritual liberation and the ultimate equality of all mankind would subvert the values and institutions that were the cornerstones of southern society. Discipline and control were vital to the maintenance of social order. Their first concern was with blacks worshiping without white supervision. Free blacks and the independent African Methodist churches were suspected of implanting rebellious thoughts in the minds of slaves, and the Denmark Vesey plot and the Nat Turner uprising in Virginia in 1831, both of which involved black religious figures, reaffirmed the slaveholders' apprehensions. Even when theology was not involved, the church as a physical facility served as a community center that slaves could use to subvert the system. Such was the case when slaves in Kentucky, led by Elijah Marrs, used a local church as the headquarters for an attempt by twenty-seven persons to arm themselves and escape from bondage.[42]

Whites' feelings of alarm about independent African churches and their influence on the slave population led them to intrude more and more into the religious activities of slaves. Masters often encouraged the Christian instruction of the servants on their plantations, either performing the instruction themselves or arranging for white ministers to do it. Most often, slaves attended the same services as local whites. They were segregated in the sanctuary, but they heard the same sermon, sang the same hymns, were bound by the same code of ethics, in many Baptist churches were baptized together with whites, and were listed on the church rolls along with white members of the congregation. Occasionally, masters demanded that their slaves regularly attend church services and enforced the dictate. John Hyrne Tucker, who owned plantations in the Georgetown district of South Carolina, required his slaves to attend church services, and his overseer checked the roll to be certain that all the slaves were present. An unexcused absence was punished by depriving the miscreant of his or her weekly allowance of molasses, bacon, sugar, or to-

41. Donald G. Mathews, "Charles Colcock Jones and the Southern Evangelical Crusade to Form a Biracial Community," *Journal of Southern History*, XLI (1975), 299–320.

42. *Ibid.*; James M. McPherson, *The Negro's Civil War: How American Negroes Felt and Acted During the War for the Union* (New York, 1965), 206–207.

stress duty. In their sermons to slave congregations they delivered the message that slaves were *slaves* because it was God's will, and their duty was to obey their worldly and heavenly masters. One former slave from Texas many years later recalled that he and his fellow plantation slaves often heard about their Christian duty to obey Massa. The message that was drummed into them was "Obey your massa and missy, don't steal chickens and eggs and meat, but nary a word 'bout havin' a soul to save." The idea that slaves must be obedient if they hoped to realize heavenly rewards did not come only from the mouths of white people. Many a black preacher "jus' talk what he done heard de white preachers say." Black preachers had to serve both their white masters and their black congregations by respecting their masters' demands while providing the uplifting message that their own religious beliefs and the needs of their congregations required. But because the two were usually antithetical, the preachers often found themselves in a precarious and frustrating pre-dicament. Black congregations that worshiped in the open did so at the sufferance of their masters, and preachers in those situations often spoke the words their masters demanded. This, however, should not be taken to mean that they failed in their responsibilities to their fellow slaves. An-drew Bryan of Savannah was an example of the many successful slave preachers who earned the support of their masters by deftly avoiding giv-ing offense to them and as a result was allowed to preach an uplifting and self-affirming message to his followers in their own church. And of course one cannot always take what the slave preachers said about duty and responsibility to Massa when they were under the scrutiny of whites to mean that slaves should be submissive. Slaves were adept at implanting double meanings in their language. Instruction in proper behavior when around the master of the plantation was often a lesson in "puttin' on old Massa." Lewis Favor, a Georgia slave, regularly joined the other slaves on his plantation at services in the white church. As they sat in the rear and listened to the white minister preach, they heard his admonition: "Don't steal your master's chickens or his eggs and your backs won't be whipped." Afterward, the slaves' own black preacher was permitted to preach to them, and Favor heard the very same words: "Obey your mas-ters and your mistresses and your backs won't be whipped." The white minister obviously was preaching a version of the Christian command-ment not to steal that the master class was eager to apply to slaves for the purpose of controlling their behavior. They wanted the slaves to be sub-missive to white authority and not to undermine the discipline that a profitable plantation system demanded. But who can be certain that the black preacher, employing the same words, was not merely advising expedient behavior, not exhorting slaves to be obedient but rather instructing them how to behave to avoid punishment?[45]

The slave preacher was one of the most influential members of the plantation community and of slave society in general. Through him the people heard the gospel that did so much to sustain them in their travails. He intoned it in a rhythmical preaching style reminiscent of Africa and in an African-American dialect with gestures that evoked the powerful emotional and physical responses characteristic of slave worship. He presided over the worship service and provided comfort and counsel to members of the congregation. Like so many elements in the slave church, the preacher reflected both African and European-American religious traditions. William E. B. Du Bois regarded him as the "Priest or Medicine-man" who preserved African beliefs and practices and embedded them in the slave church. "He early appeared as the healer of the sick, the interpreter of the Unknown, the comforter of the sorrowing, the supernatural avenger of wrong, and the one who rudely but picturesquely expressed the longing, disappointment, and resentment of a stolen and oppressed people." The slave church was not a messianic institution, and as Eugene D. Genovese has pointed out, the preachers did not project themselves as revolutionaries or saviors; yet they, like their African counterparts, mediated between the natural and supernatural forces that controlled their lives and their followers'.[46]

Many slaves resented having to attend church services conducted by whites. They hated repeatedly being told "Obey de massa, obey de overseer; obey dis, obey dat," while their masters and overseers oppressed and physically abused them. They disliked having to sit in the rear of the church or in galleries set apart exclusively for them. They cherished meetings of their own where they could relax and enjoy the form of worship that pleased them and uplifted their spirits. Thus slaves held their own religious meetings, whether furtively or openly with the approval of their masters. Frederick Law Olmsted attended a church service with a racially mixed congregation near Savannah and noticed that the blacks in attend-

45. George P. Rawick, ed., *Texas Narratives* (Westport, 1972), Pt. 1, p. 35, Vol. IV of Rawick, ed., *The American Slave: A Composite Autobiography,* 19 vols.; Rawick, ed., *Georgia Narratives* (Westport, 1972), Pt. 1, p. 323, Vol. XII, *ibid.*

46. Du Bois, *Souls of Black Folk,* 342; Stuckey, *Slave Culture,* 61, 256–58; Genovese, *Roll, Jordan, Roll,* 271–79.

ance were subdued. "The exercises at this time," he noted, "seem to have no reference to them." But he also observed other blacks waiting outside the church, who "were expecting to enjoy a meeting to themselves, after the whites had left the house." If their masters refused to permit them to hold their own worship services, slaves would steal away into the woods and congregate in what they called hush arbors or brush arbors, which were sanctuaries constructed of tree branches or in secluded cabins. Whether they worshiped surreptitiously or with the consent of their masters, they enjoyed their own services. Black preachers related to them in their vernacular, and the singing and dancing provided them with excitement and pleasure. On the plantation in Walker County, Texas, where Carey Davenport resided, no blacks were permitted to preach. The only preaching that Davenport's master allowed was that done by white Methodist circuit riders who occasionally passed through the area. Therefore, Davenport and the other slaves had to slip away into dugouts or hollows to hold their own services. There they sang songs that came "a-gushing up from the heart." To protect themselves from discovery by their masters or patrollers, slaves often turned a kettle upside down. They believed that the pot would catch the sounds of their singing and shouts before they came within the hearing range of whites who might punish them. Cato Carter lived on a plantation near Pineapple in Wilcox County, Alabama, where slaves were permitted to conduct their own church meetings, but he knew of masters on other plantations who "wouldn' 'low them to worship atall and they had to put they heads in pots to sing or pray."[47]

Slave codes, which went to great lengths in defining a "Negro" so as to determine who was subject to enslavement, carefully distinguished between slave and free blacks. Because of the antebellum slave statutes and the different conditions that existed under them, cultural divisions evolved among people of color, most visibly and dramatically between slaves and the privileged light-skinned mulatto elite. The latter were more often educated—at least able to read and write—relatively prosperous, and concentrated in cities like Charleston, Mobile, and New Orleans. Although the elite's position in society was not as precarious as that of ordinary free blacks, its members carefully guarded their status by applying on two fronts the singular strategy of identifying with whites. One front was against the condition of slavery that threatened to engulf them

47. Rawick, ed., *Texas Narratives*, Pt. 1, pp. 68–69, 206–207, 282; Olmsted, *Journeys and Explorations in the Cotton Kingdom*, I, 265.

from below. They did not as a rule act overtly against the slave system; some were slave owners themselves. Rather, they endeavored to keep their distance from slaves. To behave like slaves might lead to their being treated as slaves. Therefore, the free blacks' attitude and behavior toward enslaved blacks showed traces of condescension and contempt. They often excluded slaves from their social institutions. In Charleston, for example, the exclusive Brown Fellowship Society established rigid barriers against the inclusion of slaves. New Orleans' elite St. James African Methodist Church specifically excluded slaves from its membership. Though free blacks avoided an incriminating proximity to slaves, they maneuvered on the second front by undertaking to minimize the distance between themselves and important whites. Of course, skin color was a nearly impenetrable barrier against black entrance into white society, but mulattoes could nevertheless gain some of the benefits of crossing the color line by winning the acceptance of whites who were in positions to bestow privileges on them and accord them respect.[48]

Several factors, some of which were beyond their control, influenced free people's chances of successfully ingratiating themselves to whites. The latter feared the outbreak of slave rebellion almost more than the wrath of God, and some mused that if, in such an eventuality, the free black population allied itself with them rather than with slaves the effect of rebellion might be minimized. Free blacks might learn about planned uprisings and reveal them to white authorities before any damage could be done. Indeed, it had been a free black man who had informed white authorities in South Carolina about the Denmark Vesey plot. Further disposing whites to grant privileges to selected blacks was the slave owners' assertion that the slave system allowed the best in the character of individual Africans to come out while it protected the masses from the destructive effects of competition with whites. Thus a few exceptional blacks might actually affirm the race ideology upon which the slave system was erected—that slavery was a benevolent institution that protected the inferior and uplifted them to their maximum potential. And, of course, whites sometimes favored their mulatto offspring and on occasion manumitted them.

48. Joel Williamson, *New People: Miscegenation and Mulattoes in the United States* (New York, 1980), 71–77; Berlin, *Slaves Without Masters*, 43, 56–57, 95, 124, 197–98, 269–73, 314, 327; Michael P. Johnson and James L. Roark, eds., *No Chariot Let Down: Charleston's Free People of Color on the Eve of the Civil War* (Chapel Hill, 1984), 12, 23, 25, 28.

Such considerations made it possible for blacks to secure the approval of whites, but vital to the attainment and preservation of high status was their emulation of white behavior. Inevitably, some blacks and mulattoes went beyond artfully cultivating habits they knew would endear them to whites and so thoroughly assimilated white values that had it not been for their color they would have been almost indistinguishable from respectable whites.[49]

Freeborn blacks generally adhered to standard Christian doctrine. In towns and cities such as Charleston, Pensacola, Mobile, and New Orleans they attended Methodist, Episcopal, and Presbyterian churches that had well-educated pastors. Free blacks in the Upper South often joined the African Methodist or Baptist churches that were active there. Their continued adherence to standard forms of European-American Protestant doctrine was largely a matter of choice. In some instances they were free to join with slaves in religious services, and some did; however, others did not because they were not permitted to or, more significantly, because their hunger for status and their determination to avoid slipping down to the level of slaves made them scorn slave religion.[50]

Thus over the course of roughly two hundred years of African-American experience, two kinds of churches evolved among African Americans, based on contrasting religious traditions. One was formally organized and governed by published rules. Its structure and theology were mostly adopted from white churches. It was denominational, Baptist and Methodist for the most part. It included northern free blacks who resented the discrimination they encountered in biracial churches and were unified by their religious beliefs and their commitment to race solidarity but also free blacks in the South, some of whom identified more with white than with slave culture. The second one was made up of the sometimes invisible churches of southern slaves. It was a folk church, the product of a primal culture, nonintellectual, experiential, and indigenous in the sense that it was the syncretistic product of a dynamic African-American culture. During the late antebellum period, the two churches were as separate from each other as most free blacks were from the bulk of their slave brethren, but emancipation changed that relationship. The two churches fused when a legion of northern missionaries swept into the South to Christianize and proselytize the former slaves and to incorpo-

---

49. Berlin, *Slaves Without Masters*, 271–81.
50. *Ibid.*, 284–303; Johnson and Roark, eds., *No Chariot Let Down*, 11, 23, 132–33.

rate slave and free black congregations into their denominations. They hoped to achieve the compatible goals of race solidarity and race betterment and, had their plans materialized, the folk churches probably would have been structurally and doctrinally integrated into the institutional churches. The religion and the rituals of black folk would have been transformed in such a way as to bring them into conformity with orthodox European-American beliefs and practices. The actual result of the missionaries' efforts, however, was quite different. In many instances, a contrast—and at times conflict—remained between the two kinds of churches and the people who attended them. The bond of race unified the churches organizationally, but a gulf of class, experience, and culture divided them.

2

The Missionaries: Organizing
the Church in the South

As word that Yankee soldiers were nearby swept through the slave quarters, an air of expectancy filled the cabins. Excitement and anxiety sharpened the people's senses as they eagerly awaited their release from bondage. They had dreamed about this moment for most of their lives, prayed mightily for it, and perhaps planned calculatingly how they would meet it when it came. When at last the moment did arrive, men, women, and children slipped quietly from their plantations to the protection of Union camps—and freedom.[1]

The way freedom came was always a little different from plantation to farm and from person to person, but regardless of who and where they were, most people had the same feelings. When the slaves of All Saints Parish, in the rice country of South Carlina, heard the boom of Federal guns they knew their liberation was at hand. Mariah Heywood later recalled those moments and some of the people's reactions to what was happening. "When the big gun shooting, old people in the yard. 'Tank God! Massa, HE COMING!' . . . 'HE COMING!' Chillun say, 'What coming? What coming? What coming, Grandma?' 'You all will know! You all will know!'" Slaves elsewhere were stunned and confused by the horrendous fighting taking place around them and by the uncertainty that lay ahead. They waited, biding their time, until Federal officials told them that they were free. Slaves in areas where there had been little fighting had no idea they were free until the war ended, when their masters finally assembled them and informed them that they were now free people.[2]

---

1. Albert V. House, Jr., ed., "Deterioration of a Georgia Rice Plantation During Four Years of Civil War," *Journal of Southern History,* IX (1943), 100–102.

2. Charles Joyner, *Down by the Riverside: A South Carolina Slave Community* (Urbana, 1984), 225–26; Peter Kolchin, *First Freedom: The Responses of Alabama's Blacks to Emancipation and Reconstruction* (Westport, 1972), 3–4; Leon F. Litwack, *Been in the Storm So Long: The Aftermath of Slavery* (New York, 1979), 184.

The emancipation of approximately four million slaves began in confusion, both in Washington and in the South. During the presidential election campaign of 1860, Abraham Lincoln had pledged that if elected he would not interfere with the South's domestic institutions, although the abolition of slavery was an objective to which many members of the Republican party had been dedicated for some time. "I have no purpose," the candidate from Illinois declared, "directly or indirectly, to interfere with the institution of slavery in the States where it exists," an assertion that, for emphasis, he repeated in his inaugural address following his narrow victory. Even after the commencement of hostilities, Lincoln avowed that his purpose in fighting the war was to preserve the Union and not to free the slaves. During the first year of the war, despite enormous pressure from the abolitionists in Congress, in his cabinet, and in the military, the president stood firm by his commitment. When General John C. Frémont ordered the emancipation of slaves in the Department of the West in August, 1861, Lincoln countermanded it. Afterward, Union military officers regarded the refugee slaves who descended upon their camps as contraband of war, an ambiguous designation that indicated that the government did not have a definite policy for handling them.[3]

Then, in July, 1862, Congress authorized the confiscation of rebel property, including slaves, and in September President Lincoln issued his Preliminary Emancipation Proclamation. Those measures showed that freeing the slaves had finally become an aim of the federal government, thus changing the nature of the war. Yet the future of slavery remained uncertain. Lincoln still hoped to shorten the war more than he hoped to extinguish slavery. He structured his proclamation in such a way as to provide for a Confederate surrender with the slave system intact. It was in fact an ultimatum combined with terms for peace. If the Confederates did not lay down their arms by January 1, 1863, their slaves would be freed. If they did surrender, which he really hoped they would do, they could keep their slaves. The proclamation was a conciliatory offer, but it stood little chance of producing a quick end to the war. For one thing, it did not satisfy southerners' appetite for victory and independence, and for another, slavery would certainly remain under attack by the abolitionists. Confident of victory, the rebels rejected Lincoln's offer, but by the spring of 1865, the Confederacy was tottering on the verge of collapse, and when it finally did surrender, its slaves were free.

3. Roy P. Basler, ed., *The Collected Works of Abraham Lincoln* (8 vols.; New Brunswick, 1953), IV, 262–63.

With the fires set by retreating Confederates still burning amid the skeletons of Richmond's burned-out buildings in early April of 1865, freedmen thronged into the streets of the rebel capital to greet the Federal troops, God's messengers bringing their redemption from slavery. They were being vindicated as human beings, and their faith in God and in the liberating gospel of African-American Christianity had been justified. God had fulfilled his promise to free them from slavery. The freedmen tramped alongside the troops, praying, dancing, and singing—"ten thousand voices," recalled one of the soldiers, proclaiming their freedom. Inside Lumpkin's Jail, one of Richmond's notorious slave markets, the inmates chanted:

> Slavery chain done broke at last!
> Broke at last! Broke at last!
> Slavery chain done broke at last!
> Gonna praise God til I die.

A few days later, fifteen hundred blacks gathered in the First African Baptist Church to thank God for their deliverance. Near Yorktown, a slave woman overheard her master relating the news of the evacuation of Richmond to members of the family. She slipped quietly away and then let her emotions burst free. "I jump up an' scream, 'Glory, glory, hallelujah I's free! I's free! Glory to God, you come down an' free us; no big man could do it.' An' I got sort o' scared, afeared somebody hear me, an' I takes another good look, an' fall on de groun', an' roll over, an' kiss de groun' fo' de Lord's sake, I's so full o' praise to Masser Jesus." For Fannie Berry, a white flag hoisted near Appomattox Courthouse signaled the beginning of a new life for her and the other slaves. "Never was no time like 'em befo' or since. Niggers shoutin' an' clappin' hands an' singin'! Chillun runnin' all over de place beatin' tins an' yellin'. Ev'ybody happy. Sho' did some celebratin'. Run to de kitchen an' shout in de winder: 'Mammy, don't you cook no mo' / You's free! You's free!'" The day of Jubilo had finally dawned; freedom was at hand.[4]

The Union triumph on the battlefields destroyed the foundation upon which both the South's social order and the oppression of blacks had rested. In the aftermath of defeat, white planters waited, some anxiously

---

4. Eric Foner, *Reconstruction: America's Unfinished Revolution, 1863–1877* (New York, 1988), 73; Michael B. Chesson, *Richmond After the War, 1865–1890* (Richmond, 1981), 57–62; New York *Times*, April 11, 1865; Litwack, *Been in the Storm So Long*, 167–71.

and others in a mood of quiet resignation, for the chaos they expected to follow. They had regarded the close surveillance of blacks and strict control of their activities as essential not only to the maintenance of an orderly and prosperous society but also to their personal safety, living as they did amid a population that might at any moment erupt into a violent rebellion. Unsupervised gatherings of blacks had always been suspect, and antebellum authorities had generally outlawed them. The small number of black churches that had been permitted to function in the South before the arrival of Federal armies testified to white fears that the liberating elements of the Christian gospel might ignite a bloody slave insurrection. But the Confederate surrender and the dissolution of discipline over blacks seemed to bring the nightmare of an uprising closer than ever to reality. The reaction of Mary Boykin Chesnut, the mistress of one of the South's aristocratic families, to hearing that her husband's slaves were brandishing arms was consistent with the widely held belief that slaves were awaiting just the right moment to rise up against their late masters. "JC finds his Negro men all have Enfield rifles," she wrote in her diary. "The next move will be on pretense of hunting public arms to disarm all white men. Then we will have the long desired Negro insurrection." [5]

Mrs. Chesnut's comments betrayed a misunderstanding she shared with other white southerners about what was taking place. The war was not the signal for a bloody uprising of the black masses against their white masters. Southern blacks had only very late—and even then marginally—been permitted to participate in the armed assault against the slaveholding regime, and those who were armed were not preparing to turn their weapons upon whites and annihilate them. It was the institution of slavery, not white people or their property, that was destroyed. With the exception of sporadic incidents of former slaves ransacking abandoned plantation houses and some isolated acts of violence against individual masters and overseers, emancipation brought no civil disorders. Whites certainly were not massacred, and unless it was in the way of military operations, even their property had not come under attack. The major exception, of course, was William Tecumseh Sherman's devastating march through Georgia and South Carolina in the final months of the war. But if the collapse of slavery neither led to the bloody reprisals

5. Kolchin, *First Freedom*, 37; C. Vann Woodward and Elizabeth Muhlenfeld, eds., *The Private Mary Chesnut: The Unpublished Civil War Diaries* (New York, 1984), 243; John Richard Dennett, *The South as It Is, 1865–1866*, ed. Henry M. Christman (New York, 1965), 190, 240.

that southern whites dreaded nor immediately dissipated their concern about the future of southern society, it did transform the relationship between white and black southerners. The specter of social revolution took dramatic shape with the return of white planters, tired and dispirited from the war, to find their neglected estates on the auction block or in the hands of northern businessmen and cities and towns choked with refugee freedmen. But the reality of what was transpiring, profound enough although hardly justifying whites' most horrible nightmares, was better depicted in scenes of planters, who still had estates to come back to, negotiating labor contracts with the same men and women they had presumed to own just a few months before.[6]

Blacks were free now, and they enjoyed options they could only have imagined a short time earlier. With a deliberateness that suggested they had planned for this moment, they immediately began exercising those options. When given the opportunity to choose between the close and intricate ties with whites that had characterized the master-slave relationship or separation from their erstwhile owners, most voted with alacrity for the latter. No longer required to attend racially mixed churches or chapels established for them by whites, thousands of blacks began organizing their own autonomous congregations. The months that followed emancipation marked the beginning of an exciting new era for the black church, a time during which it began to mature and to take on new forms and functions.

Freedom, however, seldom came easily or neatly packaged. Rather, it usually arrived entangled in a web of negative implications. Problems that would haunt the freedmen long afterward were sometimes obscured from immediate view by the joyous celebrations that went on in the wake of the Civil War and by the appearance that, compared to the white ruling class, who in many ways were in eclipse, the former slaves stood on the bright side of events. But all of their hearty rejoicing could not alter the reality that freedom was a bittersweet mixture of happiness and exhilaration combined with conflict, anxiety, and uncertainty. Frustration and disappointment were in store as former slaves and those who had once been their masters—and still possessed considerable power over them—stepped toward the future entertaining very different and usually opposing notions of what freedom meant. Blacks took an expansive view and

6. Kolchin, *First Freedom*, 32; Litwack, *Been in the Storm So Long*, 145–47; Willie Lee Rose, *Rehearsal for Reconstruction: The Port Royal Experiment* (New York, 1964), 358–62.

looked forward to full citizenship, whereas whites were determined to minimize the consequences of emancipation and to maintain as much of the old order, based on white supremacy and control of black labor, as possible. "He's helpless, and ignorant, and dependent," remarked a white South Carolinian shortly after the Confederate surrender, "and the old masters will still control him." That view was shared by many whites throughout the South, and it promised to make the attainment of full freedom for blacks very difficult indeed.[7]

Apart from discrepancies in how blacks and whites defined freedom, there was another problem that complicated emancipation. The Civil War brought into the South a bewildering assortment of northerners. Multitudes of these newcomers came as soldiers, many were recruited as teachers and missionaries, and still others were drawn by the prospect of investing profitably in southern agriculture. Some of the northerners served as agents of the Bureau of Refugees, Freedmen, and Abandoned Lands, which Congress established in 1865 to assist the freedmen in the difficult transition from slavery to freedom. These Yankees included many who sympathized with the former slaves and whose compassion for them as human beings trapped in a cruel and degrading system drew forth great exertions on their behalf.[8]

Not all of the northerners were friendly, however. An abhorrence of blacks prevailed among them, as it did among southern whites. Elizabeth Botume, a northern teacher, observed it among those of her countrymen present with her in South Carolina. "It was by no means confined to the old Southerners," she reported, "but was largely shared by Northern adventurers, a host of whom had followed the army." Businessmen who purchased or supervised the operation of abandoned plantations and hired blacks as laborers often treated them in the same harsh, insensitive way that the freedmen's late masters had. The military was particularly troublesome. On grounds that slaves could not legally own property, Union officers confiscated the freedmen's mules, wagons, and other possessions. Hostile Yankee soldiers, who believed they had fought against the forces of disunion and not for the liberation of slaves, despised the

---

7. Litwack, *Been in the Storm So Long,* 221–91; Foner, *Reconstruction,* 77, 231; Whitelaw Reid, *After the War: A Southern Tour, May 1, 1865, to May 1, 1866* (Cincinnati, 1866), 84.

8. Rose, *Rehearsal for Reconstruction,* 123–24, 377; Jacqueline Jones, *Soldiers of Light and Love: Northern Teachers and Georgia Blacks, 1865–1873* (Chapel Hill, 1980), 39–48.

freed persons as much if not more than they hated the Confederates. They frequently abused them; they brutally assaulted them and stole and destroyed their property. One group of soldiers in Virginia entertained themselves by taking two "niger wenches," turning them "upon their heads, & put[ting] tobacco, chips, sticks, lighted cigars and sand into their behinds." Military authorities conscripted freedmen, without pay, and severely punished—and sometimes shot—those who resisted. Such treatment caused the freedmen to regret the soldiers' arrival. As a white visitor in Fayetteville, North Carolina, noted, "they prayed about as hard for Sherman to go as they had prayed for him to come." [9]

Even northerners who regarded themselves as the freedmen's friends often labored under perceptions of their character that grew out of negative racial or cultural stereotypes. Few of them had ever been in the South before or had contact with blacks, but because of their own cultural chauvinism, they could hardly help but assume that the culture of black southerners was inferior to their own. Such paternalism was common among, but certainly not limited to, Freedmen's Bureau agents, whom one black minister referred to as "great tyrants." John W. De Forest, who served as a Freedman's Bureau agent, had written during the height of abolitionist agitation in the 1850s that the slaves "are not worth all the hullabaloo that is made about them. They are kept ignorant and animal, say the abolitionists. Granted. But their great, great grandfathers in Africa were four times as ignorant and at least twice as animal." Such opinions did not prevent individuals like De Forest from supporting the end of slavery or from upholding the right of the freedmen to equality before the law, but they often hindered their efforts to help the freedmen advance in society. Their prejudices were often revealed in their handling of disputes between the freedmen and local whites. When a field hand in Bedford County, Virginia, complained to the local Freedmen's Bureau agent that his employer had beaten him, the agent suggested that he must have been sassy. "No, boss," the man replied; "never was sassy; never *was* sassy nigger sence I'se born." The agent dismissed the case as a waste of his time. "Well, now you go back home and go to your work again; don't be sassy." Then he turned to another white man who was present and

---

9. Foner, *Reconstruction*, 137–38; Elizabeth Hyde Botume, *First Days Amongst the Contrabands* (Boston, 1893), 176–77; Rose, *Rehearsal for Reconstruction*, 174, 177–78, 240–41, 266–67; Janet Sharp Hermann, *The Pursuit of a Dream* (New York, 1981), 49–50; Bell I. Wiley, *The Life of Billy Yank: The Common Soldier of the Union* (Baton Rouge, 1952), 109–15; Dennett, *The South as It Is*, 73–74.

remarked, "That's a sassy looking darkey." The agents' attitude planted understandable doubts about their friendliness in the minds of blacks. "It was a long time before these refugees could get rid of their suspicions of white people," Elizabeth Botume commented later. "Perhaps they never did." [10]

Many of the northern teachers and missionaries believed, as Laura Towne did, that the freedmen should put not only their slave experiences behind them but their customs, beliefs, and values as well. They deplored what they perceived as a degraded African-American culture and the slave system that begot it. They were dedicated to teaching the freedmen practical lessons in how to be intelligent, responsible citizens in a free society and productive wage laborers in a competitive market (as though the freedmen had never labored productively before or had not previously understood the meaning of wages), but they were also committed to instilling in them the ideals of northern white, middle-class virtue. When they encountered resistance from the freedmen, they often became clamorous, and their relationship with southern blacks developed into a frustrating contest of wills. "They *must find out* that their way is not the best way," Towne insisted. Thus emancipation introduced into the lives of southern blacks a new group of white people with whose ambivalence the freedmen had to deal, liberal and compassionate persons in the case of teachers and missionaries, who nonetheless demanded that the freedmen accept their notion of proper moral character as the price of their assistance. And that too made blacks skeptical of the northerners. As Elizabeth Botume pointed out, "It took time for the freed people to find out who were their true friends." [11]

Freedom also obliged the freedmen and their former masters to redefine their relationship. The freedmen often held mixed feelings toward their old masters. An overwhelming desire to leave behind them all the elements of slavery gripped the freedmen; yet it was difficult for some of them to turn their backs on masters they had served for a lifetime and for

10. *Christian Recorder,* December 1, 1866; John William De Forest, *A Union Officer in the Reconstruction,* ed. James H. Croushore and David Morris Potter (New Haven, 1948), xxiv; Dennett, *The South as It Is,* 177; Kolchin, *First Freedom,* 33; Botume, *First Days Amongst the Contrabands,* 55; *National Freedman,* I (1865), 328.

11. Lawrence W. Levine, *Black Culture and Black Consciousness: Afro-American Folk Thought from Slavery to Freedom* (New York, 1977), 141; Botume, *First Days Amongst the Contrabands,* 176–77. For a discussion of the background and activities of the northern teachers and missionaries see James M. McPherson, *The Abolitionist Legacy: From Reconstruction to the NAACP* (Princeton, 1975), and Jones, *Soldiers of Light and Love.*

whom they felt genuine emotional attachment. Booker T. Washington wrote that slaves found the reality of freedom more perplexing than they had thought it would be; that "deep down in their hearts there was a strange and peculiar attachment to 'Old Marster' and 'Old Missus,' and their children, which they found it hard to think of breaking off." Even as they walked away from their slave pasts, the freedmen often wished their former masters well and expressed the hope that they would make out all right under the new regime. Some freedmen even sacrificed a measure of their own advancement to help their masters recover from the effects of the war. When a former mistress in South Carolina instructed Aleck Parker to find another job because she could not afford to pay him, he answered: "Miss, I don't want no wagis! Aint I wuk fu yu sence I bin man grown, aint my fadder wuk fu Maussa fadder! En my grandfadder de same! . . . Ain't I drive yo!, de Guvna's lady all de time Maussa bin Guv'na, en now yu tink I gwine lef yu. . . . no ma'am, not Aleck Pa'ka, e aint mean enuf fu dat!" Similarly, a North Carolina slave named Daniel was reluctant to desert his mistress. For forty-three years he had operated a ferryboat across the Yadkin River near Lexington. He was no longer her slave, but when a traveler observed: "Well, old man, you're free now," Daniel responded: "I dunno, master. They say all the colored people's free; they do say it certain; but I'm a-goin on same as I allus has been." When asked if he was receiving wages for his labor, he replied: "No, sir; my mistress never said anything to me that I was to have wages, nor yet that I was free; nor I never said anything to her. Ye see I left it to her own honor to talk to me about it, because I was afraid she'd say I was insultin' to her and presumin', so I wouldn't speak first. She ha'n't spoke yet." [12]

The sudden reality of freedom presented many economic challenges to southern blacks. In the market-oriented society they were entering, certain assets were necessary to achieve a significant measure of success; yet the freedmen inherited little materially from slavery that would help them succeed. The slave statutes had imposed severe restraints on their ability to accumulate wealth and to develop self-reliance, leaving most of them destitute and dependent when emancipation came. The difficulty of their situation was apparent to the Radical Republican leader Thaddeus

12. Kolchin, *First Freedom,* 23; Litwack, *Been in the Storm So Long,* 165–66, 199–205, 330; Booker T. Washington, *Up from Slavery: An Autobiography* (New York, 1901), 40; Rose, *Rehearsal for Reconstruction,* 102; Joyner, *Down by the Riverside,* 227; Dennett, *The South as It Is,* 121–22.

Stevens of Pennsylvania. "We have turned, or are about to turn, loose four million slaves without a hut to shelter them or a cent in their pockets," he told members of the House of Representatives. "The infernal laws of slavery have prevented them from acquiring an education, understanding the commonest laws of contract, or of managing the ordinary business of life." Della Harris' mother, like many slave women, entered freedom owning "nothin' but a passel o' chillun." Their men were little if any better off, either materially or otherwise. Neither the Emancipation Proclamation nor the Thirteenth Amendment abolishing slavery had extended any political rights to the freedmen. And even though they were the only labor force large enough and skilled enough to maintain anything approximating normal levels of plantation production, obtaining wages adequate to meet their basic needs, much less their wants, was not guaranteed by emancipation. To Garrison Frazier, a sixty-seven-year-old black Baptist minister from Georgia, slavery meant "receiving by irresistible power the work of another man, and not by his consent." Freedom, by contrast, "is taking us from under the yoke of bondage and placing us where we could reap the fruit of our own labor." Insofar as that was true, blacks were not yet free because whites had no intention of giving up the principle of compulsory labor. It was true that a technically free labor system was imposed on southern planters, but through annual labor contracts they hoped to restrict the freedmen's movement from one employer to another in search of higher wages and more agreeable working conditions while securing the same obedience they had demanded of their slaves. Many planters and plantation superintendents applied the lash to control their workers just as they had done before. According to a Union army officer stationed in Arkansas, a majority of the planters "seem to think that the only way to manage 'niggers' is to whip them and make them *know their places.*" Moreover, cash and credit were scarce in the immediate postwar period, and planters fought hard to establish and maintain a rock-bottom wage structure. Reflecting the discouragement that many freedmen felt and the vulnerable position they were in, one group of men told journalist John Richard Dennett that they did not expect to earn what they deserved from whites now that they were free. "What kin we do, sah?" they asked. "Dey kin give us jes what they choose. Man couldn't starve, nohow; got no place to go; we 'bleege to take what dey give us." Consequently, freedom portended a future of economic struggle for emancipated blacks. Indeed, sometimes it was hard to tell the difference between the old slave labor system and the new free labor system.[13]

For many refugees waiting in camps for their husbands and fathers to be released from military service or for Union officials to devise a relocation program, freedom turned into a horrible nightmare of misery and death. Ill-prepared for a long encampment, the refugees suffered terribly. They had no clothes or adequate shelter to protect them from the cold. Refugee freedmen at Davis Bend in Mississippi occupied structures that one observer said were "not fit to shelter cattle in during a storm." Disease was rampant. Outbreaks of smallpox, yellow fever, cholera, and dysentery raced through the camps doing their deadly work. The military and the northern freedmen's aid societies found it impossible to provide sufficient food, clothing, housing, and medicine for the people. As always, the children and the elderly were the most vulnerable. "The poor Negroes die as fast as ever," Laura Towne wrote tearfully from South Carolina. "The children are all emaciated to the last degree and have such violent coughs and dysenteries that few survive. It is frightful to see such suffering among children." [14]

The slaves' initial response to emancipation, to a new and undefined life, therefore necessarily went far beyond merely celebrating the "Day of Jubilo," as the former slaves referred to their freedom day. Emancipation meant much more than deliverance from statutory slavery, and their reaction to freedom reflected all the uncertainty, the trauma, and the ambiguity of their new lives as well as the joy of their new status.

Their response included behavior intended to confirm their new legal status and to help them explore its furthest dimensions. As they stepped across the threshold from slavery to freedom, men and women all across the South who had lived in narrowly and often painfully circumscribed worlds indulged a powerful urge to test their new freedom, to experience what it was like to be really free. The expressions of that desire varied

13. Roger L. Ransom and Richard Sutch, *One Kind of Freedom: The Economic Consequences of Emancipation* (Cambridge, Mass., 1977), 13; *Congressional Globe,* 39th Cong., 1st Sess., Pt. 1, p. 74; Charles L. Perdue, Jr., Thomas E. Barden, and Robert K. Phillips, eds., *Weevils In the Wheat: Interviews with Virginia Ex-Slaves* (Charlottesville, 1976), 130; "Colloquy with Colored Ministers," *Journal of Negro History,* XVI (1931), 89, 91; Dennett, *The South as It Is,* 15; Gerald David Jaynes, *Branches Without Roots: Genesis of the Black Working Class in the American South, 1862–1882* (New York, 1986), 19, 39–53, 70, 109, 130–31.

14. Rose, *Rehearsal for Reconstruction,* 322, 332; Hermann, *Pursuit of a Dream,* 51–53; Botume, *First Days Amongst the Contrabands,* 32, 56, 67, 78–79.

from one person to another, but they all embodied the simple common purpose voiced by a Virginia freedman who said he "jes wanter see whut it feel lak tuh be free." An Alabama freedman told the reporter Whitelaw Reid exactly what freedom meant to him: "I's want to be a free man, cum when I please, and nobody say nuffin to me, nor order me roun." [15]

In church services and other celebrations, the freedmen commemorated their emancipation as well as the role of black soldiers in their liberation. Emancipation day celebrations provided occasions for exercising the right to gather whenever and wherever they wished, behaving as they pleased, and reveling in the glory and excitement of their freedom. Following a tradition of religious celebration, people gave thanks to almighty God for their deliverance just as they had prayed for it in slave congregations, singing hymns of thanksgiving and patriotic verses like "John Brown." But the freedmen knew how to frolic, too, and they enjoyed picnics with plenty of booze and barbecue, paraded and danced and sang deliriously through the streets, and watched black troops drill in strict formation with banners flying and weapons recently raised to help liberate families and friends borne proudly on their shoulders. In March, 1865, a few weeks after Federal troops had entered Charleston, four thousand freed people paraded through the city's streets carrying a banner proclaiming "We Know No Master but Ourselves" and bearing a coffin with the announcement "Slavery is Dead." A month later, on April 14, freedmen joined with northern teachers and politicians to observe the raising of the Stars and Stripes once again over Fort Sumter. It was indeed a glorious day, though later that evening, at Ford's Theatre in Washington, President Lincoln was fatally shot. But despite the sadness that descended over them as a consequence of "Massa" Lincoln's death, the freedmen continued to celebrate their freedom. They attended Fourth of July observances in Richmond that summer. Indeed, they and the black soldiers who were in attendance seemed to be the only ones who enjoyed the festivities. Blacks in Savannah honored the founding of Liberia with anniversary ceremonies in September. People there and elsewhere had secretly celebrated the first settlement of emancipated slaves in Africa for years and had determined, a journalist reported, "being now free, to make a grand and imposing demonstration on that day." And so they did, with speeches, sermons, prayers, and displays of happiness. These events elated the freedmen and engendered feelings of pride and satisfaction.

15. Litwack, *Been in the Storm So Long,* 192; Reid, *After the War,* 389.

They felt ennobled by their new status and by the role their troops had played in their emancipation.[16]

Emancipation day celebrations occurred in most parts of the South; however, picnics, parades, and revelry could not possibly express the broad range or the ambivalent character of the freedmen's feelings about their new condition and about their former masters. A store of bitterness and resentment had accumulated through the years of their bondage. As the end of slavery approached, many slaves anticipated that freedom would release them from any obligation to be subservient or deferential toward whites. Some expected to turn the tables on their former masters. One servant, enduring a scolding from her mistress that was plainly exhausting her forbearance but looking forward to new things to come, snapped back: "I expect the white folks to be waiting on me before long!"[17]

Not always able to transform such fantasies into reality, freed people nevertheless behaved in ways they considered consistent with their new status. They no longer lowered their eyes or doffed their caps in the presence of whites; they refrained from the customary use of the terms "Massa" or "Mistus" when addressing whites; and they expressed resentment at being called "Auntie" or "Uncle." They were not anyone's slaves any more; they were free people and not the "Auntie" or "Uncle" of any white person. Henry McNeal Turner, a Methodist minister and South Carolina native returning to Columbia late in 1865 for the first time since emancipation, was gratified by the attitude he observed among the people he met. Eager for southern blacks to develop confidence in themselves and a sense of race pride, he wanted them to assert their rights as free persons. He noted that the citizens of Columbia were "brave, independent, and fearless," and he witnessed "none of this foolish crouching before white men" that was so demeaning and typical of slave behavior. But he added, "at least I never saw any of it." And well he should have, because even though he had not noticed it in Columbia, many blacks continued to behave toward whites as they always had; indeed,

16. Litwack, *Been in the Storm So Long,* 73; Foner, *Reconstruction,* 72; Dennett, *The South as It Is,* 9–10; Botume, *First Days Amongst the Contrabands,* 75–78; *Christian Recorder,* September 1, 1866. For a discussion of the origins of emancipation day celebrations see William H. Wiggins, Jr., *O Freedom! Afro-American Emancipation Celebrations* (Knoxville, 1989).

17. William W. Ball, *The State That Forgot: South Carolina's Surrender to Democracy* (Indianapolis, 1932), 129.

Turner had seen displays of fawning and servile behavior elsewhere, and so had other observers. The ways of slavery sometimes died hard, and behavior rooted in a lifetime of experience was not easy to change, nor did all freedmen want to change it.[18]

Freedom meant that the former slaves could move about in the countryside or in towns and cities without being required to carry passes. The freedmen claimed the right to walk down the street on their own business, without being on errands for or in the company of masters or mistresses. In some localities, whites attempted to restrict their movement as they had during slavery, but such laws, like the one in Opelousas, Louisiana, requiring blacks to have passes and establishing a curfew for them, did not succeed in their intent. "We-uns kin go jist anywhar. Don't keer for no pass—go when yer want'er," one freedman proclaimed. In many cases the black soldiers were the first to experience this new freedom. James Jones was proud and boastful of his new status in southern society, noting that he now walked "fearlessly and boldly" along southern city streets and was no longer required to doff his cap upon meeting a white person "or to give all the sidewalks to those lordly princes of the sunny south, the planters' sons!"[19]

In addition to exercising their new freedom of mobility, former slaves seized the opportunity that emancipation provided to disentangle themselves from white people. This often meant putting physical space between themselves and their former masters. For freedom to have real meaning, it was imperative that they break completely from the ties that had formed the master-slave relationship. So in countless cases men and women walked away from plantations after learning of their emancipation, usually with a particular destination in mind and invariably with a determination to put as much distance as possible between themselves and their lives as slaves. Many of them did not leave home immediately, and when they did, they did not go far. Alice Battle's family stayed on their old master's plantation from May until Christmas, when they moved about nine miles away and started working on another farm. It did not matter whether their masters had been kind or abusive to them in bondage. It was slavery they were walking away from, not people. "Sorry to lef' you, massa; good-bye, massa," slaves informed a Virginia planter

18. *Christian Recorder,* November 18, 1865, January 20, 1866; Dennett, *The South as It Is,* 4, 42–43, 58; Botume, *First Days Amongst the Contrabands,* 132.

19. Foner, *Reconstruction,* 198, 209–10; New York *Times,* April 30, 1865; *Christian Recorder,* April 15, 1865.

who claimed that his "people were always well treated, and never were worked hard." When he asked them to explain why they were leaving, they answered simply, "Oh, sah, we 'bleege to go, sah." Although there were many practical reasons for leaving, separating themselves from the people and places that represented their enslavement, the old plantations and their masters, was a symbolic gesture of the freedmen's emancipation from slavery. It was important for them to make as clean a break with their past as possible. In Florida a black preacher named Richard Edwards understood that; he urged a crowd of listeners to leave their homes, arguing that if they stayed on they would never be free of the domination of their erstwhile masters. "So long es de shadder ob de gret house falls acrost you, you ain't gwine ter feel lak no free man, an' you ain't gwine ter feel lak no free 'omen. You mus' al move—you mus' move clar way from de ole places what you know, ter de new places what you don't know, whey you kin raise up you head outen no fear Marse Dis or Marse Tudder." [20]

If plantations and former masters reminded the freedmen of their old way of life, having their own churches and attending to their own spiritual needs symbolized the reality of their new freedom. Control of their churches was as much a part of being self-reliant as owning their own land and exercising legal and political rights. It held a central place in the new world that was opening up to them. "If they have been set free," reported Captain Horace James, a Freedmen's Bureau official in North Carolina, "they want their liberty to buy and sell and get gain; to select and favor their own church, school and party; to defend themselves; to hold written documents, instead of verbal promises; and to rearrange their own affairs." That biracial churches were not acceptable in the new order was evident in the comment of Charles Octavius Boothe, an Alabama Baptist minister who wrote some years later about the new relationship between whites and blacks: "The ex-master and ex-slave did not quite fit each other in the 'old meeting house,' as they had in days of yore." And it was dramatically stated in the action of the Reverend Morris Henderson, a former slave who was freed in February, 1865, and who led his Baptist congregation out of the church building in Memphis that whites had allowed them to worship in and moved into a rude shelter of

20. Kolchin, *First Freedom*, 4–8; Litwack, *Been in the Storm So Long*, 30–35, 230, 296–326; Dennett, *The South as It Is*, 14, 364–65; George P. Rawick, ed., *Georgia Narratives* (Westport, 1977), Pt. 1, pp. 43–44, Vol. III in Rawick, ed., *The American Slave, Supplemental Series 1*, 12 vols.

tree limbs and branches known as a brush arbor. Churchgoing blacks and whites began fashioning a new relationship in the months after emancipation. Not all of its intricacies were immediately apparent, but one fact was certain, at least to many freedmen, and that was that they were free now to worship alone. They could listen to and react to their own preachers in their own way, singing, dancing, and shouting as the spirit moved them. And, of course, a church structure was already in place. It needed only to be formalized, in the case of the slaves' "invisible" church, or transplanted from the North and the cities on the edges of the former slave South and adapted to the needs of the freedmen.[21]

Although the former bondsmen were elated by the changes that emancipation held in the offing and certainly hungered for the progress they hoped would be the fruit of their freedom, they continued to derive great comfort and pleasure from their traditional religious experiences and were loath to abandon them. The new independent black church not only symbolized freedom; it also provided continuity with southern blacks' cultural roots and a feeling of belonging to a caring community at a time when the social organization of the plantation was disintegrating and many of the old bonds of communion were snapping as people migrated in search of jobs and family members. "Their long silent preachers *want* to preach," wrote a northern teacher, "& the people prefer them." They yearned to listen to their own preachers shout out the gospel using the vocabulary and syntax of black dialect and with the enthusiasm that showed that God was present in and speaking through them. They wanted to revel in the glorious message that like the people of Israel they too had been led through the wilderness and delivered from bondage. The people trusted their preachers to lead them into an uncertain future. Slave preachers had shared with their people the trials of servitude, and most freedmen were confident that their own preachers could advise them in both spiritual and worldly matters better than white ministers could. A white minister in Wytheville, Virginia, wrote to the African Methodist Episcopal church that freedmen "are very anxious, indeed, to see a minister of your Church, and learn from him what they had better do as to church relations." A gathering of Virginia Baptists, representing twenty-eight churches and more than fourteen thousand members, discussed the pastorate of black churches. Afterward, one member recorded that

21. *Freedmen's Record*, I (1865), 143; C. O. Boothe, *Cyclopedia of Negro Baptists in Alabama* (Birmingham, 1895), 34; T. O. Fuller, *The History of the Negro Baptists of Tennessee* (Memphis, 1936), 73–74.

through the course of the discussion "it was manifest that the churches of the Association are decidedly in favor of having *colored pastors.* . . . Amen and Amen, was the hearty response." Writing in the 1880s, T. Thomas Fortune, a former slave who had become editor and publisher of the New York *Age,* noted that blacks had concluded it was "best to have nothing but colored ministers in their own pulpits." [22]

Leaving the white-controlled churches of antebellum times was an exercise in disengagement from the humiliating features of slavery and from contemptuous and condescending whites. Their own churches, regardless of the practices and the nature of the service, were an important emblem of the control that black people of the South now hoped to exert over their lives. No longer would they be required to obtain permission to conduct religious meetings or to have a white person present as had been common in antebellum times. "Praise God for this day of liberty to worship God," exclaimed one black man. "Bless God, my son, we don't have to keep watch at that door to tell us the patrollers are coming to take us to jail and fine us twenty-five dollars for prayin' and talkin' of the love of Jesus. Oh no, we's FREE!" Establishing and maintaining their own churches developed pride and self-respect and affirmed their capacity to be self-reliant. The Florida preacher Richard Edwards told his followers: "You-al is jis' as good as enny body, an' you-all is jis es free!" Their churches confirmed his assertion. Summing up the significance of the movement toward independent churches among the freedmen some years later, Matthew Gilbert, a Baptist minister from Tennessee, reflected on the importance of proving their worthiness in a society that was free of slavery but in which hostile and prejudiced whites still had the upper hand. He wrote that "the emancipation of the colored people made the colored churches and ministry a necessity, both by virtue of the prejudice existing against us and of our essential manhood before the laws of the land." [23]

22. George P. Rawick, ed., *Texas Narratives* (Westport, 1972), 35, Vol. IV of Rawick, ed., *The American Slave: A Composite Autobiography,* 19 vols.; Litwack, *Been in the Storm So Long,* 461; *Christian Recorder,* September 1, 1866; Colored Shiloh Baptist Association of Virginia, *Minutes of the Second Annual Session of the Colored Shiloh Baptist Association of Virginia . . . 1866* (Petersberg, Va., 1866), 6; T. Thomas Fortune, *Black and White* (New York, 1884), 69–70.

23. Rawick, ed., *South Carolina Narratives* (Westport, 1972), Pt. 1, p. 241, Vol. II of Rawick, ed., *American Slave, A Composite Autobiography,* 19 vols.; Rawick, ed., *Texas Narratives,* Pt. 1, p. 199; Litwack, *Been in the Storm So Long,* 297, 465; Matthew Gilbert, "Colored Churches: An Experiment," *National Baptist Magazine,* I (1894), 165.

Of all the ways the former slaves displayed their newly acquired freedom, leaving the white-controlled churches and forming their own religious organizations was perhaps the easiest and most gratifying. Abandoning their old plantation homes was seldom accompanied by celebrations or rejoicing. It was a determined act that frequently brought them up against some form of resistance. Gathering in their own congregations, however, conducting their own services, and listening to their own preachers had a warm and comfortable feel to it and was usually a happy occasion. Charles Corey, a white Baptist missionary working among the freedmen of Charleston shortly after emancipation, observed a group of blacks rejoicing at being able to gather, as the Old Testament prophets had foretold, under "their own vine and fig tree" and joyfully proclaiming that thereafter "none shall make us afraid." Whites often noted, usually scornfully, the emotional excitement of black worship. John W. De Forest, the Freedmen's Bureau agent, thought of the freedmen's prayer meetings as "little better than frolics." But behind the disdain for and lack of understanding of black religious forms that prompted such remarks was an accurate description of the euphoria that prevailed in most black religious meetings.[24]

Founding their own churches carried fewer negative repercussions and provided more substantial rewards to the freedmen than leaving the plantations, farms, shops, and town houses of their former masters for new ones, also owned by whites, who were just as determined as they had ever been to control the blacks' labor and behavior. Leaving the plantation was not always easy or pleasant, regardless of how mild or harsh the slave experience had been, because it meant deserting friends and familiar places where sometimes generations of their families had lived and died. Whites employed violence and intimidation to try to prevent the freedmen from leaving the plantations. Former slaves who departed the old places and later decided because of loneliness or the inability to secure work to return sometimes discovered that their former masters would not hire them back. They may have been freed from the exploitation of slavery, but they were still vulnerable to the vindictiveness of resentful planters, not to mention more severe reprisals by marauding whites whose rage over losing the war and having to accept the emancipation of slaves drove them to retaliate against the freedmen's "impertinence" and un-

24. Charles H. Corey, *A History of Richmond Theological Seminary: With Reminiscences of Thirty Years' Work Among the Colored People of the South* (Richmond, 1885), 26; De Forest, *Union Officer in the Reconstruction*, 99.

willingness to work under the same conditions as before. Forming their own churches was typically a satisfying if not an altogether pleasant experience that carried little of the ambivalence of leaving the home place and seldom met with much resistance from southern whites. The freedmen were generally able to provide themselves with the church environment they wanted free from the sense of betrayal and disillusionment that marred other aspects of their new freedom.[25]

But if forming their own churches gave the people satisfaction and commonly occurred with the acquiescence of local whites, it could also elicit acts of white violence. Indeed, no black person, institution, or black-owned building, especially in the rural areas, was immune to attacks by angry whites who hated the "uppity" freedmen and sought vengeance for their defeat. White vigilante groups like the Ku Klux Klan aimed to nullify the effect of emancipation through the use of terror—including murder or the threat of it—to intimidate blacks and force them to accept white supremacy. Acts of violence happened all across the South and were as much a part of the postwar scene as northern carpetbaggers, New England teachers, and a war-torn landscape. Federal troops, in the towns and cities where they were usually stationed, afforded blacks some protection against white attacks, as did agents of the Freedmen's Bureau; beyond those enclaves, however, law enforcement was in the hands of local white councils and militia that could not or would not protect blacks from violence. Not only were the Federal troops unable to provide rural blacks with much protection against assaults, but they also sometimes abetted or even committed acts of violence against blacks. Much of this violence was politically motivated as whites attempted to prevent blacks from taking part in government. Because blacks used their churches for political meetings and ministers often became political leaders, churches and clerics fell victim to white violence. Gun-wielding bushwackers burned down buildings and terrorized congregations and church leaders. Even in the cities, where the freedmen were generally safer from white violence, they and their churches came under attack. In the race riots that shook New Orleans and Memphis in 1866, church buildings were destroyed and ministers were among the casualties. Even where acts of violence were not aimed directly at the church or its leaders, the ideals

25. Kolchin, *First Freedom*, 22; Litwack, *Been in the Storm So Long*, 309–10, 321–22, 323–24, 329; Edmund L. Drago, *Black Politicians and Reconstruction in Georgia: A Splendid Failure* (Baton Rouge, 1982), 111; Foner, *Reconstruction*, 119–23.

of peace and love that they symbolized did not shield them from the generalized hatred and brutality of whites. In Opelika, Alabama, a young black preacher named Robert Alexander was waylaid, brutally assaulted, and nearly killed by a group of whites. He may have been attacked because he was a leader of the black church or merely because he was black, but in any event his being a man of God did not protect him from bloodthirsty white thugs.[26]

Northern missionaries played an important role in the early development of the independent black church. The largest number of evangelists were Baptists and Methodists, with a sizable contingent of Congregationalists and fewer Presbyterians. Most of them were white. These denominations conducted their missionary work through such groups as the American Baptist Home Mission Society, the Methodist Freedmen's Aid Society, and the American Missionary Association. A smaller number of missionaries represented the African Methodist Episcopal and African Methodist Episcopal Zion churches. They did not have the financial resources their white brethren enjoyed, but they appealed to the freedmen of the South in a way that the white missionaries could not.

Missionary activity among the southern black population followed in the wake of advancing Union armies and commenced when Federal forces established their presence in the Chesapeake and Potomac River areas of Virginia, Newbern and Wilmington in North Carolina, and the Sea Islands of South Carolina during the second year of the war. Military chaplains, especially those assigned to black regiments, not only performed ministerial duties among the troops but also served as missionaries among the slaves who fled from their plantations and sought protection and freedom in the Federal military camps. The African Methodist Episcopal minister Henry M. Turner was the first black appointed to the chaplaincy of a regiment of black troops. He ministered to soldiers in his unit and to the freedmen in North Carolina during the war. Another

---

26. Dennett, *The South as It Is,* 109–11, 183, 222–23, 245, 255; U.S. Senate, *Testimony Taken by the Joint Select Committee to Inquire into the Conditions of Affairs in the Late Insurrectionary States,* 42nd Cong., 2nd Sess., *Georgia Testimony,* I, 354, II, 690; Herbert Shapiro, *White Violence and Black Response: From Reconstruction to Montgomery* (Amherst, 1988), 5–29; *Christian Recorder,* July 28, August 18, 1866; James Gilbert Ryan, "The Memphis Riots of 1866: Terror in a Black Community During Reconstruction," *Journal of Negro History,* LXII (1977), 243, 249; Litwack, *Been in the Storm So Long,* 279, 469.

chaplain, David Stevens of the AME Zion church, preached to military and civilian congregations in Portsmouth.[27]

Northern white-controlled churches quickly became involved in missionary work. Eager to bring the Christian gospel and moral instruction to the liberated slaves, leaders of the American Baptist Home Mission Society of New York voted in 1862 to take immediate steps to supply contraband slaves with Christian instruction by means of missionaries and teachers as fast and as far "as the progress of our arms and the restoration of order and law shall open the way." Assuming that southern slaves had been denied access to the gospel of salvation, the society geared itself up for a major evangelical effort to put them on the path to redemption. Through a Christian education the former slaves, whom their masters had taught only the lessons of sin and irresponsibility, could be transformed into moral beings. Thus the strategy of these Christian soldiers was to wage war against the evils of ignorance and immorality that oppressed the South's freed people even after emancipation. "We must educate them, send missionaries to them and make their religious fervor intelligent."[28]

The society's missionaries began arriving in Beaufort, South Carolina, during the spring of 1862 and set out immediately to evangelize the freedmen, whose masters had fled from plantations in the Sea Islands of South Carolina below Charleston when Federal forces had established a base at Port Royal in November, 1861. They were participants in a visionary program known as the Port Royal experiment that intended to prepare slaves for freedom. A group of abolitionists, including Secretary of the Treasury Salmon P. Chase, had organized the enterprise and recruited supporters from among freedmen's aid and missionary societies in Boston, New York, and Philadelphia. The individuals who were attracted to this experiment shared an abolitionist lineage, and not surprisingly they were eager to assist slaves in making an orderly transition to freedom even before the government's emancipation policy had crystallized. But they divided sharply into evangelicals who took a holistic approach to assistance for the freedmen and more materialistic nonsectarians whose

27. *Christian Recorder,* October 24, November 28, 1863; New York *Age,* September 8, 1888.

28. American Baptist Home Mission Society, *Baptist Home Missions in North America, Including a Full Report of the Jubilee Meeting, and a Historical Sketch of the American Baptist Home Mission Society Tables, 1832–1882* (New York, 1883), 397; American Baptist Home Mission Society, *Report* (New York, 1865), 9.

aim was to revolutionize southern agriculture. Business-minded reformers saw the project as a chance to transform slaves into efficient wage
laborers. They believed that creating a "free peasantry" would prove the
abolitionist assertion that free labor was more profitable than slave labor.
The missionary societies associated with the project focused on educating
and reforming the moral character of the freedmen. "The great work,"
one evangel proclaimed, "is to *unlearn* them and learn them *from,* the
vices, habits and associations of their former lives." These missionaries
and teachers, labeled Gideonites by skeptics who thought them excessively sentimental, were joined by more of their brethren in succeeding
years. Within three years the American Baptist Home Mission Society
had sixty-eight missionaries in the southern field and had spent $5,000
on the evangelization of the freedmen. Although the society's responsibility was missionary work, its members shared the enthusiasm of their
more secular colleagues with respect to the evolving political goals of the
North in the Civil War. With its missionary enterprise among the South's
freedmen under way, society officials contemplated the "entire reorgani-
zation of the social and religious state of the South." [29]

The Baptist missionaries who followed Yankee armies into the South
did not lack sectarian competition. Evangelists representing three Methodist denominations were striving at the same time to recruit southern
blacks and to unite them with the northern Methodist organizations. Federal occupation of areas along the Atlantic coast, including Port Royal,
early in the Civil War opened the way for African Methodist Episcopal,
African Methodist Episcopal Zion, and Methodist Episcopal missionaries. Representatives of these denominations, sponsored by their respective
mission societies, began arriving in occupied areas during the summer of
1862. In June Benjamin Tucker Tanner, who had recently resigned the
pastorate of the Fifteenth Street Presbyterian Church in Washington and
had joined the AME church, organized St. John's Chapel and Sunday
school among the blacks of Alexandria, Virginia. In August another
AME missionary, George A. Rue, passed through Washington on his way
to Newbern, North Carolina. [30]

Momentum for aiding their southern brethren built rapidly among the
African Methodists after the Preliminary Emancipation Proclamation.
Henry M. Turner, then still pastor of Israel AME Church in Washington,

29. Rose, *Rehearsal for Reconstruction,* 217–19, 235.
30. *Christian Recorder,* March 22, July 5, 19, August 9, 1862.

promptly called on the AME church to act on behalf of freed slaves, revealing his strong personal as well as racial bonds with southern blacks. Turner had been freeborn in South Carolina in 1833. His father was a mulatto, and his mother claimed descent from African royalty. He grew up in Columbia and Abbeville, was educated by an assortment of white and black people, including some lawyers in Abbeville, joined the Southern Methodist church at the age of sixteen, and became a licensed preacher at twenty. He moved to New Orleans in 1857, where he came under the influence of two AME ministers, Willis R. Revels and John M. Brown. Turner joined the African Methodist church, studied the classics, English literature, Latin, Greek, Hebrew, and theology, and advanced rapidly through the ranks of the church hierarchy until he became an elder. Bishop Daniel Alexander Payne stationed him in Washington in 1862. Although standing only five feet five inches tall, he was a powerfully built man with a combative personality. Turner understood that the church was carrying out its missionary campaign within the framework of a massive northern assault against secession, armed rebellion, and now slavery, but he did not want whites to take control of the education and uplift of the freed slaves. That role properly belonged to blacks themselves. He was also eager for them to take a prominent position in the ranks of soldiers bearing arms and the cross into the South. He helped to recruit black troops for the army and appealed to race solidarity in arguing for an active black missionary program in the South. "Every man of us now," Turner exclaimed, "who has a speck of grace or bit of sympathy, for the race that we are inseparably identified with, is called upon by force of surrounding circumstances, to extend a hand of mercy *to bone of our bone and flesh of our flesh*." It was not until early the next year, however, that any African Methodist missionaries answered his call and joined their white brethren in South Carolina.[31]

When the Baltimore Conference of the AME church met in April, 1863, C. C. Leigh of the Methodist Episcopal church asked if there were any ministers willing to volunteer to go to South Carolina and work with freed slaves. Leigh was also an official of the New York National Freedmen's Aid Society, an organization closely associated with the American Missionary Association, which recruited missionaries and teachers for the Port Royal project. Leigh told presiding Bishop Daniel A. Payne, "The

31. New York *Globe,* April 21, 1883; New York *Age,* September 8, 1888; *Christian Recorder,* October 4, 1862.

field is yours; go and occupy it." Two AME ministers, James D. Lynch of Georgetown, D.C., and James D. S. Hall of New York, answered the call. They departed New York on May 20 aboard a steamship destined for Port Royal. Three other AME ministers who later traveled to South Carolina, Daniel A. Payne, Benjamin T. Tanner, and Richard Harvey Cain, stood on the wharf and wished them well as the ship steamed out of the harbor. Arriving at Hilton Head early on the evening of May 23, Hall and Lynch boarded another vessel that carried them to Beaufort, where they were quartered.[32]

Hall, who had a successful ministerial career but never distinguished himself either before or after his missionary experience, remains a little-known figure; however, the twenty-four-year-old Lynch was a very different case. He had been born in Baltimore of a slave mother and a free black father. After purchasing his wife's and son's freedom, the elder Lynch sent James to Kimball Union Academy in New Hampshire. Following graduation he attended the AME church's Wilberforce University in Ohio. In 1858 he joined the Presbyterian church but soon transferred his membership to the African Methodist Episcopal church. He labored as a minister for a time in Illinois and afterward was assigned to the Ebenezer AME Church in Georgetown. In 1863 he was one of the rising stars of the African Methodist ministry. Though a young man among the hierarchs of the church, he possessed a mature self-confidence and always made a positive impression on those he encountered. He was articulate and compelling whether writing letters as a correspondent of the AME church's *Christian Recorder* or preaching from the pulpit. His sermons and public addresses were models of discourse, informed and well organized. But his greatest skill was a remarkable ability to weave spells over both the educated people of the North, who were the main financial contributors to the church, and the simple, uneducated folk among the South's refugee population.[33]

As Lynch and Hall docked in South Carolina, the councils of the Lincoln administration and the military command in the Department of the South were making decisions destined to shape the definition of freedom for blacks in the postwar era. In those deliberations moral justice was

32. Clarence E. Walker, *A Rock in a Weary Land: The African Methodist Episcopal Church During the Civil War and Reconstruction* (Baton Rouge, 1982), 48–49; Rose, *Rehearsal for Reconstruction,* 152, 218; *Christian Recorder,* May 30, June 6, 1863.

33. Charles S. Smith, *A History of the African Methodist Episcopal Church* (1922; rpr. New York, 1968), 46; *Christian Recorder,* November 24, 1866.

often sacrificed to the business interests of influential northerners. Beginning in March, confiscated estates were sold at public auction rather than distributed among the blacks who had formerly worked them. So instead of becoming small landowners, most of the people were working for wages under the direction of white supervisors from the North. Many of the men were conscripted into the army, often without being permitted to notify their families of their whereabouts. By summer, the army had raised two regiments of black troops in the islands, Colonel Thomas Wentworth Higginson's 1st South Carolina Volunteers and Colonel James Montgomery's 2nd South Carolina regiment. A third unit of black troops in the department, the 54th Massachusetts commanded by Colonel Robert Gould Shaw, was composed of northern blacks. In June and July, the black soldiers saw significant action, including a controversial raid on the little Georgia town of Darien and the courageous but futile assault on Battery Wagner, which was part of the Union offensive against Charleston. In the Battery Wagner engagement, Colonel Shaw was killed and almost half of the 54th became casualties in the cause of freedom, but the fitness of blacks for soldiering could no longer be questioned and the troops' conduct under fire gave considerable force to the claim that blacks deserved full citizenship as well as freedom. Notwithstanding the honor won by the black troops, however, the rewards that they and their families gained were meager, and distrust of Yankees continued to grow.[34]

Bishop Alexander Wayman was instrumental in organizing Methodist congregations in Virginia, where the missionaries had fairly easy access to the freedmen in areas of Federal occupation. Wayman secured permission from military officials late in 1863 to travel from Baltimore to Norfolk. Members of St. John's Chapel had sent to the Baltimore Conference for a missionary who could help them affiliate with the AME church. Wayman met with several hundred Methodists when he arrived and welcomed them into the church. Presently, he brought Bishop Payne and John M. Brown, a successful missionary in Missouri and Louisiana, to the city. St. John's became the first AME congregation in the state.[35]

Meanwhile, missionary work among the freedmen in the Port Royal area continued under the direction of Mansfield French, a Methodist clergyman, and Edward Pierce, a Massachusetts lawyer, who directed the

34. Rose, *Rehearsal for Reconstruction*, 214–16, 242–60.
35. Daniel A. Payne, *Recollections of Seventy Years* (Nashville, 1888), 154–56; Israel L. Butt, *History of African Methodism in Virginia; or, Four Decades in the Old Dominion* (Hampton, 1908), 32–35, 224.

Port Royal experiment. The missionary program was aimed at teaching the freedmen "civilization and Christianity." James Lynch was assigned to St. Helena and Ladies islands, but he also established churches among the freedmen on Hilton Head. In Beaufort and at Hilton Head he found thousands of freedmen working on cotton plantations; many were receptive to him and his effort to organize churches. "There is no difficulty in so doing," he noted; "the elements are here, though rough. I expect before three months we will have organized a dozen societies." At Mitchellville, a refugee camp located about a mile from Hilton Head, he found twelve hundred to fifteen hundred blacks striving to establish churches, and he organized an AME congregation among them. At Helenaville he encountered about eight hundred more freedmen and organized yet another congregation. Lynch's primary missionary responsibility was to provide for a permanent church organization as part of the larger objective of establishing Christian communities among the freedmen. He worked with amazing intensity to organize churches and to license local preachers, who were to continue to conduct services on an ongoing basis after he had moved on to other areas. It was a step-by-step process that built the church steadily in membership, number of congregations, and licensed clergymen. Lynch reported, "I licensed two local preachers, and two exhorters who had previously been verbally licensed; last Sabbath I received twenty into the church; we now number one hundred and seventy-three." [36]

James Hall also labored among the freedmen at Beaufort and Hilton Head and organized them into AME congregations. After spending several months in South Carolina, Hall was transferred to a church in Washington, but Lynch remained in the South. [37]

In December, 1864, while he was in Beaufort, Lynch heard that General William Tecumseh Sherman's army had completed its march from Atlanta to the sea and had occupied Savannah. Obtaining a pass from the local military authorities, he set out by transport vessel for the old coastal city. He arrived there a few days later, along with Mansfield French, and began immediately to enroll blacks in the AME denomination and to work with John W. Alvord of the American Tract Society on a program to aid freedmen who were eager to establish their own schools. Sherman's

36. Rose, *Rehearsal for Reconstruction,* 21–41; Walker, *Rock in a Weary Land,* 82; *Christian Recorder,* June 6, 27, July 25, 1863; *Freedmen's Record,* I (1865), 13–15.
37. *Christian Recorder,* February 17, 1865.

march had liberated thousands of slaves in Georgia, presenting the northern missionaries and teachers with an enormous challenge. Their numbers were few, and they had to cover a lot of territory and bring thousands of freedmen into the fold. "The field in Savannah," Lynch reported, "is now the most important point along the eastern coast. How long I can be here, I do not know. My work in South Carolina calls loudly for me. We want more ministers of our Church sent down this way." Like most AME missionaries, Lynch felt acutely both the limited financial support that was available to the church's emissaries and the overwhelming task of organizing so many freedmen into congregations.[38]

Representatives of the African Methodist Episcopal Zion church were also among the first wave of northern missionaries to sweep into the South to work among the freedmen during the Civil War. Andrew Cartwright, a former slave who had escaped to the North and joined the church, moved to Virginia in 1863 as a preacher and established the first AME Zion congregation in the South. Earlier that same year, Superintendent Joseph J. Clinton had directed John Williams to go to Newbern, then recently occupied by Federal troops, to organize a congregation among the freedmen. After almost a year, however, Williams still had not departed, and the impatient Clinton dispatched James W. Hood to take up the field. Hood was a thirty-two-year-old Pennsylvanian who had been stationed at Bridgeport, Connecticut, after completing a three-year term as a missionary in Nova Scotia. He received his instructions in December, 1863, and left for North Carolina, where he arrived late in January. At Newbern he discovered some four hundred black former members of Andrew Chapel of the Methodist Episcopal Church, South, who were ready to attach themselves to one of the African Methodist denominations. The congregation had been under the pastoral care of a white missionary representing the Methodist Episcopal (ME) church for about a year. Hood defeated the attempts of two rival AME missionaries and the ME missionary to recruit the congregants and entered their names on the roll of the AME Zion church. A few weeks later Hood added a second congregation to his denomination, this one in Beaufort. When Williams finally arrived in Newbern and discovered that the field there was already occupied by several missionaries, he moved on to Roanoke Island and later to James City, a refugee camp across the Trent River from Newbern, and established Zion Methodist churches in both places. In May Clinton

38. *Ibid.,* January 21, 1865.

joined his two missionaries, and through the summer others followed. The work was arduous and contained an element of danger. An outbreak of yellow fever carried off some of the missionaries and discouraged the survivors, but Hood, Clinton, and ten others remained and gathered on December 17, 1864, to form the North Carolina Annual Conference, the first African Methodist conference below the Potomac River, which proved to be a bastion of Zion Methodism in the South.[39]

The physical and emotional strain on the missionaries who traveled through the South during and immediately after the war was extreme. Fatigue, disease, and the sweltering summer heat taxed their strength and endurance. Travel was difficult, particularly in the interior regions, because of the devastation caused by the war. Most southern railroads had suffered at least some damage: rails in many areas were torn up, rolling stock was destroyed, and those trains that were still running at the close of the war were usually crowded with passengers borne along in cars with seats and windows torn out of them. For many missionaries, probably most, travel by rail was not an option. Isaac P. Brockenton, a Baptist, traveled about in South Carolina, covering up to twenty miles at a time on foot. Henry Jones, an AME minister, walked ninety miles from Wilmington, North Carolina, to Conway, South Carolina, dressed in his long-tailed Prince Albert coat, to organize churches. The climate was hard on the missionaries. Northerners accustomed to cooler temperatures suffered from the miseries of labor in the tropical weather. Unlike many teachers who returned home for the summer months, the missionaries toiled all year long. Hiram R. Revels thought he understood summer heat before he came south as a missionary, "but I have now to confess that I knew but little of it. From the 1st of June till the present time the heat has not, during the whole day, been even moderate. Mentally and physically, it has nearly prostrated me. Had I not been so busy, I would have been sick long since."[40]

39. James W. Hood, *One Hundred Years of the African Methodist Episcopal Zion Church* (New York, 1895), 85–87, 185–88, 289–99; David H. Bradley, *A History of the A.M.E. Zion Church* (2 vols.; Nashville, 1956–70), I, 55; David L. Williams, *Black Americans and the Evangelization of Africa, 1870–1900* (Madison, 1982), 39; *Christian Recorder*, July 1, 1865; *Census of Religious Bodies: 1906* (2 vols.; Washington, D.C., 1910) I, 540, 542–62.

40. Thomas Holt, *Black over White: Negro Political Leadership in South Carolina During Reconstruction* (Urbana, 1977), 84; *Christian Recorder*, August 19, September 9, October 7, 1865.

Added to the physical stress was the tension between the missionaries and local whites. Their most extreme hostility, described by one northern missionary as "a perfect hatred," was more often directed at white than at black missionaries. Southern whites detested the Yankees, who represented the imposition of northern authority, riding boldly into Dixie in the company of Federal troops and endeavoring to inculcate their repugnant northern values in the "darkies," educating them to become citizens equal to whites and luring them out of the southern white churches and into northern denominations. But missionary work was risky for black churchmen as well. Whites had always employed violence to control blacks, and they continued to use violence or the threat of it to intimidate "uppity niggers" and maintain white hegemony. If the unarmed harbingers of the new order traveled much beyond the security of Federal soldiers almost anywhere in the South they exposed themselves to danger. George A. Rue, an African Methodist missionary, narrowly escaped trouble in Goldsboro, North Carolina. He reported that it was not "prudent to go very far east of New Bern yet." Before he could spread the gospel into surrounding areas, he testified to church officials in the North, the military would have "to do some more of their fine work." Even months after the end of the war it was still unsafe for missionaries to travel in some areas of the South. Hiram Revels came very near falling victim to murderers and robbers while traveling between Vicksburg and Jackson, Mississippi. "It is an undisguised fact," he wrote, "that no man can safely go beyond the lines of the Freedmen's Bureau, without endangering his life."[41]

Early in May, 1865, almost a month after the flag of the United States had been raised once again over Fort Sumter, Daniel Payne, a bishop in the African Methodist Episcopal church, returned to his native Charleston. This frail-looking and eccentric man had been absent from the city for thirty years. During the early 1830s, as a free person, he had conducted a school for black children, but when the South Carolina legislature prohibited such schools, Payne emigrated to Pennsylvania. There he taught school and attended a Lutheran seminary. After joining the AME church, he became one of its bishops and ultimately its most revered patriarch since the days of Richard Allen. Returning to Charleston in the

41. Kolchin, *First Freedom*, 115; Jones, *Soldiers of Light and Love*, 50; *Christian Recorder*, September 9, October 7, 1865; Foner, *Reconstruction*, 119–21.

wake of Union armies and the emancipation of the city's slaves, Payne preached in Bethel Lutheran Church, "the house of God in which I was awakened to a sense of my sinfulness when a child of only nine years." Most of the white communicants had fled into the interior with the approach of the Federals, and the church building had been appropriated by blacks.[42]

Once a gem among southern antebellum cities and a hotbed of secession, Charleston now showed the signs of defeat and bore the scars of months of bombardment by Federal batteries. The roofs of many of its fine waterfront buildings had been blasted by incoming artillery rounds, windows were shattered, and pavements had been torn up in erecting the city's defenses. The pallid faces of white citizens reflected hunger and defeat. Many of the old landmarks that Payne may have remembered were still there—the war damage was actually fairly light compared to elsewhere—but some of them betrayed the political consequences of the late struggle. Fancy hotels and fine restaurants that had once welcomed local grandees now catered to Union officers. A nearby racetrack, previously a playground for sportsmen, contained the graves of fallen soldiers. The AME missionaries, however, were exuberant. Present with Payne that spring were James Lynch, who had recently returned to the city from Savannah, William Bentley, Theophilus Gould Steward, and Richard H. Cain. Bentley, a venerable preacher who was widely known in Georgia, had met Lynch in Savannah, and Lynch had recruited him for the AME church. Steward, born in New Jersey in 1843, had been serving as a pastor in Camden when he was transferred to South Carolina. He was assigned to the territories of Beaufort, Sumerville, and Marion. Cain, the other AME pioneer who was in Charleston to celebrate the freedom of slaves in Dixie and the return of the AME church to South Carolina, was an exceptionally energetic man, physically robust, intellectually gifted, and striking in appearance with long, full sideburns. A native of Virginia, he had been taken by his parents to Ohio when he was a small boy. He converted to Methodism in 1841, joined the AME ministry in 1844, preached in several places in the Northwest, and later came to the attention of Payne, who discovered him preaching in Indiana in 1856. Recognizing "a young man of great uncultured talents," Payne sent the "crude

42. Payne, *Recollections,* 162–63; Charleston *Courier,* March 2, May 19, 1865; *Christian Recorder,* April 22, 1865.

and unpolished" preacher to the church's Wilberforce University and later placed him in the pulpit of the Bridge Street AME Church in Brooklyn. He installed Cain as the pastor of an AME church in Charleston.[43]

African Methodist leaders intended for South Carolina to be the center of missionary activity among the freedmen of the Southeast. Indeed, Payne was in Charleston for the express purpose of organizing the missions in North and South Carolina into an episcopal conference, the church's first such district in the heart of the old slaveholding South. The conference would direct further missionary activity in neighboring areas.

During the war, northern missionaries had been largely limited to areas of Federal occupation, where troops afforded protection. Their activities were thus restricted to the coastal areas of Virginia and the Carolinas, along with New Orleans and locations on the Mississippi River. But when the war ended and more evangelists arrived, missionary activity penetrated deeper into the vitals of the South. From South Carolina missionaries fanned out into Georgia. In June the indefatigable Lynch was back once again in Georgia, this time in Augusta, after a "long, tedious and perilous" trip up the Savannah River. Conditions there were fairly good, at least compared to Richmond, Columbia, Vicksburg, and Atlanta, which had suffered heavy destruction. Northern investment was keeping commerce alive, and the city's citizens, including blacks, were working hard to move ahead after the war. But the effects of the conflict were clearly noticeable. The economy was suffering; supplies were plentiful, but the money to buy them was not. And there was tension between blacks and whites. Among the latter, Lynch noticed scant loyalty to the Union. Among the former, there was anxiety, although the arrival of black troops brought a feeling of some security. Lynch found the local blacks to be "industrious and enterprising people," and he was confident that they "will take care of themselves." There were six black churches— two Methodist, three Baptist, and one Presbyterian. One of the Methodist congregations had about twelve hundred members and a black minis-

43. Reid, *After the War,* 57–58, 66–68; *Christian Recorder,* June 3, October 14, 1865; Smith, *History of the African Methodist Episcopal Church,* 505; Payne, *Recollections,* 331–32; Bishop T. M. D. Ward, "Quadriennial Address of the Board of Bishops of the A.M.E. Church," *A.M.E. Church Review,* V (July, 1888), 59; New York *Freeman,* June 13, 1885, January 22, 1887; Alexander W. Wayman, *Cyclopedia of African Methodism* (Baltimore, 1882), 155–56; William J. Simmons, *Men of Mark: Eminent, Progressive and Rising* (1887; rpr. New York, 1968), 866–71.

ter who had recently been ordained by the Methodist Episcopal Church, South. Lynch enrolled both congregations in the AME connection before departing the city and the South for Philadelphia to become editor of the *Christian Recorder.* While he was toiling in Augusta, other missionaries, including William Gaines and his brother Wesley John, were proselytizing and organizing the freedmen in other parts of the state. The Gaines brothers were both former slaves. Wesley later became an AME bishop, and William might have achieved that lofty rank if not for his premature death later in 1865.[44]

From their headquarters in South Carolina, AME missionaries directed considerable energy toward Florida. In May the newly formed South Carolina Conference, which included Florida, made William Stewart, a former slave who grew up in Jacksonville, the principal pastor of the Florida district. In 1862 he and his wife and children went as refugees to Beaufort, where he attended a school for blacks and joined the AME church. Stewart arrived back in Jacksonville in June and soon established a church a few miles away. Before long he had organized churches in Quincy, Monticello, Aucilla, and Lake City. He then moved to Tallahassee and found a congregation of 165 members awaiting him, whom he added to the tally. In February, 1866, Charles H. Pearce, whom the conference appointed presiding elder of the district, arrived in the state. Pearce quickly rose to become the most powerful early influence on the growth of the AME connection in the state.[45]

In Mississippi before the end of the war, a black evangelist named "Pappy" Adams asked the AME church's Missouri Conference to send a missionary to Vicksburg. The conference dispatched Page Tyler, who previously had been in charge of the Alton, Illinois, circuit, to Mississippi as a missionary. Tyler and Adams founded Bethel Church among black Methodists in Vicksburg. Hiram Revels, another AME missionary who arrived in the state in 1865, was placed in charge of the church as its pastor. Revels had to struggle to build the congregation, not against apa-

44. *Christian Recorder,* July 1, 8, 1865; Dennett, *The South as It Is,* 264; George A. Singleton, *The Romance of African Methodism: A Study of the African Methodist Episcopal Church* (New York, 1952), 105–106; Wesley J. Gaines, *African Methodism in the South, or, Twenty-five Years of Freedom* (Atlanta, 1890), 48–49, 205–206, 224–28.

45. New York *Freeman,* March 27, 1886, says that Stewart was not transferred to Florida until 1867. His name sometimes appears as Steward. See Joe M. Richardson, *The Negro in the Reconstruction of Florida, 1867–1877* (Tallahassee, 1965), 84–85.

thy or hostility so much as against the effects of the war on the ravaged city. Simply getting to the church for worship services was an ordeal for many members of the congregation who had to pass through the heavy fortifications that had been constructed by Union and Confederate forces during the long siege preceding its capture by Ulysses S. Grant. They had to traverse streets that had been "cut to pieces" by artillery bombardment and were regularly washed out or turned into quagmires by heavy rains. Revels' perseverance and that of his congregation paid dividends, however, in the satisfaction of seeing their church grow and prosper. The testimony of a member of Revels' congregation indicates the difficulty both the missionaries and their followers encountered. "We are trying to do the best we can," wrote Sarah Woodson, "both spiritually and temporally, and our church is rather in a good and prosperous condition. Our pastor has done all he could for us under the circumstances, and we would be glad to have him another year, if we can get him." Revels also traveled to Jackson, where he welcomed a Methodist congregation of about 150 persons into the fold. Another minister, John W. C. Pennington, was assigned to Natchez. Neither Revels nor Pennington, however, but Thomas W. Stringer became the church's most successful pioneer in Mississippi. Stringer had been a minister in Ohio until sometime after 1846, when he moved to Canada. After assisting in the formation of the British Methodist Episcopal church, he journeyed to Mississippi in 1865. He helped to found the AME church in Jackson and participated in the first annual conference in the state. He became presiding elder of the conference and held that position until his death in 1893.[46]

African Methodist missionaries had pushed all the way to Texas by early 1866. Although black chaplains had been ministering to both occupation troops and civilians, the first regular AME missionary in the state was M. M. Clark. Like most of his colleagues, Clark had been a minister in the North and in the border states before emancipation. After serving as a missionary in Louisiana and Alabama in 1865, he arrived in Galveston, where he met Emanuel Hammitt. Hammitt was in the city to receive ordination as a deacon in the Methodist Episcopal Church, South. Clark persuaded him to join the AME church instead

46. Revels A. Adams, *Cyclopedia of African Methodism in Mississippi* (Natchez, 1902), 12–13, 132, 147, 190–93, 204; Vernon L. Wharton, *The Negro in Mississippi, 1865–1890* (New York, 1965), 262; *Christian Recorder*, August 5, September 9, October 7, November 25, December 2, 1865.

and put him to work organizing the freedmen into congregations. Houston Reedy, another missionary, organized another AME church in Galveston.[47]

Black missionaries thought themselves uniquely suited to the task of evangelizing the freedmen. AME officials asserted that their church was "an instrument in the hands of God," leading the race out of the degradation of slavery. The bond of race and experience united the missionaries with the freedmen in ways that whites could never be. They all had felt the weight of the white man's boot. Many missionaries, like Henry M. Turner and Daniel A. Payne, had been born in the South. Some, like William and Wesley Gaines and William Stewart, had been slaves. They believed the black church was more faithful to Christian principles than the white church. All blacks had been victims of the dehumanization of the slave system to which the white southern church had accommodated itself. Even in the North, indeed in the white-controlled churches, racial discrimination was widespread. The missionaries welcomed the opportunity to forge a union with their southern brethren to realize the full promise of freedom, and though they welcomed white assistance, they resented white missionaries insinuating themselves into the freedmen's religious affairs with the intention of controlling or reforming their churches.[48]

The AME and AME Zion missionaries' chief rivals in recruiting southern blacks to Methodism were the representatives of the northern-based Methodist Episcopal church. The northern church had shown only casual interest in cultivating southern blacks during antebellum times, although it had contained a vocal antislavery element. As the Civil War drew to a conclusion, however, the freedmen increasingly occupied the thoughts of northern Methodists. But so did the vision of a reunited Methodist Episcopal church, divided since the 1840s over the issue of slavery. Therefore, it was toward southern whites, whom the northern church regarded as their errant brethren, that it directed its strongest appeals immediately after the war. But when the southern Methodist church made clear that it was in no mood for a reconciliation with Yankee Methodists, the northerners redirected their attention to the freedmen. Church

---

47. *Christian Recorder,* October 21, 1865; Singleton, *Romance of African Methodism,* 106; John W. Blassingame, *Black New Orleans, 1860–1888* (Chicago, 1973), 150; Hightower T. Kealing, *History of African Methodism in Texas* (Waco, 1885), 26–35.

48. Smith, *History of the A.M.E. Church,* 520.

officials proposed union with the African Methodist organizations, and its missionaries began feverishly working to organize freedmen into congregations. A large proportion of the northern church's missionary budget went to support missionary activity among the former slaves. Although it firmly adhered to a policy of not admitting blacks to the bishopric, the church established many black congregations. Within three years of the Confederacy's demise, the church had organized nine new annual conferences in the South and reported a black southern membership of ninety thousand.[49]

The Methodist Episcopal church enjoyed numerous advantages over its African Methodist rivals and appealed to the freedmen in several ways. It was wealthy and well organized. Its missionary program was bountifully endowed and effectively planned, focusing on the spiritual needs of the freedmen but not to the exclusion of education and the attainment of civil and political rights. The Methodist Freedmen's Aid Society was an active participant in the Port Royal experiment. The church's success in attracting southern blacks was largely owing to the energy and resourcefulness of its missionaries and to their ability to convince blacks that their goal was racial integration. God's kingdom was not segregated, northern churchmen asserted, and neither was the Methodist Episcopal church. "There will be no galleries in Heaven," proclaimed one cleric, referring to the separate seating arrangements that had existed in the biracial churches of the antebellum South. "Those who are willing to go with a church that makes no distinction as to race or color, follow me." The reason given for the exclusion of blacks from the office of bishop was that they were not yet fit for such a high position because of their educational deficiencies. It was an inviting message to many blacks, especially those who did not want to isolate themselves from white society and most especially when it came from the mouths of whites who vociferously declared their support for the freedmen in their struggle for the full fruits of freedom. This appeal was particularly successful in South Carolina, where the church made no distinction based on race in the organization

49. Ralph E. Morrow, *Northern Methodism and Reconstruction* (East Lansing, 1956), 125–28; Francis B. Simkins and Robert H. Woody, *South Carolina During Reconstruction* (Chapel Hill, 1932), 374–75; Sylvester Weeks, ed., *A Life's Retrospect: Autobiography of Rev. Granville Moody* (Cincinnati, 1890), 443–44; William Warren Sweet, *Methodism in American History* (Nashville, 1961), 283; Methodist Episcopal Church, General Conference, *Journal of the General Conference, 1868* (New York, 1868), 362; Walker, *Rock in a Weary Land*, 83–84.

of its congregations and its records included virtually no reference to race.[50]

But even more important to the ME church's success among the freedmen was that it often secured buildings in which they could worship, a service for which they were grateful. In November, 1863, the War Department empowered the church to occupy buildings in which disloyal ministers had been pastors. Church buildings formerly owned and occupied by whites could be turned over to the black congregations that were organized by ME missionaries and formally enrolled in the denomination. That was indeed an exciting prospect to freedmen who would otherwise be hard-pressed to obtain property.[51]

Many of the Methodist Episcopal missionaries, most of whom were white, not only succeeded in recruiting blacks as church members but also earned the staunch loyalty of their black congregations when African Methodist missionaries tried to persuade them to move over to their denominations. One of those ME missionaries was T. W. Lewis, the pastor of three churches in Charleston. When Richard H. Cain of the AME church wrote a letter to the *Christian Recorder* criticizing Lewis for trying to prevent congregations from joining the AME connection and accusing him of taking advantage of his control of church property, Lewis' supporters came to his defense, saying they wanted to "ward off the blow so maliciously aimed to wound the feelings, and traduce the usefulness of our kind and deservedly esteemed pastor." The substantial number of black members of ME congregations attests to its appeal to freedmen who wanted independence from their former masters and a close relationship with northern whites whom they considered their friends. The church's comparatively low standing among blacks, however, signifies that most Methodist freedmen preferred their own separate churches over those managed by either northern or southern whites.[52]

Presbyterians and Congregationalists also evangelized among the South's freed population. Although they appealed to higher-status blacks and mulattoes, neither of those churches was notably successful in con-

50. Kealing, *History of African Methodism in Texas*, 25–26; Morrow, *Northern Methodism*, 130; Joel Williamson, *After Slavery: The Negro in South Carolina During Reconstruction, 1861–1877* (Chapel Hill, 1965), 182–84; Simkins and Woody, *South Carolina During Reconstruction*, 376–77.

51. Walker, *Rock in a Weary Land*, 84.

52. *Christian Recorder*, July 29, 1865.

verting freedmen to their views or in organizing congregations among them. They were white-controlled denominations and did not offer blacks autonomy. The missionaries' strenuous efforts coupled with their marked failure to win black converts stand as further testimony to the freedmen's commitment to an independent church.

The Presbyterian church had divided along sectional lines during the war just as the Baptists and Methodists had done. At war's end, white Presbyterians in the South, calling themselves the Presbyterian Church in the United States, like other southerners, mostly resigned themselves to the prevailing power of the Union and the loss of slavery. The venerable Georgia Presbyterian Charles Colcock Jones's son John wrote to his mother after Appomattox that he feared some in the South were "clinging too much to a property which has never been very profitable, and which *has passed its best days* for ease and profit." But their piety did not give them any clearer understanding of the harm slavery had done. Mary, the elder Jones's widow, declared that "Northern philanthropy and cant may rave as much as they please," but the "*facts* prove that [only] in a state of slavery such as exists in the Southern States have the Negro race increased and thriven most." [53]

Church leaders hoped that the freedmen would feel an attachment to their former masters and to Presbyterianism. They approached the freedmen as their benefactors and focused on the spiritual union that crossed the social chasm within the church. The General Assembly stated the church's position regarding the freedmen at its meeting in 1865: "As slaves the colored people never stood in any other relation to the Church than that of human beings lost with us in the fall of Adam." They were "redeemed with us by the infinitely meritorious death and sacrifice of Christ, and participate with us in all the benefits and blessings of the Gospel." White Presbyterians claimed that they "rejoiced" in the prospect of associating with the freedmen "in Christian union and communion in the public services and precious sacraments of the sanctuary" and resolved that "whereas experience has invariably proved the advantages of the colored people and the white being united together in the worship of God,

53. Presbyterian Church of the United States of America, General Assembly (hereinafter cited as PCUSA), *Minutes of the General Assembly of the Presbyterian Church in the United States of America, 1860* (Philadelphia, n.d.), 256–60; Robert M. Myers, ed., *Children of Pride: A True Story of Georgia and the Civil War* (New Haven, 1972), 1244, 1292.

we see no reason why it should be otherwise now that they are freemen and not slaves." [54]

They may have been willing to share the "precious sacraments of the sanctuary," but they still did not consider blacks their equals. The fear of social upheaval led them to insist on the segregation of black members. The church's General Assembly stated its expectation that the freedmen would be "guided and controlled by their old and true friends" and would be "well content to occupy their old position" within the church. They intended to present the freedmen with a gospel that, like many sermons to slaves, muted any implication of social equality, or, as a committee of the Charleston Presbytery phrased it, was "unadulterated by admixture with political theories" and speculations as to "natural rights." Blacks were segregated by congregation, and the black congregations were under the supervision of whites. Blacks were permitted to exhort, but although technically not excluded from the ordained ministry they were effectively barred from the ranks of the regular clergy. There was no provision for educating black ministers until 1876. [55]

Church historian Andrew E. Murray has written that its leaders "must have been incredibly blind not to see that the emancipated Negroes would never settle for anything less than full equality." A black Presbyterian urged others to "come down out of the gallery to the ground floor in your own church," and the freedmen did exactly that. The Concord Presbytery observed that its black communicants had "melted away . . . like snow before the rising sun." A missionary in South Carolina reported that "the large negro membership is . . . much scattered, and, I dare say, few can ever be gathered together again. They are, I am told, much carried away and misled by ignorant preachers of their own color." Likewise, the Atlanta Presbytery admitted that its black membership "has to a large extent left us." Some of them doubtless departed the church for

---

54. Presbyterian Church of the United States (hereinafter cited as PCUS), General Assembly, *Minutes of the General Assembly of the Presbyterian Church in the United States, 1865* (Augusta, Ga., 1865), 370–71.

55. Ernest Trice Thompson, *Presbyterians in the South* (3 vols.; Richmond, 1963–73), II, 195–222, 310–11; PCUS, Charleston Presbytery, "Minutes of the Charleston Presbytery of the Presbyterian Church in the United States," April 12, 1867, April 10, 1868, in Austin Presbyterian Theological Seminary Library, Austin, Texas; PCUS, General Assembly, *Minutes of the General Assembly, 1866* (Columbia, S.C., 1866); Franklin C. Talmadge, *The Story of the Presbytery of Atlanta* (Atlanta, 1960), 107.

the new Baptist and Methodist churches; others joined the northern Presbyterian church.[56]

Like other northern-based churches, the Presbyterian Church in the United States of America, which the northern church was called after the Civil War split, attempted to proselytize the freedmen and organize black congregations during the war. By 1870 northern Presbyterians had established several black presbyteries in the South, but the number of congregants was small.[57]

Gayraud S. Wilmore has written that whatever one may think about African Americans and Presbyterianism, "it cannot be said that they came together naturally." Several factors combined to account for the church's limited success among blacks. In battling against popular Baptist and Methodist missionaries Presbyterians espoused the same doctrines that had failed to arouse "the spirit" among slaves in earlier times. Although basic Presbyterian theology was similar to that of African-American Baptist and Methodist churches, there were important differences in the atmosphere of worship, in ceremony, and in the requirements for entering the ministry. With the exception of a few freedmen and a fair number of former free persons, blacks did not respond positively to the church. New School Presbyterians, like Baptists and Methodists, stressed the centrality of spiritual conversion to salvation, but they discouraged the dramatic displays of God's presence that were so common among and valued by black folk. Furthermore, of all the evangelical denominations, they placed the greatest value on an educated ministry, a requirement that ordinarily eliminated blacks. And most of the freedmen did not have a great appreciation—or tolerance—for the intellectual and ethical discourses that were prominently featured in Presbyterian services. Still vivid in their recollections were the sermons they had heard in their masters' Presbyterian churches, which had been intended to make them obedient slaves. Cornelius Garner, a Virginia slave who grew up near Norfolk, later remembered that "de churches whar we went to serve God was 'Piscopal, Catholick, Presbyterians, de same as Marster's church only we

56. Andrew E. Murray, *Presbyterians and the Negro—A History* (Philadelphia, 1966), 146–47, 150; PCUS, Charleston Presbytery, "Minutes of the Charleston Presbytery," April 12, 1867; Talmadge, *Presbytery of Atlanta,* 106; Thompson, *Presbyterians in the South,* II, 204–209.

57. Jessee B. Barber, *Climbing Jacob's Ladder: The Story of the Work of the Presbyterian Church U.S.A. Among the Negroes* (New York, 1952), 39; *Census of Religious Bodies: 1916* (2 vols.; Washington, D.C., 1919), I, 558–76.

was off to usselves in a little log cabin way in de woods." The preaching he and his fellow slaves heard there "'twan't nothing much. Dat ole white preacher jest was telling us slaves to be good to our marsters. We ain't keered a bit 'bout dat stuff he was telling us 'cause we wanted to sing, pray, and serve God in our own way. You see, 'ligion needs a little motion—especially if you gwine feel de spirret." Some blacks thought of the Presbyterian church as the white people's church, and whereas the black elite was attracted to it, the freedmen were not. And because it appealed to the educated and well-to-do black and mulatto upper-crust, it struck the freedmen as being too aristocratic for them.[58]

The difficulty that the Presbyterian church had in conducting missionary work among blacks was compounded by the apathy of rank-and-file communicants back home. Northern churches were not notably generous in their support of missionary work. In 1867 a total of 526 Presbyterian congregations contributed financially to evangelical work among southern blacks, but 1,982 did not. Even though it was a time of economic prosperity in the North and the pinnacle of Radical Reconstruction fervor, missionary work among the freedmen, in the words of a church committee on freedmen, "has not been sustained in a manner at all commensurate with its importance." On the whole, white Presbyterians seemed to be more interested in reestablishing a unified church than in aiding the freedmen. They were fearful that attempts to evangelize the freedmen would be detrimental to the process of reunification because they might antagonize white southerners. Accordingly, church leaders expressed their desire to avoid "all unpleasant collision with the Southern churches" over the issue of evangelizing the freedmen.[59]

When they attempted to relate to the freedmen and earn their affection, the mostly white northern Presbyterian missionaries encountered the former slaves' sensitivity to white racial prejudice and paternalism. The slave experience had conditioned blacks to the racial views of southern whites, but northern missionaries also transmitted racial biases, although sometimes very subtly. For instance, the General Assembly acknowledged its obligation to care for the freedmen's spiritual condition by observing that the former slaves "imploringly appeal to our sympa-

58. Gayraud S. Wilmore, *Black and Presbyterian: The Heritage and the Hope* (Philadelphia, 1983), 54; Perdue, Barden, and Phillips, eds., *Weevils in the Wheat*, 100; Willard B. Gatewood, *Aristocrats of Color: The Black Elite, 1880–1920* (Bloomington, 1990), 285.

59. PCUSA, *Minutes of the General Assembly, 1866* (Philadelphia, n.d.), 76; *ibid.*, *1867* (Philadelphia, n.d.), 446; *ibid.*, *1871* (Philadelphia, n.d.), 510.

thies as the weaker to the stronger and wiser race." According to H. N. Payne, the field agent of the Board of Missions, the face of the "prostrate helpless man is black" while "the strong beautiful hand reaching out to him is white." The freedmen picked up such signals easily and reacted strongly against them. The northern evangelical churches' paternalism was but a transparent veneer on negative racial stereotypes. A Mississippi man complained about the "cruel and wicked injustice" of racial prejudice among northern missionaries and teachers: "When slavery had fallen, we thought our last foe was vanquished, and that our greatest trouble would be to get along with the whites of the South. Experience, however, has taught us that this is not the case." That man's disillusionment followed an incident in which a black woman was refused a seat at a table with white teachers. "If this had come from some of our Southern people, we could have passed it by unnoticed; but as it has come from a Northern Copperhead preacher and his clique, we feel that we would be doing violence to ourselves, and to our good friends at the North, who have been laboring for our welfare . . . if we were to remain silent under this usage." The racial attitude he complained of was evident not only among Presbyterian missionaries, but its existence among them handicapped their attempt to proselytize blacks.[60]

The church won some converts during the early years of freedom—mainly from among higher-class people—and it did have some black ministers. One of them, Jonathan C. Gibbs, performed notable missionary work among the freedmen in South Carolina in 1865. Gibbs arrived in Charleston in July and quickly earned the high esteem of the citizenry as pastor of Zion Presbyterian Church. But in the final analysis, Presbyterianism was not constituted to make it a major element in the emerging black church.[61]

Congregationalists fared even less well than Presbyterians in recruiting blacks, notwithstanding their history of involvement in the antislavery movement and their passionate commitment to social reform and the uplift of freedmen. Congregationalists came to the South primarily as educators. They were commissioned by the American Missionary Association, a nonsectarian organization with unofficial ties to their church and one of several public and private agencies involved in educating for-

60. *Christian Recorder*, May 5, 1866; PCUSA, *Minutes of the General Assembly, 1866,* 76; Murray, *Presbyterians and the Negro*, 192.

61. *Christian Recorder*, August 5, 1865, September 8, 1866; Holt, *Black over White,* 89.

mer slaves during Reconstruction. Although the AMA's principal role in the work among the freedmen was to establish and operate schools and to sponsor teachers, the organization did not strictly differentiate between secular and religious instruction. The AMA officially undertook the evangelization of the freedmen as well as the task of providing them with a "moral" education and literacy skills. Many of the male AMA-sponsored teachers not only were exceedingly pious but had ministerial experience, and they instructed the freedmen in "universal" principles of Protestant morality, established Sunday schools, and conducted revival meetings. Still, the AMA gave a higher priority to education than to evangelization. Teaching duties filled most of the teachers' daytime hours and many of their evenings as well. Some missionaries urged the AMA's directors to assign religious work a more prominent position on the association's agenda, but they were not successful and many were frustrated because they could not devote the amount of time they wanted to preaching and organizing congregations.[62]

As was true with Presbyterians, the Congregationalists' campaign to recruit black adherents was culture-bound in a way that lessened its chances of success. A wide gap separated the values of middle-class New England and midwestern whites who dominated Congregationalism from the lowly freedmen of the South who were the objects of the northerners' reformist endeavors. And each group was largely intolerant of the other. Congregationalists were constantly trying to root out the sin in man's soul, but the freedmen craved excitement and a sense of joy and vindication in their religion. As former slave Barney Alford explained, "I believe in shoutin', en I'se kno when yer git happy in de Lord yer got er rite ter tell it." Congregationalists could not accept such behavior as a legitimate expression of Christian piety. They regarded African-American religion as nothing more than primitive emotionalism lacking any moral basis. As evangelical abolitionists, the Congregationalists had always presumed that slaves were immoral. In their opinion, the institution of slavery had prevented its victims from developing their moral sense, and that had been the essence of its sinfulness. The missionaries' own moral code stressed self-restraint and, in particular, control of one's body; the freedmen's ecstatic behavior—shouting, dancing, and clap-

---

62. Henry Kelsey to Edward P. Smith, February 17, 1869, Lois Santley to E. M. Cravath, November 8, 1870, in American Missionary Association Archives, Amistad Research Center, Tulane University (hereinafter cited as AMA Archives); Jones, *Soldiers of Light and Love,* 14–48.

ping—was offensive both to them and, they thought, to God. They came to the South with preconceived notions of the freedmen's spiritual condition and often saw only what they already believed. Writing to Lewis Tappan from Decatur, Alabama, William G. Kephart of the AMA confessed that his expectations about the religious condition of the freedmen had been confirmed: "The religious type of the freedmen I have found everywhere the same. It is precisely what I had expected to find it—an excessive effervescence of emotional feelings with very little intelligent understanding of even the first elementary principles of the gospel." Kephart's perception of the freedmen's religious views colored his outlook for the success of missionary activity: "It will require much patience, labor, and prayer, to remove this mass of *rubbish* from their minds before a better superstructure can be reared, and it will be a long while before the work can be accomplished." The missionaries aimed their educational and evangelical efforts at correcting the pernicious effects of slavery on the South's black population, but these efforts attacked the freedmen's most basic values and beliefs. Congregational missionaries could not hope to compete with Baptist and Methodist preachers, especially black ones, who were more tolerant of folk culture and often embodied it themselves. Regardless of how earnestly or energetically they devoted themselves to it, their attempt to convert the freedmen to beliefs that had little meaning to them was hopeless. Henry S. Kelsey reported correctly to AMA officials from Mobile that prospects for a Congregational church among the freedmen there were not bright.[63]

In addition to this unpromising opposition of cultural values, racial and class factors further hampered the AMA's efforts to promote Congregationalism among southern blacks. The freedmen responded best to teachers and preachers of their own race. Referring to attempts by the white missionaries in Alabama to influence the religious activities of blacks, Henry Kelsey observed, "The colored people are somewhat Sensitive & jealous on this point." The AMA hierarchy, however, was not quick to send black teachers into the field and was actually negatively disposed toward them. Field secretaries in New York, Cincinnati, and Chicago who commissioned the missionaries preferred persons who were

63. Joe M. Richardson, *Christian Reconstruction: The American Missionary Association and Southern Blacks, 1861–1890* (Athens, Ga., 1986), 141–59; Rawick, ed., *Mississippi Narratives* (Westport, 1977), Pt. 1, p. 31, Vol. X in Rawick, ed., *The American Slave, Supplemental Series 1*, 12 vols.; W. G. Kephart to Lewis Tappan, May 9, 1864, Henry S. Kelsey to Edward P. Smith, January 20, 1869, in AMA Archives.

well-educated, experienced, and morally upright as defined by the standards of their own middle-class values. Few blacks, with their background as members of a degraded and isolated group in American society, could meet those criteria. As a result, the AMA indirectly but effectively ruled out blacks as teachers and missionaries. In Georgia, for example, 5 percent of the association's teachers were black. Race and class bias also infected the teachers in the field and stirred the freedmen's suspicions. Recently freed slaves accepted white teachers largely because there were relatively few black ones. But because they already had their own black preachers, they were little inclined to accept northerners who offered themselves as reformers. Black ministers led the opposition to the missionary activities of white Congregationalists. The Congregationalist missionaries frequently complained about black preachers turning the people against them. Henry Kelsey wrote: "There is much suspicion on the part of the colored preachers and churches concerning us, and . . . it will not meet with their approval if we attempt to establish churches of our order. They are quite willing to have their children Educated & morally impressed, but the result of all our labor they wish to garner." Likewise, Enoch K. Miller grumbled that black preachers in Arkansas were "jealous" of white ministers and did "all in their power to monopolize the attention of the freedmen." [64]

AMA missionaries had a reputation—not altogether undeserved—of horning in on established congregations, attempting to woo members away and recruiting the better-educated black ministers. Joseph W. Healy, an AMA missionary in New Orleans, tried to organize a congregation in association with an AMA normal school, but he was unable to find anyone to assume the pastorate. "We need a pastor who will draw the educated and wealthy colored people of the city," he wrote to George Whipple, the AMA's corresponding secretary. He had a person in mind, but other commitments prevented the man from coming to New Orleans for more than five months a year. Healy then decided to recruit John Turner, the very popular pastor of St. James AME Church, who possessed "large and pure influence among the colored people in the city and state."

64. Jones, *Soldiers of Light and Love,* 14–48; Henry Kelsey to Edward P. Smith, March 15, 1869, in AMA Archives; Enoch K. Miller to William M. Colby, July 31, 1867, in Records of the Superintendent of Education for the State of Georgia, 1865–70, U.S. Bureau of Refugees, Freedmen, and Abandoned Lands, Record Group 105, National Archives (hereinafter cited as Freedmen's Bureau Records); Jerry John Thornbery, "The Development of Black Atlanta, 1865–1885" (Ph.D. dissertation, University of Maryland, 1977), 78–79.

That elite congregation was divided over an order from the hierarchy to admit former slaves to membership, and many members, including Turner, were considering leaving the church and maybe the denomination as well. "Providence seems to have provided us *the* man," Healy reported optimistically to AMA officials. Turner, he wrote, "is dissatisfied with the Episcopacy, and would, I have no doubt, gladly assume the charge of the University church; and, if he should, would at once gather around him a large and influential number of colored families." In the end, Turner did not abandon his congregation or the AME church, but by resorting to such tactics, AMA missionaries generated suspicion and resentment among blacks throughout the South.[65]

Some Congregational missionaries at least partly succeeded in overcoming the obstacles between them and their goal of evangelizing blacks. Diligent missionaries used what free time they had to immerse themselves in the religious affairs of the freedmen. They preached to black audiences and recorded some conversions; however, the larger and more stable Congregational churches were located near AMA schools, whose students they could use to inflate the size of their congregations, and in urban areas of the South, where a relatively large number of the educated blacks lived. There were Congregational churches in New Orleans, Montgomery, Atlanta, Savannah, and several other cities and towns. But the use of schools to indoctrinate pupils was another source of black suspicion and resentment directed at the AMA and probably contributed to black resistance to Congregationalism. In 1878 the AMA counted 64 Congregational churches and 4,189 members in the South, but for the most part the missionaries' endeavors were unrewarded by black converts, and the denomination's growth was painfully slow. By 1885 there were 118 Congregational churches in the South and 7,512 members, about 6,000 of whom were black.[66]

The Catholic church showed little interest in mission work among the freedmen. The reasons were complex and not often stated explicitly. Partly it was because the Church was dominated by immigrants, many of whom had felt the antagonism of abolitionists before the Civil War. Rac-

65. J. W. Healy to George Whipple, March 26, 1869, in AMA Archives.

66. Henry Kelsey to Edward P. Smith, March 23, 1869, Kelsey to the Secretaries, May 6, 1869, G. Stanley Pope to Edward P. Smith, April 9, 1870, *ibid.*; *Christian Recorder,* September 8, 1866; Thornbery, "Development of Black Atlanta," 104–16, 151, 182; Joe M. Richardson, "The Failure of the American Missionary Association to Expand Congregationalism Among Southern Blacks," *Southern Studies,* XVIII (1979), 65.

ism was also a factor, with both the clergy and the laity showing scant appreciation for or understanding of African Americans. Limited resources and few missionaries willing to labor among the freedmen also hampered missionary work. Many southern bishops had supported the antebellum South's slave system and now exhibited the same fierce resentment of northern political domination as most other white southerners. These all added up to neglect of a field of parishioners, in areas like Maryland, coastal South Carolina, and Florida, and in cities like Mobile and New Orleans, who had been Catholics during slavery. Freedmen who might be converted to the Catholic faith were also ignored. At its Plenary Council in 1866, the Church committed itself to missionary work among African Americans. Five years later, in 1871, Father Herbert Vaughan brought the first missionaries from Saint Joseph's Society of the Sacred Heart for Foreign Missions in England (known as Josephites) to conduct evangelical work exclusively among blacks. But these steps proved to be more of a show than anything of substance. Segregation of black congregants and a strong opposition among whites to admitting blacks to the clergy discouraged African Americans from converting and caused freedmen who had been Catholics during slavery to fall away from the Church now that freedom had arrived.[67]

The black missionaries who came south concentrated much of their effort on preaching to the freedmen, organizing congregations, and enrolling groups in their denominations. But they performed many social services for the freedmen as well. Among the rites of passage over which they presided, besides the induction of persons into the Christian faith, were the marriage of couples and the burial of the dead. From his station in South Carolina, James D. S. Hall reported the product of ten days' labor: "I have married four couples; buried two, one of whom was Robert Small, Jr.; baptized twenty-six, of whom five were infants, and nineteen grown persons, eleven of them by immersion." Still another function was to help reconstruct broken families. Slavery had placed great strain on black families. Slave marriages had no legal sanction, and the separation of husbands from wives had been common. Transactions of sale had

67. Randall M. Miller, "The Failed Mission: The Catholic Church and Black Catholics in the Old South," in *Catholics in the Old South: Essays on Church and Culture,* ed. Randall M. Miller and John L. Wakelyn (Macon, 1983), 149–70; Cyprian Davis, *The History of Black Catholics in the United States* (New York, 1990), 58–86, 127, 132; Stephen J. Ochs, *Desegregating the Altar: The Josephites and the Struggle for Black Priests, 1871–1960* (Baton Rouge, 1990), 33–34, 36–56.

also separated parents from children. Through the network of churches the freedmen sought to locate and be reunited with long-lost loved ones. The AME church's weekly newspaper the *Christian Recorder* regularly carried notices of parents trying to locate children from whom they had been separated or of people searching for other loved ones.[68]

Northern missionaries were unquestionably important contributors to the expansion of the black church in the South, but they did not do it alone. The freedmen were responsible for much of it themselves. Despite the abolitionists' charge that slave owners had prevented slaves from hearing the Word of God and therefore had denied them the way to salvation, many slaves had access to Christian churches, either those of their masters or their own "invisible" churches. As a consequence, the clergymen who journeyed into the South found many freedmen who already subscribed to a Christian faith and some who were more or less organized into functioning congregations. Hiram Revels, an AME missionary, discovered that when he arrived in Jackson, Mississippi, in the summer of 1865. If he expected to encounter a demoralized population with minds filled with religious "rubbish" and unacquainted with Christian beliefs and ethics, he must have been greatly surprised because what he saw in the black community was "a noble people. They are pious and zealous in the cause of righteousness, hospitable and benevolent." Indeed, such was the experience of most missionaries.[69]

Some of the missionaries, however, did not appreciate the freedmen's religion as much as Revels did and could not admit that it represented a true Christian faith. Missionaries and teachers complained again and again about the excessive emotionalism of black worshipers and about the scriptural ignorance of their preachers. A Baptist missionary on St. Helena Island was "very much puzzled" by "the religious feeling" of the freedmen there. Others employed less ambiguous terms to describe the freedmen's religion. Laura Towne, a northern teacher in South Carolina, described black patterns of worship as "savage." These perceptions were not limited to white evangels. Black teachers and missionaries were appalled by the state of black folks' religion. Charlotte Forten, a teacher from Philadelphia, called the religious gatherings on the Sea Islands of South Carolina "barbarous." Henry M. Turner criticized a black preacher on Roanoke Island because he spent all his time preaching about

---

68. *Christian Recorder*, June 27, 1863. The paper regularly carried such advertisements during the months following emancipation.

69. *Ibid.*, August 5, 1865.

"Hell fire, brimstone, damnation, black smoke, hot lead, etc." while the "more powerful message of Jesus was thoughtlessly passed by." This, Turner believed, represented a "lower class" of ideas and "a much cruder notion of God and the plan of salvation" than those held by other congregations. Black missionaries usually attributed the defects they saw in the existing religion of the recently freed persons to the effects of slavery, whereas the whites sometimes tended to regard them as racial traits. But none of these critics had much respect for the religion the slaves carried with them into freedom.[70]

The black missionaries who journeyed into the South at the end of the Civil War came hopefully though naïvely intending to teach the freedmen not just Christianity but Christianity as they understood it. They bore with them values that stressed self-restraint, were based on European-American Protestant theology, and included a Puritan work ethic. And they came with preconceived notions about the freedmen and their beliefs. They thought most freedmen were intemperate, superstitious, and immoral. In the expressions of the freedmen's religiosity they perceived the consequences of slavery's degradation, not a unified and coherent system of beliefs. They expected the freedmen simply to adopt the gospel as they interpreted it and their forms of worship. These unrealistic expectations were based on several widely held assumptions. The first one, reflecting both cultural chauvinism and a vivid northern imagination, was that African-American religion was superstition rather than legitimate theology. They believed that a vast majority of the former slaves clung to exotic superstitions "which belonged to the fetish worship of savage Africa, and not of Christian America." Another, which was largely wishful thinking, was that the freed people were calling out to them—a "Macedonian cry"—to teach them the way to salvation. A third assumption, which was the most correct, was that Christianized blacks would follow them into their organizations. Many conversions to Christianity can be credited to the missionaries, but a large number of freedmen only wanted the missionaries to assist them in organizing their churches, not to reform the way they worshiped.[71]

70. Elizabeth Ware Pearson, ed., *Letters from Port Royal Written at the Time of the Civil War* (Boston, 1906), 36; Rose, *Rehearsal for Reconstruction,* 92; Charlotte Forten, "Life on the Sea Islands," *Atlantic Monthly,* XIII (1864), 593–94; *Christian Recorder,* July 1, 1865; Walker, *Rock in a Weary Land,* 58.

71. G. W. Nichols, "Six Weeks in Florida," *Harper's New Monthly Magazine,* XLI (1870), 663; *Christian Recorder,* November 21, 1863.

Many congregations of freedmen antedated the missionaries' arrival and were led by licensed preachers and sometimes even by ordained ministers. In those cases the only change that occurred with the coming of the missionaries was that the local churches were enrolled in denominational organizations. The First African Baptist Church of Savannah, for instance, was older than any other black congregation in the country, older than most of the churches represented by the missionaries. The Third African Baptist Church in Savannah had a history stretching deep into the antebellum past. Its pastor, N. I. Houston, was one of the first blacks to greet James Lynch and the other northern missionaries who entered the city after the Federal occupation in December, 1864. The congregations that Alexander Wayman enrolled in the AME Church in Norfolk and Portsmouth, Virginia, had pastors, including Richard Parker, a preacher in the Norfolk church. Among the first sights to greet James Lynch and James D. S. Hall upon their arrival at Hilton Head in 1863 was a baptismal service being conducted by Peter Murchison, the black minister of a local Baptist congregation. There were three Baptist and two Methodist churches in Augusta at the end of the war. All three of the Baptist congregations had black preachers. The Methodist congregation, which James Lynch received into the AME connection, had for some time been under the pastoral care of Samuel Drayton, a cleric who enjoyed the high regard of local white church authorities as well as that of northern missionaries. He was one of the few black preachers to have been ordained by the white church. Lynch regarded him as "a very good preacher, and a man of more than ordinary tact and energy." The other Methodist church was Trinity Church, whose pastor was Edward West. It was affiliated with the Methodist Episcopal Church, South.[72]

In rural areas there were countless congregations that slave preachers had led in the old days and continued to gather and conduct religious services for as frequently as possible with the coming of freedom. Those preachers may not have been licensed by established denominational authorities, but they nevertheless ministered to organized congregations. Henry M. Turner, chaplain of the 1st Regiment of United States Colored Troops, reported from Roanoke Island in the summer of 1865 that the Baptists "are not disposed to claim relations to an organized body whatever, but are simply Baptists." Somewhat chagrined, he recorded that

72. *Christian Recorder,* June 6, October 24, 1863, January 21, July 1, September 9, 1865, January 20, 1866.

their preachers performed religious sacraments whether they enjoyed proper authority or not: "They have two or three churches of their own with colored pastors, but none are ordained; still they baptize and marry with as much boldness as if properly authorized."[73]

Many times, however, the black congregations that existed at emancipation were without pastors, having been left in that condition by the whites who had previously provided them with preachers and then fled before the advancing Union armies. Many of these were hardly congregations at all but were rather more like conglomerations of worshipers thrown together in the towns, cities, and refugee camps that attracted freedmen from surrounding areas. This confusing and stressful situation existed in Helenaville, South Carolina, where the black residents who professed religion or attended church services included Methodists, Presbyterians, Baptists, and Episcopalians. James Lynch discovered them worshiping together, "or what is nearer the truth," he said, "quarreling together," when he came as a missionary in 1863. As other missionaries attempted to do in other locations, he endeavored to sort out the pieces and recruit them all to his African Methodist church. If he was bewildered by the medley of worshipers he found before him, they were also curious about him. "The first Sabbath I preached to them, they began to wonder among themselves as to what denomination I belonged. This was soon settled by my telling them that I was a minister of the A.M.E. church sent by Gen. [Rufus] Saxton, and as such I organized the church under our discipline." The freedmen happily assented to that arrangement, with the exception of some of the Baptists.[74]

But if these groups were a diverse collection of unorganized and unsupervised worshipers, some were also comfortably ensconced in the church buildings of the white congregations that had vacated them. The situation at Helenaville struck Lynch as strange. The Baptists, Methodists, Presbyterians, and Episcopalians were all meeting together in an abandoned building that had housed a white Episcopal congregation until near the end of the war. But that state of affairs was commonplace among the freedmen in the waning months of the war and during the confused period that followed. In Beaufort, South Carolina, blacks worshiped in another abandoned Episcopal church. In April, 1865, only days after the Confederate capital fell into Union hands, the First African

73. *Ibid.*, July 1, 1865.
74. *Ibid.*, July 25, 1865.

Church occupied the building in which Virginia's white leaders had voted to secede from the Union four years before.[75]

The sharp break with the past symbolized by black congregations worshiping independent of whites, and doing so in church edifices where during slavery they had been segregated and shunted into balconies, made a profound impression on visitors and no doubt on the former slaves themselves. Such incongruous scenes were indicative of the fractured order of southern society; native white southerners were threatened with dispossession of their property as well as their social position and political power, and blacks occupied places and positions they were unaccustomed to and where they were not usually seen. In Charleston, in March, 1865, Elisha B. Weaver, the editor of the *Christian Recorder,* preached to a congregation in a church that in former times had belonged to whites, an honor that neither he nor any other black person had ever enjoyed before. "The change," he observed, "is a striking one. Those members who formerly had to take seats in the gallery, now occupy the whole church." He was the first black man who had ever preached from that pulpit, "and you may imagine the pleasure and satisfaction exhibited by the congregation."[76]

The freedmen's legal right to ownership of vacated church buildings, however, was not established merely by occupying them. The question of what, if any, right the freedmen had to church property was a difficult one, and the government's answer to it was ambiguous. Many northerners contended that the southern planters' wealth was the result of extorted slave labor, but few, even including abolitionists, advocated the distribution of abandoned rebel property to the freedmen. Both the Congress and President Lincoln had agreed on confiscation of property as a penalty to be imposed on southern rebels, but throughout the war the government avoided implementing the policy on a universal basis. Southern property included church buildings as well as plantations, but the government was not consistent in dealing with church property. In January, 1863, Lincoln implied that confiscation did not apply to church buildings, stating that the government should not become involved in running the churches in the South. "When an individual, in a church or out of it, becomes dangerous to the public interest," the president said, "he must be checked; but the churches, as such, must take care of them-

75. *Ibid.,* July 25, 1863, July 29, 1865; *Freedmen's Record,* I (June, 1865), 95.
76. *Christian Recorder,* April 22, 1865.

selves." Nevertheless, the War Department, on November 30, 1863, authorized military commanders in the South to turn over to officials of the Methodist Episcopal church all church edifices belonging to the Methodist Episcopal Church, South, not presided over by loyal ministers. This order, which Lincoln endorsed despite his earlier, contrary statement, applied only to Methodist-owned buildings. It furnished the ME church with considerable leverage in its competition with the AME and AME Zion churches and bred resentment among the African Methodist missionaries. It also denied many Methodist freedmen the use of those church buildings. Early in 1865, James Lynch reported from Charleston that African Methodism there had a strong following but that the Methodist Episcopal church was attempting to force them from their church buildings: "Rev. T. W. Lewis, representative of the M.E. Church, is making a strong effort to hold the property by military order, which the Secretary of War gave to Bishop Janes about eighteen months since. But we are going to test the matter. Certainly two thousand Methodist members are not to be forced from their churches because they do not choose to follow Mr. Lewis." The African Methodists argued vociferously that the abandoned church buildings belonged to them, particularly those that had been regularly used by the slaves, because the southern whites had forfeited their claim to them when they fled their homes and because the slaves had built them and in some cases they had been used exclusively by black worshipers.[77]

When white southerners returned to their homes after the war, they asserted their claim to the church edifices, including those in the possession of ME church officials, and forced the freedmen out. Indeed, as part of his evolving Reconstruction policy, Lincoln granted amnesty to rebel southerners who took a loyalty oath, and incorporated in the grant was the restoration of confiscated property, including churches. Slave laborers had constructed many of those buildings, had used them, and had even paid for them, but because whites held the titles, the freedmen had no legal right to them. Their struggles to obtain ownership were usually fruitless. Prevailing laws pertaining to property clearly benefited white owners, and neither the freedmen's moral assertions nor the extraordinary circumstances of southern rebellion could compel Federal authorities to transfer property to the freed people.[78]

77. Basler, ed., *Collected Works of Abraham Lincoln,* VII, 178–80, 182–83; *Christian Recorder,* May 6, October 21, 1865.
78. Basler, ed., *Collected Works of Abraham Lincoln,* VIII, 264.

The legal maze that protected white churches from the claims of black congregations was virtually impenetrable. No matter how doggedly blacks pursued their claims, whites always erected a successful line of defense. A white congregation in Jackson, Mississippi, for example, did not challenge a black Methodist congregation's ownership of a church building but did claim the land on which it stood. A black missionary there admitted that "our people have nothing to disprove that claim. It is so near to the white church, not more than twenty-five yards, that the latter contend that it must and shall be removed." Hiram Revels' experience in Vicksburg, where he attempted to obtain title to church property, was a tale of immense frustration. When he arrived in Vicksburg as an AME missionary, he did not know that his congregation did not have a church of its own. He soon discovered that they had been worshiping in a building owned by whites and that they would probably be forced out of it. Within a few months he confronted his fears: "The thing which we so anxiously anticipated we are now realizing. We are thrown out of our place of worship." The white southern Methodists had indeed taken possession of the building, and the blacks had no place to worship. "I regret to have to say that we are not able to find a vacant church, hall, or even a room, of sufficient size in which to meet for the time being." The people did obtain temporary use of a barracks that they equipped in the best fashion they could, but they had no assurance of being able to continue using it for very long. And even if local whites permitted them to stay, their problems would not be solved because the building was inadequate for their needs. Revels reported: "If we had the right to occupy it permanently . . . we would not be able to keep our congregation, simply because it is too small, and in every respect unfit for this purpose. Therefore, we must, in order to sustain our cause here, make every possible effort to get another and more suitable place." The people appealed to General Henry W. Slocum, commander of Federal troops in Vicksburg, for assistance, and he responded with enough lumber for them to erect a temporary frame structure. But that did not end their predicament. The materials were free so it would cost them very little to construct a building. But they could not obtain title to the land. "We would now be engaged in erecting the house," Revels explained, "but for the fact that we have reason to believe that the (white) Trustees of the Southern M.E. Church, who alone can give a deed for our ground, will refuse to give one that would place the people and property under the control of the bishop and Conference of the A.M.E. Church." Actually, the congregation had already paid for the property before emancipation but had never obtained a deed because under Mississippi law blacks were not entitled to own property. The problem was further compounded by the absence from the city of those whites in whose names the legal title was registered. Revels lamented, "Before, and since the close of the war, I tried to procure a deed for the ground in question, but failed, on the ground that none but the Trustees of the (white) church could give legal deed, and the majority of them being away from Vicksburg till very recently, we had to delay an application till now." [79]

The white Methodists of Vicksburg were not acting solely out of spite or a spirit of vindictiveness. Some of the leaders of the white congregation promised to help the blacks build a church and permitted them to use the basement of their church until the new building was completed. "But so far as my knowledge extends," Revels remarked, "our people, from a painful recollection of their past and a happy realization of their present ecclesiastical relations, determined to decline the offer." The freedmen's determination to make their own way without the assistance of local whites exceeded their desire for an adequate church building. [80]

As the events in Vicksburg showed, although whites did reclaim their church property, they often assisted the freedmen in obtaining new places in which to worship. Sometimes southern whites donated old buildings to blacks or helped them finance and construct new ones. The Tallahassee *Sentinel,* a Republican party newspaper, appealed to local whites' keen sense of self-interest as well as to racial stereotypes in urging them to support the construction of black churches and schools. Whites generally, whether northerners or southerners, believed that blacks were demoralized and disposed to thievery, and if they could be reformed, whites would be made more secure against stealing. "Aid them to build their churches and schools and you will thus build the surest protection around your dwellings and your henroosts," the paper pleaded. The solicitation produced $100 for a local Baptist church. Some whites genuinely wished the freedmen well and did what they could to help with the construction of churches. A white man named Anderson Dickens, who lived near Raleigh, North Carolina, gave blacks some land on which to erect a church. That he was probably not acting in his own self-interest is borne out by the fact that he was dragged from his bed one night by a gang of white

79. *Christian Recorder,* August 5, October 7, 1865.
80. *Ibid.*

thugs and forced to burn down the building. Elias Bryan, a white farmer from Chatham County, North Carolina, built a church for blacks on a small piece of land that he owned. When he subsequently sold the tract, he neglected to exempt the building so the blacks lost both the building and the land. Bryan made it up to them, however, by erecting another church on a nearby lot. In some cases white church officials offered to sell property to blacks and sometimes proposed giving it to them if they would remain affiliated with the white church. But most of the time the freedmen were hard-pressed to raise the money necessary to purchase the buildings and the land and were unwilling to pay for the property with their ecclesiastical independence.[81]

For most black congregations, both those that had existed in slavery and the new ones organized by the missionaries, obtaining a place to conduct their church services was a struggle. Before they could obtain suitable buildings, many of them were forced to work out borrowing or sharing arrangements with other congregations. One congregation in Vicksburg succeeded in obtaining use of an unoccupied church building. Nelson Fitzhugh wrote that the church "is getting on as well as can be expected under existing circumstances. We were, during the summer, turned out of the church building of the white M.E. Church, but the Presbyterians kindly permitted us to use one of their churches." Affairs in Charleston were not as promising for Methodists, however. After being denied the use of abandoned property by the Methodist Episcopal church, blacks worshiped for a time with members of the Zion Colored Presbyterian Church. Richard H. Cain, who had been installed in the summer of 1865 as the pastor of that African Methodist congregation, noted that the arrangement continued until Jonathan C. Gibbs became pastor. "The Methodists," Cain reported, "were turned out without a day's warning, the written agreement disregarded, and a new order of things instituted, much to the dislike of many of the best friends of our unity, as a people in the city."[82]

Misfortune sometimes descended on the freedmen from unexpected sources. Congregations that obtained church property lost it to such hazards as mortgage foreclosure, fire, or the devastation of war. It often was extremely difficult for the people to recoup such losses, and from time to

81. Robert L. Hall, "Tallahassee's Black Churches, 1865–1885," *Florida Historical Quarterly,* LVIII (1979), 191; U.S. Senate, *Testimony to inquire Into Conditions in the Late Insurrectionary States, North Carolina Testimony,* II, 13–14, 76.

82. *Christian Recorder,* September 9, August 5, 1865, September 8, 1866.

time they were compelled to ask for help. When General William T. Sherman's army marched through South Carolina early in 1865, devastating the countryside along the way, the soldiers destroyed a black church in Columbia. For a time the people held services in the South Carolina College chapel, but by autumn the arrangement had been canceled. The congregation had no money with which to obtain a new building and was forced to appeal for help. "We are all very anxious to have a church," pleaded John Horton, a member of the congregation, "and we would like our brethren at the North to help us if they possibly can. We are in a poor, helpless condition, but still are trying to do all that we can." [83]

In their quest for meetinghouses the freedmen found various relief agencies helpful, especially the Freedmen's Bureau, the freedmen's aid societies of the North, and the northern missionary societies. They worked together to provide educational opportunities for the freedmen. Agents, supervisors, and teachers helped in purchasing or constructing churches because the buildings doubled as schoolhouses. Moreover, many of the agents and teachers also were ministers and were concerned about freedmen who had no place to worship. In Georgia, Freedmen's Bureau agent W. H. Robert secured a building for some Baptist freedmen. Baptists in Andersonville, Georgia, held their services in a new church obtained through the bureau. And in Mitchellville, on Hilton Head Island, a preacher named Lymas Anders erected a church building with money he solicited from local blacks, troops from the 32nd Regiment of U.S. Colored Troops, and white teachers representing the New England Freedmen's Aid Society. The teachers gladly contributed to the effort because the building, like many others across the South, would serve as a school and dormitory for teachers as well as a church for the freedmen. [84]

The freedmen's pleasure at receiving assistance from the northerners was diminished, however, in some communities, like Natchez, when blacks who desired both schools and churches faced the unhappy prospect of choosing one or the other. And sometimes the agencies that procured the buildings refused to turn the title over to the freedmen. [85]

The struggle to obtain usable accommodations frequently became a stern test of a congregation's resourcefulness. E. J. Adams, a missionary

83. *Ibid.*, September 30, 1865.

84. *Ibid.*; W. H. Robert to G. L. Eberhart, January 28, 1867, in Freedmen's Bureau Records; *Freedmen's Journal*, I (January, 1865), 13–15.

85. *Christian Recorder*, December 2, 1865; *Freedmen's Record*, I (December, 1865), 92.

in Charleston, was fortunate in his search for a building. He reported, "I have succeeded in obtaining one of the finest church buildings in this city, though damaged considerably with shells, for the purpose of carrying on religious worship and Sabbath school operations, and the building up of a congregation." Many congregations had to make do with considerably less. The fledgling Ezra Presbyterian Church in Savannah held its first services in an old gristmill. A congregation in Richmond convened for services in Lumpkin's Jail, a notorious antebellum slave market. Bethel Church of Adel, Georgia, conducted its services in an abandoned railroad boxcar. A Baptist congregation in Austin, Texas, met in a barbershop, and the Metropolitan AME Church there occupied a local opera house on Sundays. In the absence of even such crude or bizarre facilities as these, congregations in rural areas erected shelters constructed with tree branches. In slavery times such hush arbors had served as sanctuaries from watchful whites; now they were makeshift meeting places. The shelter covered only the pulpit and perhaps a few rows of rough-cut wooden benches. Mose Banks belonged to a congregation that gathered in a brush arbor in Arkansas. He later recalled that on cold winter days the congregation would build a fire in the middle of it and sit on small pine logs and sing and listen to the preacher.[86]

Some congregations, particularly those in larger towns and cities, were able to buy or build large and impressive church buildings and furnish them comfortably and even lavishly by contemporary standards remarkably soon after the end of the war. They also were able to finance the projects themselves, resorting to a variety of devices to raise the money. James Lynch described one Methodist church in Augusta, Georgia, as a commodious and appealing building located in an attractive setting: "The church property is worth eight thousand dollars. The church is a good, substantial building, very tastefully finished inside and admirably planned, having three aisles, a capacious altar, and a pulpit, with the usual fault of being too high; it is located in a very attractive part of the city, and on a large lot neatly fenced. The building is comparatively

---

86. *Christian Recorder*, August 5, 1865; Works Progress Administration, County Church Records, Cook County, Georgia, Box 44–1, in Georgia State Archives, Atlanta; William E. B. Du Bois, ed., *The Negro Church: Report of a Social Study Made Under the Direction of Atlanta University* (Atlanta, 1903), 72; J. Mason Brewer, *An Historical Outline of the Negro Church in Travis County* (Austin, 1940), 18, 22, 35; Rawick, ed., *Arkansas Narratives* (Westport, 1972), 102, Vol. VIII of Rawick, ed., *American Slave: A Composite Autobiography*, 19 vols.

new." He did not describe the other Methodist church in town except to note its secure financial and legal situation: "This Church is out of debt, and the deed so drawn up that there is no likelihood of any question ever being raised as to the rights of property." After being turned out of Zion Presbyterian Church in Charleston, Richard H. Cain, who quickly earned a reputation as a church builder, undertook a project of major proportions on behalf of his African Methodist congregation. It was a wood-frame structure designed to seat at least two thousand people. The architect was Robert Vesey, the son of Denmark Vesey, the Methodist exhorter who had been executed after the discovery of a planned slave uprising. The church cost $10,000, and only blacks were employed in its construction.[87]

The women members of a Methodist church in Natchez, like their sisters in many other churches, raised much of the money needed to purchase their building. It would not be an exaggeration to say that the securing of property, the construction of buildings, and the expansion and maintenance of these buildings were the direct result of the vital role that women played in the development of the church. The place of black women in postwar southern society was defined both by the history of black women in Africa and America and by contemporary gender roles. It essentially reflected their subordinate relationship to men. The church, to an extent, reinforced the traditional division of labor along gender lines by excluding women from the ministry and other offices within the church organization. But from within their subordinate position women exerted a powerful influence on the organization and management of the institution. The women of the congregation played a key part in raising funds to pay for the construction of church buildings. In addition to special collections taken during worship services, they organized events such as bake sales, carnivals, and balls to earn money, especially in churches located in towns and cities. The women of larger urban congregations formed auxiliary societies through which they organized campaigns to raise money. The women of Memphis' Beale Street Baptist Church organized the Baptist Sewing Society in 1865 and directed their efforts at raising money to erect a permanent church building. Their power as fund-raisers was evident when within nine months they had raised more than $500, and within two years they had generated enough revenue to enable the congregation to pay off a $1,000 mortgage on a building site and put

87. *Christian Recorder,* July 8, October 14, December 2, 1865.

away another $1,000 in a savings account in the Freedmen's Savings and Trust Company.[88]

By the end of 1866 the independent black church had gained a firm foothold in the South, evincing the new status of the former slaves. From the Carolina coast to the plantations of Texas the freedmen had withdrawn from the old biracial churches of slavery times as they tried out the feel of freedom. Missionaries representing several northern churches, both black and predominantly white, followed Union armies into the South and competed vigorously for the allegiance of former slaves. Expecting to find masses of heathens living in a primitive spiritual condition, many were surprised to find a largely Christianized population. But both black and white missionaries shared the values of middle-class society and were appalled by many of the peculiar beliefs and practices they observed among the Christianized former slaves. Thinking them highly superstitious and overly emotional, the missionaries tried hard to reform them—with uneven results. Their main business, however, was bringing congregations of freedmen into their denominations and helping them obtain buildings in which to hold church services, and in that endeavor they succeeded. Black people, however, struggled with varying degrees of success during the first months of freedom to obtain church property of their own. The first years of freedom were a time of exuberance and great determination to become free in a very real sense, and, at least as far as their churches were concerned, they garnered many rewards.

88. *Ibid.*, December 2, 1865; Jacqueline Jones, "'My Mother Was Much of a Woman': Black Women, Work and Family Under Slavery," *Feminist Studies,* VIII (1982), 235–70; Kathleen C. Berkeley, "'Colored Ladies Also Contributed': Black Women's Activities from Benevolence to Social Welfare, 1866–1896," in *The Web of Southern Social Relations: Women, Family, and Education,* ed. Walter J. Fraser, Jr., R. Frank Saunders, Jr., and Jon L. Wakelyn (Athens, Ga., 1985), 182, 201.

3

Expansion and Consolidation

In October, 1871, a member of a joint select committee of Congress that was investigating conditions in the South questioned Thomas Allen, a black minister from Marietta, Georgia, about the new churches that were forming. Allen was asked if he thought black people preferred religious associations with themselves or with whites. He responded matter-of-factly that most "prefer to have them to themselves." Although it was obvious by then that blacks were establishing their own churches—the flow of blacks from biracial into the black organizations that began with the arrival of the northern missionaries during the latter stages of the war increased in volume over the next few years—the question put to Allen pertained to an important issue: whether blacks truly wanted churches of their own or were being maneuvered into segregated churches by whites who refused to associate with them in their new condition as freed people. It was true that some blacks had been reluctant to withdraw from white churches and also that whites were searching for ways to distance themselves from liberated blacks so as to ensure white supremacy. Thus at least some of the legislators must have wondered whether separate churches were truly a manifestation of the blacks' desire for freedom or merely an indication of a developing pattern of racial segregation. The answer, which seems obvious now, was not so clear—or so readily accepted—then. It was, as Thomas Allen testified, that, with some important exceptions, blacks were voluntarily leaving the churches of their former masters and establishing congregations of their own.[1]

1. U.S. Senate, *Testimony Taken by the Joint Select Committee to Inquire into the Conditions of Affairs in the Late Insurrectionary States*, 42nd Cong., 2nd Sess., *Georgia Testimony*, II, 616. Although the question of whether blacks were voluntarily forming separate churches is not now and has never been a point of dispute among historians, a larger question concerning the origins of racial segregation in the South certainly is. C. Vann Woodward initiated the controversy with *The Strange Career of Jim Crow* (New York,

The black church emerged from the turbulence of the Civil War and the initial exertions of the northern missionaries during the weeks and months that followed more unified than when it had a northern branch made up of free people and a southern branch composed of slaves. The postemancipation period was one of vigorous activity for the church, highlighted by sustained growth and an important shift in location. The number of southern black churches, as well as individual church members, increased substantially during the next several years. The base of the black church shifted from the North to the South, making it a more introverted institution. Instead of looking toward Dixie from a northern vantage point, as it had done before the war, or reaching out to the freed slaves through its missionaries, it became firmly established amid the people of the former slave states. More and more, the freedmen rather than middle-class northerners shaped its identity and linked its destiny with theirs. Church hierarchs concentrated increasingly on the institution's internal development, although missionary activity, reflecting an awareness of people and conditions outside of the church community, continued at a lively pace. Thus for the next several years the black church not only continued to experience substantial growth in membership but it also expanded its organizational apparatus. The church's prosperity, as denoted by enrolled members, property holdings, and influence in the community, reflected the extended opportunities available to southern blacks with the abolition of slavery and with the power of government behind them.

Not enough reliable data exist to show accurately and in complete detail the extent of the black exodus from the white-controlled churches or to record the number of people who had not been associated with

---

1955), and his work has continued to provide the focus of the debate. He suggested that institutional racial segregation evolved from a white southern reaction to the end of slavery but did not flower until the end of the nineteenth century. Some scholars have challenged this view, including Richard C. Wade in *Slavery in the Cities: The South, 1820–1860* (New York, 1964) and Joel Williamson in *After Slavery: The Negro in South Carolina During Reconstruction, 1861–1877* (Chapel Hill, 1965). Others, like Charles E. Wynes in *Race Relations in Virginia, 1870–1902* (Charlottesville, 1961) and Frenise A. Logan in *The Negro in North Carolina, 1876–1894* (Chapel Hill, 1964), have supported it. Still others, especially Howard N. Rabinowitz in *Race Relations in the Urban South, 1865–1890* (New York, 1978), have sought to redefine the debate. For a review of the controversy see Rabinowitz, "More Than the Woodward Thesis: Assessing *The Strange Career of Jim Crow*," *Journal of American History*, LXXV (1988), 842–56, and C. Vann Woodward, "Strange Career Critics: Long May They Persevere," *ibid.*, 857–68.

formal congregations before the war and who became church members afterward; however, illustrations drawn from across the South, along with some scattered statistics, demonstrate clearly that a massive black withdrawal took place. They also illuminate the process by which the black church expanded during the decade following the arrival of northern missionaries.

Church growth gained impetus with the arrival of the missionaries, who worked among the freed people for several years after the war ended. But to attribute the magnitude of the growth in church membership to their efforts alone would exaggerate their role and underrate the dynamic quality of local churches. Although they recruited many new members, the northern missionaries' primary contribution to the continued progress of the church was in releasing the great creative energy of southern blacks themselves. A large number of the new congregations during the late 1860s and 1870s were organized through the initiative of native southerners with little or only indirect help from the northern missionary societies.

Although emancipation caused the dislocation of many former slaves, it did not dissolve all of the social relationships that had fostered a sense of community in antebellum times. Whether or not church gatherings had been at the absolute center of the social life in the slave quarters, they were vital parts of the slave community. Members of church groups had relied on religious meetings to help them cope with the harshness of their lives, and they held their congregations together or formed new ones after freedom. One of the first acts of many religious people after emancipation was to organize church congregations. Not only did they continue to draw spiritual satisfaction from the church as they had before, but they used the congregation as a political forum for discussing and acting on issues that affected the community. As practically the only black social institutions at the onset of freedom, churches provided many services— from education to recreation—and they functioned to maintain the cohesion of communities against the destructive effects of people uprooting themselves and resuming their lives among new neighbors in unfamiliar places. Even after the appearance of schools, lodges, and literary societies in the new black urban communities, churches held a prominent place in community life.

In Atlanta, where the nine thousand black residents in 1870 exceeded the city's total population at the beginning of the war, churches were immediately evident in the black settlements. Although only a third of the city's blacks lived in identifiable black neighborhoods, the eight churches were located in these enclaves, contributing to community cohesion within those settlements and drawing the six thousand blacks living outside of the neighborhoods into the developing black community within.[2]

Liberated slave exhorters were often catalysts in the formation of new churches or in their integration into denominational organizations. Slave preachers retained the allegiance of their followers after emancipation, leading them into affiliation with the independent black denominations. Within a short time after emancipation, wrote Elizabeth Botume, the religious leaders of the South Carolina Sea Islands had "established churches in all the towns, with branch societies in the country." People continued to withdraw from the white-controlled churches and sought to obtain a new pastoral leadership of their own choosing. A former slave preacher named James Page founded a church among the people whom he had exhorted when they had all been slaves in Tallahassee. Another former slave, John Jasper of Fluvanna County, Virginia, also a preacher before emancipation, established the Sixth Mount Zion Church in Richmond. Freedmen in Camden, South Carolina, seceded from the white-run Baptist church there and formed the Mount Moriah Baptist Church.[3]

Atlanta's two oldest black churches originated in the antebellum period, and their pastors successfully conducted them through the hazards and uncertainties of the war and emancipation. In the 1840s, local Methodists organized their own church and even purchased land and constructed a building on it, an act of autonomy slaves were seldom permitted. The congregation gathered in the building for church services and other activities through the war until late 1864, when Union soldiers who occupied Atlanta set it on fire. The pastor was Joseph Wood, and after the war he endeavored to rebuild the church, which had been severely damaged but not totally destroyed. Wood and his congregation allowed the American Missionary Association to operate a school in the leaky, dilapidated building in return for a stove for heating. In 1867, under the

2. Jerry John Thornbery, "The Development of Black Atlanta, 1865–1885" (Ph.D. dissertation, University of Maryland, 1977), 146–47.

3. Elizabeth Hyde Botume, *First Days Amongst the Contrabands* (Boston, 1893), 272; Robert L. Hall, "Tallahassee's Black Churches, 1865–1885," *Florida Historical Quarterly*, LVIII (1979), 190–91; George B. Tindall, *South Carolina Negroes, 1870–1900* (Baton Rouge, 1966), 187; Alrutheus A. Taylor, *The Negro in the Reconstruction of Virginia* (Washington, D.C., 1926), 189.

pastorate of Wesley J. Gaines, the congregation moved to a new location in the black settlement of Shermantown, on the eastern edge of the city.[4]

A lay preacher named Frank Quarles organized the first black Baptist congregation there. Quarles, who had been born in Virginia and acquired by a slave trader who moved him to Thomasville and then Atlanta, was ordained by white church officials in 1862. He established a black congregation that held separate worship services until 1864, when the arrival of General Sherman and the burning of Atlanta sent the local population, black and white, into flight. Returning after the war, as Joseph Wood had, to rebuild his church, Quarles likewise worked out an arrangement with the AMA by which it would erect a building on the property for use as a school during the week; the Baptists worshiped in it on Sundays. The arrangement lasted for about six months, until local white residents began to complain about the black church in their neighborhood. The white Baptists who owned the property sold it but purchased a new lot for what was then called Friendship Baptist Church adjacent to Jenningstown on the west side of the city.[5]

Most of the churches in the postbellum period, however, were founded after the war. Like infant creatures born in the wilderness, they were fragile and struggled for survival in perilous surroundings. Some grew large and strong, others remained small and feeble, and many died prematurely. Weak central authority, especially among the Baptists, along with a highly competitive and sectarian environment within the black church, made it especially easy for the freed people to organize and obtain official recognition for their congregations, a situation they favored and took full advantage of. According to denominational canon, however, the licensing of preachers and the ordaining of ministers had to be performed by established authorities, and that too the people generally endorsed. Thus Monroe Boykin, another former slave, and his parishioners were free to establish their church in Camden, but the pastor received his ordination from two northern missionaries.[6]

The ecclesiastical career of Pierre Landry, a native of Ascension Parish, Louisiana, exemplifies how blacks, on their own initiative, retreated from the restrictive environment of their former masters' churches and formed their own congregations. Landry, the child of his white master and a slave

4. Thornbery, "Development of Black Atlanta," 139–43.
5. *Ibid.*, 140–41.
6. Tindall, *South Carolina Negroes*, 187.

mother, had been raised as a Roman Catholic. He was confirmed in the church at Donaldsonville, a member of a large class of both white and black youths, and he later remembered vividly the confirmation service and the powerful effect it had on him: "The Sacraments were administered on an Easter Sunday morning, and I shall never forget the impressiveness of the services that day. The august presence of the Bishop who confirmed the class was to me typical of extraordinary grandeur, pomp with power, and when it was my time to kiss the signet ring of His grace, the jewel appeared to me as a blazing mirror in which were reflected the burning candles of the resplendent altar." But in 1862, at the age of twenty-one, he converted to Protestantism through the influence of a group of Methodist slaves. The appeal of the Methodist community was powerful enough to dissolve the hold that the Catholic church had had on him for so long. The group, eighteen in number, had been sold to a slave owner in Louisiana and practiced their faith under the leadership of a local preacher and class leader. After his conversion, Landry became a member of the church society and continued to worship with them until the end of the Civil War.

By then, the Methodist Episcopal church had begun to organize its missionary activities in Louisiana and had established an episcopal district that included Louisiana and Mississippi. The Donaldsonville congregation chose Landry to petition the annual conference for the appointment of a regular pastor to serve them and others in Ascension Parish who wished to join the Methodist church. The presiding bishop selected a black man, Thomas Kennedy, to be the pastor of the Donaldsonville church. Landry recalled: "On Rev. Kennedy assuming charge of the work at Donaldsonville where there were no members other than the colony mentioned, I assisted him in his labors. And being a former Catholic and having a large number of friends who followed me into the Methodist Church, the present St. Peter's Church was founded." Subsequently, Landry and Kennedy established Methodist missions at Ashland, Bayou Goula, Napoleonville, Woodlawn, and Vioron. Landry was chosen as a lay delegate from Louisiana to the General Conference in 1872. Following his ordination, he became pastor of St. Peter's Church.[7]

Methodist Episcopal missionaries in Louisiana represented the clerical authority that legitimized Landry's organizational activities and those

7. Pierre Landry, "Autobiographical Sketch" (Typescript in Dunn-Landry Family Papers, Amistad Research Center, Tulane University).

of the other Methodists of Ascension Parish. But the impetus for the expansion of the church into that part of the state came not so much from northern missionaries as from the freedmen themselves and their desire to bring the church under their own control.

Churches proliferated through the recruitment of new members, the enrollment of newly organized congregations, and the division of congregations. A tendency for elements within congregations to secede was evident early in the period. Francis L. Cardozo, a teacher working under the auspices of the American Missionary Association in Charleston, commented on this trend among the city's churches. In attempting to unify them for political purposes, he was frustrated by "a strict tendency to division." Groups of congregants often withdrew from parent churches because of disagreements over church policy or personality clashes. Disputes between the minister and one or more of the elders in a church often triggered a secession, as when William Troy, the minister of the Second Colored Baptist Church of Richmond, disagreed with the elders over church policy. Some of the members left and organized the Sharon Baptist Church. Troy himself left Second Church later on in another disagreement and founded the Moore Street Baptist Church. Virtual freedom from centralized control made it particularly easy for Baptist congregations to divide and to form new churches, but the trend was not confined to that denomination. Methodist congregations also experienced schisms. In New Orleans' elite St. James AME Church, a group of fifty or more members dissented from an episcopal decision admitting new members to fellowship. Church leaders did not admit freedmen, but the presiding bishop ordered that membership be available to freed as well as former free persons. Among the dissidents were the church's pastor, John Turner, and a deacon, Jacob Norager. After months of appeals failed to reverse the ruling, thirty-two of the dissidents, including Norager, departed St. James and organized the "upper-crust" Central Congregational Church.[8]

Similar conflicts and the frequent divisions within congregations led to a reputation for contentiousness that the church's critics exploited to denigrate it. Scholars also have cited this divisiveness as an example of

8. J. W. Healy to G. W. Whipple, March 26, 1869, in American Missionary Association Archives, Amistad Research Center, Tulane University (hereinafter cited as AMA Archives); Lucille L. Hutton, "This Is a Grand Work: A History of Central Congregational Church (United Church of Christ), New Orleans, Louisiana, 1872–1977" (Typescript in Central United Church of Christ Records, Amistad Research Center).

the disunity of black communities. But congregations often divided for reasons that reflected the growth and location of communities and were indicative of a strong sense of community spirit rather than of factionalism. Two important trends were evident in the division and expansion of churches. First, as freedmen migrated from plantations into the towns and cities of the South after the war and settled in new black neighborhoods, the established churches initiated intracity missionary programs to serve those neighborhoods and to promote community cohesion. Many of the larger urban churches established branches to serve rural rsidents and forge bonds among them. Second, segments of some of the older urban congregations that grew very large and were unable to serve all of their members effectively broke off and established their own neighborhood churches. Joseph Wood, for instance, the pastor of Bethel AME Church in Atlanta, one of two antebellum black congregations in the city and located in the eastside settlement of Shermantown, organized a congregation in the southside neighborhood of Summer Hill, some distance from Bethel. When a group of Bethel's members who lived in northwest Atlanta got tired of traveling back and forth from their homes in Shermantown to church, they formed Shiloh AME Church closer to their homes. Friendship Baptist Church also responded to the increased number of Baptists in the city after the war by assisting in the organization of five new churches. These divisions did not reflect conflict or factionalism within the church, but rather were responses to changes in the population and a desire on the part of ministers and church members to maintain community cohesion. They occurred largely to locate churches conveniently for their members.[9]

The number of offspring from original churches sometimes reached staggering proportions. Out of the Ebenezer Baptist Church of Richmond, for example, came Shiloh Baptist Church and St. John's Baptist Church. Four churches in Raleigh emerged from the First Baptist Colored Church. And from the Pine Grove Church in Aberdeen, Mississippi, issued Bethel, Pleasant Valley, Baptist Grove, New Grove, Ebenezer, Daniel, and Lakeville Baptist churches.[10]

The principal black churches, Baptist and Methodist, did not grow evenly with each other or consistently throughout the South in the period

9. Thornbery, "Development of Black Atlanta," 146–63.

10. Francis L. Cardozo to M. E. Strieby, April 12, 1866, in AMA Archives; Rabinowitz, *Race Relations in the Urban South,* 203; Vernon L. Wharton, *The Negro in Mississippi, 1865–1890* (New York, 1965), 258.

after the Civil War. In the first months of missionary activity, Methodists gained an edge in South Carolina, which the denomination maintained; at the same time, Baptists gained the upper hand in Virginia. In May, 1867, when AME officials organized the Virginia Annual Conference, only 3,500 members were enrolled, and the number grew very slowly in the ensuing years. In 1880 the conference had only 5,919 members. The AME church also struggled for members in Mississippi. The AME church was larger on the whole than the AME Zion; the latter outnumbered the former in North Carolina, but it was significantly less strong elsewhere. In the Louisiana Conference, for example, membership declined from 10,124 in 1871 to 1,680 in 1879, which James Hood blamed on unfortunate choices of men to work as missionaries in the area.[11]

The largest number of churchgoing people in the postbellum period were Baptists. Isaac Brinckerhoff, a white northern missionary working to establish churches among the freedmen of South Carolina, Georgia, and Florida, guessed that perhaps nine-tenths of those who professed religion were already Baptists at the conclusion of the Civil War. Of the remaining tenth, he surmised, "nearly all are Baptists in sentiment." Although Brinckerhoff grossly exaggerated the number of adherents, he was right that Baptist theology and polity had a very strong appeal to the masses. The northern and southern churches' estimates of the number of Baptists at the time of the Civil War range from 150,000 to 400,000. Black church records are too sparse to draw any solid figures from them. Federal census reports in 1890 provide the earliest reliable data about black church membership after emancipation. Although those figures obviously do not give absolute numbers for the immediate postwar period, they do suggest the relative strength of black denominations for the earlier time if one assumes that no dramatic shift occurred between the 1860s and 1890. In 1890 over half (approximately 54 percent) of those southern blacks who belonged to all-black churches were Baptists. In some states Baptists were even more predominant. They were particularly strong in Virginia, for example, where 83 percent of the black communicants were Baptists, the highest proportion in all of the southern states. In Louisiana, 62 percent of black churchgoers were Baptists, in Mississippi, 61 percent, and in Texas and Arkansas, 60 percent. Some states, however, had very small percentages of Baptists. In Maryland, for

11. Taylor, *Negro in the Reconstruction of Virginia*, 180; Wharton, *Negro in Mississippi*, 260; James W. Hood, *One Hundred Years of the African Methodist Episcopal Zion Church* (New York, 1895), 312.

example, where the Methodist denominations had strong, aggressive organizations, only 13 percent of black communicants were Baptists. In Florida, 32 percent of the churchgoers were Baptists, in South Carolina and Tennessee, 40 percent, and in Missouri, 44 percent.[12]

That there were appreciably higher percentages of Baptists in some areas suggests that local conditions affected the people's religious beliefs and determined their church affiliation. Certainly the denominational orientation of significant whites influenced the church affiliation of blacks. Large numbers of slaves had become Christians because of their Baptist masters. Slaves commonly joined the churches of their masters or ones that were accessible to them on antebellum plantations. Sometimes the demands of their masters and mistresses gave slaves no choice of what church to attend. Rachel Bradley nearly always accompanied her mistress to church meetings and caught the spirit of evangelical revivalism as a result. "Old missis used to go off to church and revivals and she'd take me along," she remembered. "When they got to shoutin' I'd shout too." Youngsters were swayed by their parents as well. "I jined church long time er go," recalled Sol Webb of Alabama, "cause my Mother and Daddy b'longed and I jist followed them." People tended to remain in the churches they had joined before the war. Because slaves did not usually travel beyond the boundaries of their plantations and received few stimuli from outside of their local communities, those who were converted to Baptist Christianity were likely to remain in the fold for a long time, even after emancipation. But there were many reasons why people changed their church membership. Ellen King, for instance, joined a Methodist church in Mobile, Alabama, but when she moved to Mauvilla she found no Methodist congregation there. So "I joined the Baptist church." Some people rejected their religious upbringing and joined another church

12. Isaac Brinckerhoff, "Thirty Years Among Freedmen: Mission Work Among the Freed Negroes of Beaufort, S. Carolina, St. Augustine, Florida, and Savannah, Georgia, 1862–1894" (MS in American Baptist Historical Society, Rochester, New York); American Baptist Home Mission Society, *Baptist Home Missions in North America, Including a Full Report of the Jubilee Meeting, and a Historical Sketch of the American Baptist Home Mission Society Tables, 1832–1882* (New York, 1883), 421; *Eleventh Census, 1890: Churches,* 172–77, 403–34; Logan, *Negro in North Carolina,* 164–65; Taylor, *Negro in the Reconstruction of Virginia,* 182–93. The statistics on church membership in the 1890 census derived from reports submitted by church officials. It is doubtful that their figures are accurate because often congregants were not removed from the rolls for nonattendance or if they joined other denominations. Furthermore, sectarian impulses may have tempted reporters to inflate membership figures.

when they had a freer choice as adults. George Simpson was raised as a Presbyterian but later became a Methodist. Pierre Landry had been raised as a Catholic in Louisiana but converted to Methodism.[13]

African-American denominational identification was not merely a hand-me-down from whites. Many blacks were Baptists for reasons entirely apart from the religious convictions of significant whites in their lives. Although there is no way of knowing precisely what proportions of either blacks or whites in the antebellum South were Baptists, it appears doubtful that the ratios were similar. Many of the largest slave owners were Episcopalians, Presbyterians, and Methodists. Furthermore, census data from the late nineteenth century indicate that there were significant differences between the proportions of whites and blacks who belonged to the same denominations. The percentage of Baptists among the black churchgoing population was appreciably higher than among whites. Nor can the prevalence of black Baptists be accounted for solely by the evangelical endeavors of white Baptist missionaries. They had been remarkably effective in converting people during the revivals early in the nineteenth century, but missionaries of other evangelical denominations, particularly Methodists, labored just as assiduously to convert blacks without as much success. During the closing stages of the Civil War and afterward, no group was more industrious in evangelical activity than the Congregationalists, whose intense efforts should have enlisted many more converts than they did. Black church affiliation was not based on chance, nor was it a replica of white patterns of church association, and it certainly was not the result of white evangelization alone.[14]

Other factors help to explain black southerners' propensity to become Baptists. Baptist theology blended particularly well with African religious traditions. The Baptists' insistence on baptism by immersion clearly distinguished them from other evangelical denominations and resembled some of the river ceremonies common in areas of West Africa where many slaves had come from. More important, Baptist polity attracted blacks who wanted independence from white control. The principle of

13. Charles L. Perdue, Jr., Thomas E. Barden, and Robert K. Phillips, eds., *Weevils in the Wheat: Interviews with Virginia Ex-Slaves* (Charlottesville, 1976), 100; George P. Rawick, ed., *Arkansas Narratives* (Westport, 1977), 1, Vol. II of Rawick, ed., *The American Slave: A Composite Autobiography, Supplemental Series 1*, 12 vols.; Rawick, ed., *Alabama Narratives, ibid.*, 234, 442; Rawick, ed., *Missouri Narratives, ibid.*, 221.

14. *Census of Religious Bodies: 1906* (2 vols.; Washington, D.C., 1909), I, 156–290, II, 43–153.

congregationalism allowed for the accommodation of a wide range of beliefs and practices. The Baptist community of churches had no outside authority to impinge on a congregation's freedom. And because individual congregations had the authority to call and dismiss their preachers, Baptists could usually get preachers who preached the gospel as they wanted it preached. Congregationalism also facilitated the proliferation of Baptist churches by allowing new congregations to form and old ones to divide. All of the considerations that made the evangelical Baptist church popular among slaves also appealed to them as freedmen. And as the number of missionaries (many of them black by the late 1860s and 1870s) working among the black population increased after emancipation, so did the number of converts.[15]

The number of blacks in racially mixed Baptist churches fell proportionately as membership in the new, independent black churches grew, indicating not only that nonbelievers were being converted by Baptist missionaries but that blacks were withdrawing from biracial, white-controlled churches. In Georgia, for instance, enrollment in white-controlled Baptist churches dropped from 27,734 in 1860 to 5,745 in 1870. Conversely, membership in identifiable black Baptist congregations grew from a few hundred in 1860 to 38,878 in 1870. In South Carolina by 1874, only 1,614 blacks remained in biracial churches. By 1867, 21,000 members of congregations were affiliated with the Virginia black state convention of missionary Baptist churches.[16]

At first, white church leaders seemed to want the freedmen to remain in the old churches. Disavowing any animosity toward them and denying that they had ever been anything but friends and benefactors to the former chattels, the delegates to the Alabama Baptist State Convention affirmed their paternalistic friendship by asserting that the freedmen's "highest good will be subserved by their maintaining their present relation to those who know them, who love them, and who will labor for the promotion of their welfare." Many whites doubted that blacks possessed the ability to organize and maintain holy churches. They believed that, if left alone, the blacks would lapse into emotionalism, superstition, or

15. Sterling Stuckey, *Slave Culture: Nationalist Theory and the Foundations of Black America* (New York, 1987), 34.

16. Rufus L. Spain, *At Ease in Zion: A Social History of the Southern Baptists, 1865–1900* (Nashville, 1967), 51; Francis B. Simkins and Robert H. Woody, *South Carolina During Reconstruction* (Chapel Hill, 1932), 385; Taylor, *Negro in the Reconstruction of Virginia*, 185.

heathenish forms of worship. The *Religious Herald,* the official voice of the Southern Baptist Convention, expressed doubt that freedom had provided blacks with the "intelligence and self-control demanded in conducting the business and discipline of the Church." Whites worried about losing control over the former slaves. One Virginia minister told fellow members of the Goshen Baptist Association that control over their religion was practically the only authority they still had over blacks, and if that was lost all discipline over the freedmen would disappear. The desire to retain the old social order was so strong that whites deluded themselves into believing that the freedmen would really want to remain in fellowship with them. As late as 1872, the white Georgia state convention counted eight black district associations of churches and 39,212 black congregants among its members even though none of them had any official connection with the organization.[17]

But most whites, whatever their denomination, were not deluded when it came to assessing the freedmen's attitude toward biracial churches. They recorded the decline in black membership and drew the obvious conclusion that they could not halt the exodus. Nor, all things considered, did they want to. Their yearning for the old days and the old ways was curbed by their distaste for associating with blacks who would not accept a subordinate status. New and inescapable realities shaped race relations in the South, but white ecclesiastics were intent on preserving as much of the old order as possible. They wanted the freedmen to remain in the old churches, but they expected them to accept an inferior status. If blacks were willing to accept the old order—and some were—they were welcome to stay; if not, whites were content to let them go their own way. Thus officials of the Antioch Baptist Church in Savannah allowed blacks to attend church services but required them to occupy a section at the rear of the sanctuary as they had during slavery. And a member of the Goshen Association advised his brethren to "let the Yankees and negroes take care of themselves."[18]

As blacks moved out, whites placidly invoked the banal assertion that

17. Spain, *At Ease in Zion,* 48–49; H. Shelton Smith, *In His Image, But . . . : Racism in Southern Religion, 1780–1910* (Durham, N.C., 1972), 226; *Religious Herald,* October 19, 1865; *Christian Recorder,* September 22, 1866; Georgia Baptist State Convention, *Minutes of the Fiftieth Anniversary of the Georgia Baptist State Convention . . . 1872* (Atlanta, 1872).

18. Robert E. Perdue, *The Negro in Savannah, 1865–1900* (New York, 1973), 29; *Christian Recorder,* September 22, 1966.

slavery had been God's will, not their own, and that they had always met their Christian obligation by caring for the slaves' welfare. They continued to maintain that the two races could live amicably. White southern Methodists and Baptists reacted the same way. "If they elect to leave us," white southern Methodist leaders in Mississippi declared, "let them go with the assurance that as heretofore we have been, so will we continue to be their friends." G. W. Nolby, a white southern Methodist, carried that message personally to a black congregation in Richmond. Amid mutual expressions of goodwill and friendship, he affirmed that the blacks' redemption and elevation were in their own hands more than ever before, adding, according to a reporter, that southern Methodists "intended still to stand by them, to be their friends and to help them as they had ever done." [19]

Whites' resignation to the departure of blacks did not mean that they abandoned the freedmen altogether. Many denominational leaders urged their churches not to forsake their former servants and leave them to superstition or, worse, the influence of Yankee missionaries. Regardless of their motives or their perception of the freedmen's religious condition, many whites remained paternalistically involved in the spiritual affairs of blacks who shared their world. White Baptist leaders in Texas stated their opinion that if not cared for the freedmen would naturally lapse into superstition and primitive emotionalism. The white Texas state convention resolved to "render this people both material and moral aid, directly and indirectly." The Alabama state convention asked, "Shall we abandon them to the inevitable fate of the masses, if uncared for by the white man—indolence, superstition, and the rapid return to barbarism—or shall we leave them to the teachings of others who are strangers to their character, and who, however pure in their motives and purposes, must from the very nature of things, labor under many and serious hindrances to success?" They voted to accept responsibility for the freedmen, remarking, "The changed relation of the Negro does not release us from our religious obligations to them." [20]

19. Methodist Episcopal Church, South, Mississippi Annual Conference, *Minutes of the Annual Session of the Mississippi Conference . . . 1865* (Jackson, 1866), p. 26; *Christian Recorder*, December 2, 1865; Hunter D. Farish, *The Circuit-Rider Dismounts: A Social History of Southern Methodism, 1865–1900* (Richmond, 1938), 163–208; Ralph E. Morrow, *Northern Methodism and Reconstruction* (East Lansing, 1956), 63–70; Smith, *In His Image, But . . .* , 229–32.

20. *Christian Recorder*, June 16, September 22, 1866; Baptist General Association of Texas, *Proceedings of the Third Meeting of the Baptist General Association of Texas, July,*

Many whites did considerably more than merely acknowledge their duty to the former slaves. They contributed money and time to the organization of black congregations. They endeavored to assist black missionaries in converting the freedmen and establishing Sunday schools and secular schools and thereby achieved the twin objectives of undercutting the northern missionaries and satisfying their own consciences. To promote Christian brotherhood, most white conventions invited delegates from black churches to attend their annual meetings. The Virginia convention seated black delegates and made "suitable provision" for their "hospitable and appropriate entertainment" during the session. The Alabama politician and layman Jabez L. M. Curry, like many other white Baptists, met with groups of freedmen and offered them advice on how to organize churches and also on how to raise the money that was necessary to construct buildings. Gradually, white southerners came to feel comfortable with the new arrangement. In Virginia, some whites emphasized the importance of easing racial tensions and accepting the proposition that the "colored Baptists of the State constitute an important part of Zion." [21]

The local congregations were the building blocks of black Baptist polity. Soon after the appearance of independent Baptist churches, however, congregational leaders began organizing associations of churches that sent representatives to annual state conventions. The purpose of district and state organizations was to coordinate communication and cooperation among local congregations in missionary, educational, and welfare activities. They supported missionaries who preached the gospel and organized new churches, founded and operated schools, and maintained funds for the tuition payments of qualified pupils, the financial support of retired ministers, their widows, and orphans, and to feed the needy. The associations and state conventions challenged the autonomy of local congregations but had very little real authority over them and so represented no serious threat to the principle of congregationalism.

District associations made their appearance almost as soon as independent black congregations were organized; some black associations actually antedated the Civil War. The Baptist denomination's rapid growth

---

1870 (Houston, 1872), 17; Alabama Baptist State Convention, *Minutes of the Alabama Baptist State Convention . . . 1866* (Atlanta, 1866), 13–14.

21. *People's Advocate*, June 14, 1879; Alabama Baptist State Convention, *Proceedings of the Fifty-sixth Annual Session of the Alabama Baptist State Convention . . . 1879* (Eufaula, Ala., 1879), 25; J. L. M. Curry, Diary, March 21, 1868 (MS in Manuscript Division, Library of Congress).

after emancipation resulted in more associations. In 1863 representatives from five churches in Norfolk, Williamsburg, Hampton, and Chesapeake City gathered in the First Baptist Church of Hampton to form the Norfolk Union Baptist Association. In May, 1864, they held their first annual meeting. In 1865 seven churches in the vicinity of Richmond formed the Shiloh Association, which by 1868 encompassed seventy-five churches, while Norfolk Union had thirty-seven and the Valley Association seventeen. In 1865 Baptist churches in eastern Georgia, South Carolina, and Florida formed the Zion Association. Associations also appeared in North Carolina soon after emancipation; delegates from three churches in Bladen County formed Gray's Association. Samuel Peterson and Fred Long led the organization of the old Eastern Missionary Baptist Association at the "slab chapel" in the black town of James City. At about the same time, William H. Banks came from Virginia to Wilmington, where he took over the pastorate of First Baptist Church. Banks occupied that pulpit until a dispute within the congregation forced him to resign. Joined by William Greene, he organized Ebenezer Church in Wilmington and then several others in New Hanover, Dublin, Sampson, and Bladen counties. In 1872 representatives of eighteen of the churches met at Ebenezer Church and created the Middle District Association.[22]

Most associations sent representatives to state conventions that served the same theoretical purpose as the district organizations, only on a larger scale. Their basic objective was to unify churches under a standardized discipline and to widen the community of Baptist believers. Their primary activity was to facilitate missionary work by sending preachers out among the population to convert sinners. The Virginia Baptist State Convention gave as its purpose the "diffusion of the Gospel of Jesus Christ" by cooperative enterprise in supporting missionaries, forming congregations, distributing literature, founding Sunday schools, and establishing secular schools. It also maintained pension and scholarship funds that assisted the needy. North Carolina and Arkansas Baptists both formed state conventions in 1867. A year later, ministers of the Norfolk Union and Shiloh associations met to organize the Baptist State Convention of Virginia. Also in 1868, representatives of twenty-seven

22. Garnet Ryland, *The Baptists of Virginia, 1699–1926* (Richmond, 1955), 303–305; Zion Baptist Association (Georgia), *Minutes of the Third Annual Session of the Zion Baptist Association . . . 1868* (Savannah, 1868); J. A. Whitted, *A History of the Negro Baptists of North Carolina* (Raleigh, 1908), 75, 81, 86–87.

churches met in Montgomery to form the Colored Baptist State Convention of Alabama.[23]

Mississippi Baptists organized a state convention in 1869. One of its architects was Henry P. Jacobs of Natchez, whom one historian called "perhaps the most effective organizer the Negro Baptists of the state ever possessed." Jacobs had followed the missionary Jesse F. Boulden into the Natchez pulpit. Boulden came to Mississippi in 1865 from the Northwest Baptist Missionary Convention, an organization representing black Baptists in Illinois, Ohio, Kentucky, Missouri, Indiana, and Michigan. He departed Natchez after being called to a church in Columbus. He had not supported the formation of the state convention, and from his base in Columbus he established new churches, organized district associations, and finally in 1872 brought together representatives from 226 churches and 21,000 members in northern Mississippi into the rival General Missionary Baptist Association. In 1890 the Missionary Baptist Association merged with the convention that Jacobs had founded, thus bringing together some 900 churches and more than 79,000 Baptist church members.[24]

By 1874, Texas Baptists had formed a state convention. As was true elsewhere in the South, black Texans were still trying to adjust to freedom and whites were searching for ways to maintain their supremacy. It suited the interests of both groups for blacks to have their own independent churches. Black Baptist leaders sought the advice of their southern white brethren in church organization, and whites responded by helping them. Blacks now issued a special invitation to whites to attend the first meeting of their new state convention and to help them organize it. Several whites accepted, and the new organization took its place among state Baptist conventions.[25]

South Carolina had no statewide organization until 1876, when representatives of the three existing district associations convened under the

23. Virginia Baptist State Convention, *Minutes of the Eighteenth Annual Session of the Virginia Baptist State Convention . . . 1885* (Portsmouth, Va., 1885), 3; Ryland, *Baptists of Virginia,* 305; Whitted, *History of the Negro Baptists of North Carolina,* 34; Carter G. Woodson, *The History of the Negro Church* (1921; rpr. Washington, D.C., 1972), 177–78; C. O. Boothe, *Cyclopedia of Negro Baptists of Alabama* (Birmingham, 1895), 37, 114.

24. Wharton, *Negro in Mississippi,* 259–60; Patrick H. Thompson, *The History of Negro Baptists in Mississippi* (Jackson, 1898), 58, 143, 152, 154.

25. J. M. Carroll, *A History of Texas Baptists: Comprising a Detailed Account of Their Activities, Their Progress, and Their Achievements* (Dallas, 1923), 355–56.

leadership of Isaac P. Brockenton and Edward M. Brawley at Shiloh Church in Charleston. The convention's first regular session met in 1877.[26]

Women constituted a majority of the membership and were a powerful element in the church. In keeping with the "cult of true womanhood" that prevailed at the time and confined the wives and daughters of business and professional men to roles supportive of their husbands, fathers, and church leaders, however, their influence did not come from the forefront of the church, the pulpit, but rather from the pew. Rural and urban working-class women were less affected by middle-class social conventions, but even though they outnumbered men among church members, they were limited to nonministerial positions within the church. Women played a very important role in planning the meetings of district associations and state conventions and in arranging accommodations for the representatives of member churches who attended the meetings. Association and convention gatherings were often social affairs as much as business meetings, and the women of the host churches labored hard to feed and entertain the visiting ministers. They also organized separate women's societies in conjunction with local congregations and district associations, but it was not until the 1880s that they began to organize their own statewide conventions. The first Baptist women's state convention was founded in Kentucky in 1883. It had the support of male church leaders such as William J. Simmons, an influential figure in the state, who recognized the effectiveness of women's societies in raising money for church activities and convinced his male colleagues to allow the sisters to form a separate organization. The Kentucky example set a pattern that women in other states quickly followed. Many of the women who led the convention movement, including Virginia Broughton of Tennessee, like some of the male organizers, were graduates of colleges and training schools established by northern churches. Broughton was a member of Fisk University's first graduating class. These women assimilated the Christian values and middle-class mores of their mentors, which included the feminine role of service to the community, particularly in providing moral and educational leadership.[27]

26. South Carolina Baptist Missionary, Education, and Sunday School Convention, *Minutes of the Third Anniversary of the Baptist Educational, Missionary, and Sunday School Convention of South Carolina . . . 1879* (Columbia, 1879), 3–4; Joe M. King, *A History of South Carolina Baptists* (Columbia, 1964), 259.

27. Evelyn Brooks, "The Women's Movement in the Black Baptist Church, 1880–1920" (Ph.D. dissertation, University of Rochester, 1984), 18–82.

Missionary work, Sunday school activity, and care for the needy within the community were particular areas of women's involvement. Initially, their role was largely to raise money, and they did so well at it that preachers became dependent on the women's organizations to finance the church-building and school-building programs that always redounded to the ministers' credit and enhanced their professional reputations. But the women soon grew dissatisfied with their subordinate position and demanded an enlarged role in church operations. Not only did they complain about the roles men assigned them in the church, but some from the elite class also grumbled about self-centered men who restricted their activities outside of the church. One Georgia woman noted that a man was likely to protest against her studying law or medicine or obtaining other work to earn money. "But whenever it came to church affairs, especially in raising money for the church he quietly puts his hands in his pockets and steps aside leaving it for the women to do." Women also demanded more support from ministers for their church work, especially for social welfare programs among the poor and disabled in the community. They took charge of teaching in church schools, and they became effective church missionaries, visiting people in their homes to conduct Bible readings and prayer meetings. They offered instruction to poor and peasant families in hygiene, housekeeping, and nutrition.[28]

Association and convention meetings across the South followed a common pattern. They lasted three or four days, beginning on Thursday or Friday and concluding with services on Sunday. The delegates, called messengers, represented the member churches, and they brought along with them statements of the financial and religious condition of their churches as well as annual dues. In addition to membership fees, the messengers and their churches were expected to contribute to association and convention home and foreign mission programs, schools, and welfare projects. Conscientious messengers attended committee meetings and three scheduled business sessions each day. The general sessions were open to the public. They were governed by elaborate rules, mastery of which the officers demonstrated with considerable pride and the spectators viewed with admiration, and featured speeches by local pastors, both white and black; addresses and sermons by the presiding ministers; and reports from the organizations' standing committees. Picnics, huge meals, and excursions to places of interest nearby added to the pleasure

28. *Ibid.,* 98–101, 109–14.

of seeing old friends and created an atmosphere that, although broken by controversy from time to time, was generally agreeable.[29]

For Baptists regional and statewide agencies were components of a system of church polity that they adopted from whites, but these associations and conventions contradicted the principle of congregationalism that stood at the center of Baptist organizational theory, and in their association and convention constitutions and bylaws, church leaders addressed the issue of congregationalism versus hierarchy and resolved conflicts between the two. In theory, associations and conventions possessed no coercive authority over their member churches and therefore did not impinge on congregational autonomy. The Cedar Grove Baptist Association in North Carolina, like most of its kind, could only "advise and aid the churches" in the achievement of common objectives. It could not lawfully "interfere with the internal affairs of the churches."[30]

In practice, though, both associations and state conventions did possess coercive power over their constituent congregations, which they derived from the benefits they imparted to their members and from their authority as ordaining agencies. They could expel members and thereby deprive them of the fruits of fellowship. Membership in one of these agencies not only brought the benefit of association with other born-again Christians but also the money in the form of pensions to preachers or their survivors, scholarships for students, funds for missions, Sunday schools and secular schools, and also the opportunities for career advancement, power, and prestige afforded by positions sustained by associations and conventions.[31]

The associations and state conventions were unstable organizations because of the Baptists' strong commitment to congregationalism and their vulnerability to ministers who might tear congregations away from them. The principle of congregationalism weakened the bonding properties of the associations, and disputes between ministers were an ongoing problem. In Mississippi, for example, Baptists attempting to organize a state convention were unable to win the support of Jesse F. Boulden because of the inclusion of some congregations that he deemed "dis-

---

29. Berean Valley Baptist Association (Virginia), *Minutes of the Fourteenth Annual Session of the Berean Valley Baptist Association . . . 1896* (Washington, D.C., n.d.), 6; Northern Neck Baptist Association (Virginia), *Minutes of the Twentieth Annual Session of the Northern Neck Baptist Association . . . 1897* (Washington, D.C., 1897), 10, 14.

30. Cedar Grove Baptist Association (North Carolina), *Minutes of the Eighth Annual Session of the Cedar Grove Baptist Association . . . 1875* (Raleigh, 1875), 1.

31. *Ibid.*; Thompson, *History of Negro Baptists in Mississippi*, 97, 168.

orderly." Boulden then formed a rival group, the Baptist General Association. Later on, the state convention had difficulty deciding whether to discipline a dissident minister who had become involved in a dispute with his congregation. The convention ordered that he be dismissed from the pulpit and tried to replace the deacons of the church as well. The offending minister organized a "bogus convention" and generated sufficient opposition to the regular state convention that the latter's missionaries began reporting "negativism" among the people in certain areas of the state and considerable trouble in Adams County "owing to the workings of bogus parties against this Convention." [32]

As the South moved farther from the experience of the Civil War, the Methodist denominations prospered in much the same way the Baptists did. Methodist membership increased significantly, and church officials expanded their denominational apparatus throughout the former slave states. Before the Civil War, the African Methodist Episcopal church had approximately 20,000 members; by 1866 it claimed 75,000, virtually all of the increase in the South. The church's growth was especially impressive in South Carolina, which serves as an illustration of its performance throughout the South. Membership in the South Carolina Conference numbered 22,388 in 1866, and the church's ministers quickly multiplied that number. The conference claimed 47,891 members in 1867, and by 1878 it was so large that it was divided. Georgia and North Carolina became separate conferences, and South Carolina was divided between the Columbia Annual Conference, which took in the northern counties, and the South Carolina Conference, encompassing the remainder of the state. The Georgia Conference divided in 1873, creating the North Georgia Conference, and ten years later divided again, producing the Macon Conference. When the Florida Conference met for the first time in 1867, it claimed 4,800 members. It grew significantly afterward, boasting 11,600 members, 25 traveling elders, 48 traveling deacons, and 244 local preachers by 1871. [33]

32. Thompson, *History of Negro Baptists in Mississippi*, 58, 143, 152, 154.

33. *Eleventh Census, 1890: Churches*, 46, 543, 559, 604; *Christian Recorder*, July 1, 8, 21, 1865; Simkins and Woody, *South Carolina During Reconstruction*, 386; Williamson, *After Slavery*, 191; Charles S. Smith, *A History of the African Methodist Episcopal Church* (1922; rpr. New York, 1968), 504–509; Tindall, *South Carolina Negroes*, 190; George A. Singleton, *The Romance of African Methodism: A Study of the African Methodist Episcopal Church* (New York, 1952), 105–106; Wesley J. Gaines, *African Methodism in the South, or, Twenty-five Years of Freedom* (Atlanta, 1890), 48–49, 205–206, 224–28; Joe M. Richardson, *The Negro in the Reconstruction of Florida, 1867–1877* (Tallahassee, 1965), 84–85.

AME Zion missionaries also continued their efforts to establish churches throughout the South. Superintendents Joseph J. Clinton, Samson D. Talbot, and John J. Moore organized annual conferences. Clinton formed the Louisiana Conference in March, 1865, originally containing churches from New Orleans westward into Texas and eastward to Georgia and Florida. Eventually, it spawned conferences in Alabama (1867), Georgia (1867), Florida (1869), and Texas (1881). The Virginia (1866), South Carolina (1867), Tennessee (1868), and West Tennessee and Mississippi (1869) conferences were outgrowths of the North Carolina one. Talbot organized the Kentucky Conference in June, 1866, and conferences in Arkansas (1870) and Missouri (1889) issued from it. By 1870 there were eleven AME Zion annual conferences in the former slave states.[34]

Most of the freedmen who joined AME or AME Zion churches had previously belonged to the Methodist Episcopal Church, South. In 1860 the southern church had approximately 207,000 black communicants; by the end of the war most of them had deserted it for one of the African Methodist churches or the Methodist Episcopal church. For example, black membership in the Virginia Conference fell from 7,500 in 1860 to 1,200 in 1866. Membership in South Carolina declined from 50,000 to 16,000, in Georgia from 27,400 to 15,000, and in Mississippi from 17,500 to 5,400. By the end of the war, southern Methodist officials had made some concessions to black parishioners to retain their hold over them. For instance, several black congregations worshiped under the leadership of black preachers, some of whom had been ordained by white bishops, an obvious acknowledgment of the freedmen's demand for autonomy. But despite that liberal façade, racial discrimination remained as embedded as ever in the church's polity, and it still did not permit its black congregations to own property or to exercise any power in denominational affairs. In the midst of rising black expectations brought about by emancipation and the appeals of African and white Methodist Episcopal missionaries, such conditions were intolerable to most black Methodists.[35]

34. Hood, *One Hundred Years of the African Methodist Episcopal Zion Church*, 299, 312–13, 327–30, 336; David H. Bradley, *A History of the A.M.E. Zion Church* (2 vols.; Nashville, 1956–70), I, 175–78, II, 60–61.

35. Charles H. Phillips, *The History of the Colored Methodist Episcopal Church in America* (Jackson, 1898), 25; Richardson, *Negro in the Reconstruction of Florida*, 83; Smith, *In His Image, But . . .*, 229–30.

Nevertheless, approximately seventy thousand blacks did not immediately sever their ties with the southern church. The white church's refusal to transfer title to buildings to blacks who wanted to join the African churches kept them in the white-controlled organization. Church officials made it clear to congregations that occupied those meeting-houses that if they joined the African church they would forfeit the property. Heeding the warning, many black parishioners had remained under the authority of the southern church, although most continued to worship in separate congregations. By the spring of 1866, black withdrawal from the southern church and the missionary effort among the freedmen motivated the church to develop a plan for dealing with its black members. At its General Conference in New Orleans, a delegation from the AME church, including M. M. Clark, a veteran missionary, John Turner, the immensely popular pastor of St. James AME Church in New Orleans, and Charles Burch, proposed that the church deed all buildings used by blacks to the African Methodists. Although the presiding bishop refused to introduce the African Methodists formally to the conference, he did direct the assembly to respond to their petition. The conference acknowledged that its black members desired their own church organization and congratulated itself on having already provided for black ministers, districts, and annual conferences among its black parishioners. The bishops indicated that they would approve a union with the AME church, suggesting that the African Methodists possessed greater wisdom and experience in dealing with church matters than the southern church's black congregants. The proposal was little more than an abstraction, however, and no detailed terms of a merger ever resulted. The whites were not seriously interested in consolidating with the African Methodists, although they did prefer the African Methodists over their northern Methodist Episcopal rivals and were happy to keep channels of communication with the African church open.

The conference reached out to the AME delegation in a pledge to cooperate on matters pertaining to the "religious welfare of the colored people." That meant that it would content itself with allowing blacks to choose between the southern Methodist church and the African Methodists. This gesture was intended to generate goodwill between southern and African Methodists while isolating the northern Methodist Episcopal church. The African Methodists would not attempt to induce blacks to leave the southern church, and it in turn would not try to prevent blacks from joining the AME church. But although they would be permitted

continued use of the church buildings they occupied, they would not receive legal title to them.

The third part of the plan contained the essence of what the southern
Methodists' wanted. The bishops continued to be obsessed with a desire
for dominion over their black former members. The only card they had
to play was the church's ownership of the property that meant so much
to freedmen. The bishops offered those blacks who remained with the
church two choices. They could stay in the white-controlled churches as
they had been before emancipation—highly unlikely but at least a hypo-
thetical possibility—or they could opt to form separate congregations,
have their own preachers, and manage their own affairs through districts,
annual conferences, and even their own general conference. The bishops
did not promise to turn church property over to those who remained in
the church, but they were evidently prepared to do so if the parishioners
would not affiliate with any other Methodist organization.[36]

AME officials responded optimistically to the proposal, reading more
into it than was actually there, especially about church property. Elisha
Weaver, the former editor of the *Christian Recorder,* wrote that "the
Methodist Episcopal Church South has passed a resolution to turn all
their colored members over to us, with their church buildings." Praising
the "Christ-like spirit" of the proposal as he understood it, Weaver said
"it ought to be cherished and fostered until we can all worship together,
on terms of perfect equality. We say, most emphatically, that this will be
the means of much union and prosperity between our Church and the
M.E. Church South. For pursuing this course, it will be a pleasure for us
to invite the ministers of the South to preach in our pulpits. May God
speed the good cause onward." James Lynch, who had left the missionary
field and now was the *Christian Recorder*'s editor, also responded to the
proposal. He had been a persistent critic of the southern church because
of its policy regarding church property and had vented his indignation
over the bishops' refusal to introduce the AME delegation to the General
Conference. But he was an advocate of racial accommodation and could
not help viewing the proposals sanguinely. Although not beguiled into
believing that the southern church had committed itself to transferring
property to the AME church, he did acclaim its "liberal policy" and believed that progress in relations between the two organizations had been
made at the General Conference. "Certainly this much has been gained;

36. *Christian Recorder,* September 8, 1866.

that henceforth we can pursue our work of labor and love in all parts of the South gathering in those colored Methodists who may desire to unite with us; without provoking the hostility of ministers of the M.E. Church South." [37]

In actuality, the southern Methodist church never seriously contemplated turning its property over to the African Methodists. What it hoped to accomplish—and succeeded in doing—was to keep as many black Methodists as possible under its control. By retaining control of church properties but allowing those members who remained under the authority of its bishops to use them, it contained its losses to about 60 percent of its prewar membership, a substantial attrition but no doubt less than it would have been had the church turned the buildings over to the African Methodists. And by presenting even the illusion of conciliation to the African Methodists, whose leaders had become distinctly more inclined to align their church with the southern Methodists than with their rivals in the ME church, it formed something of a defense against the latter's missionary activities. Southern Methodist hierarchs believed that it was better, for the sake of southern whites and their ability to control the South's black population, that those who did leave the southern Methodist church join the AME church rather than the hated Methodist Episcopal church, but in the final accounting, the southern church lost more than it hoped it would. When its General Conference met in Memphis in 1870, virtually all of its black members had chosen to organize separate churches and conferences. Therefore, the bishops decided to set their black members free. The Colored Methodist Episcopal church (CME) was granted complete autonomy and received the prize of the church property that the southern Methodist church had withheld from the AME church. [38]

Among the blacks who created the Colored Methodist Episcopal church were William H. Miles, Richard H. Vanderhorst, Lucius H. Holsey, and Isaac Lane. Miles had the greatest initial impact. Manumitted by his owner in 1854, he joined the southern Methodist church a year later. After the Civil War he moved to Ohio, where he joined the AME Zion

---

37. *Ibid.*, May 5, 12, 1866.

38. Farish, *Circuit-Rider Dismounts*, 163–208; Morrow, *Northern Methodism and Reconstruction*, 63–70; Smith, *In His Image, But . . .*, 229–32; Clarence E. Walker, *A Rock in a Weary Land: The African Methodist Episcopal Church During the Civil War and Reconstruction* (Baton Rouge, 1982), 94–99; Phillips, *History of the Colored Methodist Episcopal Church*, 22–23.

church. Later he returned to his home state of Kentucky, was a charter member of the Kentucky Annual Conference, and became pastor of the Central Street Church in Louisville. He was instrumental in the appointment of Jermain W. Loguen, another former Kentucky slave, to be superintendent of the Kentucky Conference, but Loguen removed him from his Louisville church and sent him traveling as a missionary. Miles quit the church then and returned to the white Methodist Church, South. After organizing a black conference in Kentucky in 1868, he attended the first General Conference of the CME church as an alternate delegate. A "plain, positive man," he remained quiet throughout most of the conference meetings until called upon to deliver a sermon. Then, according to the church's early historian, he so impressed the delegates with his message that they elected him their first bishop.

Richard Vanderhorst, Miles's senior by fifteen years, was one of five sons born of a slave couple in Georgetown, South Carolina. As a boy he had been a body servant, and one of his tasks was to carry his mistress' hymnal and Bible to church, sit through the service, and carry her things back home again. At his parents' request, he was apprenticed to a carpenter, and in 1834 or 1835 he moved to Charleston, where he joined a southern Methodist church. After emancipation he joined the AME church and participated in the first South Carolina Annual Conference in 1865. The years of Reconstruction found him in Georgia, whence he came to the CME General Conference. The reason for his switch from AME to CME is not clear. In appearance Vanderhorst was tall, dignified, and, as someone put it, "black enough for any of us." Known as "old man eloquent," he was a better preacher than administrator. Fifty-seven years old and worn out when elected to the bishopric, Vanderhorst survived less than two years in office.

Lucius H. Holsey was in many ways the most remarkable of the church's early leaders. His ascent through the ranks was little short of phenomenal. The son of a slave woman and her white master, James Holsey of Georgia, young Lucius worked after emancipation on a small farm near Sparta. Having received religious training from a southern Methodist clergyman, he obtained a license to preach in 1868 and became a delegate from Georgia to the General Conference. His forceful personality and administrative talent led to his elevation to the episcopacy by a special session of the conference in 1873. He was then only thirty-five years old.

Isaac Lane was born a slave in Jackson, Tennessee, in 1834. He acquired a little learning surreptitiously, joined the Methodist church, and became a licensed exhorter. His ordination as a deacon in 1866 was followed two years later by an eldership. Like the others, Lane attended the organizing conference in 1870, where he impressed many delegates. The conference made him a bishop in 1873. Patriarchal in appearance, with a flowing, silvery beard, he was especially active in educational work and was responsible for the founding of Lane College in Jackson.[39]

From the outset relations between the Colored church and the African churches were strained. African Methodists referred to the CME as the "rebel church" or the "old slavery church" because of its cordial relationship with white Methodists and its readiness to accommodate white supremacy. Unlike the AME and AME Zion churches, which actively participated in Reconstruction politics, the CME church avoided involvement. Lucius Holsey wrote that although CME ministers were often members of political parties, "as ministers of the gospel, we make no stump-speeches and fight no battles of the politicians." Holsey believed that friction between blacks and whites in the postwar South could best be ameliorated through cooperation; "hence, we seek the friendship of all, and especially and particularly the fatherly directorship of the Methodist Episcopal Church, South." Furthermore, the African Methodist groups did not look favorably upon another denomination that would divide black Methodists further. Among the more subtle expressions of hostility was a statement by the AME bishops in 1873 regarding the creation of the Colored Methodist Episcopal church: "We confess that we would have been more pleased if, in the providence of God, you could have seen clear to have united with us, instead of increasing the number of independent organizations of African Methodists by one." Other attacks were more direct. The *Christian Index,* the official newspaper of the CME church, reported several instances when brethren were forced to endure persecutions "of their African friends" and even burnings of CME buildings.[40]

From time to time the Methodists talked of a union of the various

39. Phillips, *History of the Colored Methodist Episcopal Church,* 51, 196–204, 213–22.

40. William B. Gravely, "The Social, Political and Religious Significance of the Formation of the Colored Methodist Episcopal Church (1870)," *Methodist History,* XVIII (October, 1979), 3–21; Milton C. Sernett, ed., *Afro-American Religious History: A Documentary Witness* (Durham, 1985), 237; Phillips, *History of the Colored Methodist Episcopal Church,* 51, 192–204, 213–22.

church organizations because of the inefficiency of three independent black denominations along with black organizations within the Methodist Episcopal church. During the 1860s, representatives of the AME and AME Zion churches met to discuss the possibility. These two were the most likely to consolidate because of their doctrinal similarities and because neither had ties with any white denomination. Opposition to union was strong, however, particularly among leaders of both churches. Merger would likely result in consolidation of episcopal offices, and none of the hierarchs wanted to relinquish the power he enjoyed. Furthermore, the denominations differed on the term of office for its bishops. AME bishops served for life whereas AME superintendents served four-year terms. Despite ongoing discussions and prodding from laypersons, church leaders were never able to reconcile their differences and consolidate their denominations.

Mergers with the northern and southern Methodist churches were also considered. Some African Methodists were uncomfortable with the separation of their church from the white denominations. In the years immediately after emancipation, the prospects for a racially unified nation seemed brighter to them than ever before. They hoped for an integrated society in which black and white churches would move closer together. They thought the African churches isolated blacks from the mainstream of American life, and white segregationists exploited them to widen the gap between the races. The accommodationist and integrationist James Lynch suggested that the word *African* be dropped from the church's name, believing that it called attention to an invidious separation of blacks from whites in religious as well as social affairs. Most African Methodists, however, saw nothing harmful in the label. Indeed, the term *African* defined a common people and linked them with a heritage that lived in African-American culture. Moreover, it represented the continued opposition to racial exploitation and the salvation of all people of African descent. George A. Rue, another AME minister, was convinced that it had a positive effect on blacks' continuing struggle for freedom. "What is there so detestable in that word?" he asked. No other name "seems to be so frightful to our oppressors as the word African. It is a terror to evil-doers, and is destined to loose the captive from his chain, through the power of God's great arm." Lynch countered by arguing that "all intelligent colored men of the South believe it best to cultivate the sympathy and regard of the whites. Nay, more conciliate them whenever it can be done without sacrificing their manhood, and this is wise." Blacks, he contended, had to strengthen ties with whites who possessed power, wealth, and influence. "We cannot throw ourselves in the opposite side of the scale. . . . We must unite with our white friends, who believe in the equal rights of man; and act on the principle that we are one of the elements of the American people." Although the conciliatory attitude that Lynch exhibited was widespread through the AME church, there were no serious attempts to unite with either the Methodist Episcopal church or the Methodist Episcopal Church South.[41]

White southern Presbyterian leaders faced a situation similar to that of the Baptists and Methodists. Their desire to retain black members had not kept the freedmen from leaving the church so they decided to ease them out and into one of their own in hope of continuing to exercise considerable influence if not direct control. One white southerner hit the mark that most Presbyterians were shooting for when he observed that "the white people of the South deem it a matter [of] *first* importance to maintain their present social ascendancy, and they cannot take an active interest even in religious work, if that work threatens to disturb this ascendancy." Allowing the freedmen to drift into the northern or independent black churches would not further that end. Southern and northern Presbyterians were engaged throughout the second half of the nineteenth century in a struggle not only for influence over the freedmen but also for status as the most righteous church. Some southern whites likened the northern church to the Antichrist. The "nominal church" had destroyed Christ, and now the "nominal church" in the North threatened to do the same to the freedmen by diverting their attention from ultimate salvation and filling their heads with notions of "natural rights." In 1874 the General Assembly began setting up separate and independent black organizations within the church. Black congregations were permitted to form presbyteries. Two or more presbyteries might then organize a synod. Synods would finally unite in the creation of an independent black General Assembly.[42]

41. *Christian Recorder,* April 8, May 6, June 24, 1865, January 27, 1866, September 24, 1870; *A.M.E. Church Review,* II (July, 1885), 87–88; F. Douglass to W. J. Wilson, August 8, 1865, in Philip Foner, ed., *The Life and Writings of Frederick Douglass* (5 vols.; New York, 1950–55), IV, 172–73.

42. Andrew E. Murray, *Presbyterians and the Negro—A History* (Philadelphia, 1966), 150; Presbyterian Church in the United States (hereinafter cited as PCUS), Charleston Presbytery, Minutes of the Charleston Presbytery of the Presbyterian Church in the United States, April 10, 1868, in Austin Presbyterian Theological Seminary Library, Austin, Texas; PCUS, General Assembly, *Minutes of the General Assembly of the Presbyterian Church in the United States, 1874* (Richmond, 1874), 517–18.

The Cumberland Presbyterian church had broken away from the Presbyterian church in 1810 over issues growing out of the great revivals at the opening of the nineteenth century. At the time of the Civil War, the Cumberland church had approximately twenty thousand black members. After emancipation, they too desired a separate and independent church. Blacks in Tennessee organized the first separate synod in 1861, but in 1869 the white-controlled church provided for the departure of its entire black membership, and the first General Assembly of the Colored Cumberland Presbyterian church met five years later.[43]

The Protestant Episcopal church, like the Presbyterian churches, enjoyed no great popularity among the masses of southern blacks. Antebellum elite mulattoes in places like Washington and Charleston had chosen to be Episcopalian, an emblem of high status, but the bulk of the black parishioners attended because it was their masters' church. With emancipation, many former slaves deserted their masters' Episcopal churches for the new independent Baptist and Methodist churches. White Episcopalians expressed amazement at this "strange defection." In Virginia, they charged that the freedmen had fallen under the spells of "so-called spiritual pastors" who "plainly teach their congregations that there is no religion in the Episcopal Church." In South Carolina, the church reported a decline in black membership from roughly three thousand to three hundred during the eight years after 1860. A missionary in Alabama reported an 80 percent decline in black members from 1865 to 1868. Nor did church leaders expend much effort in trying to arrest the flow. In 1871 the Arkansas diocesan convention resolved "to organize a plan by which the claims of the Protestant Episcopal Church may be brought before the colored people of this State." Eight years later, however, Bishop H. N. Pierce pointed out that nothing had yet been done to implement the plan.[44]

Once again, the reasons for blacks' desertion included a desire for freedom and independence and the racial prejudice and discrimination

43. *Census of Religious Bodies: 1916* (2 vols.; Washington, D.C., 1919), II, 576–78.

44. Michael P. Johnson and James L. Roark, eds., *No Chariot Let Down: Charleston's Free People of Color on the Eve of the Civil War* (Chapel Hill, 1984), 6, 65; Protestant Episcopal Church, Committee on Home Missions to Colored People, *9th Annual Report* [1873–74] (New York, 1874), 6; George F. Bragg, *A History of the Afro-American Group of the Episcopal Church* (Baltimore, 1922), 126; Protestant Episcopal Church Diocese of Alabama, *Proceedings of the Thirty-seventh Annual Convention of the Protestant Episcopal Church in the Diocese of Alabama . . . 1868* (Selma, 1868), 17; Protestant Episcopal Church Diocese of Arkansas, *Proceedings of the Primary Convention . . . 1871* (Little Rock, 1873), 8, 37.

that haunted the church. Moreover, the conservative philosophy of the Episcopal church taught Christians to obey God and to accept the station in life into which he had placed them. Churchmen believed that the freedmen needed to be given "such sound religious teaching as shall make them faithful 'to do their duty in that state of life which it has pleased God to call them.'" During the 1860s and 1870s, ordinary blacks who remained in the church were usually organized as missions presided over by white ministers and sustained and controlled by neighboring white congregations. The blacks were generally not represented in diocesan councils. Those who were members of white-dominated congregations worshiped separately, ordinarily on Sunday afternoon or in the evening. Where blacks and whites worshiped together, segregated seating was the rule. Bishop Pierce of Arkansas, describing plans for a cathedral in Little Rock, told the diocesan convention that blacks would find its seats as comfortable "as are furnished for the whites." But, he hastened to add, the "two races will not be in any way mingled together, for this would be for both alike unpleasant." [45]

This expansion and internal development of the black church occurred at a time when the economy was struggling to recover from the devastating effects of war and emancipation. Blacks were striving to redefine their place in the economy. Their primary objective was the self-reliance their masters had denied them during slavery. Blacks now had the right to sell their labor for whatever it was worth. They might still be employed by white people, but many refused to be exploited the way they had been under slavery. In the autumn of 1865, Elisha B. Weaver, traveling by steamboat from St. Louis to New Orleans, conversed with a freedwoman from Grand Gulf, Mississippi. Weaver was an African Methodist minister and the editor of the *Christian Recorder*. He was journeying to New Orleans to attend a church conference and took notes on conditions as he found them among the freedmen along the way. The woman "informed us that she was now free, and intended to make good use of her freedom, and whoever she worked for must pay her every Saturday night, or if they didn't, she would not work for them." [46]

Unfortunately, the prospects for realizing even those modest expecta-

45. Freedmen's Commission of the Protestant Episcopal Church, Report, June, 1868, p. 2, in Historical Society and Archives, Episcopal Theological Seminary of the Southwest, Austin, Texas; Protestant Episcopal Church, Diocese of Arkansas, *Journal of the Seventh Annual Council of the Diocese of Arkansas . . . 1879* (Little Rock, 1879), 37.

46. *Christian Recorder*, November 18, 1865; John Richard Dennett, *The South as It Is, 1865–1866*, ed. Henry M. Christman (New York, 1965), 39–40.

tions, let alone self-sufficiency and prosperity, were not very bright. Agricultural wages were woefully low even though demand for plantation labor was high. Disastrous crops from 1866 through 1868 led to a shortage of cash and extremely tight credit in the South. Planters endeavored to keep labor costs down, defer payment of wages until the end of the year after the crop was in, and pay in kind or with a share of the crop. Not surprisingly, the freedmen looked for better work than they had been required to perform during slavery, but whites generally thought they preferred to be idle and had to be coerced to work. Carl Schurz, after inspecting the South on behalf of Andrew Johnson, reported to the president that the comment he most often heard from white planters was that "you cannot make the Negro work without physical compulsion." To stabilize the work force, the military, the Freedmen's Bureau, and local authorities combined in 1865 to require that freedmen agree to year-long labor contracts or face arrest as vagrants and compulsory work on plantations, threats that applied exclusively to blacks. Planters were obligated to pay at least prevailing market wages, but they regarded the contract-labor system as similar to indentured servitude and demanded loyalty and servility from their laborers. Struck by the similarity between the contract-labor system and slavery, the New Orleans *Tribune,* a black newspaper, asked indignantly: "Is slavery abolished? If abolished, let us follow the rules of free labor. If not abolished, let us know it." [47]

Most black southerners saw ownership of land as the key to freedom. "They have the important idea fixed in their minds," wrote the African Methodist minister Jonathan J. Wright, "that if they get a piece of land of their own, they will not be obliged to work for their old masters again." That bourgeois objective lay at the center of the former slaves' concept of freedom; it was what would differentiate their lives now from the way they had been in slavery times. It represented the self-reliance and sense of privacy that slaves never enjoyed. Without it, being free assumed a different and distinctly unsatisfying character. "What's de use of being free?" an elderly man asked Whitelaw Reid. "What's de use of being free

47. Gerald David Jaynes, *Branches Without Roots: Genesis of the Black Working Class in the American South, 1862–1882* (New York, 1986), 37, 45–53, 65–68, 70, 109; Peter Kolchin, *First Freedom: The Responses of Alabama Blacks to Emancipation and Reconstruction* (Westport, 1972), 33–36; Carl Schurz, *Report to the President, Senate Executive Document No. 2,* 39th Cong., 1st Sess., 16; New Orleans *Tribune,* December 31, 1867; Eric Foner, *Reconstruction: America's Unfinished Revolution, 1863–1877* (New York, 1988), 53, 57, 85–87, 107–10, 199–201.

if you don't own land enough to be buried in? Might juss as well stay slave all yo' days." Another man explained, "All I wants is to git to own fo' or five acres ob land, dat I can build me a little house on and call my home."[48]

Many people expected the federal government to assist them in acquiring land by parceling out confiscated plantations. Their expectations seemed to be borne out in January, 1865, when General William T. Sherman, whose assault on Georgia and South Carolina contributed substantially to the final defeat of the Confederacy, issued a special field order that divided abandoned land between Charleston and the St. Johns River into forty-acre tracts and gave possessory title to the freedmen. They eagerly responded to the general's order, establishing farms on the abandoned plantations in time for the spring planting. Ulysses L. Houston, a Baptist minister from Savannah, led a group of freedmen who settled on land on Skidaway Island. "We shall build our cabins, and organize our town government for the maintenance of order and the settlement of all difficulties," he exclaimed. Through the summer the Sea Islands were under cultivation by blacks, with scarcely a white person in sight. As they prepared to harvest the cotton crop in the fall, blacks in the Sea Islands and elsewhere who had been working for wages anticipated receiving their allotments of land. Many of them refused to enter into contracts for the next year because they were convinced that they would soon own their own farms.[49]

Their optimism had scarcely begun to rise when a grim reality settled over them. Shortly after assuming office following the assassination of Abraham Lincoln, President Andrew Johnson began granting pardons to southerners who had aided the Confederacy, and these pardons included the restoration of their property. Johnson's plan was to reconstruct the South not on a foundation of blacks and southern Unionists, as many Republicans intended, but rather on conservative southern businessmen and landowners who had opposed secession even though they may have abided by the decision to leave the Union and may even have actively supported the rebellion after the Civil War began. Although his lenient pardon and restoration policy was initially aimed at one particular group of southern landowners, it eventually included virtually all members of

48. *Christian Recorder,* December 30, 1865; Whitelaw Reid, *After the War: A Southern Tour, May 1, 1865, to May 1, 1866* (Cincinnati, 1866), 564.

49. Willie Lee Rose, *Rehearsal for Reconstruction: The Port Royal Experiment* (New York, 1964), 331; Dennett, *The South as It Is,* 186–89; Reid, *After the War,* 335–36.

the landed class regardless of their position on the secession issue, restoring their lands and squeezing out the claims of the freedmen. Even the Radical Republicans had misgivings about distributing southern plantation land to freedmen, whom they believed were too ignorant and indolent to make it flourish. Although they may have sympathized with the sentiments expressed by Charles Sumner when he wrote that the "great plantations . . . must be broken up, and the freedmen must have the pieces," their greater concern was that southern agricultural production be put in the hands of people who knew how to manage it effectively, namely, the white planters. The freedmen's economic fate was being sealed by friend and foe alike.[50]

A journalist traveling down the Atlantic coast during the summer of 1865 noted that the freedmen "may be very ignorant, but it is quite evident that they know, or think they know, who their friends are." The truth was that they did not always know. The realization that the land distribution program would not be fulfilled came painfully to the freedmen in Chesterfield County, Virginia, and taught them a lesson about the untrustworthiness of their northern white friends. A carpetbagger, playing on their expectations and the unfortunate fact that their wishes had clouded their judgment, claimed to be a government agent distributing Confederate land. "He had a badge an' ev'ything," recalled Lewis Clarke, one of the county's black residents. "Said de gov'ment sent him." The northerner walked into church one Sunday and told the people that he wanted to know who needed land. "Course dey all needed it, even de preacher." He said he wanted to know "where was de secesh lands in de county." A group of blacks accompanied the "'bagger" to the estate of Jack Turner, a local landowner who had died during the war. He showed them a sack full of stakes that he had brought with him for marking off individual plots of land. "Took out dem pegs an' tole de Negroes to go 'haid pick dere land." All they had to do was select their piece and stake it off. But then came the catch, which some of the people recognized and others did not. The man said a person would have to pay one dollar to acquire the pegs. Some of the people paid him the money, others did not. Then one day sometime later, according to Clarke, "Yankee troops come ridin' out from Richmond lookin' fo' dat 'bagger. Said he didn't

50. Foner, *Reconstruction*, 184–85, 190–91; Jaynes, *Branches Without Roots*, 11, 13–14; *Freedmen's Record*, I (December, 1865), 191–92; Louis Gerteis, *From Contraband to Freedmen: Federal Policy Towards Southern Blacks, 1861–1865* (Westport, 1973), 183–92.

belong to de gov'ment, an' didn't have no right sellin' no lan' or givin' it away." It was a painful lesson—and an eye-opener too. Land distribution was no more than a poor man's dream.[51]

In Georgia and South Carolina, where the expectation of owning land had actually begun to materialize with Sherman's field order, there may not have been any fraud, but the freedmen's disappointment was even more bitter than if they too had been tricked by some slippery carpetbagger. The president's policy of granting pardons wholesale crystallized during the summer, and he directed General Oliver O. Howard, commissioner of the Freedmen's Bureau, to inform the freedmen that the land they were farming, which they assumed was theirs, did not belong to them. Rumor preceded Howard's arrival on Edisto Island in October for a meeting with the freedmen, and when he appeared at the old brick church, which the people used for their worship services as well as a public meetinghouse, and which, ironically, would also soon be restored to its original white owners, the atmosphere was highly charged. As he prepared to speak, "strong evidence of dissatisfaction and sorrow were manifested from every part of the assembly." Noise and confusion prevailed until a "sweet-voiced" woman began singing a hymn and calmed the crowd. Howard recalled, "Then I endeavored as clearly and gently as I could to explain to them the wishes of the President, as they were made known to me in an interview had with him just before leaving Washington." His words devastated his listeners, whether they had anticipated them or not. "My address, however kind in manner I rendered it, met with no apparent favor," and the kindhearted but obedient soldier, who personally objected to the president's policy, could only listen sympathetically to their anguished entreaties. "Why, General Howard," one man asked, "why do you take away our lands? You take them from us who have always been true, always true to the Government! You give them to our all-time enemies! That is not right!"[52]

In Hampton, Virginia, officials enlisted the local church to assist them in dispossessing the freedmen. They engaged a local preacher to persuade people to accept the land decision. A white southerner named Jeff Sinclair and the preacher, a Reverend Taylor, "the mos' powerful colored man in

51. Foner, *Reconstruction*, 176–277; Reid, *After the War*, 82; Perdue, Barden, and Phillips, eds., *Weevils in the Wheat*, 72.

52. Rose, *Rehearsal for Reconstruction*, 327–28, 331; *National Freedman*, I (April, 1865), 82–83; Oliver O. Howard, *Autobiography of Oliver Otis Howard* (2 vols.; New York, 1907), I, 238–40.

town," went about exhorting the people to sign an affidavit to the effect that the land they were farming did not belong to them unless they could purchase it. "Dey couldn't buy," Matilda Carter remembered, "so dey had to pay ten dollars a year rent fo' livin' on de lan. Rev'en Taylor was dar to help to make folks sign. What he said to a Negro was law." [53]

Thus the planters recovered their land; in return, the freedmen were offered an opportunity to contract for wage labor or to rent land. They were entitled to the current crop, the government assured them, and to a house if they should decide to stay on. But most of them were left as landless as at the time of emancipation. "No white folks didn't leave me nothing but de wide world to make a living," Anna E. Crawford sighed. The people viewed the decision to deny them land as a betrayal, one that slashed deep into their souls and etched a profound distrust of northern whites. [54]

Without a program of land distribution, it was difficult for the freed people to obtain property. They had little cash with which to purchase farms, and lenders were leery of extending credit to them. Southern whites as a rule were so loath to sell land to blacks that in the Mississippi Valley, according to the northern journalist and traveler Whitelaw Reid, "the man who would sell small tracts to them would be in actual personal danger. Every effort will be made to prevent Negroes from acquiring land; even the renting of small tracts to them is held to be unpatriotic and unworthy of a good citizen." In 1865 the Mississippi legislature enacted a measure that prohibited blacks from leasing or renting land except in incorporated areas. By the end of the 1870s, blacks owned less than 10 percent of all the acres under cultivation in the cotton South. [55]

Without land, the options remaining to most ordinary people in the countryside were wage labor and some form of tenancy. Many who labored on cotton plantations preferred the latter because it at least had the appearance of bringing them closer to the goal of economic self-reliance. Within limits imposed by merchants, who were their main source of credit, they were free to grow whatever crops they chose and to organize their own time and labor. Tenancy also enabled the freedmen to live and

53. Perdue, Barden, and Phillips, eds., *Weevils in the Wheat,* 69.

54. Howard, *Autobiography,* 239–40; Perdue, Barden, and Phillips, eds., *Weevils in the Wheat,* 77.

55. Roger Ransom and Richard Sutch, "The Ex-Slave in the Post-Bellum South," *Journal of Economic History,* XXX (1973), 133; Reid, *After the War,* 564–65; *Christian Recorder,* December 23, 1865.

work as families. Cash wages on a daily basis would have provided them with considerable flexibility and made that option attractive; however, planters preferred to make share payments after harvest. Moreover, as wage laborers they were often compelled to work in large gangs under an overseer, a situation reminiscent of slavery. In neither case did they enjoy much prosperity, nor did they advance very rapidly toward economic self-reliance. White landlords were averse to renting land to blacks on a cash basis because they assumed there was a high risk of default. Low wages persisted because of the scarcity of cash and the planters' insistence on paying blacks less than they paid white laborers. All of that combined with crop failures during the first few years after emancipation and depressed agricultural prices in the 1870s to keep blacks impoverished and indebted.[56]

The dismal economic picture was not without some signs of progress, however, and some individuals achieved a measure of prosperity. During the late 1860s and the 1870s, black agricultural workers gained greater control over the conditions of their labor, obtaining higher wages and larger shares of the crops. A few freedmen managed to obtain land, buying it either individually or cooperatively. Blacks in Georgia had acquired three hundred thousand acres of land by 1874. For many, even a modest landholding engendered confidence about the future. "I dug a heap o' dirt in slavery time," Squire Harris told an interviewer as he recalled his transformation from slave to freedman, "and atter freedom I got me a acre o' land, run away wid my gal and ma'yed her, and settled down to make a livin."[57]

Although it happened infrequently, white landowners sometimes failed to reclaim their estates, in which case blacks were in a position to gain legal title to it. Refugee freedmen in a camp located across the Tar River from Tarboro, North Carolina, were able to obtain legal right to land formerly owned by whites and founded the town of Princeville there.

56. Foner, *Reconstruction*, 102–10; Eric Foner, *Nothing but Freedom: Emancipation and Its Legacy* (Baton Rouge, 1983), 8–12, 18–19; Dennett, *The South as It Is*, 40, 205, 214; Ralph Schlomowitz, " 'Bound' or 'Free'? Black Labor in Cotton and Sugarcane Farming, 1865–1880," *Journal of Southern History*, L (1984), 567–96; Gavin Wright, *The Political Economy of the Cotton South: Households, Markets, and Wealth in the Nineteenth Century* (New York, 1978), 158–80; Ransom and Sutch, "The Ex-Slave in the Post-Bellum South," 131–48.

57. Edmund L. Drago, *Black Politicians and Reconstruction in Georgia: A Splendid Failure* (Baton Rouge, 1982), 130; George P. Rawick, ed., *Georgia Narratives* (Westport, 1977), Pt. 1, p. 305, Vol. IV of Rawick, ed., *American Slave, Supplemental Series I*, 12 vols.

In an even rarer example of economic progress in agriculture—although it was short-lived—blacks at Davis Bend on the Mississippi River succeeded in becoming large landowners. Benjamin Montgomery, a former slave, negotiated the purchase of the plantations of Confederate President Jefferson Davis and his brother Joseph. Montgomery and his family not only operated three plantations at Davis Bend but rented out land to other freedmen and owned the store that supplied the inhabitants of the colony with tools and other supplies.[58]

Although farmers and agricultural laborers made up the bulk of the black population for a long time after emancipation, many freedmen and a substantial proportion of the former freeborn population migrated to towns and cities in search of work. A sizable proportion of those were unskilled laborers. They worked as manual laborers, draymen and hackmen, and dockworkers. They worked long and hard but earned paltry wages, seldom enough, if they were family men, to provide for wives, children, and other relatives. Many women were forced to enter the work force, generally as domestic servants and washerwomen. Although most nonagricultural laborers were unskilled, some notable though certainly not spectacular advances took place in black occupational and economic status. The number of skilled workers, although only a small minority of the black work force and generally limited to old trades such as blacksmith, bricklayer, carpenter, and shoemaker, steadily increased. Proprietors such as grocers, restaurant operators, barbers, and undertakers made up an emerging entrepreneurial class. These groups constituted a black middle class. A few physicians, dentists, and lawyers joined with teachers and preachers to form an occupational and social elite. In many cities, the professional elite dominated African-American society; in smaller towns, artisans were the dominant group.[59]

Most artisans and entrepreneurs struggled on the margins of economic survival. Their condition by the end of the 1870s could be called successful or prosperous only if measured—as it should be—against the

58. Joe A. Mobley, "In the Shadow of White Society: Princeville, a Black Town in North Carolina, 1865–1915," *North Carolina Historical Review,* LXIII (1986), 340–84; Janet Sharp Hermann, *The Pursuit of a Dream* (New York, 1981), 152.

59. Orville Vernon Burton, "The Rise and Fall of Afro-American Town Life: Town and Country in Reconstruction Edgefield County, South Carolina," in *Toward a New South? Studies in Post–Civil War Southern Communities,* ed. Orville Vernon Burton and Robert C. McMath, Jr. (Westport, 1982), 166; Kolchin, *First Freedom,* 131–32, 163–67; Rabinowitz, *Race Relations in the Urban South,* 61–96; Thornbery, "Development of Black Atlanta," 195–207.

difficulty of overcoming the many obstacles in their path and hardly compared with that of middle-class whites. Their economic advancement was hindered by opposition from local whites who resented their competition and insisted that they were unfit for anything but manual labor. The comment of one white Atlantan typified the attitude of whites toward black mechanics. He confided in the British traveler Sir George Campbell the opinion that the Negro "is not fit to rise higher; he has no 'judgment,' and does not make a skilled mechanic." Accordingly, whites established barriers to the advancement of black artisans and professionals. But despite their being denied membership in local unions, having limited employment opportunities, and suffering high rents, some Richmond blacks—like those in other towns and cities—did make progress, and by one account they were "prospering as well as might be expected under the circumstances." [60]

For the most part, skilled workers and storekeepers filled jobs that were either unsuited to whites or served the black communities exclusively. Illustrating the community orientation of black artisans was the Louisville Board of Health's solicitation in 1866 of black undertakers to construct all the coffins and provide all the burial services required by blacks in the city. In Charleston and New Orleans, mulattoes who had been born free and had prospered as merchants and craftsmen remained conspicuous among an expanding African-American middle class. The low wage scale and limited means of urban blacks during the 1860s and 1870s, however, produced generally meager earnings for black tradesmen of either bond or free background. [61]

The elite black aristocracy was centered among the freeborn mulattoes living in such cities as Washington, Baltimore, Charleston, Mobile, and New Orleans. Like the middle-class tradesmen and skilled workers, they did not compare in wealth to their white counterparts, but their high-prestige jobs, their education, and above all their refinement and gentility set them apart from the masses of blacks and made them role models for aspiring members of their race. [62]

60. Sir George Campbell, *White and Black: The Outcome of a Visit to the United States* (London, 1879), 378; Rabinowitz, *Race Relations in the Urban South*, 63; *Christian Recorder*, December 2, 1865.

61. *Christian Recorder*, March 10, 1866; Rabinowitz, *Race Relations in the Urban South*, 61–96.

62. Willard B. Gatewood, *Aristocrats of Color: The Black Elite, 1880–1920* (Bloomington, 1990), 7–29, 69–95.

Church leaders assumed the function of advisers in the freedmen's uphill struggle to attain economic autonomy, offering remedies for their present condition and suggestions for improvement. The local untrained clergy were usually in the same economic fix as the freedmen in their congregations, and although what counsel they gave their flocks is largely unknown, we can assume that they preached perseverance and the prospect of heavenly rewards for faithfulness to God and hard work. The denominational hierarchs and the pastors of larger, urban congregations, whose experience and education gave them a broader outlook than that of their rural colleagues, tended to advise the freedmen to remain on the farms and plantations and not to congregate in the cities, to educate their children, and to endeavor to become skilled farmers and craftsmen. Too many freedmen were crowding into towns and cities; there were not enough jobs for all the new arrivals, and the result would certainly be increasing misery, a continued dependence on benevolence, and a drift into criminal or immoral behavior. With the paternalism that was a ministerial characteristic, they often assumed not just that the freedmen could not find a way out of their economic predicament but also that they would not recognize what was in their best interest if they saw it.[63]

Editorials in the AME *Christian Recorder,* which during the 1860s and 1870s was the only black church newspaper that circulated through the entire South, reveal the tone as well as the content of much of the church's advice to the freedmen. In December, 1865, Elisha Weaver sermonized under the title "Advice from the Editor of this Paper to the Many Freedmen throughout the South." Most freedmen should not migrate to the cities because, he believed, they were unaccustomed to city ways and did not know how to earn a respectable living there. "Dear brethren, in this lamentable condition you gather in listless and idle squads on the street-corners, without money, and totally ignorant of the customary way of getting employment in large cities." Unable to provide for themselves, they would most likely be tempted to follow the path of errancy. "You may, and probably will resort to the taking of that which is not your own. If you succeed in what the law terms the first offense, you will become emboldened, and will try your hand again for the second time, and thus continue on in your career of unbridled crime." Over and above the humiliation they would bring to themselves, they would draw

---

63. Jaynes, *Branches Without Roots,* 236; Ransom and Sutch, *One Kind of Freedom,* 44–47.

the whites' scorn down upon the race as a whole because their enemies would cite their crimes as "verification of the unprincipled doctrine they would inculcate." They were getting themselves into a sorry situation. "But, my brother freedmen, I now, as a friend, tell you that I have a remedy for all this, and I think you will agree with me as to its efficacy. It is this: Leave the cities, and push your fortune. Rent farms, and raise cotton, corn, wheat, hogs, cows, sheep and horses. Take a portion to market every year, sell it and get your money. Be sure to lay by your surplus funds until you have enough to buy a little farm of ten, twenty, or a hundred acres, or more, as the case may be." In promoting these bourgeois values, Weaver made it clear that he did not oppose in principle blacks' seeking their fortunes in the city. Those who had the necessary skills as well as the proper inclination belonged there. "Many of those who have good trades can probably make more by being in the city than they could in the country. Our exception also extends to those who prefer keeping groceries, dry goods, or follow dress-making, etc. Some of our people can get along anywhere. Their magic touch turns everything to gold." [64]

The following autumn James Lynch called on parents to provide their children with training in the mechanical trades. Lynch believed that the opportunities for race advancement were increasing. "We desire now," he wrote, "to speak of the importance of parents giving their children useful trades, whereby they can earn a living." Noting that mechanics in northern cities had all the business they could handle, he assumed that a similar demand existed in the South and that black youth should be trained to take advantage of it. Instead of unskilled or domestic labor, southern blacks should learn a trade because it would bring greater material and psychological rewards. "It is better that a boy should grow up a competent blacksmith or carpenter or skilled in any other branch of mechanical art, than that he should be a waiter, barber, bootblack, dock-laborer, or the keeper of a one-horse restaurant. He will think more of himself, and be more respected, if he possesses a trade." He would be more important to the community as a tradesman because he would be more useful. Lynch felt that most southern blacks could not afford to aspire to professional status, although both professional men and efficient farmers were needed to strengthen the race. "Professional life may be chosen by some, but it is only the few who can enter it and be successful, because it requires costly attainments as well as a superior order of talent. The profes-

64. *Christian Recorder,* December 16, 1865.

sional men of any race comprise a small number. Agriculture demands our attention, but no one is better calculated by physical development and disciplined labor to become a successful farmer, than a mechanic."[65]

It is impossible to ascertain precisely what effect such renderings had on the people as a whole. Newspapers such as the *Christian Recorder* reached the clergy and many other members of the black middle class, who as preachers, teachers, and role models were in a position to influence the attitudes and behavior of ordinary people, but it is impossible to distinguish between the church's influence and that of others because church leaders, secular leaders, and benevolent whites advocated the same strategies for personal growth and race advancement. Schools such as Hampton Institute were established to help train youths as artisans and farmers and reflected some of the same basic views that Lynch professed. To be sure, freedmen continued to clog the towns and cities in obvious disregard of Weaver's advice, struggling for jobs and suffering the miseries of poverty and discrimination that he warned against. Although church leaders urged the freedmen to remain in the plantation system that had been the cradle of slavery and was known for white racial violence, this was probably good advice for freedmen who were unable to find employment in towns and cities. Disease and mortality rose noticeably among the freedmen after emancipation, and although public and private agencies conducted relief programs, many of the needy went unaided. The most important federal government agency for distributing direct relief to the freedmen was the Freedmen's Bureau, but it assisted less than 5 percent of the black population of the former slave states. There were simply too many needy, and after the first few months following the war, blacks were increasingly forced to compete with indigent whites for scant relief. Racial tension and violence were only one consequence of that situation. The federal government regarded direct relief to the freedmen as a temporary measure, and the Freedmen's Bureau began reducing its outlays of food and supplies following the first winter after the war, hoping to induce blacks to leave the cities and return to the rural areas.[66]

65. *Ibid.*, September 22, 1866.
66. Kathleen C. Berkeley, "'Colored Ladies Also Contributed': Black Women's Activities from Benevolence to Social Welfare, 1866–1896," in *The Web of Southern Social Relations: Women, Family, and Education*, ed. Walter J. Fraser, Jr., R. Frank Saunders, Jr., and Jon L. Wakelyn (Athens, Ga., 1985), 188–89; Robert Bremner, *The Public Good: Philanthropy and Welfare in the Civil War Era* (New York, 1980), 125; Gerteis, *From Contraband to Freedmen*, 183–92.

When the Freedmen's Bureau stopped providing direct relief, it turned over the responsibility to local authorities and to blacks themselves. The churches took up a considerable portion of that burden. The missionaries and local pastors became the custodians of such programs as the Freedmen's Sanitary Commission and Hospital Fund in Memphis, financed by tax levies on local blacks. But social welfare had never been a major role for men in African-American society, and, feeling uncomfortable with it, the preachers quickly turned over the administration of those programs to the women of the congregation.[67]

Slaves had always taken care of their sick and disabled and taught their children the skills of plantation life and labor, and most of the work fell to slave women. Gender roles among slaves were subject to the dictates, and sometimes the whims, of slave owners, but to the extent that the masters had allowed them to, women had acted as the nurturers and caretakers of the slave family. It was natural for them to carry on in that capacity once freedom came. Those feminine roles were reinforced by the teachings of white missionaries and educators, who professed a middle-class ethic and preached the "cult of true womanhood." Through auxiliary societies that operated in association with local congregations, groups like the Daughters of Zion of Avery Chapel in Memphis and the Baptist women's district associations, church women solicited funds for charity, school tuition, medical care, and old-age pensions. Women spearheaded the benevolent activities of the church. They not only led the societies as officers, but they also maintained their bank accounts and exercised exclusive authority to deposit and withdraw money. The benevolent societies were more common in the towns and cities of the postwar South than in the rural areas, and women of the privileged classes were conspicuous members. The leaders of the women's societies were not always members of the elite groups or professional classes, whose aspirations for high status and acceptance by whites often caused them to turn their backs on what they referred to as the "submerged masses." Rather, the leaders of the church societies were freedwomen who toiled as skilled or unskilled workers and sympathized with those like themselves who were in need.[68]

Throughout the late 1860s and early 1870s, despite the many disap-

67. Berkeley, "'Colored Ladies Also Contributed,'" 190.

68. Eugene D. Genovese, *Roll, Jordan, Roll: The World the Slaves Made* (New York, 1972), 502–23; Elizabeth Fox-Genovese, *Within the Plantation Household: Black and White Women of the Old South* (Chapel Hill, 1988), 152–59, 167–69; Berkeley, "'Colored Ladies Also Contributed,'" 191–95.

pointments and frustrations, church leaders maintained a buoyant view of the people's prospects. Even though the race suffered injustice and endured economic hardship, the ministers expressed confidence that advancement would continue. As violent attacks on blacks by whites mounted in North Carolina, an African Methodist minister, Samuel Williams, wrote: "The rebels are very bitter. It is dangerous for a colored man to venture out alone at night; and in the surrounding country it is dangerous even in daylight." He was sorry also to report that "these people are still somewhat oppressed by their former masters." Whites charged enormous rents for houses "and are endeavoring to carry out the argument that the colored people are not able to take care of themselves. Still the people are stemming the current, hoping for a better day." Another African Methodist preacher, James C. Embry, expressed optimism about the future. He admitted that wages earned by black laborers in Bowling Green, Kentucky, were lower than in just about every other region of the South, but the energy of the people there "is attested by the perseverance of these men of labor, and the acquisition of property, in spite of low prices and the tightness of the class of whites they have to deal with." [69]

Clerics were just as rosy about the continued growth of the church as they were about the prospects for economic progress. But the real questions were whether the impecunious black population could support the expansion of such a large and redundant institution and whether blacks needed a church on so grand a scale. There was considerable overlap within the independent black church with three independent Methodist denominations competing for members and churches fragmenting at the whim of egotistic ministers or displeased congregants. Some churchmen advocated consolidation rather than expansion of the church. One proponent of a union of the African Methodist Episcopal and African Methodist Episcopal Zion churches argued that "the gospel cannot be supported as affairs now stand," with ministers preaching essentially the same doctrine, demanding support, and financially crippling black communities. Southern blacks did make some economic progress in their first steps from slavery to freedom, despite being set free without land and with few of the skills that a rapidly industrializing society demanded, but the road to security and self-reliance was long and hard. To succeed in their journey they needed education; it was a key that could unlock the

69. *Christian Recorder,* February 17, October 27, 1866.

doors to higher-paying jobs. Furthermore, individuals and the black community would not be economically viable until they became influential in the politics of Reconstruction. For it was in the statehouses and the Congress that the destiny of black southerners was being determined. Before southern blacks could hope to become economically self-reliant they would have to secure protection from exploitation by white businessmen and landowners. They had to win recognition as full citizens of their state and nation, and they would have to become politically powerful before whites would recognize their rights and help them fulfill their freedom.[70]

70. *Ibid.*, December 1, 1866.

4

The Church and Reconstruction

Southern blacks were determined to make the most of their freedom and to define it as broadly as possible. They were not content with being idle, as many whites charged, although they were certainly reluctant to work under the same conditions that had marked their enslavement. Nor were they satisfied with the freedom to move from place to place, even though it was gratifying to be able to negotiate for employment wherever it might be found and to search for and be reunited with loved ones. Freedom meant much more than that, and it meant more than having control over their churches. They wanted land, and even though the expectation that the government would provide them with a parcel of their old masters' plantations quickly evaporated, they continued to struggle, with the encouragement of their leaders, to acquire farms of their own. The freedmen had two additional objectives that also reflected their ideas about the meaning of freedom. These were to become educated and to obtain full citizenship, that is, the right to give testimony in court, to serve on juries, to vote, and to hold public office. These goals of both freed and freeborn blacks were also sources of controversy between the defeated yet defiant white former Confederates and Radical Republicans in the North.

One of the freedmen's strongest and most immediate aspirations, obtaining an education, was deeply rooted in their deprivation throughout the long years of bondage of the opportunity to learn much beyond what was necessary to perform their assigned tasks. Belying the common assertion that Africans were not capable of book learning and had no interest in it, slaves craved knowledge, sought it out, and deeply resented being denied it. One former slave said he could never forgive his master for having "robbed me of my education." From colonial times, slaves had endeavored to learn how to read and write, as was evident in the slaveholders' determined effort to prevent it. In part, the whites' attitude

142

toward education was based on racial considerations; they preferred that neither slave nor free blacks be schooled. They resisted anything that obscured caste lines, but above all they realized that it would be far more difficult to keep an educated population shackled to the plow than an uneducated one. By denying slaves the opportunity to acquire literacy skills, the master class hoped to keep them isolated from the outside world and from information and ideas that might make them rebellious or simply less productive laborers. Whites imagined literate slaves forging passes and thereby undermining plantation discipline, and they suffered even sharper anxiety about slaves reading abolitionist literature, communicating among themselves, and devising and actuating plans of rebellion. The scares of the 1820s and early 1830s, when educated blacks were implicated in plots against the slave system, intensified these feelings. The constant and very immediate threat of mass slave revolts resulted in the enactment of strict legislation in many states banning the education of slaves. The punishment for slaves caught trying to read or write was harsh, ranging from whippings to cutting off offenders' fingers.[1]

But at least some slaves (probably no more than about 5 percent) learned to read and write despite the whites' many precautions. Ironically, to a certain extent whites themselves were responsible for promoting slave learning. Some masters acquiesced in their slaves' education, occasionally even tutoring their most trusted servants. Perhaps it was a lark—like training a pet; or maybe it was prompted by a more serious motive such as a religious master or mistress feeling obligated to teach slaves to read the Bible. The white southerners' role in their slaves' education, however, should not be exaggerated. Rarely did masters deliberately instruct their slaves. When slaves learned, it was generally despite their masters' opposition. It was virtually impossible to prevent white children from teaching slave children through their contact as playmates, or adults, sometimes inadvertently, teaching adult slaves rudimentary literacy skills through working and more casual associations. What was remarkable about the slaves' education, though, was their desire to teach themselves without any assistance from whites and their perseverance in doing so even at the risk of being caught and punished. They did not have to be told the value of education, nor did they wait passively for whites to teach them. They were motivated by their own natural curiosity, and

1. Winthrop D. Jordan, *White over Black: American Attitudes Toward the Negro, 1550–1812* (Chapel Hill, 1968), 133–34; Eugene D. Genovese, *Roll, Jordan, Roll: The World the Slaves Made* (New York, 1972), 561–66.

they could infer the power of learning from the measures their masters took to prohibit it. The cynical side of their natures told them that when a white person said that something was not good for them, the reverse was probably true. Surely, if the master class was determined to deprive them of an education, it must be of great value. Actually, they did not have to rely on such inferences to grasp the value of education. They had developed their own understanding of its relevance to their freedom, and somehow there had always been at least a few slaves who had discovered the truth, who had learned to read and write and who taught others.[2]

Once emancipated, men and women and boys and girls flocked from the slave quarters to the new schools that northern missionaries set up for them. This was a different response to freedom than having a parade or walking down the street without a pass just to feel free. Their thirst for knowledge, W. E. B. Du Bois later remarked, was "too persistent and durable to be mere curiosity or whim." They sought to satisfy a profound need, one that they related directly and centrally to their new freedom. Black men and women of the postwar South regarded literacy as a passport to their rightful station in American society. They desired for themselves and their children advancement to citizenship equal to that of whites, not defined by whites and entombed in ignorance, and they were certain that education would help them achieve it. "Freedom and school books," a black journalist wrote in 1865, "go hand in hand." Ordinary people knew that they could not break the grip of white dominance and function as free persons without first learning to read and write and to perform basic arithmetic calculations. Contract laborers had to be able to read the documents they signed so they could avoid being cheated. To succeed as tradesmen they would have to maintain accurate records. And if they obtained the right to vote, as they hoped, they would have to read and understand the ballot. An uneducated person was still a slave; an educated one was free.[3]

2. Alwyn Barr, *Black Texans: A History of Negroes in Texas, 1528–1971* (Austin, 1973), 23; W. E. B. Du Bois, *Black Reconstruction in America* (New York, 1935), 638; Genovese, *Roll, Jordan, Roll*, 563–66; Jacqueline Jones, *Soldiers of Light and Love: Northern Teachers and Georgia Blacks, 1865–1873* (Chapel Hill, 1980), 59; Herbert G. Gutman, *The Black Family in Slavery and Freedom, 1750–1925* (New York, 1976), 371.

3. Peter Kolchin, *First Freedom: The Responses of Alabama's Blacks to Emancipation and Reconstruction* (Westport, 1972), 84–86; *Freedmen's Record*, I (December, 1865), 193; W. E. B. Du Bois, "Reconstruction and Its Benefits," *American Historical Review*, XV (1910), 797; James D. Anderson, *The Education of Blacks in the South, 1860–1935* (Chapel Hill, 1988), 17–18.

Education also carried an important religious significance; it provided access to the Bible, which religious people regarded as the ultimate source of knowledge and understanding. During slavery, their white masters had interpreted the Scriptures for them with an eye to maintaining a submissive labor force. Now they wanted to read God's unexpurgated word and imbibe its good news. One black preacher told his congregation: "Breddern and sisters! I can't read more'n a werse or two of dis bressed Book, but de gospel it is here—de glad tidings it is here—oh teach your chill'en to read dis yar bressed Book. It's de good news for we poor coloured folk." The ability to read the Bible had practical effects as well. They looked to it for the wisdom to solve everyday problems. "You kin read the Bible," insisted a black woman who was soliciting help from a northern teacher, "an' you knows more'na me." If they could read it themselves, they would be less reliant on others.[4]

At the end of the war, the question was not whether blacks wanted an education but how they would get it. There was no established system of public education in the South. Southern whites had never shown much interest in the public schooling that began to develop in the North during the 1830s. Especially in the industrializing Northeast, a proletarian working class, impoverished and including many immigrants, stood in striking contrast to the rest of society and was a cause of concern for educators, revivalists, and civic leaders alike. The working poor could not support their own education, that is, moral instruction in Protestant values as well as intellectual and physical development. If they were not educated at the public's expense, they would continue as an illiterate, culturally distinct, and immoral underclass outside the mainstream of society, weakening the community's moral fiber and contradicting the ideal of national unity. In the South, however, where an agrarian social and economic order prevailed, the white elite preferred the rigidly stratified society that northern reformers sought to avoid. The traditional plantation and caste systems of the South remained entrenched long after the seeds of industrial capitalism and the ideal of social egalitarianism had taken root in the North. Southern rice, sugar, and cotton plantations demanded long hours of backbreaking labor, and planters believed that such work could be extracted only under compulsion; it could not be purchased. For the white planter class, a submissive labor force was an

4. Leon F. Litwack, *Been in the Storm So Long: The Aftermath of Slavery* (New York, 1979), 471; Elizabeth Hyde Botume, *First Days Amongst the Contraband* (Boston, 1893), 126.

absolute necessity, and keeping workers ignorant and unlettered would go a long way toward ensuring their submissiveness. Because the southern working class was largely black, racial considerations also caused the white planter class to abhor the thought of public schools like those of the North that would shorten the distance between whites and blacks and weaken the racial justification for slavery. The planters were generally able to provide for their own children's schooling and saw little need for public education. Thus the combined force of economic, racial, and class considerations, unmitigated by republican or egalitarian ideals, deflected the antebellum planter class from the democratic model of public education.[5]

After the war, southern whites were no more inclined to support universal public education than before. The white elite, hoping to preserve as much of the antebellum social and economic order as possible, set about to rebuild southern agriculture and continued to believe that coercion and repression were the best ways of guaranteeing a reliable and productive labor force. Despite military defeat, whites had not forsaken the basic tenet of slavery, natural law decreed that one group should submit to the authority of another. They intended to confine blacks to the working class and were convinced that education would spoil them and thus be a counterproductive ingredient in the recipe for the South's economic recovery. As Carl Schurz noted, white southern planters generally believed that "learning will spoil the nigger for work."[6]

From the beginning of freedom, blacks showed not only a fierce determination to obtain an education but also a clear preference for their own schools and teachers. They aspired to freedom from white control and to self-reliance, but to "set up housekeeping for themselves," as Charles Octavius Boothe, a Baptist minister and church historian, described it, they had to look beyond their families, friends, and communities for assistance. They were not equipped to educate themselves because so few slaves had learned to read and write, and they did not possess the financial resources required to pay teachers and maintain school buildings.

5. Jones, *Soldiers of Light and Love,* 87, 113–14; Genovese, *Roll, Jordan, Roll,* 561–62.

6. Kolchin, *First Freedom,* 34; Ronald Butchart, *Northern Schools, Southern Blacks, and Reconstruction: Freedmen's Education, 1862–1875* (Westport, 1980), 181–88; Roger Ransom and Richard Sutch, *One Kind of Freedom: The Economic Consequences of Emancipation* (Cambridge, Mass., 1977), 54–55, 97–99; Jonathan Weiner, *Social Origins of the New South: Alabama, 1865–1885* (Baton Rouge, 1979), 35–73.

Nor were northern blacks, on the whole, much more literate or financially able to help provide for the freedmen's education. Whites, however, did have the resources to provide schooling, a fact that blacks acknowledged and gave priority over the ideal of fending for themselves. "It is estimated that there are 800,000 colored children in the heretofore slave states," reasoned James Lynch, the African Methodist Episcopal missionary; "it will take ten thousand teachers to instruct these, and this will cost, if the teachers are paid but $200 annually, $2,000,000. Who will pay the ten thousand teachers? Who will furnish the two million dollars?" Only their white friends, he believed, had the ability to meet such an enormous need.[7]

Assistance in providing schools for blacks did flow from the North, which had historically considered education the key to a free society. Private agencies such as the American Baptist Home Mission Society, the Methodist Freedmen's Aid Society, the American Freedmen's Union Commission, and the American Missionary Association drew on the human and material resources of the North to establish freedmen's schools early in the Civil War. In the spring of 1862, northern missionaries established a school at Fortress Monroe, Virginia, that was taught by a free black woman, Mary Peake. Teachers established numerous schools among the freedmen at Port Royal in the Sea Islands. As the war drew to a close, many people in the North enthusiastically supported the idea of aiding the freedmen through education. The freedmen demonstrated their appreciation for that largesse by attending schools set up for them in South Carolina, in New Orleans, and in Virginia during the latter stages of the war. During the months following the Confederate surrender, schools operated and supported by northern whites spread rapidly through the hinterlands of the South. In forming the Freedmen's Bureau, Congress gave it a mandate that included overseeing the establishment of common schools for the former slaves.[8]

But the freedmen generally looked to their own educated people to teach them. They regarded schools as community institutions; they wanted to be taught by teachers from their own communities. "Our people will not be satisfied until they have colored teachers," the Methodist minister Thomas W. Stringer wrote from Vicksburg. Schools run for and by blacks in the South predated the Civil War. They were usually

7. *Christian Recorder*, September 9, 1865.

8. Butchart, *Northern Schools*, 3–114; *Christian Recorder*, November 22, 1862; Jones, *Soldiers of Light and Love*, 3–48.

located in cities and, insofar as they educated slaves, were clandestine, but they were formal schools nonetheless and were patronized by both free blacks and urban slaves. Such schools operated in Charleston, Savannah, Augusta, and New Orleans and were carried on after emancipation. For the most part, however, the freed people had to begin from scratch in building schools and staffing them with teachers. One of the first things southern blacks did following the arrival of Federal troops was to provide schools for their children. Only a few days after General Sherman's army marched into Savannah, black citizens organized the Savannah Educational Association, and soon, aided by James Lynch, Mansfield French, and John Alvord, they had hired ten black teachers.[9]

The churches assumed a prominent role in planning for and implementing programs of personal and racial uplift through education. As one of the few institutions that was able to provide organization and cohesion within the southern black population in the immediate postwar years, they were in a position to perform many useful functions on behalf of education. They mustered the personnel and furnished some of the money and other supplies that were required to operate schools. Educated clergymen or their wives and members of their congregations served as teachers. Church buildings functioned as schoolhouses. Congregations raised funds to pay teachers' salaries, purchase books, or rent additional space for classrooms and to accommodate teachers. There were a few preachers (mainly the old slave preachers in rural areas) who thought education was irrelevant to black life or was a tool of the Devil, but most saw in it, as the people generally did, an important means of race advancement and were powerful advocates of an educated population. A committee of the Virginia Baptist State Convention promised to "exert all . . . power and influence to awaken an interest among the people and cause them to see and feel the necessity of education, and arouse them to a willingness to put forth all their ability to push forward the cause of education, with all its meaning."[10]

The black missionaries were nearly as active in establishing schools as they were in forming new congregations among the freedmen. Most considered themselves responsible for providing for community development

9. *Christian Recorder*, April 6, 1867; Jones, *Soldiers of Light and Love*, 59, 62; John W. Blassingame, "Before the Ghetto: The Making of the Black Community of Savannah, Georgia, 1865–1880," *Journal of Social History*, VI (1973), 470–71.

10. Virginia Baptist State Convention, *Minutes of the Eighteenth Annual Session of the Virginia Baptist State Convention . . . 1885* (Portsmouth, Va., 1885), 28–29.

as well as preaching the gospel. Their school programs offered education grounded in community values. The schools had black teachers and were free of white control. In aiding in the establishment of schools, church leaders were also meeting their ecclesiastic responsibilities. Reading the Bible was an important part of the moral training and religious upbringing of children, and establishing and running schools enabled the preachers to meet their responsibility to care for the spiritual welfare of members of the community.

Sunday schools were traditional parts of Protestant churches. Although their basic purpose was religious instruction, they provided lessons in basic literacy skills as well. Booker T. Washington later remembered that in his hometown of Malden, West Virginia, Sunday schoolers studied the spelling book as diligently as they did the Bible. Sabbath schools were very popular among the children. A black soldier wrote from Plaquemines Parish, Louisiana, about a Methodist Sunday school there. "You can see," he said, "the little children are taking a good interest in it." Church missionaries and members of their congregations also established day schools and night schools associated with the churches. James Lynch reported in July, 1863, a "large and flourishing" day school among the freedmen at Helenaville, South Carolina, along with a Sabbath school. The day school served 142 pupils and the Sabbath school 160, "old and young." When Alexander Wayman came to Norfolk and Portsmouth in the autumn of the same year, he found several Methodist and Baptist congregations conducting schools with as many as a thousand pupils enrolled. There were fifty Sunday schools in Alabama by 1867 and 4,268 scholars.[11]

Although most of the early missionaries were, like Lynch, Wayman, James Hood, Henry Turner, Jonathan Gibbs, and Jesse Boulden, well-educated and sometimes college-trained, they seldom conducted classes in the schools, choosing instead to recruit teachers from the North, from among the educated free black population of the South, or from their own families. The teachers who were employed in the Protestant church day and Sabbath schools typically were women. Catholic orders of black nuns such as the Oblate Sisters of Providence, the Sisters of the Holy Family, and one known as Our Lady of Lourdes, conducted schools in Maryland and Louisiana. Superintendents were usually males.

11. Booker T. Washington, *Up from Slavery: An Autobiography* (New York, 1901), 30; New York *Globe,* May 10, 1884; *Christian Recorder,* July 25, October 24, 1863, April 29, 1865; Kolchin, *First Freedom,* 87–88.

Churches that did not operate schools often helped maintain those established by the northern missionary and freedmen's aid societies. Aware of the influence of the churches in the black communities and the necessity of winning local support, politically astute officials of these societies consulted with local church leaders when they set up schools. Not only was local support important to the northern societies, which had limited funds and tried to spread them as widely as possible, but local opposition could make running a school for black children very difficult. Church leaders often opposed the activities of the northern groups because they employed mainly white teachers and because some of them attempted to proselytize among the local blacks and thus presented competition for communicants. Northern white school superintendents or teachers who carefully cultivated a powerful local preacher might find the black population more responsive to their endeavors than if they were less attentive or more antagonistic. G. L. Eberhart, the Freedmen's Bureau superintendent of education, directed Alfred Mason, a northern minister who was preparing to open a freedmen's school in Georgia, to call local blacks together and have them select five of their most intelligent representatives to serve as school directors. "If there be more than one religious denomination among the freedmen," he wrote to Mason, "so arrange it as to have all represented in the board." The directors would be charged with providing money to meet the school's expenses. Obviously, the local churches could frustrate the effort if their support was not sought. Congregations could give the northern societies space in their churches for classrooms, which was hard to find elsewhere. Blacks supplied a significant number of the buildings that Freedmen's Bureau schools occupied, and most were either church or other buildings owned by local congregations. When school officials did not secure local support, church leaders were likely to withhold use of their buildings and then frustrate the northerners by establishing rival schools.[12]

Imperfect though they were, poorly lighted and ventilated and furnished with benches rather than desks for students, the church houses were often the only public buildings the freedmen owned and that could

12. Cyprian Davis, *The History of Black Catholics in the United States* (New York, 1990), 104–10; G. L. Eberhart to Rev. Alfred Mason, November 14, 1866, C. A. de la Mesa to Col. C. C. Sibley, May 21, 1867, in Records of the Superintendent of Education for the State of Georgia, 1865–70, U.S. Bureau of Refugees, Freedmen, and Abandoned Lands, Record Group 105, National Archives (hereinafter cited as Freedmen's Bureau Records); George R. Bentley, *A History of the Freedmen's Bureau* (Philadelphia, 1955), 170, 172, 179.

be put to use as schools. In rural areas and in small towns throughout the South, the people were poor, and congregations could afford only small, simple buildings that were sparsely furnished. G. Thurston Chase, a northern teacher in North Carolina, conducted classes in a church that was "made of staves split out by hand." The entire building was only "about as large as a moderate-sized room" in which pupils of widely varying ages and different classes had to be kept disciplined all day long, day after day. Rough pine benches, hardly conducive to schoolwork, served as seats. Teachers had to cram as many as seventy-five or a hundred restless, squirming, and sometimes inattentive children and teenagers into such spaces and try to get them to sit still for hours on end on the hard, uncomfortable seats. Some situations were even worse. A teacher in Marietta, Georgia, taught her pupils in a church that had adequate space, but soldiers had torn out the pews and broken out the windows. Her pupils had no place to sit, and icy winds and heavy rains blew through the room, adding to the discomfort. Even in the larger and sturdier church buildings in the cities, which congregations allowed to be used as schools, the conditions were often extremely difficult. Classes were typically conducted in basements, which were usually dark, damp, and dingy.[13]

By 1880 the AME General Conference reported that it was operating 2,345 Sunday schools, employing 15,454 teachers and other officers, and serving 154,549 pupils. In addition, it owned 88 schoolhouses and 193,358 books and pamphlets in libraries. The other Methodist organizations and the Baptists also operated regular schools and Sunday schools. As a journalist pointed out, the church and its schools were supported entirely by its members. It was not a "pampered favorite" of white philanthropists but "leaned upon itself for brains, money, and Christian sympathy." White philanthropy was meddlesome and intrusive, and it provided largesse only "when white men stood at the helm."[14]

A serious conflict between the freedmen's desire to be self-reliant and the practical necessity of accepting help from whites developed early in the postwar era. In accepting assistance from friendly whites, blacks did not intend to yield control of their lives, but for various reasons control was precisely what whites, both northerners and southerners, wanted. Some white teachers and administrators understood the distinction that

13. *Freedmen's Record,* I (December, 1865), 96, III (October, 1867), 54; Eli Semble to G. L. Eberhart, October 18, 1865, in Freedmen's Bureau Records.

14. New York *Globe,* May 10, 1884.

the freed people made between assistance and control. A white teacher in Savannah, William Channing Gannett, acknowledged that local blacks possessed "a natural and praiseworthy pride in keeping their educational institutions in their own hands." They resented white control. "What they desire is assistance without control." The truth of that observation, along with the whites' reluctance to relinquish control, caused considerable tension between the freedmen and their white benefactors and controversy among African Americans.[15]

Because of the meddlesome and domineering propensities of northern whites, as well as the hostility of white southerners, black leaders, in striving to protect themselves and their freedom immediately after the Civil War, chose to rely on the principle of justice before the law. Fair and just laws were more trustworthy than their self-proclaimed but unproven friends. There were actually several facets to that strategy. One was personal pride. African Americans were tired of arrogance and paternalism and of other people presuming to think and act for them and determining what their interests were and how best to protect and promote them. The New Orleans *Tribune,* a mulatto-operated newspaper, expressed that feeling clearly: "The age of guardianship is past forever. We now think for ourselves, and we shall act for ourselves." "We simply ask," said a group of South Carolina blacks in 1865, "that we shall be recognized as *men.*" But they were also convinced that no one could understand their needs and aspirations who had not suffered the brutality and humiliation of slavery. Outsiders would inevitably act in accordance with their own wishes or would view the freedmen's needs through the prism of their own cultural biases. It was difficult, if not impossible, for whites to know what blacks themselves felt. In opposing the selection of a white man as editor of a newspaper that would cover the Mobile black community, one person declared: "There is none but colored men that can truly sympathize with the race! None but those who have been subjected to the degrading influence of slavery that can truthfully lay our grievances before the world and claim its sympathy." Still another reason for placing their trust in the law rather than in paternalistic whites was their apprehension about the moral frailty of human beings. White southerners had demonstrated over the course of many generations that their personal profit could take precedence over the most fundamental rights of their fellow human beings, and many northerners had shown a similar tendency to

15. *Freedmen's Record,* I (December, 1865), 92.

place self-interest above altruism. Blacks believed that laws that respected neither color nor previous condition of servitude would free them to act as their own agents. The rule of law rather than of men would guarantee their liberty.[16]

Although they emphasized their rights under the law, black leaders acknowledged the practical necessity of joining with whites in building an integrated, biracial society. They were a numerical and unfranchised minority in the country, and political reality required that they form alliances with whites in the interest of progress. The black political leadership had to decide whether in practical political terms the race's future was more intimately linked with the North or the South. On one hand, as sons and daughters of the same soil, black and white southerners shared a mutuality of interest in the postwar South. Black labor was as indispensable to the reconstruction of the southern economy as were the organizational and entrepreneurial skills of planters and merchants. Many black leaders hoped to "harmonize" the feelings of black and white southerners by appealing to the Christian, law-abiding element of the white population to recognize the principle of justice under the law as well as the ideal of fair and equitable wages. They rejected any notion of migrating to the North, where it was said that prejudices "shut the colored man out of every avenue of employment." On the other hand, some spokesmen had no confidence that southern whites would respond to appeals to conscience because they believed that whites, at least those who had formerly been their masters, possessed no conscience. "We must despair of this generation," reported the New Orleans *Tribune*, "for this generation has handled the whips and sold human flesh in the market, and they are corrupt." Allied with that skepticism was a perception that northern whites had the most to offer them. They were close to the source of power in Washington, had education and experience, and were already distributing largesse through the Freedmen's Bureau and a welter of private benevolent associations.[17]

Black leaders believed that African Americans must obtain political power in the form of suffrage. Freedom meant nothing if it did not include voting, officeholding, and all the other political and legal rights that were associated with citizenship. Agitation for recognition of their civil

16. New Orleans *Tribune*, February 1, July 18, 1865; *Christian Recorder*, October 28, 1865.

17. *Christian Recorder*, October 28, 1865; New Orleans *Tribune*, June 4, 1865; Litwack, *Been in the Storm So Long*, 512, 515.

and political rights began to build in late 1864 and gained momentum during 1865 and 1866. A National Convention of Colored Men met in Syracuse, New York, in October, 1864, to bring national leaders' attention to the issue of citizenship rights for African Americans. A National Equal Rights League, with branches in several states, kept the effort alive. Mass meetings followed by a series of statewide conventions in 1865, attended by elected representatives of southern blacks, lobbied constitutional conventions and legislatures in the former Confederate states and the Congress in Washington for equal rights, which they insisted flowed from their status as "true and loyal citizens of the United States." [18]

African Americans in Edgecombe County, North Carolina, were among the first to hold a mass meeting for the purpose of laying out their claim to citizenship based on their loyalty, proven during the Civil War when they had offered their lives in defense of their country. Black soldiers had paid for their rights as citizens, they averred, with their blood at Milliken's Bend, Port Hudson, Battery Wagner, and other battlefields. As citizens, they had the right to equal treatment under the law, along with direct representation in government through the ballot. Summoning images of honored American patriots, they revived the revolutionary issue of taxation without representation, pointing out that such a wrong had justified the rebellion against British tyranny and was precisely what they were forced to endure as long as their property was taxed without their having the right to vote for the representatives who enacted the tax measures. It was "diametrically opposed to republican institutions to tax us for the support and expenses of the government, and deny us, at the same time, the right of representation." They trusted that "law-loving" men everywhere would recognize their rightful claims and support them in securing justice under the law. [19]

The conventions took place at the same time as all-white state constitutional conventions and legislatures met under the Johnson administration's program of Reconstruction. It then appeared that the states and not

18. Thomas Holt, *Black over White: Negro Political Leadership in South Carolina During Reconstruction* (Urbana, 1977), 16; Charles Vincent, *Black Legislators in Louisiana During Reconstruction* (Baton Rouge, 1976), 29–47; *Christian Recorder,* October 28, 1865.

19. *Christian Recorder,* October 28, 1865. Blacks in Charleston and on St. Helena Island in South Carolina held similar mass meetings that fall. See Holt, *Black over White,* 14. On the Revolution analogy see Edmund L. Drago, *Black Politicians and Reconstruction in Georgia: A Splendid Failure* (Baton Rouge, 1982), 73–74.

the government in Washington would be making the vital decisions regarding the civil and political rights of blacks. For that reason, the black gatherings adopted a strategy of placating southern whites. Most leaders agreed that a conciliatory approach to obtaining their rights, petitioning southern whites for recognition of a few rights rather than demanding everything all at once, was the best course of action. They concentrated on persuading law-abiding whites to support their petitions for basic justice. The conventions put down in the mildest terms what blacks understood to be their rights and in the strongest ones their goodwill toward their former masters and the absence of vindictiveness in their hearts. The resolutions that the conventions adopted scrupulously avoided inflammatory language or radical demands; the majority of delegates represented themselves as long-suffering but loyal and forgiving citizens who wanted to live together with their former masters in dignity and harmony. Thus, following the advice of Martin R. Delany, the widely known and respected black abolitionist, now a Freedmen's Bureau agent, who urged them to be firm about their legal rights but to defer the issue of land distribution until later, black leaders hoped to secure basic civil rights while convincing whites that they were not a threat to their political position or economic well-being in a reconstructed southern society.[20]

Although the conventions represented the freedmen as well as free-born people of color and allowed free expression of ideas by anyone in attendance, they were dominated by coteries of men, mainly the elite. Conspicuous by their numbers (twenty-four out of forty-six delegates to the South Carolina convention and a large proportion in Louisiana) and in framing the resolutions adopted by the conventions were members of the elite antebellum class of property-owning and privileged mulattoes. Distinct differences in interest and attitude divided them from the black former slaves and were clearly reflected in their positions on issues discussed in the conventions. For example, taxation without representation was a greater concern to property owners like themselves, who feared arbitrary seizure of their estates, than to landless peasants. Similarly, the conventions' avoidance of any demand for confiscation and distribution of Confederate property suggests a bourgeois attitude toward property rights that one would expect to be more ingrained in the affluent than among the impoverished peasantry. An obsession with decorum and with

20. Litwack, *Been in the Storm So Long*, 502–24; Foner, *Reconstruction*, 112–18; Holt, *Black over White*, 16–22; Victor Ullman, *Martin R. Delany: The Beginnings of Black Nationalism* (Boston, 1971), 329.

whites' reactions to the way they looked, behaved, and phrased their resolutions was as much a sign of the elite's self-consciousness as a coldly
calculated political strategy to obtain the greatest concessions from white
power brokers. The mulatto elite identified with white society and tried
to avoid being associated with blacks. Alabama mulattoes, for instance,
opposed segregation on railway cars not because it was discriminatory
but because it forced them to sit with common blacks. Thus, hidden beneath the conciliation and moderation that the conventions fostered in
their relations with whites were important divisions within the African-
American population, cleavages that held considerable potential for tension and divided purpose in the postemancipation period.[21]

Class differentiation, however, was not simply a dichotomy between
mulattoes and blacks. Although color was a factor in defining social
classes, other determiners, including wealth, education, occupation, and
background, were also significant, sometimes more so than the amount
of white blood that flowed through one's veins. Many blacks, in some
cases freeborn and in others privileged slaves, enjoyed elite status by virtue of their property holdings or their high-status positions as teachers
and ministers. In some states, including Alabama and Georgia, and in
such cities as Memphis, they, rather than the mulattoes, dominated the
elite. There was also a small middle class, mostly artisans who were former slaves, in African-American society. Slowly but steadily expanding
and upwardly mobile, the middle class, like the elite, often perceived its
interests as more closely associated with those of whites than of the "submerged masses" of freedmen.[22]

Ministers and the churches they led were very important in the political leadership of the black community. The ministers enjoyed high status
and were members of the political elite either because of their wealth,
their education, or their role of providing advice in worldly as well as
spiritual matters. They had been both secular and religious leaders during
slavery, and no other group had yet emerged to challenge them. They
enjoyed the people's trust. The preachers' paternalism also thrust them

21. Holt, *Black over White,* 15–23; Vincent, *Black Legislators in Louisiana,* 48–70,
219; Litwack, *Been in the Storm So Long,* 513–14; Kolchin, *First Freedom,* 137–43.

22. Kolchin, *First Freedom,* 163–67; Drago, *Black Politicians and Reconstruction in
Georgia,* 37–39; Armstead L. Robinson, "Plans Dat Comed from God: Institution Building
and the Emergence of Black Leadership in Reconstruction Memphis," in *Toward a New
South? Studies in Post–Civil War Southern Communities,* ed. Orville Vernon Burton and
Robert C. McMath, Jr. (Westport, 1982), 93.

into political leadership. Thomas Allen, the Georgia Baptist minister, explained that most freedmen were too ignorant to act alone in politics. "In my country the colored people came to me for instructions, and I gave them the best instructions I could. I took the New York Tribune and other papers, and in that way I found out a great deal, and I told them whatever I thought was right." Another Baptist, James M. Simms, believed that ministers like himself "were almost the only ones capable of looking out after our people." They were interested in the people's political well-being. "And my profession as minister-missionary was the only one in which I could go to our people and freely advise them." In the absence of any other effective grass-roots political organizations, the churches were the only means by which political leaders could organize and mobilize the constituencies that elected delegates to the conventions. Not surprisingly, church congregations often elected their own ministers to represent them. Once elected, and owing to their experience as popular leaders, their oratorical skills, and their command of parliamentary procedure, the ministers were naturals to take charge of the conventions. They often presided over the sessions, chaired the committees that drew up resolutions and petitions, and influenced the nature and outcome of debate on the floor. Many of the conventions assembled in church buildings.[23]

The minister-politicians tended to be conservative and conciliatory in their outlook and approach to the issues of Reconstruction. Some of them had been slaves and had long before learned through hard experience how to accommodate their followers' needs to the whites' demands. Others were members either of the middle class or the black aristocracy. Many were mulattoes. Their class interests led them to espouse a bourgeois ideology that regarded hard work, frugality, and the slow but steady accumulation of wealth as the stones that paved the road to advancement. Their Christian faith made them trust God to overcome racial hatred and injustice. They believed that God commanded them to love their enemies and to be conciliatory toward them; thus James Lynch noted that whites might deny blacks justice for a while but not for long, "for there will be an army marshalled in the Heavens for our protection,

23. Robinson, "Plans Dat Comed from God," 71–102; Litwack, *Been in the Storm So Long,* 502–24; U.S. Senate, *Testimony Taken by the Joint Select Committee to Inquire into the Conditions of Affairs in the Late Insurrectionary States,* 42nd Cong, 2nd Sess., *Georgia Testimony,* Vol. VII, Pt. 6, p. 615; *House Miscellaneous Documents,* 40th Cong., 3rd Sess., No. 52, p. 9.

and events will transpire by which the hand of Providence will wring from you in wrath, that which should have been given in love."[24]

Meeting in September, 1865, in the Loyal AME Church of Raleigh, also known as the Lincoln Church in honor of the martyred president, whose life-sized effigy behind the pulpit was still draped in black mourning ribbons, about 150 people chosen largely from Edgecombe County but including nearly every other region of North Carolina discussed their needs and how best to meet them. Although the impetus for calling the convention came from militant blacks who pressed the group to demand that the state's constitutional convention, which had convened at the same time in the same city, grant complete and immediate civil and political equality to blacks, a more moderate and acquiescent attitude prevailed under the leadership of James W. Hood, the AME Zion missionary who had come to the state from Connecticut two years before, and James Harris, a North Carolina native. Hood was elected president of the convention. He presided over the debates and helped set the tone of the meeting. He hoped to forge a union with southern whites that would further the common interests of both races. His strategy was to allay white fears and avoid antagonizing them by limiting the delegates' demands. Although Hood spoke of the people's legitimate right to testify in courts of law, to be admitted to the jury box, to serve as counsel for blacks involved in litigation, and to cast ballots, he admitted that they "may not gain all at once." Harris likewise argued the necessity of seeking an accommodation with white southerners.

The convention drafted a petition to the all-white state constitutional convention that read more like a supplication than a demand. It "most respectfully and humbly" presented "the situation and our wants as a people." Addressing white resentment of the slaves' alleged betrayal of their masters, the petition stressed that most slaves had been "obedient and passive" during the conflict, "calmly waiting upon Providence" rather than rising up in insurrection. Candidly acknowledging that they had no independent political power, they said they preferred to establish and maintain ties with their southern friends rather than seek the support of northern agencies, whose presence they knew was only temporary. They asked specifically for public education for their children, legal recognition of their marriages, and care for the helpless among them. "Is this asking too much?" They said virtually nothing directly about such

24. Drago, *Black Politicians and Reconstruction in Georgia*, 25–26.

inflammatory issues as entry into the jury box, the right to practice law, or the franchise.[25]

Southern whites faced a golden opportunity in late 1865 to reach an accommodation with their emancipated slaves on terms that would have been decidedly favorable to them. Black demands were moderate, and they were obviously hoping for an accommodation. As yet there were few indications of any alliance between southern blacks and Republicans in the North on a more radical list of demands relating to their political status. Indeed, in the North, ideas about Reconstruction and what if anything should be done to extend citizenship rights were still only the tangled threads of a future policy. Congress was not yet mobilized behind any program that went beyond the very lenient Johnson plan that had just begun to take shape. This plan offered amnesty to disloyal southerners who pledged their future allegiance to the republic and required pacified states to draft new constitutions abolishing slavery and repudiating secession but did not guarantee that blacks would be educated at the public's expense or granted the right to vote. Some Republicans in the House of Representatives and Senate opposed presidential Reconstruction and backed a measure sponsored by Benjamin Wade and Henry Winter Davis that would require southern state constitutions to extend equal rights under the law to blacks, but they shared no consensus about black suffrage. Some of them went beyond the Wade-Davis proposal and favored a restricted franchise for blacks, based on literacy tests. Only a few, however (to whom the label Radical Republican was eventually attached), like Thaddeus Stevens and Charles Sumner advocated unrestricted voting rights for all blacks. Almost any white southern concession that went beyond abolishing slavery, even if it did not include black voting, would have satisfied enough Republicans in the Congress to avert unified opposition to what southern whites really wanted, which was continued rule in the region and virtually complete control of the black population.[26]

Southern whites chose to ignore the petitions of the colored men's conventions because they were under no immediate pressure to accept them. They did what they had to do and very little more. Under the terms of presidential Reconstruction, the constitutional conventions that met after the surrender in 1865 repudiated the earlier ordinances of secession, prohibited slavery, and, after President Johnson instructed them to do so,

---

25. *Christian Recorder,* October 28, 1865.
26. Litwack, *Been in the Storm So Long,* 536–37; Foner, *Reconstruction,* 221–27.

repudiated all debts incurred in support of the rebellion. But as members of the same class as the old secessionists—and often former slave owners themselves—the Unionists and white antisecessionists who dominated the conventions scarcely personified the winds of change on the subject of race. The ideology that had prevailed in state government during antebellum times remained. The delegates took no action on the petitions from the colored men's conventions, ultimately referring the issues raised in them to the new legislatures, and their collective silence spoke loudly of their individual convictions. Indeed, numerous delegates voiced their scorn for Radical Republican ideas about the rightful status of blacks. In typical fashion, one delegate to the North Carolina convention, who like most white southerners insisted that he understood black people and described himself as "a friend of the Negro," believed that "this is a white man's country and a white man's government." He opposed black suffrage, black testimony in court, miscegenation, "and other articles of the radical faith." Instead of making any concessions to blacks or to liberal Republicans in Congress, the delegates acted to reconstruct as much of the old order as possible. "Under the pressure of Federal bayonets," Mississippi's governor Benjamin Humphries declared, and "urged by the misdirected sympathies of the world," the people of Mississippi had abolished slavery. "The Negro is free, whether we like it or not; we must realize that fact now and forever. To be free, however, does not make him a citizen, or entitle him to political or social equality with the white race." [27]

When the state legislatures convened and took up the "nigger question," they showed little interest in anything but the disorganization of black labor and fantasies about miscegenation. Far from establishing public school systems, providing for black testimony in court, or granting black suffrage, the new state legislatures enacted highly restrictive measures designed to force the freedmen to work and to keep them on the plantations rather than migrating to the cities. These Black Codes, as the laws were called, required African Americans to contract to work by January of each year or be arrested as vagrants. Those who did not pay the fines imposed for the crime of vagrancy could be sold into labor. They were forbidden to own firearms or other weapons. The laws treated all people of color alike, making no distinctions based on class or skin tone.

27. Foner, *Reconstruction*, 193–96; Dennett, *The South as It Is*, 165; Vernon L. Wharton, *The Negro in Mississippi, 1865–1890* (1947; rpr. New York, 1965), 83–84.

The Mississippi code, for example, stated that "all freedmen, free negroes and mulattoes in this State, over the age of eighteen years, found on the second Monday in January, 1866, or thereafter, with no lawful employment or business . . . shall be deemed vagrants."[28]

The white southerners' response to the blacks' demands spurred an alliance of mutual self-interest between freedmen and freeborn blacks and mulattoes, providing the basis for a more politically solid black community. White southerners' obstinacy and rejection of the colored people's petitions also offended moderate Republicans in the North and helped galvanize the various philosophies represented in the party into an ideology of action on behalf of blacks. Not only were conservative whites legislating blacks into a quasi-slavery, but they were employing intimidation and violence to keep them subservient. Two riots, in Memphis and New Orleans, in the spring and summer of 1866 resulted in considerable injury, death, and the destruction of property (including the wounding of one local black preacher and the death of another in New Orleans and the burning of several churches in Memphis). The riots outraged blacks and their white sympathizers and discredited the Johnson administration's Reconstruction program.[29]

President Johnson's actions also contributed to the formation of a consensus among Republicans in Congress in support of voting rights for blacks. Although he had initially declared that treason was "odious" and should be punished, Johnson soon decided to grant pardons to former Confederate leaders and extend recognition to the governments they led. His offenses against Republican ideals alienated most factions within the party. He backed the southern white leadership on all issues relating to race. He vetoed an extension of the Freedmen's Bureau and a civil rights bill in 1866. He urged the former Confederate states not to ratify the proposed Fourteenth Amendment guaranteeing citizenship rights against state encroachment. The result of "my policy," as black leaders scornfully labeled the president's program, was a set of regimes in the southern states governed by unremorseful former slave owners who may have opposed secession but had actively supported the Confederacy and what it had stood for.

In the congressional elections of 1866, Republicans campaigned to convince voters to repudiate Johnson's program and support civil and

28. Wharton, *Negro in Mississippi*, 85.
29. *Christian Recorder*, August 18, 25, 1866; Foner, *Reconstruction*, 261–64.

political rights for blacks. In Congress they had blocked southern delegations elected under the new state governments from taking their seats.
Now they hoped to win a large enough majority in both houses to allow
them consistently to override presidential vetoes, as they had done in re-
passing the Freedmen's Bureau and civil rights bills. The elections resulted in a resounding Radical Republican victory, "the most decisive and
emphatic victory ever seen in American politics," trumpeted the *Nation*.
It gave them power to legislate the terms of a new program of southern
reconstruction. Senator James W. Grimes of Iowa explained the balance
of power between Congress and the president: "The President has no
power to control or influence anybody and legislation will be carried on
entirely regardless of his opinions or wishes." When the new Congress
convened in 1867, it began Reconstruction all over again. Suspending
civilian government in most of the former Confederate states, Congress
demanded that new constitutional conventions be held, with election of
delegates to be based on manhood suffrage but excluding those southerners who had participated in the rebellion. With the Republican-controlled
Congress now in command, blacks began to play a more direct role in
shaping their social and political environment, and under Radical control, the federal government took steps to end the organized violence
against blacks, to turn the Freedmen's Bureau into an agency for blacks
rather than southern whites, and to provide for the education of the
freedmen.[30]

Southern blacks showed great interest in and enthusiasm for Radical
Reconstruction, particularly their enfranchisement and their impending
participation in the drafting of new state constitutions. They avidly supported the Republican party and worked diligently to form local Union
League groups that mobilized support for the party, but the representatives they chose for the state constitutional conventions, state legislatures,
and Congress came from an elite group of businessmen, professionals,
skilled craftsmen, and landowning farmers. A majority of the delegates
to the constitutional conventions from 1867 to 1869, for example, were
mulattoes and had never been slaves. Contrary to the image of an illiterate and unsophisticated black buffoon that many whites represented as
typical of those the Republicans had elevated to power, most members of
the conventions and state legislatures were literate and capable of making
rational decisions on the complex issues that confronted them. But as had

30. Foner, *Reconstruction*, 268, 271; *Nation*, November 15, 1866.

been true in 1865, class identification was as strong among them, if not more so, than race, and at least at the outset, they represented the interests of the elite rather than those of impoverished and oppressed black folk. That made it easy for them, perhaps too easy, to form political alliances with conservative whites who also joined the Republican party. Although many of these elite representatives initially voted with the conservatives and moderates on such issues as voting rights, taxes, and property matters, most eventually came to realize that their class and personal interests depended on overall race advancement, and consequently they supported the Radical Republican program of political, social, and economic reform that promised to turn the South's social and political systems upside down.[31]

Because of its traditionally holistic view of its role in the community the black church slipped easily into the front lines of Reconstruction politics. Its politicization made it a major force in the advocacy and exercise of black citizenship rights during the late 1860s and early 1870s. Without the African-American church, as AME minister Wesley J. Gaines testified to a congressional committee, "there would have been no black political movement." The churches served as venues for political rallies and Republican party meetings, and many ministers preached the message of the party about as often as the gospel of spiritual salvation. Local Union Leagues, organizations of Republican party members pledged to the principle of equal rights, often met in church buildings. Thomas Allen repeatedly reminded his congregation that "they had been freed by the Yankees and Union men" and "they ought to vote with them; to go with the party always." A white observer in Georgia noted of the ministers there that "their preaching is often political in nature." So politicized was the church and so enthusiastically did its ministers enter the political arena that, according to one preacher, "politics got in our midst and our revival or religious work for a while began to wane." The preachers reflected not only the people's enthusiasm for politics and their hopes for full citizenship but also the general expectation that they would be political leaders. That feeling was not unanimous, however, and occasionally preachers alienated their congregations by becoming too involved in political activity and neglecting their ministerial responsibilities. Ulysses L. Houston, a

31. Richard L. Hume, "Negro Delegates to the State Constitutional Conventions of 1867–69," in *Southern Black Leaders of the Reconstruction Era,* ed. Howard N. Rabinowitz (Urbana, 1982), 129–53; Vincent, *Black Legislators in Louisiana,* 48–58; Holt, *Black over White,* 36–71.

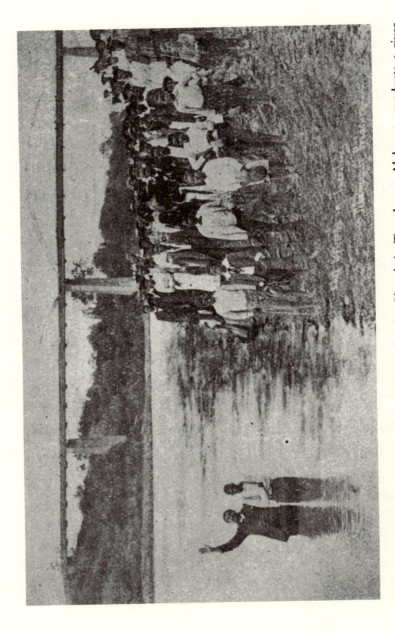

Rev. L. S. Steinback, pastor of the African Baptist Church in Tuscaloosa, Alabama, conducts a river baptism.

From C. O. Boothe, *Cyclopedia of Negro Baptists in Alabama* (Birmingham, 1895)

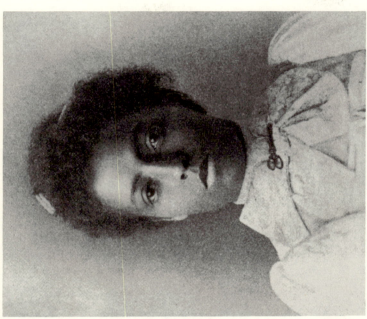

Mrs. Dinah Smith Jordan, Women's Missionary Society of Alabama

From C. O. Boothe, *Cyclopedia of Negro Baptists in Alabama* (Birmingham, 1895)

Mrs. Rebecca Pitts, of the Alabama Women's State Convention

From C. O. Boothe, *Cyclopedia of Negro Baptists in Alabama* (Birmingham, 1895)

This sketch of generals Steedman and Fullerton conferring with freedmen in their church at Trent River settlement first appeared in *Harper's Weekly,* June 9, 1866.

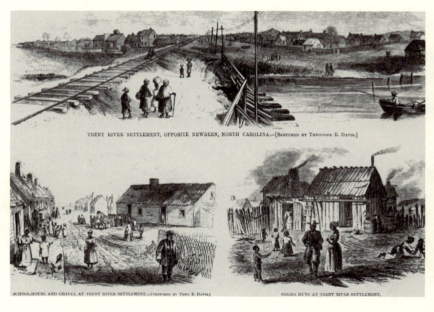

TRENT RIVER SETTLEMENT, OPPOSITE NEWBERN, NORTH CAROLINA.—[Sketched by Theodore R. Davis.]

SCHOOL-HOUSE AND CHAPEL AT TRENT RIVER SETTLEMENT.—[Sketched by Theo. R. Davis.]

NEGRO HUTS AT TRENT RIVER SETTLEMENT.

Sketches of the Trent River settlement show an overview of the area opposite Newbern, North Carolina (top), the schoolhouse and chapel (lower left), and some huts (lower right). These sketches first appeared in *Harper's Weekly,* June 9, 1866.

Francis Grimké, Presbyterian minister

From D. W. Culp, *Twentieth Century Negro Literature* (1902; rpr. New York, 1969)

Bishop Henry McNeal Turner
From D. W. Culp, *Twentieth Century Negro Literature* (1902; rpr. New York, 1969)

Bishop James W. Hood, African Methodist Episcopal Zion Church

From D. W. Culp, *Twentieth Century Negro Literature* (1902; rpr. New York, 1969)

Daniel Alexander Payne, African Methodist Episcopal bishop

From Daniel A. Payne, *Recollections of Seventy Years* (Nashville, 1888)

John Jasper, Virginia Baptist minister

From William E. Hatcher, *John Jasper: The Unmatched Negro Philosopher and Teacher* (New York, 1908)

Charles Octavius Boothe, Alabama Baptist leader

From C. O. Boothe, *Cyclopedia of Negro Baptists in Alabama* (Birmingham, 1895)

Emanuel K. Love

From E. K. Love, *A History of the First African Baptist Church of Savannah from Its Organization, January 20th, 1788, to July 1st, 1888* (Savannah, 1888)

African Methodist Episcopal ministers Benjamin W. Arnett, Wesley J. Gaines (top row), Benjamin Tucker Tanner, and Abraham Grant (bottom row)

From Daniel A. Payne, *Recollections of Seventy Years* (Nashville, 1888)

Rural church in South Carolina
Courtesy University of South Carolina Library, South Caroliniana Collection

A "praise house" in South Carolina

Courtesy University of South Carolina Library, South Caroliniana Collection

Shiloh Baptist Church, Birmingham, Alabama, *ca.* 1870

From C. O. Boothe, *Cyclopedia of Negro Baptists in Alabama* (Birmingham, 1895)

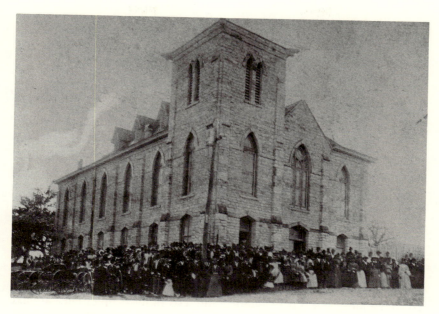

Wesley Chapel African Methodist Episcopal Church, Austin, Texas
Courtesy Austin History Center, Austin Public Library

St. John's Orphanage in Texas, operated by the St. John's Baptist Association of Texas
Courtesy Austin History Center, Austin Public Library

Georgia Baptist minister, actually lost his congregation because of his political activism.[32]

Ministers were conspicuous members of the state constitutional conventions during 1867 and 1868 and, following ratification of the constitutions, were prominent among the blacks elected to seats in the state legislatures. They also held appointed positions from the state down to the county and municipal levels of government. Sixteen of the nineteen black delegates to the Georgia constitutional convention were ministers, as were at least twenty-eight of the sixty-nine blacks who served in the legislature during Reconstruction. Seven ministers were delegates to the 1868 Florida convention, and at least five were elected to the legislature. Forty-two of South Carolina's black legislators between 1868 and 1876 were ministers, and many others held a variety of county and municipal offices.[33]

One is hard-pressed to imagine a more natural group of political leaders. "A man in this state," explained Charles H. Pearce, an AME minister and a political activist in Florida, "cannot do his whole duty as a minister except he looks out for the political interests of his people. They are like ships out at sea, and they must have somebody to guide them; and it is natural that they should get their best informed men to lead them." As a group, ministers were as competent as the other black delegates and legislators, and their skills as orators and church administrators, the contacts that some of the missionaries among them had with powerful northerners, and the paternalistic relationship that they established with those under their charge made them ideally suited to serve as delegates, legislators, and political organizers. Furthermore, many enjoyed their churches' financial support—more or less anyway—and could better afford to spend time doing political work than most blacks, who were struggling to make a living. They represented established and often dynamic constituencies, and their relationships with their congregations put them in a

32. U.S. Senate, *Testimony to Inquire into Conditions in the Late Insurrectionary States, Georgia Testimony,* Vol. VII, Pt. 6, p. 615; Drago, *Black Politicians and Reconstruction in Georgia,* 72–73; Foner, *Reconstruction,* 282.

33. Drago, *Black Politicians and Reconstruction in Georgia,* 37–39, 46–47, 72–73; Joe M. Richardson, *The Negro in the Reconstruction of Florida, 1867–1877* (Tallahassee, 1965), 177–98; Holt, *Black over White,* 84, 229–41; William C. Hine, "Black Politicians in Reconstruction Charleston, South Carolina: A Collective Study," *Journal of Southern History,* XLIX (1983), 562, 570; Hume, "Negro Delegates to the State Constitutional Conventions," 139–40.

good position to mobilize voters. Traveling through their districts tending to their congregants' needs and winning new adherents provided excellent opportunities to win the people's trust and to exchange political views with them. Indeed, doing church business and electioneering were often one and the same. Isaac P. Brockenton of Darlington spent the year before his election to the South Carolina constitutional convention crisscrossing his district preaching sermons, performing various other ministerial duties, and politicking. As a group, the ministers had little experience in dealing with governmental matters, but it is evident in the fact that black voters elected and reelected them that they were trusted.[34]

Several individual ministers stood out in the crowd of Reconstruction politicians because of their flair for attention or their special skills and articulateness in dealing with issues. On issues of race and economic development, they represented a range of ideologies, from radical to conservative, as well as the opposing strategies of militant confrontation to cautious accommodationism. In Florida, the highly respected, Dartmouth-educated Jonathan Gibbs, a Presbyterian minister, served as secretary of state and superintendent of education. Charles H. Pearce, a former slave and an African Methodist missionary, held a seat in the state senate from 1868 until 1872 and was a formidable power in Leon County politics.[35]

In the Georgia constitutional convention and in the subsequent legislature, preachers such as AME luminary Henry M. Turner and Baptists James M. Simms and Ulysses L. Houston led the black delegation. After serving as an army chaplain during the war, Turner was attached to the Freedmen's Bureau and assigned to Georgia. Dissatisfied with the bureau, he resigned from the army and channeled his boundless energy into political activity. He became a leading Republican party organizer. At this point in his career he brimmed with optimism, as many black politicians did, believing that the country was moving toward eliminating race prejudice, and he threw himself enthusiastically into the effort to organize and mobilize the black vote in the state. Referring to himself as "a minister of the gospel and a kind of politician—both," he was elected to the state constitutional convention in 1867. Naïvely confident that the state's biracial Republican party could lead Georgia into a new era of prosperity

34. Richardson, *Negro in the Reconstruction of Florida*, 177–98; U.S. Senate, *Testimony to Inquire into Conditions in the Late Insurrectionary States, Florida Testimony*, Vol. XIII, p. 171; Holt, *Black over White*, 84.

35. Richardson, *Negro in the Reconstruction of Florida*, 177–98.

without being deflected from its course by divisive race issues and not particularly outspoken as a delegate, Turner voted on the basis of class rather than race on the issues that came before the body. He supported measures that protected the rights of property owners, established a poll tax and educational requirements for voting, and would have pardoned Confederate President Jefferson Davis, positions that were more consistent with the interests of a bourgeoisie and planter aristocracy than of a landless and still oppressed black proletariat. After he was elected to the state legislature in 1868, however, he became a more vigorous defender of the rights of ordinary black citizens. Although Republicans dominated the legislature, blacks were a minority, and a conservative coalition of white Republicans and Democrats held the balance of power. Increasingly suspicious of whites, Turner became more active as a legislator than he had been as a delegate to the constitutional convention. He sponsored bills funding public education for blacks and providing for their physical and economic protection. He and the other members of the black delegation were expelled from the legislature by the white majority, who did not want to share power with blacks, and even though he was readmitted in 1870, the experience disillusioned and radicalized him. "I am here to demand my rights," he declared on the floor of the legislature just before his departure, "and to hurl thunderbolts at the man who would dare to cross the threshold of my manhood." Turner no longer sought to conciliate whites. Convinced that blacks would never have justice in America, he began to advocate emigration as the best way for African Americans to develop pride and self-confidence.[36]

In Louisiana, as in other states, businessmen and professionals led the black delegations to the 1867 constitutional convention and the Reconstruction legislatures. Four black ministers played active and constructive roles in political affairs. One of them was Curtis Pollard, a Baptist preacher from Madison Parish. When he was elected as a delegate to the constitutional convention he was fifty-eight years old and a successful farmer. He served for eight years in the state senate.[37]

Another church leader who made a mark on Reconstruction politics

36. Robert E. Perdue, *The Negro in Savannah, 1865–1900* (New York, 1973), 52–68; Clarence E. Walker, *A Rock in a Weary Land: The African Methodist Episcopal Church During the Civil War and Reconstruction* (Baton Rouge, 1982), 122–24; John Dittmer, "The Education of Henry McNeal Turner," in *Black Leaders of the Nineteenth Century,* ed. Leon F. Litwack and August Meier (Urbana, 1988), 254–59.

37. Vincent, *Black Legislators in Louisiana,* 53.

in Louisiana was Pierre Landry, who, though not ordained until 1880, was an active layman in the Methodist Episcopal church and largely responsible for establishing Methodist congregations in the state. Landry's political career commenced with his election as mayor of Donaldsonville. After serving a single one-year term, he was elected president of the Ascension Parish police jury, and Governor Henry C. Warmoth appointed him tax collector. In 1872 he launched his career in the legislature, serving two years in the House of Representatives and then four years in the Senate. Like most African-American leaders at the time, he approached race relations from an integrationist position. That Landry was especially accommodating to whites, however, was apparent in his decision to affiliate with the Methodist Episcopal church rather than with either of the African Methodist churches. It was also evident in his steady effort to gain their approval and support in his political campaigns. "In all of these elections," he wrote, "my colleagues were men of the very best blood of the State of Louisiana and I was honored by their support and their votes." Criticized by Radicals for his alliance with those whom they saw as politically conservative and he regarded as "the best class of southern white men who composed the wealth, culture and intelligence of this State," Landry justified his political career by arguing that accommodating powerful whites afforded blacks their best opportunity for advancement: "I have nothing to regret for having labored with such a people so as to better the condition of my own race, by making it possible to live together in peace." No doubt with conservative whites' approbation, he was elected in 1879 to the constitutional convention that drafted the constitution which ended Reconstruction in Louisiana and to the House of Representatives again in 1882 under the restored regime of conservative whites.[38]

Several ministers distinguished themselves in Reconstruction Mississippi. Jesse F. Boulden, a Baptist, whose congregation was located in Columbus, was an important Republican party organizer. Among blacks elected to the constitutional convention, the three men who demonstrated the greatest ability were preachers. J. Aaron Moore was a Methodist Episcopal missionary who organized several churches in the area around Meridian. After attending the convention, he was elected to the state senate and finally settled in Jackson and became a blacksmith. Henry P. Ja-

38. Pierre Landry, "Autobiographical Sketch" (Typescript in Dunn-Landry Family Papers, Amistad Research Center, Tulane University).

cobs was a native of Mississippi, born a slave, who learned to read and write from a mentally deranged man whom he looked after and then wrote a pass for himself and escaped with his family to the North. He returned to Mississippi during the war as a Baptist missionary and was amazingly successful in organizing churches and district associations in the state. As a member of the convention, Jacobs displayed considerable energy in his work on committees and on the floor. He supported measures establishing equal rights for blacks on conveyances and in all other public places, although all that he and his supporters were ultimately able to achieve was a general statement in the bill of rights that the rights of citizens should not be abridged. The most influential of all the black delegates to the convention was Thomas W. Stringer. An AME minister, he, like Moore, Jacobs, and the numerous other churchmen who were active in Reconstruction politics, was well-known around the state because of his work in organizing churches, and in the convention he addressed the issues that pertained particularly to African Americans. He led an effort to include in the constitution a provision for compulsory school attendance; however, the body deferred to the legislature on the matter of public education and his measure was lost. Stringer, again like many of his ministerial colleagues, revealed a willingness to compromise on issues that were especially controversial. For example, he once voted against a motion that separate schools be provided for black pupils, but he later reversed himself and voted against another measure that would have condemned segregated schools.[39]

When the Mississippi constitution of 1868 finally went into effect, Moore, Jacobs, and Stringer all were elected to seats in the legislature. Another churchman, the AME missionary Hiram R. Revels, used his ministerial position to propel himself into a seat in the United States Senate to fill the unexpired term of Jefferson Davis. During the campaign for ratification of the constitution in 1868, another new arrival quickly captured the attention of blacks and whites alike. He was James D. Lynch, the AME cleric who had suddenly resigned his position as editor of the *Christian Recorder,* left the denomination and joined the Methodist Episcopal ministry (which he had vigorously attacked during his career as a missionary in South Carolina and Georgia), and moved to Mississippi to enter Reconstruction politics. Lynch had criticized both the Methodist

39. William J. Simmons, *Men of Mark: Eminent, Progressive and Rising* (1887; rpr. New York, 1968), 707–12; Wharton, *Negro in Mississippi,* 148–50.

Episcopal church and its southern counterpart, the former for its refusal to treat blacks and whites equally and the latter for not relinquishing title to church property occupied by black congregations, but he had also consistently called on blacks and whites to work together to establish an integrated, biracial community. Such was his message during the ratification campaign. "The colored people are as anxious as any people in our broad land," he instructed whites, "to see political passions subside. . . . We desire to live in peace with our ex-masters—we recognize the mutual dependence of the one on the other; and to open a breach between the races is repugnant to every feeling of our natures." Lynch was an active Republican party organizer, was nominated for and elected to the office of secretary of state in 1869 (the first black to hold such a high office in Mississippi), and won and retained the respect and admiration of even his Democratic opponents. Indeed, a Democratic newspaper gave him grudging endorsement when it referred to him as "the most popular carpet-bagger in the State—the best educated man, and the best speaker, and the most effective orator, of that party, in Mississippi; and withal, as much of a gentleman as he can be with his present white associations." That was an amazing testimonial considering the passion and racial animosity that infused the political dialogue of the time. Lynch's enormous potential was never completely tapped, however. In 1875 Republican party members moved to nominate him for a seat in Congress, but a white Republican rival brought charges of adultery against him, allegations that lent credence to other stories about his drunkenness that had already begun to circulate. Denied the nomination, the man once called "the Henry Ward Beecher of the colored race" died suddenly, and a brilliant career ended.[40]

In South Carolina the indefatigable Richard H. Cain avidly joined the struggle for land reform and civil rights. The pastor of two large congregations in Charleston and the presiding elder of the district, Cain was an exceptionally successful minister. But church work could consume only a portion of his vast energies. He was elected a delegate to the constitutional convention of 1868, then to the legislature, and finally in 1872 to the first of two terms in Congress. He shared with Hiram R. Revels, another AME minister, the distinction of being among the few blacks elected to Congress during Reconstruction. In addition to his political

40. William C. Harris, "James Lynch: Black Leader in Southern Reconstruction," *Historian*, XXXIV (November, 1971), 40–61; John R. Lynch, "Communications," *Journal of Negro History*, XVI (1931), 106; Wharton, *Negro in Mississippi*, 152, 154–55.

and ministerial careers, Cain published and edited a newspaper known as the *Missionary Record*.[41]

Throughout Reconstruction, most of the minister-politicians held moderate political views, sometimes more so than the rank-and-file membership of their churches. Believing that political power was crucial to the progress of the race and faced with the reality of their minority status and the need to form alliances with whites, they often placed political objectives above the freedmen's need for land, education, and government assistance. The ministers criticized the federal government for its reluctance to extend voting rights to them following emancipation, and they expressed outrage at the violent attacks suffered by black people in the unreconstructed South. James M. Simms of Georgia vowed to enforce "the law of retaliation" against whites: "Let no man or set of men think that the loyal citizens BUT MORE PARTICULARLY THE COLORED, will tamely submit to be attacked and murdered." As Andrew Johnson's southern policy crystallized during the summer and autumn of 1865, church leaders spoke out angrily against the president. But on the primary issues that affected blacks directly, land distribution and education, they were generally conciliatory. Those who served as delegates to state constitutional conventions and Reconstruction legislatures conceded the right of white landowners to retain ownership of property despite the argument by more militant blacks that slave labor had given that property its value and that whites owed the former slaves at least a portion of it. The churchmen advocated public education for blacks as well as whites, adopting the community-based northern system as a model. In response to whites' reaction against sending their children to schools with black children, the minister-legislators generally agreed to segregated schools and voted against mandatory school attendance requirements. Church leaders were notably aggressive only on the issue of civil rights.[42]

The reason for the moderation of Reconstruction minister-politicians lay partly in their social class background. As members of a black bourgeoisie that had traditionally accepted the values associated with white middle-class society, which included the sanctity of property rights and a strategy of conciliating whites in order to attain and achieve status in

41. Holt, *Black over White*, 16, 18, 108, 112, 126, 129, 131, 132, 165.

42. Drago, *Black Politicians and Reconstruction in Georgia*, 86–90; Vincent, *Black Legislators in Louisiana*, 48–70; Holt, *Black over White*, 126–51, 162, 186, 190, 191; Wharton, *Negro in Mississippi*, 149.

society, church leaders felt comfortable with an accommodationist approach to dealing with whites in southern state legislatures.[43]

But beyond their class interest, these were pious men whose Christian beliefs taught them to be generous and to eschew vindictiveness. They believed in the ideal of forgiveness and in their obligation as Christians to emulate God to the extent that their human condition enabled them to do so. They trusted in his omnipotence and in his faultless justice. If there were any punishment to be meted out to those who persisted in abusing the liberated people, Almighty God himself would dispense it. Commenting on Andrew Johnson's veto of the Freedmen's Bureau bill, Elisha Weaver noted that in substance it "really amounts to the same as if he had said to the colored people in the South and elsewhere, 'I don't care if you are all killed off, or kept down forever.'" The people must take hope in the Republicans in Congress who voted for the bill, he mused, but in the end "they should put their firm and abiding trust in God, He who stayed the building of the Babylonian tower. He may yet see fit to overturn the modern Babel at Washington, and crush the ingrate serpents' heads that sting the hand that feed[s] them." The ministers saw God's hand in virtually everything that happened in the world, even much that appeared to be evil. Many held to the belief that slavery itself had been part of God's plan for the redemption of Africans. Henry M. Turner believed that, "not that it was in harmony with his fundamental laws for one man to rule another, nor did he ever contemplate that the Negro was to be reduced to the status of a vassal, but as a subject for moral and intellectual culture." Slavery was the means by which the heathens of Africa had been introduced to Christianity and civilization. According to God's plan, slave owners were supposed to be the slaves' guardians, obligated to edify and then release them. They obviously had violated that trust, and slavery had turned into a "reactionary curse" on the white man as well as a burden to the African. "It rebounded back upon the white man while it degraded the status of the black." Emancipation represented the imposition of divine justice on the South, and Reconstruction in Turner's view held the promise of being like a conversion experience for whites, when they would confess to their wicked and evil ways, repent, and live in harmony with their black brethren. From that vantage point, it is easy to understand Turner's idealism and his willingness to be firm

43. Holt, *Black over White*, 36–43, 49, 59, 62, 70.

but conciliatory toward whites as he exhorted them to seek their redemption through cooperation.[44]

The minister-politicians also deferred to whites as people more experienced than they were in matters of politics and government. As Turner observed, "You know that the black people of this country acknowledge you as their superiors, by virtue of your education and knowledge."[45]

But there were exceptions to the moderation of the minister-politicians. Some ministers were so conciliatory that they could not be called moderate. Among them were Pierre Landry of Louisiana and Alexander Bettis, the pastor of Mt. Canaan Baptist Church in Edgefield County, South Carolina. Bettis assured white conservatives of blacks' willingness to be cooperative even when federal support began to weaken and white violence directed at black and white Republicans in the state mounted. His efforts were not without positive rewards. If Bettis ever felt the same optimism that Henry Turner had once exuded regarding the likelihood of an integrated, biracial society based on the ideals of equality and cooperation, he did not show it. He could see that there were definite limits to his white neighbors' toleration of freedom and opportunity for blacks. Whites in Edgefield County—and elsewhere—understood the relationship between political power and social and economic status. Their chief concern in the immediate postemancipation period was that social and economic lines dividing the races were obscured. By conceding to a black man his political rights, as one man stated, "you instantly advance his social status." Whites resisted black political advances because they believed that once progress started building momentum it could not easily be halted. "Once break down the barrier between the races, as to political rights," another explained, "on any qualifications whatever, and every succeeding election would continue to demolish more and more of the barrier until after a while there would be no barrier at all." Short of strong and consistent federal government intervention—which was not forthcoming after the first months of Radical Reconstruction—blacks were not likely to make much headway, and indeed antagonizing whites too much would only cause themselves more trouble. On the positive side, however, as some scholars have pointed out, by accepting the white demand that blacks be segregated, Bettis and other accommodationists contributed to the development of independent black institutions. A ra-

44. *Christian Recorder*, March 10, 1866; Savannah *Colored American*, January 13, 1866.

45. Drago, *Black Politicians and Reconstruction in Georgia*, 45.

cially integrated society in which African Americans had access to social institutions on the same basis as whites was not a realistic prospect in the postemancipation period, even during the era of Radical Reconstruction. The only real option that African Americans had was to develop their own social institutions. Those institutions, particularly the churches, did much during the late nineteenth century to support African Americans and to foster their self-consciousness and pride.[46]

Some preachers, however, defied the power of conservative local whites regardless of whether they enjoyed the support or protection of northern officials. Henry M. Turner became radicalized by his treatment at the hands of whites in the Georgia legislature (Republican and Democrat) in 1868. "I made a great blunder," he confessed, in supporting conservative measures in the constitutional convention. Accusing white Republicans of cowardice, pusillanimity, and treachery, he told them, "You may expel us, gentlemen, but I firmly believe that you will someday repent it." After he left government, he helped blacks organize for their own protection. He was disgusted by the indifference the Republican party showed its black members: "This seems to be the only government on the earth that cannot protect its citizens." Whites repeatedly beat and murdered blacks. "And yet when you appeal to the government for protection, it is so weak and powerless it cannot give any." A country, he said, that could not protect its citizens from lawlessness had no reason to call itself a nation. "I almost hate the land that gave me birth; and if there is not a speedy change, I shall publicly proclaim myself a rebel to my so-called country." Turner was the sort who sent southern whites into paroxysms of anxiety and rage, as was Nick Williams, a South Carolina preacher, who, according to white testimony, gathered crowds of black workers from their labor in the fields and filled them with subversive and rebellious ideas about political and social equality. He reportedly urged blacks to vote only for other blacks and to demand the lands owned by white planters and former slave owners. "Land we must have or we will die." It is hard to tell whether Williams was actually as much of a rabble-rouser as whites claimed he was or whether their reports revealed more about their anxieties than about Williams. "No one can imagine," a white witness reported, "unless he was present among us, the excitement among the negroes. All labour is suspended; our fodder withers in the

46. Vernon Burton, "Race and Reconstruction: Edgefield County, South Carolina," *Journal of Social History*, XII (Fall, 1978), 31–56; Rabinowitz, *Race Relations in the Urban South*, 127.

fields whilst crowds attend the reverend gentleman everywhere he goes." But such reports were persuasive enough to cause a Freedmen's Bureau agent to have Williams arrested for causing disturbances.[47]

Of course, activist ministers and congregation members ran the risk that they would evoke violent and destructive white rage. As Congress' commitment to the Radical Reconstruction governments (and through them the South's black population) waned during the 1870s, white violence directed at blacks and their white supporters mounted. Whites burned churches, threatened and sometimes assaulted offending preachers, and put the people on notice that they were determined to put an end to black political activity. In one state after another, white Democrats began to realize that they could recapture political power from the alliance of black and white Republicans. As John Cobb, a Sumter County, Georgia, planter and Democrat, put it, "We need never fear negro franchise." Ultimately, coercion and intimidation would restore the Democrats to power. "We can control it with little trouble—the only trouble before was that we did not know how to go about it. . . . Every man who voted the Radical ticket in this county was watched & his ticket marked & all are now known & they will never cease to regret it, as long as they live."[48]

The eventual collapse of state governments set up under congressional direction after 1867, a process known as Redemption by most white southerners, was a disheartening experience for blacks. The illusion of a racially integrated society evaporated along with federal government support for the Republican state governments. Blacks were on their own. They had their freedom and they possessed the franchise, and now they were expected to make the most of it.

The northern retreat from the goals of Radical Reconstruction was accompanied by a diminution in white northern missionary activity among blacks in the South. In part, this was the result of the dwindling financial resources available to the northern missionary societies. Officials of the American Baptist Home Mission Society, for example, frequently complained that it could not raise enough money to sustain its

47. Drago, *Black Politicians and Reconstruction in Georgia*, 45; Walker, *Rock in a Weary Land*, 134; *Christian Recorder*, November 25, 1875; Litwack, *Been in the Storm So Long*, 551–52.

48. U.S. Senate, *Testimony to Inquire into Conditions in the Late Insurrectionary States, North Carolina Testimony*, Vol. II, pp. 13–14; Drago, *Black Politicians and Reconstruction in Georgia*, 148.

missionaries in the South. In 1869 James B. Simmons, the society's agent in Georgia, wrote to John A. Rockwell of the Freedmen's Bureau apologizing for the society's failure to send many teachers, who commonly doubled as missionaries, into Georgia. It had sent only five teachers up to that time, but, he said, sometimes the work in one state had to be delayed to ensure that it continued across a broader front. But there were other reasons for the deemphasis on direct missionary activity. By the 1870s both northern and southern Baptists had shown some readiness to work cooperatively rather than competitively in assisting black Baptists to establish and organize their churches. In 1870 the Home Mission Society unanimously adopted a resolution asking "that all remembrance of the late deplorable conflict in arms between two sections of this country shall be blotted out by the blood of Jesus." Northern Baptist activity among southern blacks reached a peak immediately after the Civil War and then steadily declined. As early as 1865 the Home Mission Society had begun to deemphasize direct missionary work. At that time there were only nine missionaries in South Carolina and five in Georgia, two of the states with the largest black populations. By 1879 there were only twenty-one Home Mission Society missionaries working in the entire South.[49]

Many blacks soon reached the conclusion that it was more realistic for them to expect their destinies to depend on an accommodation with southern whites rather than alliances with northern whites. A developing, albeit limited, reconciliation between northern and southern Protestant churches was only further reason for them to achieve their own accommodation with the native whites with whom they had lived and worked all their lives. In 1876 the Colored Baptist Association of Louisiana and Texas resolved to "come to our white fellow-citizens holding out the 'olive branch' of peace and good will. We call upon them to assist us in our efforts to become useful citizens and intelligent Christians." In Alabama, blacks admitted that there still was room for more Christian love between whites and blacks, but there also was much about which to be hopeful. "It must be confessed that a love which is able to live and grow through the quakes, wrecks and ruins which we severally and jointly have passed

49. American Baptist Home Mission Society, *Baptist Home Missions in North America, Including a Full Report of the Jubilee Meeting, and a Historical Sketch of the American Baptist Home Mission Society Tables* (New York, 1883), 406, 412, 414; Joel Williamson, *After Slavery: The Negroes in South Carolina During Reconstruction, 1861–1877* (Chapel Hill, 1965), 376; James B. Simmons to John A. Rockwell, n.d., in Freedmen's Bureau Records.

through, is a love of wonderful strength." Although it was not always seen, "this love which is now unfolding itself from white men toward black men, and from black men toward white men, has lived in some smothered form during all the bitter days of our apparent antagonism." [50]

By the mid-1870s, Reconstruction had run its course. The disputed presidential election of 1876 between the Republican Rutherford B. Hayes and the Democrat Samuel J. Tilden was resolved by an agreement to withdraw federal military support for Reconstruction. The struggles for education and for legal and political rights, which stood at the center of the Radical Reconstruction program and represented the aspirations of freedmen and former free persons, took very different turns. Educational opportunities in the South slowly but steadily improved, but the Republican party's betrayal and white southerners' determination to maintain their unquestioned supremacy put black rights in extreme jeopardy. The churches had been deeply involved in both of these areas of race advancement. They allowed schools to operate in their buildings, and their missionaries organized and sometimes taught both Sunday and secular schools. These efforts placed the church in the middle of the campaign to provide education for southern blacks. Ministers played a conspicuous and constructive role in the political campaigns of Reconstruction. They were present in large proportions in the colored people's conventions, in the Reconstruction constitutional conventions, and in state legislatures. Two ministers, Hiram Revels of Mississippi and Richard H. Cain of South Carolina, represented their states and African Americans in Congress. That so many ministers represented their districts in government stands as convincing evidence that the people trusted them to make important decisions affecting their daily lives. Clearly the church was the most powerful and important social institution in the black community during the crucial Reconstruction period. It provided leadership in vital areas of development. The crucial question for the future, though, was how effectively the church would be in dealing with the issues that confronted blacks after the withdrawal of federal government support, when they were left largely on their own to establish an acceptable relationship with their white former masters.

---

50. Colored Baptist Association of Louisiana and Texas, *Minutes of the Eighth Annual Session of the Colored Baptist Association of Louisiana and Texas . . . 1876* (Marshall, Tex., 1876), 14–15; Colored Missionary Baptist Convention of Alabama, *Minutes of the Eighth Annual Session of the Colored Missionary Baptist Convention of Alabama . . . 1875* (Montgomery, 1875), 21.

5

The Church and Black Nationalism

The idealism of the Reconstruction years engendered among blacks and many powerful Radical Republicans a common vision of an integrated society based on racial equality. To be sure, broad differences about the specific definition of equality stood between them and between elements within each group as well; nonetheless, there was enough common ground to enable them to begin building a new society. The Radical Republicans had quickly rejected the idea of providing blacks with a proprietary interest in the postwar South and the wherewithal to secure their freedom through the distribution of confiscated former Confederate land. But they had attempted through the Freedmen's Bureau to protect the freedmen from masters who were wont to prey on them and had assisted them in acquiring land either by purchase or by tenant-lease contract as a step toward realizing their dream of becoming independent farmers. Although only a few white Republicans accepted blacks as their social equals, civil rights laws in 1866 and 1875 and the Fourteenth and Fifteenth Amendments to the Constitution established the principle of legal and political equality, thereby meeting at least minimal requirements for giving the blacks full citizenship rights. At least for a while, the prospect of continued progress seemed bright.[1]

But the political climate of the country with respect to the race issue changed during the 1870s, bringing storm clouds that by the end of the century rained calamity down upon African Americans and washed away their illusions. New interests and concerns replaced race uplift as a priority in the northern press, in congressional debates, and in elections across the country. The Republican party that had once campaigned on behalf of the freedmen with an uncompromising moral fervor reached the limits

1. Eric Foner, *Reconstruction: America's Unfinished Revolution, 1863–1877* (New York, 1988), 231, 257–58.

of its liberalism long before it had succeeded in building a nonracial society. Not only did its leaders abandon their commitment to clear the freedmen's path of the debris of slavery, but conservative regimes in the southern states put up new obstacles to race advancement. White southerners launched a campaign of violence and intimidation, known as the Mississippi Plan, against blacks and their Republican friends. The subsequent collapse of state governments erected at the beginning of Reconstruction to protect the freedmen and the ascendance of former slave owners once again left blacks at the mercy of men who were determined to arrest rather than advance their progress.[2]

In the distressed southern economy, which showed few signs of recovering from wartime devastation and postwar labor dislocation, antagonistic whites continued their search for ways to control the black work force and exploit its weaknesses by limiting its options. They succeeded in confining most blacks to low-paid wage labor and sharecropping tenancy; consequently, the freedmen did not attain economic independence. The few individuals who did manage to acquire their own land faced the same unpromising prospect as southern agriculture as a whole throughout the last quarter of the nineteenth century, having to sell their crops in a declining share of the world's glutted markets. Periodically, independent farmers—and tenants—fell victim to devastating insect epidemics and floods that alternately decimated their crops and inundated their farms. The capriciousness of global market conditions and natural disasters, of course, could not be laid to race prejudice, but white landlords and merchants exploited the situation and practiced some creative bookkeeping to tighten the economic vise that kept black farmers locked in debt and tied to the land in peonage.[3]

The mood of the North's white population shifted dramatically and with great impact regarding the notion that Washington should regulate race relations in the South. During the 1870s and 1880s, all three branches of the federal government clearly signaled their belief that the people of the South themselves must work out a formula for race rela-

2. James M. McPherson, *The Abolitionist Legacy: From Reconstruction to the NAACP* (Princeton, 1975), 13–139.

3. Janet Sharp Hermann, *The Pursuit of a Dream* (New York, 1981), 214–15; Gerald David Jaynes, *Branches Without Roots: Genesis of the Black Working Class in the American South, 1862–1882* (New York, 1986), 246; Roger L. Ransom and Richard Sutch, *One Kind of Freedom: The Economic Consequences of Emancipation* (Cambridge, Mass., 1977), 13, 81–170.

tions. Congress relinquished responsibility for the welfare of vulnerable blacks after passing the Civil Rights Act of 1875, a measure that prohibited discrimination in public accommodations such as hotels, theaters, and public conveyances. Congressional Republicans were no longer able to muster majorities in favor of protective legislation. The Republican president Rutherford B. Hayes withdrew the few remaining federal troops from the South as part of the bargain that followed his disputed victory over Samuel J. Tilden in the election of 1876. And in a series of cases in 1883 the Supreme Court ruled that the Civil Rights Act of 1875 was unconstitutional. Together, those actions guaranteed the maintenance of white supremacy. A power imbalance that overwhelmingly favored whites, along with the antagonism that whites felt toward blacks in the South, left little doubt that freedom's road would be long and twisting.

During the last quarter of the nineteenth century, southern blacks encountered a daunting array of laws and practices that severely restricted their access to the institutions and social services that would make the difference between happy, satisfying lives and mere existence. Whites employed racial segregation to control the black population. Segregation laws originated and were most evident in towns and cities, where large concentrations of people of both races lived and worked in close proximity and where increasing numbers of blacks were drawn in search of jobs in the New South's mills and factories. Jim Crow, as racial segregation was known, was particularly onerous in cities that had a huge number of rigidly enforced laws and ordinances. From schools to parks to railroad and trolley cars, not only separate facilities but ones that were inferior to those provided for whites signified the inferior status to which whites assigned blacks in southern society. Segregation existed in rural areas, too, but it was not as necessary to white supremacy there because planters continued to exercise firm control over rural blacks. The worlds of blacks and whites across the South became more and more separate and antagonistic and for blacks remained largely empty, bleak, and oppressive.[4]

4. C. Vann Woodward, *The Strange Career Of Jim Crow* (3rd rev. ed.; New York, 1974); Joel Williamson, *The Crucible of Race: Black-White Relations in the American South Since Reconstruction* (New York, 1986), 44–323; Howard N. Rabinowitz, *Race Relations in the Urban South, 1865–1890* (New York, 1978); John W. Cell, *The Highest Stage of White Supremacy: The Origins of Segregation in South Africa and the American South* (Cambridge, Eng., 1982).

During the final twenty-five years of the nineteenth century, southern whites, with the tacit approval of the federal government, subverted the political gains blacks had made during Reconstruction, including enfranchisement and a high level of voting activity, participation in political organizations, and the election of large numbers of their own candidates ranging from local officials to members of Congress. They were determined to eliminate blacks from politics, and state legislatures and Democratic party organizations employed literacy tests, poll taxes, and all-white primary elections to accomplish that end. The exclusionary laws were not 100 percent effective, but a campaign of intimidation against black political participation filled in many of the loopholes. One of the whites' favorite election campaign tactics was race-baiting. Candidates harangued listeners with horror stories about black criminals and swore that blacks would never again share power in the South. In its coverage of political campaigns the white press played directly and often deliberately into the hands of race bigots, inflaming the passions of prejudiced citizens and helping to create an atmosphere so highly charged with hatred that one tiny spark could ignite into explosions of violence.[5]

The campaign of violence and depredation that whites had launched against blacks during the latter stages of the Civil War, which had intensified during the final turbulent years of Reconstruction, showed no signs of abating as the federal government retreated from responsibility for protecting southern blacks and conservative whites "redeemed" the South from justice and equality. Politics motivated much of the hostility, which was aimed at discouraging people who were politically active from voting or running for public office. But intense race hatred evoked white brutality, often in the form of random assaults. One such victim was Elder Lewis Davis of the African Methodist Episcopal church, whose only offense was possessing a dark skin. Marauding whites murdered Davis, by one account "one of the purest and holiest of men," in northern Georgia late in 1878. He had not been politically active and apparently had given no offense to whites either by his actions or his attitude. "He knew nothing, nor did he bother with anything but the souls of men," his friend and presiding elder Henry M. Turner mused. Davis became the object of a lesson in terror through which whites intended to teach all blacks that

5. Neil R. McMillen, *Dark Journey: Black Mississippians in the Age of Jim Crow* (Urbana, 1989), 35–71.

But during the late 1870s, hundreds of men, women, and children packed their worldly belongings on wagons, railroad trains, or steamboats and headed for the promised land. The destination of some of the homesteaders was Arkansas, Indian Territory, or Kansas, but others sought to go to Africa, their ancestral homeland. There were several reasons why African emigration seemed feasible to those humble people despite the great distance they would have to travel to get there. Many of them had grown up hearing stories about Africa and their African ancestors. Henry M. Turner boasted of being descended from African royalty and was correct in saying that such family traditions "doubtless had much to do in forming our African attachments." Some of them knew that earlier in the century colonists very much like themselves had followed Paul Cuffee and the AME minister Daniel Coker to Sierra Leone and had succeeded in making new lives for themselves there. This generation of settlers focused their interest on neighboring Liberia, the colony that the American Colonization Society had founded in 1822. White abolitionists had condemned the society, and blacks generally rejected it because slave owners, to whom colonization seemed like a fine way to rid themselves of unwanted blacks, supported it. But emancipation changed both whites' and blacks' attitudes toward colonization and toward the society. Whites no longer saw as much need to colonize blacks, whereas blacks no longer viewed colonization as forced deportation from their homeland and were more receptive than before to the idea of emigration. The letters and personal accounts of people who had emigrated previously or who had traveled there, which the society printed in its journal, *African Repository,* informed readers about Liberia and made emigration seem like a viable possibility. In addition, the influential propagandists Martin R. Delany and Edward W. Blyden persuaded them to emigrate. Delany had been born of free black parents in Virginia in 1812 and had settled in Pennsylvania before moving on to Rochester to work with Frederick Douglass on the abolitionist paper *North Star* and from there went to Harvard to study medicine. Becoming a proponent of emigrationism, he published a book entitled *The Condition, Elevation, Emigration, and Destiny of the Colored People of the United States, Politically Considered* and led an exploration of the Niger Valley that convinced him of the practicality of colonizing West Africa. Blyden was a native of Jamaica who migrated to Liberia in 1850 at the age of eighteen after spending several years in the United States and reaching the conclusion that there was no hope for blacks there. Both men spoke often to black audiences, urging them to leave the United States and settle in Liberia, and the African-American press publicized their speeches. Blyden worked closely with the American Colonization Society to promote emigrationism. After emancipation, the society lost much of its financial backing, but enough money still flowed into its office from its dwindling number of benefactors to enable it to send anywhere from fifty to one hundred settlers a year to Liberia, paying for their transportation as well as supplying them with provisions to last for six months after their arrival. Thus from an organization southern blacks despised, the society had become a beneficent agency of escape from oppression.[8]

Some blacks, especially members of the educated elite who believed the race should pull itself up by its own bootstraps, thought it essential that emigration be accomplished without white assistance. The first serious effort after emancipation by African Americans to settle in Africa began in 1877 in South Carolina. Interest in emigration boiled up at that time because of prevailing conditions, in particular the violence and intimidation that accompanied the elections of 1876 in the state, the dismal economic picture, and a general disillusionment with Reconstruction. Most of the leading figures in the enterprise were clergymen. Indeed, one of the most outspoken advocates of emigration in the state was Richard H. Cain, the AME missionary and extraordinary church builder, who had also been a state senator and was now the publisher of a newspaper called the *Missionary Record*. His several positions enabled him to influence others to consider going to Africa, and the idea quickly gained popularity. In January Cain wrote from Charleston of the "deep and growing interest taken by the Colored people . . . in the subject of Emigration." He added that "the Colored people of the South are tired of the constant struggle for life and liberty with such results as the 'Miss[iss]ippi Plan' and prefer going where no such obstacles are in their way of enjoying their Liberty." They were held back only because they lacked the means of getting there. Two other important figures in the emigration plan were also clergymen, Harrison N. Bouey, a native Georgian and now a Baptist

8. *Voice of Missions*, February, 1894; Edwin S. Redkey, *Black Exodus: Black Nationalist and Back-to-Africa Movements, 1890–1910* (New Haven, 1969), 18–23, 73–98. The careers of Delany and Blyden are examined in Victor Ullman, *Martin R. Delany: The Beginnings of Black Nationalism* (Boston, 1971), and Hollis R. Lynch, *Edward Wilmot Blyden: Pan-Negro Patriot, 1832–1912* (New York, 1967). For the experiences of Americans who settled in Liberia see Tom W. Shick, *Behold the Promised Land: A History of Afro-American Settler Society in Nineteenth-Century Liberia* (Baltimore, 1977).

minister and Republican probate judge from Edgefield County, who had lost a bid for reelection in 1876, and Benjamin F. Porter, pastor of the Morris Brown AME Church in Charleston. During a mass meeting held to celebrate Liberian independence, Porter proposed that blacks form a joint stock company to facilitate emigration, and before the day was over he had organized the Liberian Exodus Joint Stock Company. Porter became the new company's president and Bouey its secretary. They immediately began to raise money and recruit prospective settlers. Cain promoted the program by printing a standing editorial in his newspaper. "Ho for Africa!" ran the headline. "One million men wanted for Africa." The promotions aroused the people's imagination, but few were able to join the enterprise. Some did, however, such as George Black, who wanted to go to Liberia and give his family the "liberty which I consider very sacraid." Entire communities in South Carolina were reportedly "afflicted with the Liberia fever." The company purchased a ship, the *Azor*, and made ready for its departure. Henry M. Turner, the former AME missionary, Civil War army chaplain, former Republican politician, and convert to colonization, helped dedicate the vessel. AME bishop John M. Brown boarded the ship as the passengers embarked to consecrate a Methodist congregation among the settlers. Some 206 emigrants sailed for Liberia on April 26, 1878. Bouey was not among them, but he went the next year and became pastor of a congregation in Monrovia, preached to native people in western Liberia, and organized the Liberian Baptist Convention. Samuel Flegler led the AME congregation that settled in the promised land.[9]

But the Liberian Exodus Joint Stock Company failed to launch a wave of emigration, and its troubles actually dampened the emigration spirit. Mismanagement caused much suffering among the emigrants and the deaths of twenty-three settlers en route. None of the organizers had any experience in such an endeavor, and they knew nothing about how to plan for it. The settlers were not prepared for the hardships they encountered in the primitive and disease-infested coastal areas where they settled, and there was not enough money to train and support them until they could survive on their own. Most of them remained in Liberia, and some eventually prospered, but discouraging letters from the ones who were stranded and the disheartening stories told by returnees dampened

9. George B. Tindall, "The Liberian Exodus of 1878," *South Carolina Historical Magazine*, LIII (1952), 133–39; *Christian Recorder*, October 5, 1882; William J. Simmons, *Men of Mark: Eminent, Progressive and Rising* (1887; rpr. New York, 1968), 867, 951–53.

much of the enthusiasm for emigration to Africa. The final blow fell on the company when a court judge ordered it to auction off its vessel to settle an assortment of legal claims stemming from cost overruns it had been unable to meet. It sent no more settlers to Liberia. But even though this project failed and the impracticality of mass emigration as a solution to the problems that beset blacks became apparent, the discontent that gave birth to it was not dispelled. Indeed, conditions in the South only got worse for blacks, and emigrationists continued to expatiate on the virtues of repatriation to Africa.[10]

Emigration, whether from America to Africa, the Caribbean, or the western frontier, raised several important moral as well as practical questions for both blacks and whites. One was whether, as the emigrationists believed, blacks ought to cease submitting themselves to white injustice, or as the opponents expressed it, whether it was better to stay and defend their rights rather than surrender their livelihoods and even their American citizenship in exchange for a harsh, uncertain existence elsewhere. Those who argued that blacks should stay put, including Senator Blanche K. Bruce of Mississippi and Frederick Douglass, were mostly members of the upper-class elite who had managed to prosper in white America. Many of them were northerners or residents of Washington, D.C., who lived in an environment that was less hostile toward blacks than the South was. Emigration made little sense to them. The people who were inclined to leave were poor southern black folk. For them the prospects for freedom and personal fulfillment elsewhere, at least as recruiters presented them, were much brighter than the reality at home. But the controversy was not confined to what emigration meant to those who might choose to leave; it also raised concerns about those who would stay behind. The departure of large numbers of blacks carried implications for the economy insofar as it threatened to reduce the labor force upon which southern planters and industrial employers depended. Whites were opposed to such a loss and were prepared to go to considerable lengths to prevent it. In some cases, the whites' fear of losing their laborers caused them to make concessions on rents and wages in an effort to dissuade blacks from emigrating. Whites also circulated exaggerated reports of misery and death among those who went to Africa, and they made blacks who promoted exodus targets of violence and intimidation. Curtis Pollard, a Baptist minister in Louisiana, was only one activist whom whites

10. Tindall, "Liberian Exodus," 139–45.

harassed and finally hounded out of the South because of his assistance to other blacks who chose to move to Kansas. Whites believed that by driving off such disruptive influences they could force other blacks to remain where they were. And the price blacks would have to pay for remaining in the South was absolute submission to white power. Emigration also challenged the power structure that was developing among blacks by removing masses of people from such social and political institutions as churches, fraternal societies, and political organizations, thereby diminishing the power of the individuals who managed those institutions. It might also take away the greatest contributors to the cause of race progress. One of the more frequently heard reasons for opposing emigration was that it would draw off skilled and educated blacks and cripple the race's effort to advance toward true freedom and equality with whites.[11]

Church leaders lined up on both sides of the emigration issue. They were conspicuous among the organizers and promoters of emigration programs, and emigration probably would not have happened at all had it not been for their efforts. The local clergy in the South not only organized their congregations' emigrations but often accompanied their flocks. Some denominational leaders viewed the movement of people to new territory as a way to enlarge the power and influence of the church. The black church, like Christianity generally, was vigorously expansionist. Missions would follow the people, then regional conferences would form, and associations and eventually statewide and international organizations that would allow the church to keep pace with the spirit of expansionism that had carried it into the South after emancipation. By contrast, preachers whose congregations were more vulnerable to the appeal of emigration than they were and who would lose substantial numbers of their followers were among emigration's critics. Opposition preachers, including and especially the northern-based ministers who worried that a mass exodus would decimate the African-American population and encourage white racism, expressed a hopeful if unrealistic optimism about the future of race relations in the South, saying that hostile whites would finally wake up to the wickedness of their ways and begin to follow the Christian principle—which they often professed—of treating all people

11. Nell Irvin Painter, *Exodusters: Black Migration to Kansas After Reconstruction* (New York, 1977), 141, 143, 245–50; Charles Vincent, *Black Legislators in Louisiana During Reconstruction* (Baton Rouge, 1976), 53; *Christian Recorder,* September 28, October 19, 1882, April 12, 1883.

with love and kindness. Yet ironically, even as these preachers spoke, whites employed violence and intimidation to break up emigration schemes and tighten their stranglehold on the black population.[12]

Although emigration was an inflammatory issue, the back-to-Africa movement evoked a particularly strong response from leaders. Unlike the Kansas migration, immigration to Africa meant expatriation. It was a huge step to take, and even its proponents sometimes advised careful consideration before doing it. William H. Heard, an AME minister, argued in 1883 that blacks should not go to Africa "while there is so much that needs to be done and can be done at home." He urged people to "go West in as large numbers as the times demand." References to Africa struck powerfully responsive chords. Proponents of back-to-Africa emigration conceived of it within the framework of a Christian theology and black nationalism that appealed to downtrodden people. The theme of deliverance, featured prominently in slave religion, still ran through the southern black church after emancipation and had particular relevance following the disillusionment of Reconstruction. Many people thought emigration would bring freedom from oppression and that the redemption of Africa would follow through the civilizing influence of American emigrants. During the 1850s and 1860s, the northern ministers Henry Highland Garnet and Alexander Crummell had expressed their belief that the deliverance of black Americans from white oppression was tied to the redemption of Africa. Their "African civilization" program, through which Western culture acquired by black Americans would be implanted in Africa and used to lead the continent out of its intellectual darkness and spiritual depravity, would ultimately elevate both Africans and black Americans. If Africa were to be regenerated, Crummell argued, "the agencies to this end must come from external sources. Civilization . . . never springs up, spontaneously, in any new land. It must be transplanted." Crummell was convinced that it was God's plan to use civilized and Christianized black Americans to redeem Africa and that good deed would contribute to their salvation. Many black preachers presented emigration as the strategy through which God's plan would be implemented. They heard the voice of Providence commanding them to "return to the land of your fathers" and were eager to obey. Old Testament prophecy (Psa. 68:31, for example) foretold that "Ethiopia shall soon stretch out

12. John Dittmer, *Black Georgia in the Progressive Era, 1900–1920* (Urbana, 1977); Tindall, "Liberian Exodus," 134–35.

her hands unto God." The Reverend Benjamin Gaston, who led an effort to settle blacks in the Congo, was not the only minister who invoked scriptural allusions to justify emigration. "The Ethiopian," he declared from a dock in New York Harbor as colonists whom he had recruited prepared to embark, "shall stretch forth his hand unto God an' shall worship Him under his own vine and fig tree." [13]

Despite the scriptural rationale and the appeals to racial identity with Africa, the idea of repatriation evoked vociferous opposition from many community leaders, including members of the clergy, who objected to it on practical as well as philosophical grounds. The list of things that they saw wrong with going to Liberia was lengthy. They argued, justifiably, that the country's history was punctuated with hardship, failure, and death. None of the resettlement enterprises of the late nineteenth century adequately prepared settlers for life in a new environment. Once they arrived, they were cut adrift to fend for themselves. Malaria plagued the settlers, who had access to only meager medical facilities. And the task of reclaiming land from the forest and turning it into productive farms had proven much harder than promoters had said. A steady stream of returnees testified to failure and disillusionment. There also were allegations that Liberia condoned slavery. The indigenous people practiced slavery, and the Liberians who had come earlier from America employed a system of apprenticeship that amounted to bondage. Even if those problems could be rectified, there were many other objections. One of the strongest arguments was that the United States was their home, and blacks should remain and fight for their rights and make productive lives for themselves. It was acceptable for a few emigrationists to work as missionaries and teachers to help Africans progress and to bring recognition to the race. "This we favor," wrote Benjamin Tucker Tanner, an AME minister, "with no idea, however, of surrendering our position in America." The antiemigrationists' major point, which went to the heart of black Americans' problem of identity, was that despite being black in white America

13. Painter, *Exodusters*, 243–50; *Christian Recorder*, April 12, 1883; Gayraud S. Wilmore, *Black Religion and Black Radicalism: An Interpretation of the Religious History of Afro-American People* (2nd ed.; Maryknoll, 1983); Wilson Jeremiah Moses, *Alexander Crummell: A Study of Civilization and Discontent* (New York, 1989), 133; David L. Williams, *Black Americans and the Evangelization of Africa, 1877–1900* (Madison, 1982), 11; Edwin S. Redkey, ed., *Respect Black: The Writings and Speeches of Henry McNeal Turner* (New York, 1971, 42; New York *Times*, March 10, 1894.

and the emotional attraction to Africa, they were, after all, Americans and not Africans.[14]

During late 1882 and early 1883, a debate over African emigration raged in the pages of the AME church's newspaper the *Christian Recorder*. Several writers contributed to the discussion, but the key figures were Benjamin T. Tanner and Henry M. Turner. Tanner, who was the paper's editor, represented the northern-based establishment's view. He had been born in Pittsburgh in 1835. His father died when he was a boy, and his mother depended on his care. Working as a barber, he not only met her needs but also paid his way through Avery College and the Presbyterian Western Theological Seminary. After serving as minister for a Washington congregation of Presbyterians, he joined the AME church and established a Sabbath school for freedmen and ministered to a Methodist church in Washington during the Civil War. Afterward he operated freedmen's schools in Maryland and in 1868 was appointed to succeed James Lynch as editor of the *Christian Recorder*, headquartered in Philadelphia.[15]

Turner, a maverick churchman, whose offices were in Georgia, regarded himself as the spokesman of the common black folk of the South against the mainly northern-based hierarchs, whom he believed were ready at the twinkling of an eye to accommodate white oppression. Turner was sturdy in both body and mind, and his prodigious intellectual and oratorical powers were just beginning to ripen. He showed little willingness to accommodate to white power, preferring direct confrontation. His illusions about a harmonious, nonracial community in America had been shattered by his Reconstruction experiences, especially his expulsion from the Georgia legislature by his erstwhile white Republican allies. The Republican party's evaporating commitment to blacks had turned him into a bitter man full of contempt, not only for whites but also for sycophantic blacks to whom he often referred as "scullions" (and among whom he included the church's conservative northern leaders). He was scornful of Republicans and, in the end, the entire nation. He hated southern whites for what they were doing to his people, but he saw little to choose between them and white northerners, who as a whole sat idly by as his people's rights were stolen away. "True, I am grateful for the

14. Redkey, *Black Exodus*, 129–33; *Christian Recorder*, April 18, 1878.
15. Simmons, *Men of Mark*, 985–88.

services of a few individuals, but in the aggregate I have no thanks for either." He had abandoned political activity in favor of church work after being expelled from the legislature and in 1880 was elevated to the bishopric of his church over the opposition of many of the church's younger and more moderate hierarchs, but he continued to comment publicly on race issues. His trademark was the verbal "thunderbolts" that he hurled at the nation and its symbols. "I think my race has been treated by it with the kindness that a hungry snake treats a helpless frog," he said. He declared that the federal government's refusal to protect the rights of black citizens "absolves the negro's allegiance to the general government, makes the American flag to him a rag of contempt instead of a symbol of liberty." A vehement promoter of race pride, Turner abhorred references to color in Christian teaching that suggested an association between whiteness and purity or between blackness and evil or filth. He refused to sing the verse "Now wash me and I shall be whiter than snow" because, he said, "the Negro will believe that the devil is black" and that he "was the devil." "This is one of the reasons why we favor African emigration." He understood the corrosive effect of white cultural tyranny on black self-esteem and tried to neutralize it by rebuking those who felt no self-pride. "Every colored man in this country," he declared in an open letter to Blanche K. Bruce, "who is not proud of himself, his color, his hair, and his general make-up is a monstrosity." Insisting that all people and races, including blacks, have a right to think of themselves in the image of God, he preached that "God is a Negro."[16]

Turner had considered immigration to Africa before the Civil War, but he did not actively promote the idea until after emancipation. In 1866, even though he was still somewhat hopeful about the race's future in America, he asked the American Colonization Society for information about Africa and started making speeches on the subject. By the end of Reconstruction he had lost all hope for an American destiny: "There is no more doubt in my mind that we have ultimately to return to Africa than there is of the existence of a God; and the sooner we begin to recognize that fact and prepare for it, the better it will be for us as a people." Convinced that equality for blacks was a chimera in "this bloody, lynch-

16. *Christian Recorder,* January 15, 1875, March 25, 1880, February 22, November 8, 1883; John Dittmer, "The Education of Henry McNeal Turner," in *Black Leaders of the Nineteenth Century,* ed. Leon Litwack and August Meier (Urbana, 1988), 259–72; Redkey, ed., *Respect Black,* 77.

ing nation," he threw his boundless energy, his pen, and his prestige as a bishop in the church behind emigration.[17]

Tanner fired the opening salvo in the contest over emigration with a series of editorials condemning it and its principal proponent, Edward W. Blyden. Blyden was in the country to raise money for Liberia College, but as an ardent promoter of African-American emigration he could not pass up an opportunity to urge American blacks to settle in Liberia. Arguing that they had no future in the United States because it was not their country, he urged at least half a million, especially skilled and educated people, to return immediately to their ancestral homeland. Act according to race, he exhorted his audiences; unite with fellow blacks in Africa and become free from oppression. He also appealed to the Americans' sense of duty to help redeem Africa. Tanner's reply suggested that Blyden possessed little understanding of black Americans. They had scarcely anything in common with Africans, Tanner insisted. "To speak plainly . . . we are simply black white men." The only basis on which black Americans could relate to Africans was color; in every other way they related to America. He feared that Blyden's race ideology would encourage whites to reverse the progress of the Reconstruction era. To think of themselves as Africans instead of Americans would "estrange us from our white fellow citizens" and "change the channel of our future." Tanner felt that Africa had very little to offer black people beyond misery and degradation. Like many elite American blacks, he not only identified with white America but shared the chauvinism of nineteenth-century whites as well. The African, he asserted, was "savage, or at most, semi-civilized. . . . We know we are not, and yet by a most destructive sentiment, not a few of us insist upon linking our destiny with him, when the fates have marked out for us a destiny far different . . . an American destiny." America held forth an abundance of blessings. To trade one for the other, as Blyden suggested, would be absurd and "utterly destructive to our American destiny." He admitted that conditions were far from perfect, but instead of running from prejudice and discrimination and seeking refuge in Africa, the black man ought to exhibit the moral courage to "stand his ground and conquer it, especially when he has such ground to stand upon." Referring to the influx of immigrants fleeing from oppression in Europe, which advo-

17. Redkey, ed., *Respect Black*, 13, 42–44, 52–59; August Meier, *Negro Thought in America, 1880–1915* (Ann Arbor, 1963), 218.

cates of emigration often cited as an example for blacks, he denied that
the analogy was appropriate. The oppressions were not the same. Irish
degradation "is such as we nowhere have seen among the colored people
of this country, while our position is becoming better every day." He argued that German immigrants had lost their cultural identity after settling in America and deduced that blacks would become assimilated into
the inferior culture of Africa, much to their misfortune, if they moved
there permanently. Tanner was scornful of any supposed duty that American blacks owed to Africans. He could not understand how sacrificing
themselves would contribute to Africans' uplift. "The measure of a man's
duty to another, regardless of his race, is the measure of his duty to himself." Above all, Tanner worried that emigration would lead to a massive
depopulation of black Americans, especially talented leaders, that would
leave the remainder even more vulnerable to mistreatment than before. A
few teachers and missionaries might go, but half a million emigrants was
too many.[18]

Tanner's editorials and an address he delivered to the Pennsylvania
Colonization Society late in 1882, in which he sharply attacked both Blyden and Henry M. Turner, caused Turner to unleash a vigorous counter-
attack and a strong defense of emigration in a series of articles in the
Christian Recorder. He differentiated between the northern elite and the
plain people of the South on the basis of their conditions and needs. Writing of "the relief for which our people sigh," he meant the common
people of the South. "If the Northern Negro is satisfied with matters and
things, we of the South are far from being." The heart of his argument
was that outrages were mounting and southern blacks faced a life-or-
death threat far more serious than the bouts with malaria that Liberian
settlers encountered. "Many of us think that the acclimating headaches
of Africa, though sometimes possibly fatal, are not to be compared with
such an orgy of blood and death." He accused Tanner of dabbling in
"moral philosophy" in the comfort and security of his Philadelphia office
while black people were dying at the hands of whites in the South. He
ridiculed Tanner's assertion that conditions in the country were good for
blacks and were improving. "This is the first time in my life I have found
a colored man who had the effrontery to deny, or even attempt a partial
negation of the unhuman treatment we have suffered at the hands of the

18. *Christian Recorder*, September 28, October 19, November 9, 23, 1882, April 12,
1883.

nation's banditti." Something had to be done or the race would face ex-
tinction. "Matters cannot go on as at present, and the remedy is thought
by tens of thousands to be in a negro nationality." Turner recognized "the
fact of our American-ship" as fully as Tanner did, but he was outraged
because these Americans, who had sacrificed for the freedom and independence of their country, were yet denied the rights of citizenship and
human dignity. "We were born here, raised here, fought, bled and died
here, and have a thousand times more right here than hundreds of thousands of those who help to snub, proscribe and persecute us, and that is
one of the reasons I almost despise the land of my birth." He was disgusted by what he regarded as the detached and irrelevant theorizing of
people like Tanner: "So much for Dr. Tanner and his mistaken position." [19]

In addition to attacking Tanner for being out of touch with conditions
in the South, Turner outlined his own ideas about emigration. He argued
forcefully for empowerment within a race context. He believed no race of
people would be respected until it founded a country and set up a functioning and effective government. "This has not been done creditably yet
by the civilized negro, and till it is done he will be a mere scullion in the
eyes of the world." He wanted a refuge for black Americans. Echoing
Crummell's "providential plan," he averred that "any person whom-
soever opposes the return of a sufficient number of her descendants to
begin the grand work . . . is fighting the God of the universe face to face."
Southern blacks, he said, had a great yearning to fulfill God's promise;
they lacked only the means of accomplishing it. The American Colonization Society had offered to assist in resettling people in Africa, and "they
are our best friends and greatest benefactors." Turner argued that the federal government owed black people $40 billion "for actual services ren-
dered" in the development of the country for two hundred years and that
amount would be sufficient, if paid, to relocate from five to ten thousand
people a year. Answering Tanner's point that mass emigration would de-
stroy the future of those who chose to remain in the United States, Turner
insisted that he was not advocating mass exodus. Blacks were not prepared for that, and neither was Africa. "Such a course would be madness
in the extreme and folly unpardonable." But any who wished to go
should be encouraged and provided with the means of doing so, and with
a few thousand a year "I could establish a government, build a country

19. *Ibid.*, January 4, 25, February 22, 1883.

and raise a national symbol that could give character to our people every-where." [20]

Turner's notions about emigration exemplified his well-defined sense of nationalism, which saw black Americans joined with Africans in a common struggle for freedom and self-reliance. But in the typical fashion of nineteenth-century nationalists, his ideas were culture-bound and did not represent pan-Africanism as it would emerge in the twentieth century, accepting the validity of traditional African culture. Turner did not, for instance, think of himself as an African as Paul Robeson or even William E. B. Du Bois did, and rather than stressing what American blacks could gain from African culture, he was interested in the reverse. His feelings about Africa were intense, but his attitude toward African culture and the linkage between Africa and African Americans was ambivalent. He admitted thinking almost constantly about the land of his forefathers. "I weave Africa into all my prayers, sermons, lectures, addresses and ad-monitions." And his words certainly contained elements of pan-Africanism, especially after he made three trips there during the 1890s. There was a racial connection. Of Africans, he once observed: "These are my folks. We all came from that stock." He also identified with Africans regarding experiences of slavery. He equated the European exploitation of Africa with the enslavement of African Americans and argued that the only way for both to realize freedom was through self-reliance and self-respect. "A man must believe he is somebody before he is acknowledged to be somebody." The obvious answer was a union of the two people in Africa. "Nothing will remedy the evils of the Negro but a great Christian nation upon the continent of Africa." He dreamed of great black nations emerging from weakness and European exploitation and colonization to rank with the great nations of the world, and he envisioned African Americans contributing to that renaissance. But he visualized an African-American zion in Africa rather than native African nations built on tra-ditional cultures. Africans would be transformed and Westernized, and he did not believe that they could advance toward civilization without the assistance of African Americans. Turner always emphasized the reloca-tion of black Americans, the fulfillment of their destiny, and the logic of Africa as the place to realize that destiny. "Now what is my position?" he asked. "Simply to found and establish a country or a government some-where upon the continent of Africa, as I see no other place in the world

20. *Ibid.*, February 22, 1883.

to do it, where our young men and ladies can find a theatre of activity and usefulness, and commence a career for the future that will meet the wants of posterity, at the same time build up a center of Christian civilization that will help redeem the land of our ancestry." Thus, instead of linking the destiny of African Americans with that of independent and traditional African societies, Turner took for granted African-American domination that would remake Africans and African society based on Western culture.[21]

Reflecting the dilemma of identity felt by many emigrationists, Bishop Turner remained an American and continued to use American culture as the standard against which he measured African values, folkways, and institutions even as he denounced his country for its treatment of blacks. He preferred the term *emigration,* which implied leaving one home for another one, to *repatriation,* the word native Africans used in referring to African Americans returning to their only home—Africa. "The native African, from the kings down, cannot realize that the black man in America is at home across the sea." While he was en route to Sierra Leone and Liberia in 1891, an American ship overtook the vessel he was on. His response revealed the ambivalence of his feelings. "I was glad to see our flag, while I knew that there was not a star in the galaxy that recognized the manhood of her black inhabitants." And while in Africa, he spoke condescendingly of native languages (recording native speech in crude phonetic renderings instead of trying to discern specific words) and praised the success of African-American settlers in laying out towns and building houses with dormer windows just like those he was accustomed to back home.[22]

Usually when people accused him, as Tanner did, of seeing Africa only as a refuge for American blacks, he denied it, but at least once he defended that motive on grounds that self-interest and self-preservation constituted acceptable behavior. It was basically the same Social Darwinist rationale for imperialism that whites used. Employing the same argument that Tanner had made in criticizing both Blyden and him, he asked, "Does not our existence depend upon providing for self?" and re-

---

21. Sterling Stuckey, *Slave Culture: Nationalist Theory and the Foundations of Black America* (New York, 1987), 324–29; James Tierney Campbell, "Our Fathers, Our Children: The African Methodist Episcopal Church in the United States and South Africa" (Ph.D. dissertation, Stanford University, 1989), 57–60; Williams, *Black Americans and the Evangelization of Africa,* 52; Redkey, ed., *Respect Black,* 58, 71–72.

22. Redkey, ed., *Respect Black,* 54, 95, 131–32.

sponded, "Yes, I would make Africa the place of refuge, because I see no other shelter from the stormy blast, from the red tide of persecution, from the horrors of American prejudice."[23]

In the end, the debate neither resolved the issues that emigration had raised nor forged a consensus within the black church. Turner remained the champion of the poor masses of southern blacks and the spokesman for African emigration within the community, but a new wedge was driven between the upper-class northern wing of the church and its southern working-class counterpoint with Turner at the helm. T. Thomas Fortune, originally from Florida but now a resident of New York and editor of the New York *Globe,* was ambivalent on the matter but remarked insightfully: "We will say this much, that Dr. Tanner may speak, in his view, the prevailing opinion of northern colored men, while Bishop Turner may speak that of the South. [But] whatever may be the wishes of the thoughtful men of the race, the masses of our people in the South are growing fearfully restless." Most of the thoughtful men of the race, both integrationist and nationalist, regardless of complexion or philosophy, were opposed to Turner. Frederick Douglass had always favored assimilation. A mulatto, married to a white woman, he worked for the total absorption of blacks into American life. The religion and civilization of blacks, he wrote in an article for the *North American Review,* were "in harmony with those of the people among whom he lives." The black nationalist Alexander Crummell had become disillusioned about life in Liberia after residing there for the better part of twenty years and urged blacks to seek an American destiny, albeit as "a nation within a nation." His denominational leaders, Daniel Payne, Wesley Gaines, and most of the other AME bishops also opposed him. Even Richard H. Cain, elevated to the bishopric in 1880 along with Turner and for a time the church's director of African missions, boasted of the achievements of blacks at home and predicted a unified and thoroughly integrated nation, "no Black, no White, no Saxon, no Negro, but a great happy peaceful nation." Bishop Jabez P. Campbell, who had a southern constituency and a long interest in Africa, was Turner's principal ally among the hierarchs. Turner clearly had his finger much closer to the pulse of the masses of southern black folk than his critics did.[24]

23. *Ibid.,* 54.

24. New York *Globe,* January 12, 1883; Meier, *Negro Thought in America,* 66–67; *A.M.E. Church Review,* II (July, 1885), *passim,* and II (October, 1885), 145; *North American Review,* CXXXIX (July, 1884), 84–85; Moses, *Alexander Crummell,* 207–11.

Several events in the 1870s and 1880s related to the struggle for advancement portended a further worsening of African Americans' condition during the final years of the nineteenth century. Economic depressions increased the pressure on black farmers, laborers, and businessmen. Blacks were locked out of the most remunerative occupations and professions by the color bar, and the Supreme Court's ruling that the Civil Rights Act of 1875 was unconstitutional paved the way for the expansion of racial segregation. The barriers to biracial social interaction grew higher and higher. The Protestant Episcopal church, which had not formally segregated blacks before, did so beginning in 1883. Southern bishops, meeting in Sewanee, Tennessee, adopted a canon that provided for the maintenance of separate black congregations under the supervision of white bishops. The maturing Jim Crow system not only separated the races but oppressed and humiliated blacks, as was reflected by a municipal park sign that declared, "No niggers and no dogs allowed." The failure of the Republican Congress in 1890 to enact into law a measure, known as the Force Bill, drafted to protect black voters from harassment at the polls, symbolized the *laissez-faire* policy of the federal government regarding southern race relations. White supremacy was reaching its zenith and black freedom its nadir, and any black who dared challenge white power by standing up for his rights risked being cruelly struck down. Such indeed was the fate of three young Memphis grocers who were murdered by a white mob in 1892 for trying to defend themselves and their business from a white man who operated a store on the opposite corner and was determined to "clean them out" of the neighborhood.[25]

Nothing degraded and demoralized southern blacks more than the lynching and mob violence to which they were subjected with sickening frequency during the 1890s. In denying blacks the basic rights of justice and showing utter disregard for their lives, whites sounded the depths of their enormous contempt for blacks and revealed the magnitude of their inhumanity as well. Mobs of whites whose racial hatred knew virtually no bounds murdered more than one hundred blacks per year during the decade. They were cruelly beaten, burned, butchered, and shot to death.[26]

25. New York *Globe,* June 3, 1883; Shapiro, *White Violence and Black Response,* 105; Ida B. Wells, *Southern Horrors: Lynch Law in All Its Phases* (1892; rpr. New York, 1969), 18–19.

26. National Association for the Advancement of Colored People, *Thirty Years of Lynching in the United States, 1889–1918* (New York, 1919), 7, 10.

Lynchings and riots were not merely criminal assaults upon individual blacks committed by mobs of white hoodlums. They were symptoms of the deeply rooted racial tensions of the postwar South and signified the hatred white society felt toward the entire race. The victims were symbols, their real personalities and identities obscured by stereotypical characteristics that reflected the grotesque black image that haunted the white mind. Lynchings were crimes inflicted on the black community by a wide range of people from all strata of white society. Lower-class whites perpetrated racial violence, but otherwise respectable whites were often present in lynch mobs too. White community leaders openly defended the violence by insisting that the victims were vicious criminals, whose acts, especially the rape of white women, were so savage as to cause them to forfeit the right to a court trial. Demagogic politicians shamelessly exploited the deep prejudice and hatred harbored by whites of all classes to arouse passions during election campaigns in order to win votes. Many of the worst cases of white mob violence occurred immediately after election campaigns in which the alleged criminality of blacks had been used as a campaign issue. The white press fueled racial strife through its coverage of black crimes and by encouraging white violence. When a black newspaper in Memphis condemned lynchings that had occurred in the vicinity in 1892 and suggested that blacks might retaliate, the *Evening Scimitar* retorted that patience in the face of such threats was not a virtue and that "it will be the duty of those whom he has attacked to tie the wretch who utters these calumnies to a stake at the intersection of Main and Madison Sts., brand him in the forehead with a hot iron and perform upon him a surgical operation with a pair of tailor's shears." Rather than being motivated by black criminality, lynchings and mob violence were the result of a general race hatred. The justification whites most often gave was that lynching was necessary to teach blacks the consequences of assaulting white women, yet less than 20 percent of the lynching victims had even been accused of rape. Whites were not trying to correct blacks' behavior; they were using terror to oppress them. Mary Church Terrell, a leader of Washington society and of the campaign against lynching, noted that "it is just as impossible for the negroes of this country to prevent mob violence by any attitude of mind which they may assume, or any course of conduct which they may pursue, as it is for a straw dam to stop Niagara's flow." [27]

27. Wells, *Southern Horrors*, 4–5; Shapiro, *White Violence and Black Response*, 122.

Mob violence terrorized virtually all blacks because all were potential victims. It could come without warning, and there was no hiding from it. Alleged crimes committed by blacks drove whites into frenzies of uncontrollable rage, inspiring them to arm themselves and rampage through cities such as Memphis, New Orleans, Wilmington, and Atlanta, attacking black people wherever they found them, beating them, shooting them, and burning their homes and shops. During the New Orleans riot of 1900, which started when a black man shot an abusive white policeman in self-defense, a mob of armed white longshoremen sighted another black man walking along the levee and began chasing him with their guns blazing. Frantic, the man fled into the French Quarter, desperately trying to elude his pursuers. When he stumbled in the street and realized that he could not get away, he turned to the mob and pleaded for his life. His desperate appeals were answered with a hail of bullets that dropped him to the pavement mortally wounded. As they approached him, they fired more shots, blasting away his face, and then butchered him with knives. The police arrested no one at the scene and no witnesses came forward to identify any members of the mob. Across the South, blacks accused of crimes were dragged from jails, usually under the averted eyes of white jailers and policemen, and strung up from trees or telephone poles, shot full of holes, and set on fire. The hideous mutilations that accompanied the lynchings were graphic evidence of the hatred and determination to degrade blacks. Not satisfied with murdering their victims, the perpetrators beat them with sticks and irons until their bodies were bloody pulp, cut off fingers, toes, and genitals, shot sometimes fifty to a hundred bullets into the corpses, and incinerated the remains.[28]

The terror that gripped the black community amid this bloody wave of violence caused people to look desperately for help. Often it was nowhere to be found. Local authorities frequently abetted the mobs rather than protected the victims. The churches, institutions of peace, were ill equipped to provide a shield against the savage fury of white racism. Their leaders could only express outrage, petition the authorities for protection, and hold out the prospect of providential justice. Indeed, the clergy were often targets too. Some leaders spoke out angrily, often from

28. Ida B. Wells-Barnett, *Mob Rule in New Orleans: Robert Charles and His Fight to the Death* (N.d.; rpr. New York, 1969), 22–23. Wells-Barnett assembled statistics on lynchings and provided descriptions of several incidences of lynching, mostly taken from the press, in *A Red Record: Tabulated Statistics and Alleged Causes of Lynchings in the United States, 1892–1893–1894* (N.d.; rpr. New York, 1969).

a safe distance, against white violence and urged people to protest against it. Elias C. Morris, president of the National Baptist Convention, advised people "to be law-abiding, no matter how much they may suffer thereby," but not to suffer without protest "the inhuman treatment administered to members of our race." He declared that any person "who will not lift his voice in defense of the sacredness of the home and the chastity of the women in this country, is unworthy to be called a man." But other ministers—one is inclined to think most—adopted a strategy of lying low and avoiding language and behavior that might provoke white attacks. Baptist ministers in North Carolina resolved to "severely condemn" outrages committed against black men and women, but they further resolved "to impress upon our people the necessity of avoiding by word or action anything that will produce race conflict and strife." The Reverend T. W. Henderson visited Meridian, Mississippi, in 1899, "said to be rather a warm place for our people every once in a while." He went about his work, paying "strict attention to business" and not bothering whites in the town. The people's vulnerability deepened both their sense of helplessness and their alienation. A North Carolina woman who came face to face with mob violence in Wilmington conveyed her despair in a letter pleading for federal protection against white violence. Where else could she and her neighbors turn? White violence was running wild, and local authorities were doing nothing to stop it. She wondered, "Are we to die like rats in a trap?" Blacks once more looked to Africa as a refuge. Perhaps there they would be free of the hatred and violence that were aimed at them in the South.[29]

The idea of emigration had remained alive through the efforts of a combination of very different people with widely divergent motives. The American Colonization Society continued to send almost one hundred settlers a year to Liberia and publicized its program through the *African Repository*. In 1889 Edward W. Blyden was back in the United States aggressively promoting emigration. Liberia's neighboring European colonies, Sierra Leone on its northern border and the French on the east, had

29. Meier, *Negro Thought in America*, 73–74; Milton C. Sernett, ed., *Afro-American Religious History: A Documentary Witness* (Durham, 1985), 277; North Carolina Baptist Educational and Missionary Convention, *Proceedings of the Joint Sessions of the Baptist Educational and Missionary Convention, the Ministerial Union, the Hayes-Fleming Foreign Missionary Society, and the State Sunday School Convention of North Carolina . . . 1889* (Winton, N.C., 1890), 7; *Christian Recorder*, January 19, 1899; Shapiro, *White Violence and Black Response*, 72.

taken advantage of the Liberians' failure to develop the interior of the country and seized large chunks of territory. The government sent Blyden to recruit settlers to occupy and help defend Liberia. Although he got a cool reception from northerners, southern audiences welcomed him warmly and listened rapturously as he urged them to return to the land of their ancestors. While Blyden was making his pitch for emigration, Senator Matthew C. Butler of South Carolina introduced a bill in Congress to appropriate funds to assist blacks who wished to leave the South to emigrate. The Butler bill assumed the character of a deportation measure, though, when the segregationist John T. Morgan of Alabama endorsed it. Morgan, who also wanted the United States to establish commercial relations with the new colonies that European countries were establishing in West and Central Africa, believed that emigration might provide the basis for developing an African trade as well as for removing blacks from the South and preventing the "general amalgamation of races." Although the Butler bill failed to pass, debate over it helped revive interest in emigration.[30]

The formidable presence of Henry M. Turner, however, was most influential in rallying people to abandon a country where they were hated for an African continent that he said waited to embrace them. His ranting on the subject had kept emigration alive in the minds of black people. He was approaching the age of sixty and still hurling "thunderbolts" at his white antagonists. He wore his crankiness like a badge, but it was a brand of opprobrium in the eyes of his conservative critics. Alexander Crummell, once an emigrationist but now a staunch opponent of the back-to-Africa movement, referred to Turner as "that truculent, screeching and screaming creature." His most offensive utterance was a bitter denunciation of the United States and its flag: "I used to love what I thought was the grand old flag, and sing with ecstasy about the Stars and Stripes, but to the negro in this country the American flag is a dirty and contemptible rag." Although he had said the same thing many times before, he had achieved national stature, and his remarks were widely reported in the press.[31]

Henry Turner was the person most responsible for generating excitement among southern blacks for African emigration in 1891 and 1892, although a few other black church leaders had joined him. William H.

30. Redkey, *Black Exodus*, 47–98.
31. Moses, *Alexander Crummell*, 244; Redkey, ed., *Respect Black*, 196; Meier, *Negro Thought in America*, 218.

Heard had been a Turner disciple since Reconstruction and recently had been appointed United States minister resident and consul general to Liberia. Charles S. Morris, financial secretary of the National Baptist Convention, was another ardent and outspoken emigrationist. Turner's comments in secular newspapers, numerous speeches, and articles in the *Voice of Missions,* a paper that he started and edited from his headquarters in Georgia, kept the topic in the center of public attention. He traveled extensively through the South and West encouraging blacks to emigrate. During his African trip in 1891 and on a return visit in 1893, he sent home letters in which he touted the vast potential for success there owing to the abundance of cultivable land, plentiful natural resources, and the salubrious climate. If he were younger, he wrote from Liberia, "I would come here, and, if I had half as much sense as I have now, I would be worth a fortune in ten years." [32]

The American Colonization Society had always made strong appeals for mass black emigration and had been able to sponsor settlers in Africa. By 1892, however, the society was no longer able to finance large numbers of emigrants, and Liberia complained that too many settlers were poor, unskilled workers who competed with Liberians for jobs, did not contribute to the development of the country, and were becoming burdens. The society curtailed its emigration program. Turner then assumed more responsibility for organizing projects to send blacks to Africa. Many local southern pastors joined in, trying to line up transportation for the hundreds of people, many of them disillusioned with Arkansas, Texas, and Oklahoma, who had neither hope nor sufficient will power to stay in the South. Unfortunately, some charlatans, including many preachers, took advantage of the people's gullibility by setting up fraudulent emigration schemes. No more than a few hundred settlers actually went to Liberia during the 1890s, but the ground swell of interest showed the frustration and desperation of southern blacks.[33]

As had been true twenty years before, most church leaders, whether they were integrationists or nationalists, disapproved of emigration. Arguing that the condition of African Americans was steadily improving, they advised people to remain in the United States and work toward the fulfillment of their destiny. "Our salvation inheres in remaining here," proclaimed the AME minister H. T. Johnson, editor of the *Christian Re-*

32. Redkey, *Black Exodus,* 113, 123–24, 223–24; Redkey, ed., *Respect Black,* 131.
33. Redkey, *Black Exodus,* 127–48.

corder and an outspoken critic of racial injustice, "and making the best of the situation with a heroic faith in God and the aid of that moral philosophy in which the white man professes to believe." [34]

Despite their opposition to blacks emigrating to escape discrimination, the antiemigrationists often felt a strong affinity with Africa and its people. Their national identity was clearly American, but the majority acknowledged their African antecedents, and the racial connection that linked them to Africa was unbreakable. The same church leaders who battled Henry Turner over emigration had no trouble relating to Africans as "bone of our bone and flesh of our flesh." Clergymen who opposed both emigration and an African identity were interested in Africa because of the doctrine of universal evangelization that stood at the heart of African-American Christianity. According to AME bishop Abraham Grant, missionary work was simply "obeying the command of Christ" to carry the gospel to men and women inhabiting the four corners of the earth. "We are commissioned to preach the gospel to every creature in every land," the Missionary Baptist Convention of Georgia declared. But there was also a special relationship, a racial bond, between most southern blacks and black people elsewhere, and the church established foreign mission stations to bring those other blacks into the Christian fold. Both Baptists and Methodists supported missionaries in the African diaspora, first in Haiti and Santo Domingo and then after the war with Spain in 1898 in Cuba and Puerto Rico. Africa constituted the greatest challenge to black evangelical Protestantism, however, and the African-American churches became deeply involved in the evangelization of their ancestral homeland. "Africa," proclaimed the AME General Conference in 1896, "is the largest and most important of the fields that lie before us . . . on account of the relationship that exists between our race and the inhabitants of the Dark Continent." [35]

The church considered foreign missionary work in Africa its special responsibility and anticipated important rewards for its labor. Thomas Johnson, a Baptist missionary and former slave from Virginia, noted that

---

34. John Wesley Edward Bowen, ed., *Africa and the American Negro: Addresses and Proceedings of the Congress on Africa* (1896; rpr. Miami, 1969), 163–73; *Christian Recorder*, March 2, 1899.

35. Williams, *Black Americans and the Evangelization of Africa*, 42, 98; Missionary Baptist Convention of Georgia, *Minutes of the Twenty-seventh Annual Session of the Missionary Baptist Convention of Georgia . . . 1897* (Augusta, 1897), 43; *Home Mission Monthly*, II (August, 1880), 154.

Africans were "our own brethren in the land of our fathers." He believed that black Americans were "tied to that people by ties of consanguinity, of suffering and wrong. We can enter into the intellectual, social and moral life as no race alien to us can do." More than simply the Christian's obligation as God's servant to carry the gospel to heathens wherever they abided, the black church's mission movement was a fundamental element in a developing black nationalism that assumed the unity of all black people. It was a responsibility they felt with special keenness toward the people of Africa. "Africa is our land," said C. S. Brown of the North Carolina Baptist State Convention, "our mission field by the natural right of heredity." Through that mission church leaders hoped not only to contribute to the salvation of Africa's benighted millions but also to evoke from whites an acknowledgment that blacks and whites were moral equals. They understood the importance of missionary activity to the expansion of America's power and influence in the world, how it was a spur to imperialism and part of the rationale for the domination of heathen and non-Westernized people. Whites regarded foreign missions as emblems of their racial and cultural superiority, and so blacks, without endorsing racist imperialism, contended that their own missionary work, spreading Christianity and Western civilization to a heathen and savage continent, placed them on the same high moral and cultural plane as whites. Many church leaders supported the expansion of American influence in the world; some were unabashed cultural imperialists. Elias C. Morris of Arkansas, a Baptist leader, warned his fellow churchmen in 1899 that they could "no longer hope to retain the confidence and respect of other people of the world unless we do more for the redemption of the heathen, and especially those of our fatherland." [36]

There can be no denying the affinity that many southern blacks felt with their African brothers and sisters, but their deepest feelings were ambivalent. They spoke about the unity of all African people yet perceived themselves as very different from Africans. Beyond viewing African culture as foreign to their own, they regarded it as backward and distinctly inferior. How else is one to interpret their constant references to the "savagery" of Africans and the "benighted condition" of the millions of souls in Africa, locked in "superstition"? Such invidious distinc-

36. Williams, *Black Americans and the Evangelization of Africa*, 98–102, 136, 170; Baptist Educational and Missionary Convention of North Carolina, *Minutes of the Nineteenth Annual Session of the Baptist Educational and Missionary Convention of North Carolina . . . 1893* (Reidsville, N.C., 1893), 14; *Christian Recorder*, March 2, 1899.

tions between their own Westernized culture and that of indigenous African people, however, helped measurably in their struggle to sustain a positive self-image. African Americans' view of Africans served as an uplifting counterpoise against the humiliating ideology of white racism at home. They thought of themselves as being closer to God and to salvation than Africans, who still were slaves to idolatry and superstition. Moreover, the benighted Africans were calling to their American brothers and sisters for help, a big boost to self-pride. In the poetic phrases of Thomas Johnson, a Baptist missionary:

> "Come over and help us," is their cry,
> "Come now, oh, do not pass us by,
> We are seeking truth, we are seeking light,
> We seek deliverance from dark night.
> Can you who have the Gospel fail
> To hear our Cry, our doleful wail?"

It might not have been acceptable to emigrate and join an African society, but it was mandated by God and the conditions of blacks in white America to contribute to the uplift of Africa. "We are here," Benjamin Tanner stated over and over. "Let us stay here—at the same time do what we can to lift up Liberia." [37]

The white denominations, whose involvement in foreign missions grew by leaps and bounds with the global expansion of American power during the second half of the nineteenth century, did much to generate interest in African missions. The millions of heathens who inhabited the dark continent captured the attention of white evangelical churches. But Africa had the reputation of being a white man's graveyard because of the high incidence of disease and death among whites who went there, and, thinking that blacks were better suited to Africa's tropical climate than they were, white churches employed them as missionaries. Among the blacks who had gone to Africa under the auspices of white denominations were Lott Cary, who had been born a slave in Virginia and went to Liberia in 1821 as a Baptist missionary; Edward W. Blyden, who went initially as a Presbyterian missionary; and Alexander Crummell, an Episcopalian. Their enthusiasm and dedication to the cause of African evangelization led them to write and speak often and persuasively on be-

---

37. Lewis G. Jordan, *Up the Ladder in Foreign Missions* (Nashville, 1901 and 1903), 90; Thomas L. Johnson, *Africa for Christ, or Twenty-Eight Years a Slave* (6th ed.; London, 1892), 60; *Christian Recorder*, April 18, 1878.

half of African missions. "The hand of God is on the black man," Crummell wrote in his book *Africa and America,* "in all the lands of his distant sojourn, for the good of Africa." The white churches trained black missionaries in the schools and seminaries they established during the years following the Civil War. That training led individuals such as Alexander Camphor, who attended a Methodist Freedmen's Aid Society school in Louisiana as well as New Orleans University and Gammon Theological Seminary in Atlanta, and William W. Colley, who was trained in the Baptist Richmond Theological Seminary and sponsored in Nigeria by the Southern Baptist Convention, to serve as African missionaries. These evangelists were sophisticated and articulate, and their letters and reports as well as the lectures they delivered to American audiences after they returned to the United States aroused profound sympathy for "the teeming millions in Africa, groping in ignorance dark as the night." [38]

The emigration movement further immersed blacks in the subject of Africa and attracted them to the cause of foreign missions. Beginning with antebellum colonization, the migration of blacks to Africa had been closely associated with churches and evangelization. Paul Cuffee, Daniel Coker, and Lott Cary all went to Africa as settlers and missionaries. Cary became an agent for the American Colonization Society. Clergymen had been prominent among the *Azor* settlers in 1878. And, of course, Bishop Turner had almost single-handedly welded together the elements of emigration and the Christianization of Africa into a cause that no one in black America could ignore. [39]

The African Methodist and Baptist churches inaugurated their African mission programs in the 1870s, each erecting a denominational apparatus for conducting missionary work. The white churches were then employing fewer missionaries in Africa, leaving the mission field largely open to the independent black churches. In 1880 the Baptist missionary Thomas Johnson noted an air of excitement among blacks, who were "alive to the importance of the evangelisation of Africa." The AME church had formed a Home and Foreign Missionary Society as early as 1844 and later created the position of mission secretary. But it was not until after the emigration from South Carolina in 1878 that the church

38. Carter G. Woodson, *The History of the Negro Church* (1921; rpr. Washington, D.C., 1972), 121–23; Williams, *Black Americans and the Evangelization of Africa,* 3–15, 18, 30; Jordan, *Up the Ladder in Foreign Missions,* 93.

39. Williams, *Black Americans and the Evangelization of Africa,* 34–35, 39, 47, 49–52.

began to sponsor African missions. The AME Zion church formally entered the foreign mission field in 1880 with the establishment of the General Home and Foreign Mission Board. A native North Carolinian named Andrew Cartwright had immigrated to Liberia under the sponsorship of the American Colonization Society in 1876 and had organized several congregations among the Liberians. The church officially assumed support of the Liberian missions in 1882. The early 1880s also marked the beginning of Baptist evangelization of Africa. William W. Colley, who had served as a missionary for the white Southern Baptist Convention, organized the Baptist Foreign Mission Convention in Montgomery, Alabama, in 1880. In 1883 the convention sent six missionaries to Liberia, including Colley and his wife, J. H. Presley and his wife, Hattie, and two young seminary graduates, John J. Coles and Henson McKinney. They established the Bendoo mission station among the native people of Liberia. The Colored Methodist Episcopal church was too weak financially to undertake foreign mission work.[40]

Money was the key to success for these African missions, and women played the principal role in raising it. Fund-raising was one of the many ways in which women showed that even though men were up front and received most of the attention, they were the backbone of the church. All three of the independent black denominations that conducted missionary work formed women's foreign mission societies whose primary activity was raising money to support African missionaries. Special collections during church services and events such as bazaars and cake sales were among the ways women raised funds. At least for a while, sizable amounts of money came into the foreign mission programs. The Ladies Mission Society of the AME Zion church raised $1,000 within four years of its inception.[41]

But local congregations and the ordinary men and women who belonged to them often failed to demonstrate in tangible ways the same commitment to missionary union with Africans that church leaders felt. By the mid-1880s involvement had begun to wane and financial contributions to shrink. Missions struggled with meager support. The Baptists' Bendoo mission in Liberia fell to pieces because of a lack of financial backing and illness that took the lives of Hattie Presley and Henson McKinney. District and state organizations obligated themselves in prin-

40. *Ibid.*, 39, 45–63, 65, 67–68; Lewis G. Jordan, *Negro Baptist History, U.S.A., 1750–1930* (Nashville, 1930), 114, 154–57, 161.

41. Williams, *Black Americans and the Evangelization of Africa*, 45–46, 52, 58.

ciple to African missions but contributed scantily toward missionary enterprises. An AME committee reported in 1884 a "woeful lack of interest in mission work." AME contributions to missions fell from $34,811 during 1880–1884 to $19,001 from 1884 to 1888. The president of the Louisiana Baptist Convention told the assembled messengers from local churches in 1885 about the weak commitment within his state to African missions. "Brethren, our interest in this work must deepen," he admonished, adding that more must be done on behalf of the heathens of Africa: "Let us consecrate ourselves more fully to the work of saving the perishing millions of Africa." People did not have much money to spare for foreign missions. The impoverishment of most southern congregations was evident in sparse funding for virtually all church programs, but their financial support of local educational, missionary, and benevolence programs consistently outstripped their support for the distant African missions. The AME committee that complained of the lack of interest in foreign missions explained it by saying that Africa was "too far removed" and "too sunken in sin, too steeped in superstition and idolatry for us." Even some leaders were at best lukewarm about African evangelization. AME bishop Daniel A. Payne, leery of imposing alien cultures on vulnerable people, warned his followers about the possibility that "African Methodist Imperialism" might follow from missionary activity. African missions stood relatively low on the church's list of priorities or on those of ordinary people struggling against the many barriers erected against their advancement.[42]

By the 1890s, however, the promotional efforts of church leaders and missionaries and the renewed interest in emigration breathed new life into African missionary work. Henry M. Turner was in the vanguard of those who advocated expanded church involvement. Named bishop of Africa, Turner visited the continent three times, Liberia and Sierra Leone in 1891 and 1893 and South Africa in 1898, officially to promote and organize African missions. His letters during those visits and articles after his return appeared in the *Voice of Missions* and did a great deal to publicize the church's missionary work. Church officials grew more and more excited about missions and attributed the enthusiasm to Turner. The

42. H. B. Parks, *Africa: The Problem of the New Century* (New York, 1899), 16; *Minutes of the Thirteenth Annual Session of the Louisiana Baptist State Convention . . . 1885* (New Orleans, 1885), 12; Wilson Jeremiah Moses, *The Golden Age of Black Nationalism, 1850–1925* (Rev. ed.; New York, 1988), 15–20; Williams, *Black Americans and the Evangelization of Africa,* 35–39.

General Conference noted in 1896 that the "feeling for Africa's redemption, throughout Christendom is unprecedented" and credited Turner, who had "laid his life upon the altar for the salvation of Africa, morally, intellectually, commercially and religiously." Their excitement, in some degree, drifted down to the ordinary black folk in local congregations. A letter from an Arkansas man in the *Voice of Missions* revealed the contagious effect of evangelization promotions. After hearing a sermon by William B. Derrick, the church's secretary of missions, the writer declared: "His words on Africa enthused my soul from its greatest depths, and I myself am Africa struck. . . . Today my heart yearns for Africa, my dear nativity, and I ask God each day to bless the missionaries of Africa." The AME Zion church competed energetically with its AME brethren for status and recognition in African missionary work just as it had done in evangelizing the freedmen after the Civil War. Bishop Alexander Walters was one of the organization's most vigorous promoters of African missions, and the denomination's paper *Star of Zion* carried the cause to the people. The discouragement that followed the failure of the Baptists' Bendoo mission also lifted in the 1890s. When the Mississippian Lewis Garnett Jordan took over as head of foreign mission work in 1896, he found "a depleted treasury, the missionaries off of the field, the whole work under a cloud, the confidence of the denomination in Foreign Mission work sadly shaken." But his tireless efforts to rebuild mission work soon began to pay dividends.[43]

By the end of the 1890s, foreign missions, especially those in the evangelization of Africa, were a major activity of the black church. Financial contributions reached record levels. The AME mission department raised $36,535 from 1892 to 1896, the largest amount it had ever amassed in a four-year period and a remarkable feat considering the economic depression that blighted the country. Most of the contributions came from the South, 61 percent in 1899. At least 113 black missionaries had gone to Africa between 1877 and 1900, 65 of them representing independent black churches and at least 47 of them southerners. Of that number no fewer than 33 were women. Opportunities for women within the regular ministry of the black church were limited, but were more plentiful in missionary work. Admittedly, most of the women were the wives of male missionaries, but several were unmarried and were employed as evange-

---

43. Williams, *Black Americans and the Evangelization of Africa*, 53, 59–61; *Voice of Missions*, March, 1896; Jordan, *Up the Ladder in Foreign Missions*, 103.

lists independent of males. Regardless of their marital status, their contribution to the church's foreign mission program was noteworthy.[44]

To the extent that contemporary blacks conceived of missionary work in racial terms, and also insofar as evangelization was conducted independent of white authority, was based on the principle of self-help, and served to promote the unity and solidarity of African Americans, it was confluent with the powerful current of nationalism that ran through the black church in the nineteenth century. By the 1890s nationalism, which had been a prominent feature of the antislavery ideology of northern church leaders but had been diminished by the optimism and idealism of Reconstruction, had resurfaced to become an important theme in the thinking of southern blacks. It was driven by several forces that compelled them to acknowledge that their destiny was separate from although obviously related to that of whites. When the Republican party assumed a *laissez-faire* attitude toward the issue of race, it forced blacks to draw together and fend for themselves. Of necessity they tightened the bonds of community that enfolded them, what William E. B. Du Bois called the "veil" of race. Institutionalized racial segregation created a reality of isolation and strengthened their sense of themselves. Ironically, white nationalism, rampant in the late nineteenth century and laced with racism, served as a model for black nationalists. Fed by remarkable achievements in business and science as well as the conquest of the western frontier, including the Indians, who were being "civilized" just as African people were, it set a standard against which black nationalists often measured the achievements of African Americans and asserted their own superiority over the people of Africa.[45]

Nineteenth-century nationalism typically manifested itself either in a desire to break away from the control of external authority or in efforts to unify people who shared a common culture but were disunited politically and economically. Black nationalism in the United States grew out of both aspirations. Race consciousness and solidarity surged through the ranks of a growing number of educated and cosmopolitan leaders within the black community and led them to demand political and economic control of their lives. Aside from color, their self-awareness came from their African cultural roots, even though they may not have been consciously aware of all of them. As Sterling Stuckey has written, "The

44. Parks, *Africa*, 16; Williams, *Black Americans and the Evangelization of Africa*, 85, 182–90.
45. Redkey, *Black Exodus*, 9, 12.

impact of Africa need not be consciously 'felt' to shape values and to inform behavior." The African influence had certainly shaped the culture of the mass of black Americans, including their religious beliefs and practices. Moreover, for some, nineteenth-century black nationalism included an interest in reuniting African Americans and Africa through zionist emigration and through the agency of foreign missions. In any event, African Americans became increasingly aware of the necessity for common effort to promote the common welfare.[46]

The church also contributed to African-American unity through its ecclesiastical organizations. Independent church organizations signified African Americans' aspiration to self-reliance. Methodist churches had been nationally organized since the early nineteenth century and were among the most powerful agencies for the generation and expression of nationalist feeling. The two African Methodist denominations, bearing the defining label *African* in their names, embodied the clearest feelings of black nationalism among the Methodists. Assimilationists had from time to time voiced their objections to the designation, as James Lynch had during the Reconstruction period, arguing that blacks had become culturally American and that to focus on their distinctiveness would encourage white racism. Another name controversy flared up among African Methodists toward the end of the century when assimilationists once again urged the AME church to drop the word *African*. A response from AME minister J. T. Jenifer expressed the feelings of most members of the church. He suspected that critics of the term were ashamed of being African. But Africa was the source of civilization, he argued, "the cradle of arts and sciences; the earliest nursery of the Church of God." Africa was synonymous with greatness. "Why, then, should the Negro of this country, with African blood and of African parentage, be ashamed of Africa?" Refuting the assertion that use of the word hardened racial divisions in America, Jenifer argued that whites were responsible for the prevailing conditions and blacks had no choice but to protect themselves and advance their own cause. "To the proscribed and downtrodden colored people of this country this name was a symbol of hope; it was an *asylum and an inspiration*—a protest against religious oppression or proscription at the altar of God." The term *African* stayed.[47]

Black members of the southern Presbyterian Church of the United

46. Moses, *Golden Age of Black Nationalism*, 10–20; Stuckey, *Slave Culture*, 215.
47. Rev. J. T. Jenifer, "Why I Am an African Methodist," *A.M.E. Church Review*, VII (January, 1891), 287.

States, who had been promised a separate organization soon after emancipation, had become frustrated by white officials' slowness in granting them autonomy. By the 1890s, they had begun aggressively to press for an independent church. In 1897 representatives of the General Assembly and the black presbyteries met in Birmingham and mapped out plans for a final separation of the black congregations. In New Orleans the following year, blacks organized the Synod of the Colored Presbyterian Church of the United States and Canada, a cumbersome name that was shortened to Afro-American Synod and then changed to the Afro-American Presbyterian church. The church registered only about fifteen hundred members, a thousand fewer blacks than the white church claimed, but it fulfilled their desire to be free of white domination and the humiliation of segregation.[48]

Among Baptists the process of establishing cooperative organizations at the district and state levels culminated in the formation of national conventions by the close of the century. Free blacks in the North had organized the American Baptist Missionary Convention as early as 1840. As soon as southern Baptists achieved control of their churches they considered forming interstate conventions. In 1864 Baptists founded the Northwestern and Southern conventions. Neither was a national organization; indeed, blacks during the 1860s and 1870s did not agree about the need for a national organization. White northern Baptists appeared eager to undertake the education and evangelization of the freedmen in the South. Racial prejudice and an irritating paternalism among northern whites, however, engendered separationist feelings among black church leaders. The unwillingness of the American Baptist Home Mission Society's officials to pursue missionary work among black southerners with sufficient vigor and the fact that whites dominated the society and refused to consult black church leaders about how funds raised to aid African-American churches should be spent led some to conclude that an independent missionary convention was indispensable. Therefore, in 1866 the American Baptist Missionary Convention and the Northwestern and Southern conventions united to form the Consolidated American Baptist Missionary Convention. It achieved some initial success. At its third annual meeting in 1869, it claimed thirteen affiliated associations with seventy-two member churches. By 1870 the convention had established a

48. Ernest Trice Thompson, *Presbyterians in the South* (3 vols.; Richmond, 1863–73), II, 311–25, III, 88–89.

school for ministerial training in Richmond and schools for secular instruction in Tennessee and Mississippi. The following year the American Baptist Free Mission Society, a northern Baptist agency, gave the convention property in Haiti for missionary use. By 1870 it claimed to have appointed over a span of seven years a total of 238 missionaries to labor in twenty-four different states. These missionaries reported traveling over one hundred thousand miles, preaching in excess of seventeen thousand sermons, and converting fifteen thousand people, mostly in the South.[49]

The Consolidated Convention inevitably confronted the problem of the scarcity of money that was all too common among black organizations. The convention's treasurer complained that its work was "limited by want of means," and Congress dealt a severe blow in 1869 when it emasculated the Freedmen's Bureau, thereby ending federal assistance to the convention's schools and forcing it back upon its own meager resources and "such help as we can get from our white friends of the North." The enterprise in Haiti proved abortive because missionaries failed to raise sufficient money to erect a building. There were several other problems as well. The convention encountered considerable apathy among brethren who seemed unable to "see and understand the importance of such thorough organization and cooperation." The elitism of northern blacks offended southerners and strained the convention's solidarity. Differences over whether it was appropriate for ministers to become politicians also divided the convention. These troubles, plus competition for funds from northern Baptist and local black Baptist organizations, slowly drained the life from the convention. Traces of its existence disappear after 1877, when it had the active support of only thirty-five churches and eleven associations.[50]

Another national organization grew out of the work of William W. Colley, the Virginian who had once been employed by the Foreign Mission Board of the Southern Baptist Convention as a missionary to Africa.

49. Woodson, *History of the Negro Church*, 192–93; James Melvin Washington, "The Origins and Emergence of Black Baptist Separatism, 1863–1897" (Ph.D. dissertation, Yale University, 1979), 88–122; Consolidated American Baptist Missionary Convention, *Report of the Third Annual Meeting of the Consolidated American Baptist Missionary Convention . . . 1869* (New York, 1869), 19–20, 34–35; Jordan, *Negro Baptist History*, 276–83.
50. Washington, "Origins and Emergence of Black Baptist Separatism," 123–54; Consolidated American Baptist Missionary Convention, *Report, 1869, Report of the Triennial Meeting and (Thirty-seventh Annual Meeting) of the Consolidated American Baptist Missionary Convention . . . 1877* (Brooklyn, 1877), 34–35; Jordan, *Negro Baptist History*, 114, 277.

Colley returned to the United States in 1879 hopeful of organizing a foreign mission convention. By much travel and assiduous campaigning he was able to win the necessary encouragement and financial support to bring together in 1880 what a contemporary called "the first . . . well thought out meeting" of Negro Baptists. Unlike the Consolidated American Baptist Missionary Convention, Colley's Baptist Foreign Mission Convention, as its name implied, limited its energies to the foreign mission field, particularly Africa. Its most important functionary was its corresponding secretary (Colley was the first), whose duty it was "to travel over the various states and collect means for African missions." The convention sent at least half a dozen missionaries to Africa but had difficulty keeping them in the field. It suffered in the panic of 1893 and the subsequent depression, as did many other religious bodies, having even more trouble than before raising money. An attempt was made in 1894 to revive it by uniting with two largely regional groups, the New England Convention and the moribund Baptist African Missionary Convention of America. But the proposed tripartite union failed.[51]

Another nominally national body deserves mention because, along with the Foreign Mission Convention, it was the immediate predecessor of the most successful Baptist convention. An assemblage of Baptists called by the Kentuckian William J. Simmons gathered in St. Louis in August, 1886, to form the American National Baptist Convention. Independent of the Foreign Mission Convention Simmons' group established missions in the United States. Beginning in 1887, committees representing the two organizations met, and by 1894 the conventions had effected an informal merger.[52]

The Foreign Mission Convention met for the last time in 1894 amid discouragement and charges that its executive board had been wasteful and irresponsible. At that meeting, the convention adopted a resolution offered by Albert W. Pegues of North Carolina directing it to appoint a committee to "enter immediately into consultation" with the executive board of the American National Convention to bring about a merger of the two conventions and a third group, the National and Educational Convention, a new organization initiated by blacks who had gathered in Washington, D.C., in 1893. The three conventions fused in September,

---

51. Jordan, *Negro Baptist History*, 114–18, 154–57, 161.
52. Woodson, *History of the Negro Church*, 178.

1895, producing the National Baptist Convention of the United States of America.[53]

The National Baptist Convention's first president, its only one until after a schism in 1915, was Elias C. Morris. Born a slave in Murray County, Georgia, in 1855, he first joined a Baptist church in Stevenson, Alabama, in 1874. Later he settled in Helena, Arkansas, where he assumed the pastorate of a church. A talented and literate minister, Morris became secretary and then president of the state convention in Arkansas, helped to found and edited the Arkansas *Times,* a denominational newspaper, and established Arkansas Baptist College. He served as president of the National Foreign Mission Convention and vice-president of the American National Baptist Convention. He enjoyed politics and was a delegate to the Republican national nominating convention in 1884 and later became a close friend and ally of Booker T. Washington.[54]

The founders of the National Baptist Convention intended that it should "do mission work in the United States of America, in Africa and elsewhere abroad," with a view to fostering "the cause of education," both religious and secular, and that these tasks should be performed and managed by blacks. It was composed of representatives of Sunday school conventions and state conventions or "any one in good standing in any regular Missionary Baptist church." Implementation of its programs was supervised by several boards, each of which had a president. The boards were actually managed, however, by a corresponding secretary. They were nominally subordinate to the convention but in fact were, like the societies of the northern church, practically independent.[55]

The National Baptist Convention reflected the evolving role of women in the expansion and development of the church. The church had always tried to provide for the worldly as well as the spiritual needs of the black community, and as the black population multiplied during the second half of the nineteenth century and its problems mounted accordingly, the church attempted to respond. As had been true all along, the women of the church played the leading part in nurturing the community. Because they were a sizable majority of all communicants (nearly two-thirds), they were able to give strong direction to the church. Of course, the

53. Jordan, *Negro Baptist History,* 116–19.

54. *National Baptist Magazine,* I (October, 1894), 271–72.

55. National Baptist Convention, *Journal of the Twenty-first Annual Session of the National Baptist Convention . . . 1901* (Nashville, 1901), 3–6.

church was not the only black institution that was involved in benevolent activity. Many women's societies operated in towns and cities along with organizations affiliated with the church. By the end of the nineteenth century, the focus of benevolence had begun to shift somewhat from the grass-roots to the national level. In 1896 black women from various parts of the country met in the Nineteenth Street Baptist Church in Washington, D.C., to found the National Association of Colored Women. The formation of this group signified a drift not only upward toward the national level of organization but also away from church responsibility for social welfare. But the woman's group maintained strong links to the church and did not supplant it as the primary agency outside of the household through which women fulfilled their traditional roles as nurturers and moral leaders. In line with the movement away from local autonomy, the sisters had established district and statewide groups in the 1880s in support of missions, Sunday schools, and charity, and with the formation of the American National Baptist Convention and the subsequent National Baptist Convention, leaders of the women's movement endeavored to organize a national women's auxiliary convention.[56]

Their effort aroused opposition from men who objected not only to an expanded women's role in church affairs but also to the sisters' assertiveness. And at least some women had become aggressive. By the 1890s influential feminists, including Virginia Broughton of Tennessee and Mary Cook and Lucy Wilmot Smith of Kentucky, had begun to challenge the subordination of women. They demanded not only a louder voice within the church but expanded opportunities outside of it as well. "Emancipate woman from the chains that now restrain her," wrote Mary Cook, "and who can estimate the part she will play in the work of the denomination." Lucy Smith, pointing out that the centuries-old paths established for women detoured around modern society, claimed that "new occasions make new duties." Yet the women were not as radical as some white feminists. They did not wish to intrude on the ministerial prerogatives of men, and they generally did not dispute the notion that the feminine personality equipped women to serve as moral exemplars, to educate the young, and to perform charitable work. But their demands for

56. U.S. Bureau of the Census, *Census of Religious Bodies: 1906* (2 vols.; Washington, D.C., 1910), I, 140; Kathleen C. Berkeley, " 'Colored Ladies Also Contributed': Black Women's Activities from Benevolence to Social Welfare," in *The Web of Southern Social Relations: Women, Family, and Education,* ed. Walter J. Fraser, Jr., R. Frank Saunders, Jr., and Jon L. Wakelyn (Athens, Ga., 1985), 185, 196.

the right to participate in the business affairs of the church and to establish and operate their own separate organizations certainly identified them with the liberal movement in the late nineteenth-century Christian church. Nor were all black churchmen reactionary fundamentalists regarding women's issues. Most of them valued women's efforts on behalf of the church and some, like Lewis G. Jordan of Virginia, William J. Simmons of Kentucky, Walter H. Brooks of Washington, D.C., and Harvey Johnson of Maryland were strong supporters of the feminist cause. A male writer in the *National Baptist Magazine* noted that slaves had been emancipated, "now let us emancipate women!" But most men were conservative and closely guarded their own position of dominance in relationships with women. Under the title "Woman and Her Work," Lewis G. Jordan gave lyrical expression to the black male's concept of his sister's proper relationship to her brothers both within the church and without, and his verse made it clear just who was subordinate to whom.

> As unto the bow the cord is,
> So unto man is woman—
> Though she bends him, she obeys him;
> Though she draws him, yet she follows;
> Useless each without the other.

Women's attempts to organize state conventions had encountered opposition in some areas, and efforts to form a separate national women's Baptist convention likewise were initially derailed by the denomination's conservative males, including Simmons, who on other feminist issues was the women's strong ally. At the National Baptist Convention's initial meeting in 1895, a tentative agreement allowing women to organize a separate convention fell apart, and at the 1896 meeting in St. Louis, the messengers rejected a proposal that the sisters be allowed to form a separate convention. But persistence and "a righteous discontent" ultimately paid off, and at the convention's 1900 meeting in Richmond, when Lewis G. Jordan rallied the messengers' support, the Women's Convention Auxiliary to the National Baptist Convention was formed. Its objectives were to engage in foreign and domestic missionary and educational work and to promote Christian womanhood.[57]

After emancipation the churches had responded to the people's desire

---

57. Evelyn Brooks, "The Women's Movement in the Black Baptist Church, 1880–1920" (Ph.D. dissertation, University of Rochester, 1984), 83–87, 168–69, 174–75; Jordan, *Up the Ladder in Foreign Missions,* 144–48.

to provide for their own education by establishing schools. During Reconstruction black leaders, including churchmen, pressed for the creation of tax-supported public education for black as well as white pupils. Although the public school systems founded during the Reconstruction period were meagerly funded and usually segregated, with funding differentials that penalized blacks, they relieved the churches of much of the burden of providing schools. But the Reconstruction state governments did not provide adequately for training black teachers who would work in black schools. Many northern white societies established colleges for black students, but calls from the black community for colleges run by blacks for blacks made it clear that the people wanted to control their own education from top to bottom.

Collegiate education was another aspect of African-American life in which the churches became involved. Black-operated colleges did not appear until after Reconstruction. Qualitatively, black colleges, whether supported and administered by whites or by blacks, ranked low when compared to white schools, and most colleges run by black churches were inferior to those established and operated by whites. Lack of money, inadequate facilities, and ill-prepared students and faculties combined to assure the continuance of these disparities. According to a report of the 1902 Atlanta University Conference, only Howard University approached standards set by New England colleges. Paul Quinn College, an AME school established in Austin, Texas, and then moved to Waco, and Wilberforce University in Ohio offered instruction that was substantially below the quality of small New England institutions. Livingstone, run by the Zion Methodists, was equivalent to an average New England high school.[58]

The education and training of ministers was an important objective of the churches in sponsoring colleges. They supported several seminaries explicitly intended to train ministers. Virginia Seminary and College at Lynchburg, founded by Baptists in 1887, enjoyed a strong reputation not only among blacks but also among whites. The National Baptist Convention and the Southern Baptist Convention joined to create a seminary in Nashville, but it did not commence classes until 1920. Among a lengthy list of minor seminaries were the Baptists' Cadiz Theological Institute in Kentucky, the AME's Payne Seminary in Ohio, and the CME church's

58. Atlanta University Conference, *The College-Bred Negro: Report of a Social Study Made Under the Direction of Atlanta University in 1900* (Atlanta, 1902), 10.

Hagood and Homer seminaries. In the main, though, ministers who received formal theological training obtained it in the church-related colleges and universities, not in the seminaries. By the turn of the century, both Baptists and Methodists operated a total of sixteen colleges. Those of the Methodists were healthier, academically and financially. Wilberforce in Ohio, Morris Brown in Atlanta, Allen in Columbia, South Carolina, and Paul Quinn in Waco, all AME institutions, were a cut below Howard and Fisk academically but were at the pinnacle of black-run colleges. Wilberforce boasted the longest tradition. Bishop Daniel A. Payne had purchased the college from the Methodist Episcopal church in 1863. It claimed the strongest faculty, including such scholars as William S. Scarborough, a noted linguist, and the talented young historian and sociologist from Harvard, William E. B. Du Bois. And it owned more property than any other black-controlled college. Its virtues, however, were counterbalanced by a narrow religious dogmatism that stifled Du Bois and hastened his departure. Zion Methodists looked with pride to Livingstone College in Salisbury, North Carolina. In 1889 the New York *Age* referred to Livingstone as "one of the most remarkable Negro enterprises in this country." Livingstone was founded in 1879 on rented property under the sure-handed guidance of Joseph C. Price, a gifted orator and a major political figure, who was on the verge of greatness as a leader when he died in 1894. The Methodist Episcopal Church, South, educated blacks in Paine Institute, but the Colored Methodist Episcopal church operated two schools of its own, Lane College in Tennessee and Texas College.[59]

The crusade to bring higher education to the freedmen generated an earnest debate over the most appropriate form it should take. Initially the argument featured mostly white educators such as Samuel C. Armstrong, a proponent of industrial training for blacks, and William T. Harris, an ardent advocate of classical instruction. Ultimately, however, two black men came to lead both sides of the controversy. Booker T. Washington, born a slave in western Virginia, was Armstrong's protégé, having won

59. Wesley J. Gaines, *African Methodism in the South, or, Twenty-Five Years of Freedom* (Atlanta, 1890), 21–28; *Religious Herald*, July 4, 1889; Atlanta University Conference, *College-Bred Negro*, 6–7; Jordan, *Negro Baptist History*, 243–45; William E. B. Du Bois, ed., *The Negro Church: Report of a Social Study Made Under the Direction of Atlanta University* (Atlanta, 1903), 120, 130–33; Du Bois, *Dusk of Dawn: An Essay Toward an Autobiography of a Race Concept* (New York, 1940), 57; New York *Age*, November 30, 1889.

his mentor's admiration first as a student and then as a teacher at Hampton Institute. As principal of Tuskegee Institute, a public school for blacks in Alabama, he found himself surrounded by conservative whites who were wary of educating blacks. He assured them by word and deed that his school posed no threat to the social order. His concept of industrial training involved making southern blacks skilled and efficient workers, not political leaders who might challenge white supremacy and the sanctity of the white parlor. Washington burst onto the national scene in 1895, when he addressed the Southern and Cotton States Exposition in Atlanta and told whites that blacks did not desire to court their daughters or run southern politics and urged blacks to concentrate on becoming morally upright and economically self-reliant. What quickly became known as the Atlanta Compromise catapulted Washington into national prominence and pushed him ahead of the aging Henry Turner as the leading spokesman for southern blacks. The urbane Du Bois, northern-born and Harvard-educated, rejected Washington's assertion that black southerners were primarily laborers and should remain so, albeit with greater skill. He was convinced that higher education and a "talented tenth" of intellectual leaders were essential to race advancement. "Men we shall have only as we make manhood the object of the work of the schools—intelligence, broad sympathy, knowledge of the world that was and is, and of the relation of men to it," he contended.[60]

The churches lined up on both sides of this issue as they did on many others. Industrial training schools were a vital part of church educational programs, especially after the 1880s. In 1886 the AME church in North Carolina founded Kittrell Normal and Industrial School, one of the first such institutions created by an independent African-American church. In 1888, by agreement between the North Carolina and Virginia annual conferences, it became the North Carolina and Virginia Normal and Industrial School. Sponsors of church-related training schools echoed the arguments of Armstrong and Washington, saying essentially that African Americans had to make themselves efficiently productive if they were to improve their condition in American society. Such schools might "create

60. Henry Allen Bullock, *A History of Negro Education in the South: From 1619 to the Present* (Cambridge, Mass., 1967), 74–85; William E. B. Du Bois, *The Souls of Black Folk: Essays and Sketches* (Chicago, 1909), 41–59; Booker T. Washington *et al.*, *The Negro Problem: A Series of Articles by Representative Negroes of To-Day* (1903; rpr. New York, 1969), 34.

an era of greater usefulness among the colored, enhance their general welfare and cause better understanding and better feelings between races in these parts and as far as its influence may extend." They were operated by associations, annual conferences, and state conventions all over the South.[61]

Other church leaders acknowledged Du Bois' concept of the "talented tenth," an educated elite that "rises and pulls all that are worth the saving up to their vantage ground." Church leaders often perceived themselves as part of the "tenth," that is, as sources of inspiration and guidance to others of the race. "The Negro ministry is in fact the leaders of the race" was the comment of one church official and the opinion of many others. Leaders also stressed the need for an educated ministry that would guide the rest of the race. Members of the Northern Neck Baptist Association of Virginia believed that "the safety and preservation of the Baptist denomination must rest upon an intelligent ministry" and that "no person should be trusted to instruct the people in divine things who is ignorant of the truths which he is to teach." An association report couched in manifestly Du Boisian terms emphasized the importance of higher education in promoting race advancement: "No people ever rise higher than their aspirations. We should create a thirst for knowledge." The moderator approved and commended "the effort now being made along the lines of industrial education for the masses of our people by the schools of this country, especially the one over which Dr. Booker T. Washington presides as its honored founder and principal." But only higher education, by bringing out the potential worth of black people, could command respect and equitable treatment for the race. "It has been objected, or contended," the moderator stated, "that the Negro is not adapted to the higher education. We answer this objection by saying, that as a race we are to rise and advance by the utilization of the means and methods employed by the people who have raised themselves high in the scales of moral and intellectual being." In 1916, 90 percent of the teachers in

61. New York *Age*, April 2, 1888; Charles S. Smith, *A History of the African Methodist Episcopal Church* (1922; rpr. New York, 1968), 357–58; Israel L. Butt, *History of African Methodism in Virginia: Four Decades in the Old Dominion* (Hampton, 1908), 119; J. A. Whitted, *A History of the Negro Baptists of North Carolina* (Raleigh, 1908), 169; Northern Neck Baptist Association (Virginia), *Minutes of the Thirteenth Annual Session of the Northern Neck Baptist Association . . . 1890* (Washington, D.C., 1890), 17–18; Gaines, *African Methodism in the South*, 108–109.

church-supported schools were academic rather than vocational instruc-
tors. In Baptist schools, 95 percent were academic.[62]

The churches also aided education and the unification of the black
community by providing important media for the dissemination of ideas
and information. The churches published several important newspapers
and magazines that spread not only the Christian gospel but secular news
as well. The oldest and most successful of these was the AME's *Christian
Recorder*, which was begun in 1847 and called the *Christian Herald* until
1852. One of the best black newspapers of the nineteenth century, the
Christian Recorder printed national news, correspondence from across
the nation, editorials, and exchanges from other newspapers. Among its
editors were such prominent church figures as James Lynch, Benjamin
Tanner, and Henry Turner. In June, 1866, the AME Zion church began
publishing *Zion's Standard and Weekly Review*. In 1867 it was
superseded by a weekly known as the *Star of Zion*, which was published
in several North Carolina cities over the next several decades. The *Star's*
ablest editor was a layman, John C. Dancy, a journalist of considerable
experience and skill. Patterned after the *Christian Recorder*, it offered its
readers a mixture of secular and religious fare, including news reports
and editorial comment. The *Christian Index*, another weekly newspaper,
first appeared in 1867 as the voice of the black conference of the southern
Methodist church. In 1870 it became the publication of the Colored
Methodist Episcopal church. Another Methodist newspaper commenced
publication in the early 1890s under the direction of Henry M. Turner.
The *Voice of Missions* soon became a widely circulated monthly, promoting the cause of African emigration. Turner later became the publisher
and changed its name to *Voice of the People*. Black members of the Methodist Episcopal church published the *Southwestern Christian Advocate*.
Like the others, it was a weekly and contained articles on religious topics,
news items, and editorials. Negro Baptists also published a long-lived
weekly newspaper, the *American Baptist*, edited by a Kentucky Baptist

62. Washington *et al.*, *Negro Problem*, 45; Du Bois, *Souls of Black Folk*, 88–109; African Methodist Episcopal Church, South Carolina Annual Conference, *Minutes of the
South Carolina Conference of the Methodist Episcopal Church, South . . . 1907* (Columbia,
S.C., 1907), 37–38; Northern Neck Baptist Association (Virginia), *Minutes of the Thirty-
second Annual Session of the Northern Neck Baptist Association . . . 1909* (N.p., n.d.), 13,
27–28; U.S. Department of Interior, Bureau of Education, *Negro Education: A Study of the
Private and Higher Schools for Colored People in the United States* (2 vols.; Washington,
D.C., 1917), I, 151.

layman, William H. Steward. A variety of local publications appeared over the years, but most of them died after only a few months because conferences and conventions did not have sufficient money to operate them. Probably the best of these was the *Georgia Baptist,* published and edited by William Jefferson White, a militant nationalist and a foe of Booker T. Washington's.

More literary than the newspapers were the quarterly magazines that some of the black denominations published. In 1884 the AME church began publishing the *A.M.E. Church Review.* Benjamin T. Tanner, who moved from the *Christian Recorder,* was its first editor. The *Review* was a vehicle for fiction writers and essayists as well as theologians. It contained articles by such well-known leaders of the black community as Henry Turner, James Theodore Holly, T. Thomas Fortune, William S. Scarborough, and Kelly Miller. By the turn of the century, the *Review* had a circulation of about a thousand. A similar publication was the *A.M.E. Zion Quarterly Review,* begun in 1888. John C. Dancy of the *Star of Zion* was its editor. In 1894 the Baptists began publishing the *National Baptist Magazine,* but it lasted only a few years. Its format and content resembled those of the AME and AME Zion quarterlies. Its editor, W. Bishop Johnson, was a noted Baptist minister.

If many black church members were in agreement that redemption from economic and political oppression lay in their own hands, shared a high level of race consciousness, and exhibited solidarity in the effort to secure citizenship rights—all ingredients of nationalism—their statements and actions often betrayed sharp differences of opinion over whether separatism and self-help on one hand or the maintenance of a cooperative relationship with northern whites on the other was the best strategy for achieving their objectives. There was also debate over the strategy for cultivating the goodwill of southern whites, which was advocated persuasively by Booker T. Washington and supported by vast numbers of southern blacks.

The church was buffeted by many of the same cross-currents of opinion about race advancement that influenced the larger black community, and it was no freer of conflict over the strategies for progress than was black society as a whole. The church was not merely an otherworldly religious institution being exploited as a vehicle by ambitious black politicians who had gotten a taste of power during Reconstruction but were now being squeezed out of conventional political organizations. It was very much a part of this world, an important social institution with pronounced nationalistic tendencies, and it faced head-on the important public issue of race relations in the late nineteenth-century South. The church usually dealt mainly with issues related to institutional policy, but they were often connected to the broader political controversies of the time.

Among the questions that produced discord in the church during the post-Reconstruction years was its relationship to the white northern churches. During the Civil War and immediately afterward, northern white denominations had proclaimed their friendliness toward blacks; in thousands of individual acts of selflessness on behalf of the freedmen, members of those churches had proved themselves faithful to their leaders' declarations. But the friendship that white northern churchmen offered to the freedmen was often burdened by an arrogance and paternalism that infuriated many blacks, and led them to demand a detachment from the influence of white churches.

The general issue of whether to separate from whites assumed several specific forms. One was the rather cut-and-dried question of organizational autonomy, which was of greater importance to Methodists because of the nature of their polity than it was to the Baptists. Methodism's centralized and more authoritarian structure required that congregations be totally integrated into one denomination or another. There was little room for local congregations to maneuver or to be innovative in seeking formal association with other Methodist organizations. They had to choose between affiliation with the independent African Methodist denominations and submission to their annual and general conferences or the biracial but white-controlled northern and southern Methodist churches.

The number of black members of the two white-controlled denominations indicates that a substantial minority of black Methodists preferred to maintain ecclesiastical ties with their white brethren. The Colored Methodist Episcopal church contained blacks who had deliberately chosen not to join either one of the African denominations following the Civil War and had worked closely with the Methodist Episcopal Church, South. Accordingly, white Methodists had certain expectations, mostly fulfilled, of their CME brethren. They expected, for instance, that the CME church would not play the active political role that the African Methodist churches played in southern politics. CME leaders did tend to avoid comment on temporal issues, a policy, especially compared to those of the African churches and indeed the history of black evangelical Christianity, that suggests the church's acquiescence in the resurgent political power of southern whites. In 1874 the General Conference of the southern church expressed pleasure that "its" Colored Methodists were keeping their religious assemblies free from "that complication with political parties and demagogues that has been so damaging to the spiritual interests of the colored people of the South." In 1890, the Colored Methodist Episcopal church had 129,383 members, not an insignificant number.[63]

Baptists, with their decentralized structure and commitment to congregational autonomy, framed the question of separatism versus integration differently. Black Baptists divided over whether to remain reliant on the white northern American Baptist Publication Society for instructional booklets, religious tracts, and hymnals. By the 1890s a nationalistic and enterprising spirit directed blacks to begin publishing their own literature, but they had a strong residual loyalty to the publication society. Foreign mission work raised another issue. Separatists within the National Baptist Convention's Foreign Mission Board did not want to cooperate with whites in establishing and maintaining missions in Africa, whereas activists in Virginia and North Carolina, where a long tradition of biracial cooperation stretched back to the days of Lott Cary, argued for continuation of the relationship. The issue was complicated by the decision of the Foreign Mission Board to relocate its headquarters from Richmond to Louisville. In 1897 the integrationists established the Lott Cary Foreign Mission Society and continued to work closely with whites in the foreign mission field.[64]

Another Baptist controversy involved control of church-related colleges and schools, most of which had been established by the American Baptist Home Mission Society. The governing boards, administrations, and faculties of those schools were generally white, and by the 1890s blacks thought they should be turned over to them to manage. In these disagreements, the fundamental question was whether the black church

63. Charles H. Phillips, *The History of the Colored Methodist Episcopal Church in America* (Jackson, Tenn., 1898), 25; Joe M. Richardson, *The Negro in the Reconstruction of Florida, 1867–1877* (Tallahassee, 1965), 83; H. Shelton Smith, *In His Image, But . . . : Racism in Southern Religion, 1780–1910* (Durham, 1972), 229–30; William B. Gravely, "The Social, Political and Religious Significance of the Formation of the Colored Methodist Episcopal Church (1870)," *Methodist History,* XVIII (October, 1979), 3–21; Methodist Episcopal Church, South, General Conference, *Journal of the General Conference of the Methodist Episcopal Church, South . . . 1874* (Nashville, 1874), 459; *Eleventh Census, 1890: Churches,* 46, 543, 559, 604.

64. Williams, *Black Americans and the Evangelization of Africa,* 70.

and the religious activities of blacks would be controlled by blacks themselves or by whites and therefore was related to the basic issue of separatism or integrationism that confronted southern blacks at the close of the nineteenth century.

The tension between these opposing strategies of racial integration and self-reliant separation had been evident during Reconstruction. The issue was clearly drawn in the competition between the African Methodist denominations and the Methodist Episcopal church. African Methodists had resented the northern church because it competed directly with them for black adherents, and the Methodist Episcopal church had challenged the separatist principles of the African churches. Methodist Episcopal missionaries had appealed to the freedmen with the ideal of an integrated church. Separatism was inherent in the African Methodist churches and made them part of the evolving black nationalism of the nineteenth century, but it had not appealed to all black Methodists, as the CME church and the black congregations in the ME church testified. The separatist orientation of the AME church had deeply distressed James D. Lynch, missionary and editor of the *Christian Recorder*. He thought it was a fallacy in the argument of his separatist brethren that blacks could live their lives independent of whites. Blacks and whites, he believed, were inseparable parts of the same society. He expected blacks to enjoy the rights of American citizens, but he argued that they could not be obtained through militancy but by working to convince southern whites that it was in their interest as well as that of blacks for the two to coexist as equals. He insisted that "we have got to live together in this country, we expect to enjoy political rights, and we can never get them by force, but must depend upon the identity of interest and the prompting of fellow feeling. The white people have the physical power, political power, intellectual power, wealth and influence, while that which we possess, in comparison with theirs, is a little more than nothing." Lynch's advice revealed the most fundamental element in his approach to whites and forecast his decision to leave the AME church and join the ME church. "We must unite with our white friends who believe in the equal rights of man; and act on the principle that we are one of the elements of the American people." Although he had labored tirelessly on behalf of freedmen who were struggling to secure title to church property from the white southern Methodist church and was uncompromising in his demands on that issue, he sought an understanding with southern whites that would produce racial harmony. He had been confident that such a goal could be achieved because "there are good and great men in the Methodist Church, South, who will stand by the colored people in this matter, because they stand by the right." [65]

Whether black congregations ought to be integrated into white associations and conventions was not an issue for Baptists, who had taken the independence of church organizations for granted from the beginning of freedom. But Baptists quickly established close and rewarding relationships with the American Baptist Home Mission Society and the American Baptist Publication Society so as to receive aid from white northern Baptists. Black Baptist leaders were very direct, however, in pointing out that they would not submit to white control. The Cedar Grove Association of North Carolina stated the matter with perfect clarity: it was "opposed to any white person's having the whole control of the colored churches, but gladly receive advice from all." [66]

The questions that confronted Baptists during the time of mounting discrimination by whites and the rising militancy of black nationalists in the 1890s were twofold. One was whether denominational colleges and seminaries that had been founded, supported, and controlled by the American Baptist Home Mission Society of New York should be turned over to black organizations. The second was whether black Baptists would continue to rely on the white-run American Baptist Publication Society for religious literature used in Sunday school and church services or, instead, support the newly established Publishing Board of the black National Baptist Convention. Black Baptist leaders in the South argued bitterly over the application of the related concepts of separation and self-help to these questions with the result that, in several states, deep and bitter divisions occurred in statewide and district organizations.

During the 1870s and 1880s, the American Baptist Home Mission Society had owned and operated several schools for blacks, including Wayland Seminary in Washington (later moved to Richmond), Richmond Theological Seminary for males and Hartshorn Memorial College for females in Virginia, Shaw University in North Carolina, Augusta Baptist Seminary in Georgia, and Bishop College in Texas. In addition, the society contributed financially to the support of several other seminaries, col-

---

65. *Christian Recorder,* September 9, October 21, 1865, July 20, 1867. For an account of Lynch's political career see William C. Harris, "James Lynch: Black Leader in Southern Reconstruction," *Historian,* XXXIV (November, 1971), 40–61.

66. Baptist State Convention of the State of North Carolina, *Proceedings of the State Baptist Convention, Colored, of the State of North Carolina . . . 1870* (Raleigh, 1871), 7.

leges, and secondary schools for black students. In most cases, the presidents and majorities on the governing boards and faculties of the colleges and schools that the society owned were white. Schools that had been founded by blacks but received financial support from the Home Mission Society generally employed black administrators and faculties.

Through the 1880s, the American Baptist Home Mission Society continued to revise its missionary and educational work in the South, taking into account various stringencies and the fact that missionary activity in other parts of the country was assuming greater importance to members of the society and a correspondingly larger share of its financial resources. One such change in policy was embodied in a plan to consolidate the society's schools by designating flagship schools in each state that would be developed into respectable colleges and theological schools. "It is evidently impossible," society officials stated in 1881, "even if it were desirable, to conduct ten or twelve thoroughly equipped Theological Schools for the freedmen. One or two institutions of this character, however, are required." Other existing institutions would become secondary or feeder schools, and no new schools would be established. In every case, the flagship school would be one that the society owned and operated. The administrations and property of those colleges would remain under the society's control. As reasonable as the plan seemed to the society's officials, it drew opposition from blacks who resented continued white domination and wanted to end it. They believed that under the society's plan white domination would increase.[67]

But the school plan was not the only divisive issue for blacks. Their dependence on white northern Baptists for religious literature was another. That material was published and distributed by the American Baptist Publication Society. Even though black churches and Sunday schools were a major market for the society's literature, it did not accept contributions from black authors, an indication of white officials' negative perception of blacks and that they did not want their program of cooperation with white southern Baptists jeopardized by an offensive editorial policy. In 1889, though, under pressure from the black American National Baptist Convention, the publication society announced that it would publish articles written by three prominent black ministers, Walter H. Brooks, William J. Simmons, and Emanuel K. Love, in its journal the *Baptist Teacher*. After a strong negative reaction by southern white Bap-

67. *Home Mission Monthly,* III (June, 1881), 119.

tists, the society withdrew its offer, suggesting instead that the Brooks-Simmons-Love articles be published separately as tracts. All three of the ministers recognized the segregation implied in the society's alternative proposal and summarily rejected it. This confrontation motivated separatists to organize the National Baptist Publishing Board within the National Baptist Convention. Thus after 1895 literature written and published by blacks as well as the publications of the American Baptist Publication Society were available to black churches.[68]

Tension between black Baptists in several southern states and the northern Baptist societies became acute when the former began to express their deep resentment over discrimination by northern white Baptists. In some states, such as Georgia, the outcry was a solitary voice, but in others, notably Virginia and Texas, it was a loud chorus that caused divisions in state and district organizations as militant nationalists and more conservative blacks argued over what loyalty black churches owed the northern societies.

In Virginia the crisis began to build in 1890, when the black state convention denounced the publication society's decision not to publish the Brooks-Simmons-Love articles. Calling its policy discriminatory and maintaining that discrimination based on skin color was "incompatible with Christianity," the convention condemned the society for "sacrificing the colored brethren for the sake of gain or hope of gratifying blind prejudice." This criticism, the messengers said, was not intended to express any "unkindness" or "ingratitude," but rather a sense of "self-respect" and "violated justice." The society placated the Virginians by agreeing to publish a volume of essays by black authors, and the tension between the Virginia state convention and white northern Baptists eased. Indeed, in 1896, the convention ratified an agreement between the American Baptist Home Mission Society and the Home Mission Board of the Southern Baptist Convention negotiated at a meeting at Fortress Monroe to share the cost of maintaining missionaries among blacks, thereby formally committing itself to continued cooperation with the northern home mission society. But more rough times lay ahead.[69]

Actually, the cause of the trouble had little to do with the publication society or with cooperation in missionary activity but concerned the Home Mission Society's plan to reorganize Baptist schools in the state.

68. Washington, "Origins and Emergence of Black Separatism," 190–208.
69. *Ibid.*, 202–203.

That plan, presented to the convention in 1896, called for combining the Richmond Seminary, Wayland Baptist College, and Hartshorn College into the Virginia Union University. Another school, Virginia Seminary, located in Lynchburg and operated by blacks with financial contributions from the society, would become a secondary school affiliated with Virginia Union. That the Virginia Seminary, which had a black administration and a black faculty, would be subordinated to the proposed Virginia Union University offended the pride of many blacks. They feared that Virginia Seminary would be destroyed if the society's plan were implemented or, at the very least, the school's independence would be sacrificed. The plan, they charged, amounted to a breach of the society's agreement to support Virginia Seminary. Meeting in Lexington in May, 1899, the state convention voted to withdraw Virginia Seminary from the Virginia Union compact and rescinded its earlier ratification of the Fortress Monroe agreement.[70]

Supporters of the action of the state convention, including Gregory W. Hayes, the president of Virginia Seminary, were motivated by a maturing sense of black cultural and economic nationalism. They had come to resent the American Baptist Home Mission Society's control over their schools. Virginia Seminary symbolized black progress toward self-reliance in the generation since slavery. Hayes was especially militant, advocating the radical idea of a totally separate black nation within the United States. A majority of the delegates to the state convention favored independence from the Home Mission Society and argued for self-help rather than cooperation based on discrimination. Some district associations, like the Valley Baptist Association, endorsed the state convention's action. The next year the Valley Association went even further by resolving to support the Publishing Board of the National Baptist Convention. Messengers to the association explained that "it will inspire the youth to use literature which is the product of the brain and thought of his own race."[71]

A minority of black Baptists in Virginia favored continued cooperation with their white northern brethren and refused to abide by the decision of the majority. They did not necessarily reject the goal of black in-

---

70. *Home Mission Monthly,* XXI (January, 1899), 3.

71. *Ibid.;* Valley Baptist Association of Virginia, *Minutes of the Thirty-third Annual Session of the Valley Baptist Association of Virginia . . . 1899* (Lynchburg, 1900) 12–14, *Minutes of the Thirty-fourth Annual Session of the Valley Baptist Association of Virginia . . . 1900* (Lynchburg, 1900), 21.

dependence and self-reliance; they just did not believe that blacks were yet ready to strike out on their own. A report by the committee on education read to the messengers of the Norfolk, Virginia, Union Baptist Association in 1896 urged a pragmatic approach to the financing of education. It noted that black Baptists had white friends, who had done much "to lift us from the slums of ignorance." "Now, let us not show too much independency, but talk business," the committee members advised. "Remember we are neither Astors nor Rothschilds." The heavy and chronic indebtedness of the Virginia Seminary bore out the argument of these and other cooperationists that blacks could not afford the price of separation. The cooperationist delegates to the state convention, meeting in 1899, returned to their homes disturbed by what had happened at Lexington. A group of eight ministers composed a statement of protest addressed to the Baptist brotherhood of Virginia. In it, they described the action of the "sinners" and "irresponsible men" of the "so-called" state convention as self-defeating because "it directly rejects the good offices of our best white friends North and South, especially of the American Baptist Home Mission Society, which has been and is doing so much for us." Desiring an end to discrimination based on race, they insisted that by rejecting cooperation with benevolent whites the state convention was unwittingly inviting more discrimination. They said "it must and will widen the breach between the white and the colored people, which is now unfortunately too wide in some places to be wholesome and promising for good." Meeting in Richmond in June, 1899, the cooperationists formed the rival General Association of Virginia. At its first annual session in 1900, the group stated: "Untold good has come to us as a denomination and race by working in harmony and cooperation with those of the dominant race in this country North and South in our educational and missionary work." The organization continued to cooperate with whites who wished to assist in the advancement of the race.[72]

One of the most vehement and articulate spokesmen for separation among black Baptists during the 1890s was Emanuel K. Love of Georgia.

72. Shaeffer Memorial Association (Virginia), *Minutes of the First Annual Session of the Shaeffer Memorial Association . . . 1901* (Lynchburg, n.d.), 4–6; Norfolk, Virginia, Union Baptist Association, *Minutes of the Thirty-third Annual Session of the Norfolk, Virginia, Union Baptist Association . . . 1896* (Lynchburg, 1896), 44–45; *Home Mission Monthly*, XXI (December, 1899), 446–47; General Association of Virginia, *Proceedings of the Second Annual Session of the General Association of Virginia . . . 1900* (Richmond, 1900), 26 and *passim*.

A graduate of Augusta Institute, an American Baptist Home Mission Society school, Love spent several years as a missionary in Florida and Georgia, sponsored by the society, before becoming pastor of the historic First African Baptist Church of Savannah. Recognized for his rhetorical skills and his leadership qualities, Love became president of the independent black Foreign Mission Convention as well as of the Missionary Baptist Convention of Georgia. One of the three black ministers whose essays the American Baptist Publication Society had agreed to publish, Love became a militantly outspoken proponent of separationism and self-help and demanded control of black Baptist schools.[73]

One of the first schools that the American Baptist Home Mission Society had founded in the South was located in Augusta. In 1878 the society's officers decided to relocate the school in Atlanta because it would be more centrally located and more accessible to Georgians. Moreover, Alabama Baptists had requested financial support from the society for a college in Alabama, and its officials, who did not want to undertake another black college building program, thought that an Atlanta campus would adequately serve blacks in both Alabama and Georgia. They worked out an arrangement whereby the Missionary Baptist Convention of Georgia would contribute its tract of land for the Atlanta Baptist College. A white board of trustees governed the college, a white president, George D. Sales, formulated and administered policy, whites dominated the faculty, and the Home Mission Society managed the school's financial affairs. This organization was typical of the society's schools.[74]

Love opposed the state convention's dispossession of the Atlanta property because he had hoped that blacks in the state would build and operate their own school on the site. By 1887, Love, William J. White, and James C. Bryan were the leaders of a faction among the state's black Baptists that desired more control in the administration of the Atlanta Baptist Seminary. By 1890, Love and Bryan were calling for blacks to stop participating in the society's educational programs. White was more friendly toward the society, as were most other blacks, and in 1892 the dispute threatened to divide the state convention. The executive secretary

---

73. Washington, "Origins and Emergence of Black Baptist Separatism," 158.

74. *Home Mission Monthly,* I (December, 1878), 87–89, II (June, 1880), 112; Missionary Baptist Convention of Georgia, *Minutes of the Ninth Annual Session of the Missionary Baptist Convention of Georgia . . . 1879* (N.p., n.d.), 12; Harold Lynn McManus, "The American Baptist Home Mission Society and Freedmen Education in the South, with Special Reference to Georgia, 1862–1897" (Ph.D. dissertation, Yale University, 1953), 435–72.

of the white state convention, S. Y. Jameson, attempted to heal the breach and gathered representatives of both factions along with Michael McVicar of the society for a private meeting in his office. The rift only deepened, however, when McVicar refused to relinquish control of the college. When Love threatened to open a separate college, McVicar said that blacks had neither the financial nor the intellectual resources necessary to establish a school equal to the Atlanta Seminary. McVicar's remarks enraged Love, who stormed out of the meeting. When the black state convention gathered in Macon a few weeks later, and as cooperationists supported Charles T. Walker in the presidential balloting, the division of the state's black Baptists deepened further; however, Love, who was seeking reelection as president, won. A charge of sexual misconduct against Love in 1893 obscured the issue but inflamed the passions of the convention's messengers, meeting in Atlanta, and led to a fissure and the creation of the rival General Missionary and Educational Convention.[75]

Love was far more radical and militantly nationalist than most of the other Baptist leaders in the state, and as president of the state convention he spoke out against the domination of the Home Mission Society and its policies. In his presidential message to the Missionary Baptist Convention of Georgia in 1897, he claimed that blacks were given "no recognition in the management of the school, nor part nor share in the property." He accused the society, through "its hired agents," of "dictating and undertaking to run the Missionary Baptist Convention." His most eloquent appeal, however, was to his own brethren in an attempt to persuade the convention to start a school that would be independent of the Home Mission Society. By allowing the society to assert itself over their religious lives, he argued, they failed to realize the promise of emancipation. "We have looked to our white brethren for money to carry on our work and thereby have neglected to organize and systemize our work and enthuse our people." Blacks had become "parasites," he said. "We have not been taught that we must carve out our own destiny and that our salvation is in our own right arm." Race pride was at stake. "If you see this thing as I do, and feel about it as I do, we will soon betake us to this work—We ought to mark some place along our journey through this wilderness to let the children who are coming behind us know that we have been here." Then, in some of the strongest language of the message, Love responded

75. McManus, "American Baptist Home Mission Society," 435–72; Missionary Baptist Convention of Georgia, *Minutes of the Twenty-third Annual Session of the Missionary Baptist Convention of Georgia . . . 1893* (Augusta, 1893), 32–33, 36.

to the charges by cooperationists that the separationists were drawing the invidious color line. "He is both blind and foolish," Love said, "who does not recognize the fact that the color line is already drawn. I do not believe that any white man is color blind." He saw nothing wrong in a color line *per se;* what he objected to was "unjust discrimination" based on race. "I believe every race should recognize its racial distinction. I believe in race schools and I believe in Negro ownership of these schools. I would rather be with a Negro than with any body else on earth, and I believe no white man when he tells me that he prefers to be with Negroes to being with his own race." [76]

Love's strongest allies in the convention shared his desire for more black control of educational institutions, but, like William J. White, the influential editor of the convention's newspaper, the *Georgia Baptist,* they were prepared to accept a compromise arrangement with the American Baptist Home Mission Society. The society isolated Love when, during the 1897 annual session of the state convention, it proposed an alternative solution to the problem of ownership and control of Atlanta Baptist College. He was demanding that the society continue funding the college but turn over property and management of the school to blacks, which it refused to do. The society was holding the school's assets in trust for the Baptists in the North who had contributed toward the uplift of southern blacks, and to relinquish control of the property would violate that trust. The society offered instead to reorganize the school to give blacks representation in its administration and more authority in selection of its faculty. The moderates in the convention did not believe that they could maintain the college by themselves and agreed to add blacks to the board of trustees. The society's backers carried a motion to accept the plan, saying, "The highest educational interests of the colored Baptists of Georgia will be promoted in the best manner by uniting all of the Baptist forces of the State." [77]

Love stood virtually alone in fighting for a separate Baptist college. He did, however, win a significant though incomplete victory in a battle to have Georgia Baptist churches adopt the religious literature of the Publishing Board of the National Baptist Convention. Arguing that its material was equal in quality to that of the American Baptist Publication Society and attempting to discredit cooperationists, who favored con-

76. Missionary Baptist Convention of Georgia, *Minutes . . . 1897,* 35–45.

77. *Home Mission Monthly,* XXI (November, 1899), 431; Missionary Baptist Convention of Georgia, *Minutes . . . 1897,* 35–45.

tinuing to patronize the publication society by referring to them as "disloyal Negroes and hirelings," Love urged the convention to request that all member churches subscribe to the literature of the National Baptist Publishing Board. "It is not only as good as that which we have been taking, but it is a question of race pride and of race gain in dollars and cents and it gives employment to Negroes which they cannot hope for in a white publishing house." The convention resolved to endorse the black publishing house and recommended that all ministers and Sunday schools "patronize our Negro Publishing House by purchasing their literature thereby supporting a race enterprise as well as giving proper recognition of the ability and culture of our leading men and women." Most of the district associations in Georgia, however, continued to endorse the American Baptist Publication Society and its literature, which may be even more indicative than the school issue of the position of these churches on the question of separation versus cooperation. The prominent men of the convention were more apt than local congregations to be separationists.[78]

In Texas, a similar dispute over control of education polarized Baptists and divided the state organization. The objects of controversy were two colleges: Bishop College, founded by the American Baptist Home Mission Society in 1881, and Guadalupe College, purchased by the Guadalupe Baptist Association from the Catholic church in 1884. Tension between local Baptists and the Home Mission Society surfaced in 1888, when Bishop's white president, S. W. Culver, was accused of abusing a female student. Students boycotted the school, and the society removed Culver from the presidency. Then, in 1891, the Home Mission Society proposed that the schools in the state be reorganized with Bishop becoming the flagship. According to the plan, a twelve-man board of education, responsible to the society, would oversee a system of schools and ensure that Bishop was the focus of all college and theological instruction. Other institutions, including Hearne Academy and Guadalupe College, would become feeders. Blacks were asked not to attempt to establish a separate school of their own for at least fifty years. Several ministers, mostly from Austin and San Antonio, objected to the plan. What rankled them most was that Guadalupe would be subsumed by Bishop. Race pride and black nationalism were at the core of their feelings.[79]

78. Missionary Baptist Convention of Georgia, *Minutes . . . 1897*, 41, 52–53.

79. McPherson, *Abolitionist Legacy*, 287–88; William Beckham, *Unification; or, Why We Have Two Negro Baptist Conventions in Texas* (Nashville, 1897), 3–16.

Separatists came to the Baptist Missionary and Education Convention of Texas, which gathered in San Antonio in 1893, with an ultimatum that if the Home Mission Society's plan to reorganize the state's schools was not rejected, they would organize a rival convention. A committee of separationists that included David Abner, Jr., the son of a Texas Reconstruction legislator and formerly a faculty member of Bishop College, stated their objections to the plan. They opposed any change in the status of Guadalupe College. They did not want it relegated to a feeder institution to Bishop. Their commitment to the concept of independence through self-help, however, was qualified. They did not reject continued financial support from the society; they resented its interference in the operation of black colleges. "We hold that if the American Baptist Home Mission Society of New York is willing to aid the negro, as we believe it is . . . there is sufficient room to bestow gifts without making such restrictions as to visit and shape the policy of said school, especially as pertains to inspection, power, and formation of curriculum." The separationists demanded that the Missionary and Education Convention endorse Guadalupe College and that all money brought to the convention for the support of education be equally divided between Bishop and Guadalupe.[80]

The convention appointed another committee to answer the separationists' objections. This group included one separationist, Lee L. Campbell, the pastor of Austin's Ebenezer Baptist Church, but was dominated by cooperationists, particularly Allen R. Griggs of Dallas, who was an agent of the Home Mission Society. No one was surprised when the committee rejected the separationists' demands on the practical grounds that the society would not turn over its property to the black convention and they could not support the various schools by themselves. The separationists then bolted the convention and formed the rival General Missionary Baptist Convention of Texas.[81]

The separationists in Texas were not averse to maintaining a working relationship with white Baptists. What they wanted most was what the freedmen had sought after emancipation, that is, to have control of the educational institutions in the state along with the financial support of their white brethren. In a letter to the first annual session of the General Missionary Baptist Convention, which assembled in San Antonio in

80. Baptist Missionary and Educational Convention of Texas, *Minutes of the Twenty-first Annual Session . . . 1892* (Dallas, 1893), 30–34, *1893* (Austin, 1893), 42; Beckham, *Unification*, 9.

81. Beckham, *Unification*, 10–11.

1894, C. H. Griggs of Cuero, the convention's secretary, acknowledged the poverty of black Baptists and their need of assistance from whites. "The colored Baptists of Texas, and of the South," he said, "are poor; their heads are not towering very high above the poverty level, but the time is ripe that we should assert a few rights that all concerned should concede at once are inalienable. The right to hold property and manage the same should be conceded to us by all liberal minds, and if our dire financial distress should be made known to you inadvertently, and you, from the depth of your soul, desire to be to us the Good Samaritan, you'll step forward and show your philanthropic nature without asking to be made the controlling spirit in the matter ere your donation is made." A. L. Sledge, moderator of the Missionary Baptist Lincoln Association, expressed the resentment that he and other Texas Baptists felt toward the Home Mission Society and its black allies, who "have deprived the Negro Baptists of this State from owning and controlling Institutions of Higher Learning." Sledge supported the formation of a new state convention "who believe in Negro preachers for Negro churches, Negro teachers for Negro schools." Separationists also were solicitous of aid from the white state convention. Addressing the separationist convention in 1905, President L. L. Campbell said, "It is to be hoped that some definite plan of cooperation may be entered into between the white Baptist General Convention of Texas and our Convention." [82]

One wonders why the nationalism of the late nineteenth century never matured into a massive and powerful civil rights movement. Why did the sorrow and the bitterness of southern black folk not merge with the outrage of articulate nationalists to create a broad-based and unified campaign for freedom and autonomy? Edwin S. Redkey, who has written about black nationalism and the African exodus during the last quarter of the nineteenth century, suggests that it was because most blacks retained a positive outlook about their ultimate integration into American society: "If black nationalism was not . . . the predominant black reaction to white nationalism, the reason must be sought in the basic optimism of black Americans." Certainly the disputes within the black church over emigration and cooperation with white-controlled churches

---

82. General Missionary Baptist Convention of Texas, *Proceedings of the First Annual Session . . . 1894* (Austin, 1894), 5; Missionary Baptist General Convention of Texas, *Proceedings of the Twelfth Annual Session of the Missionary Baptist General Convention of Texas . . . 1905* (N.p., n.d.), 44; Missionary Baptist Lincoln Association (Texas), *Minutes of the Twenty-eighth Annual Session . . . 1895* (Austin, 1895), 11.

indicate a feeling that the black destiny was inextricably intertwined with that of whites. It is a complicated question, and the ultimate answer is beyond the scope of this study, but at least part of the reason why nationalism did not flower among southern blacks at that time lay in the nature of black leadership, including the race's traditional church leaders. The church was far and away the leading institution in the black community, and it embodied many of the basic ingredients of a nationalistic movement. At a time of economic stagnation, betrayal and abandonment by the Republican party, and often brutally violent discrimination, the church organized blacks in the interest of their own betterment. It offered a structure through which people, ideas, and resources could be mobilized, and it put forward a theology that helped to define African Americans culturally. It channeled emigrationist sentiment toward an African zion and sought to mobilize black Americans in a common cause with Africans to follow the Christian road to political redemption and the benefits of civilization. The church, more than any other black institution, exemplified the nationalist ideal of independence and self-reliance. But it was not able to convert social separatism and cultural nationalism into an effective political movement. Although the Christian pulpit was the workplace of some of the most eloquent spokesmen for the cause of nationalism in the nineteenth century, including Henry Highland Garnet, Alexander Crummell, and Henry M. Turner, the church and its leaders failed to galvanize a community that was deeply divided on the matter of nationalism versus integrationism. Indeed, the church was itself sundered by the divisive issues of the day. It was basically a conservative institution, not simply because of an otherworldly theology or an accommodationist attitude but because it was more a mirror of community attitudes and opinions than a shaper of them. Nationalists like Henry M. Turner, Gregory W. Hayes, Emanuel K. Love, and David Abner, Jr., in advocating political action in harmony with their nationalist beliefs, represented, despite the power of their voices, a minority point of view even in a time that Wilson Jeremiah Moses has described as black nationalism's "golden age." They could not change that fact. Moreover, by the turn of the century the church and its ministers were losing their status as political leaders of the black community. In political and economic matters, blacks were beginning to look toward a new generation of largely secular leaders.[83]

83. Redkey, *Black Exodus*, 13; Moses, *Golden Age of Black Nationalism*.

6

The Spirit of Worship

Beyond the long wooden bridge leading to St. Helena Island in 1865 stood a brick church in which local planters, their families, and their slaves had worshiped before emancipation. Some of the former slave owners had returned to the island after the war, but not to the church. The high-backed pews in which they had prayed, sang hymns, and listened to the minister preach the gospel showed no sign of their presence. But the church was not deserted; far from it. It had become the center of religious and social activity for the freedmen of St. Helena, who flocked to the low brick building every Sunday in such numbers that there often was not room enough for everyone to be seated inside.

On one Sunday morning that summer—although it was the same nearly every Sabbath—the sandy roads that wound alternately through cotton fields and stands of live oak trees to the church were clogged with worshipers on their way to services. Some were on foot, others rode on horseback, and still others, men, women, and children, were perched on carts and wagons. A few even traveled in stylish trotting buggies manufactured in the North. In the woods behind the church, owners parked their wagons and carts, unharnessed their horses, tied them to trees, and fed them. Small groups of men were standing around the wagons discussing the cotton crop and gossiping. Most of the parishioners milled about in the shaded yard between the old church and the brand new schoolhouse that stood on the other side. There were too many people to fit inside, the old deacon told the crowd. Services would be held outside. Indeed, a platform had already been erected near the entrance to the church to accommodate the preacher and the other dignitaries who were scheduled to address the congregation.

Everyone was standing up facing the platform, faces upturned, "eagah fur de Wud." They all had on their best clothes, the men wearing coats in a variety of colors, the women, who usually outnumbered male churchgoers by a margin of three to two, in straw hats, cotton gloves, bright calico dresses, and crinolines. Many of the older women wore colorful scarfs wrapped African-style—turbanlike—about their heads. Whitelaw Reid, the white journalist who was touring the South that summer, thought "they were dressed as well as the average day-laborers' families at the North." By and by, an old man, whose bent posture told of a life-time of backbreaking labor, stepped out onto the platform. Swaying gently back and forth, he began to sing "in a shrill, cracked voice." Immediately and spontaneously the congregation joined in several verses of "Roll, Jordan, Roll." Following the song, the preacher, who was a bald-headed, middle-aged man, came forward and offered a prayer that the members of the congregation punctuated with interjections of "Amen " and "Glory." Along with the sermon that morning, the congregation heard several "friends" deliver political speeches. Central Church happened to be a stop on General Rufus Saxton's itinerary. Saxton, the commander of the Department of the South, and Secretary of the Treasury Salmon P. Chase were traveling through the area to examine firsthand the condition of the freedmen. Both spoke to the audience, as did a Yankee minister. They all talked about the freedom and responsibility that had recently been bestowed on the former slaves. The power that their masters once had wielded over them was broken, the guests said, but it was up to the people to make the most of what God, through the agency of the Union, had seen fit to grant. After the services, with smiling faces, warm, sincere thank-yous to the distinguished guests, and good-byes to friends, the worshipers gathered up their children, hitched up their horses and wagons, and returned down those same sandy roads to their farms.[1]

Although Sabbath worship services were the primary church activities, the people in thousands of local congregations were involved with their churches on a daily basis. The churches were the nerve centers of their denominations, simultaneously sending pulses of humanity running upward through the institutional hierarchy and generating cohesion and a sense of belonging among people in isolated neighborhoods and settlements whom the larger society shunned because of their race. The congregations were an essential element in the personal identity through which the people defined themselves as Christians and as members of an

1. Whitelaw Reid, *After the War: A Southern Tour, May 1, 1865, to May 1, 1866* (Cincinnati, 1866), 99–111.

African-American community. In a myriad of ways, the congregation recognized the hopes and fears of the people who came together regularly to worship and to socialize and communicated them to others far away through a network of denominational agencies. They gave support and succor to people who struggled to maintain a positive self-concept against an onslaught of negative images and assertions emanating from the dominant white society and against poverty and the frustration of opportunities for advancement that were closed to them. In helping to promote a distinctive African-American identity, the congregations were vital contributors to African-American culture.

The church was the focal point of life in most communities throughout the postemancipation period. Church meetings were not breaks in the routine of daily life but integral parts of everyday existence. Mary White Ovington, one of the founders of the National Association for the Advancement of Colored People, placed the local church in perspective when she wrote, "It was not church, a place away from the world, that a boy or girl visited occasionally in busy life, but a part of home." Some event happened in or was sponsored by the church nearly every day of the week. During worship services on Sundays and at prayer meetings on weekday evenings parishioners gave full expression to their religious beliefs and practiced the ceremonies of worship spawned by their experience in American society. From humble, ramshackle church houses to cavernous brick sanctuaries, the voices of preachers and parishioners rang out in a special cadence of sermon and audience response that characterized black worship and in the sweet, fervent tones of hymns and spirituals rendered by people giving thanks to God for his love and grace. Above and beyond religion, church members and outsiders alike used the congregation to communicate information and to galvanize the people on important political issues. At picnics, excursions, and bazaars, parishioners relaxed and enjoyed themselves in the company of family and friends. By contributing to welfare and educational programs, congregations gave aid and comfort to citizens who had material needs and who were seeking to emerge from the shadow of ignorance. Although they were not altogether shielded from the intrusive eyes of curious outsiders, meddlesome reformers, and institutional disciplinarians, the congregations were free from most of the external controls that had impinged on them during slavery. No other institution in the black community encompassed the full range, diversity, and richness of African-American culture. The congregations embodied the spirit of worship and gave life and character to the church.[2]

It should be stressed that the notion of a black church is misleading because it suggests a monolithic institution. It also implies a strict racial dualism: blacks all attending their own churches and following their patterns of worship while whites did the same in theirs. The activities of local black congregations, many of which were Baptist and Methodist, did indeed incorporate many beliefs and practices that worshipers shared across denominational lines, creating the appearance of uniformity. And there certainly had been a black exodus from white churches after emancipation. But the reality of the black church was far more complex and ambiguous than the notion suggests. There were many striking differences among black congregations. These differences were the result of sociological as well as denominational factors and of the black response to whites generally and to white missionary activity, particularly during the period immediately following emancipation. Southern blacks, whose culture was a product of African traditions as well as American experiences and interaction with whites, did not all react in the same way to the missionaries who came south to organize and establish an essentially white style of worship among them. Some were far more accepting of the culture borne by the evangelists than others; they responded to their teaching and joined their churches—even those controlled by whites. Others insisted on complete independence from white control and resisted the missionaries, who attempted to remodel their values and customs. Black congregations reflected no single pattern of belief and behavior during the period of black cultural and community development that followed emancipation. Just how the local people reacted to the missionaries and how their churches functioned depended considerably on the social and economic conditions that governed their lives. Common elements such as a reaction against racial prejudice were prominent in postwar black society, but woven through it as well were richly diverse threads. Variations in where the people lived, in their social status, in the level of their education, in their economic situation, and even in their ages, gender, and color produced differences in perception, aspiration, psychological need, and group identity, which in turn entailed divergent worldviews and religious ideas. Widely varying social and economic con-

2. Mary White Ovington, *The Walls Came Tumbling Down* (New York, 1946), 71.

ditions opened cultural chasms that created contrasting identities and separate realities among them.[3]

Emancipation erased some of the lines that divided blacks, such as the one that distinguished between slave and free people. A large percentage of the latter were light-skinned, mulatto offspring of unions of whites and blacks. The difference between free people and slaves, as measured by quality of life, was often not very great; indeed, some slaves lived far more comfortably than many free blacks. The poorer free blacks often associated with slaves, but many free mulattoes not only enjoyed relatively high status but identified far more with white people than with slaves. As the destinies of individuals from widely different backgrounds converged after the war, however, the freeborn elite began to identify with people of lower status, including former slaves, in ways that produced a new unity among people of color in the South. Indeed, the fusion extended beyond the South, as northern and southern blacks and mulattoes forged new bonds.[4]

From the elite's point of view, solidarity was a necessity because whites nearly everywhere refused to make distinctions between different groups of blacks regardless of variations in education, occupation, quality of character, or shade of color. "They call everybody a negro," noted one black leader, "that is as black as the ace of spades or as white as snow, if they think he is a negro or know that he has negro blood in his veins." Political issues involving economics, education, and voting rights divided blacks from whites rather than the black elite from the "submerged masses." "Educated or ignorant," a white man in Richmond told journalist Whitelaw Reid, "rich or poor, the niggers must be kept down." So members of the black elite were obligated to work for the advancement of the race generally because if they did not bring the common people up to their level of achievement and respectability, whites might force them down to the level of the plain folk. Their own well-being depended on allying themselves with lower-class blacks on issues that otherwise would have divided them. This was particularly noticeable in the struggle for political rights. For example, in 1864 the New Orleans *Tribune*, published and edited by members of the city's freeborn mulatto community,

3. Joel Williamson, *The Crucible of Race: Black-White Relations in the American South Since Emancipation* (New York, 1986), 44–50.

4. Joel Williamson, *New People: Miscegenation and Mulattoes in the United States* (New York, 1980), 76–91.

known as the *gens de couleur,* supported a legislative proposal to extend voting privileges only to former free mulattoes and blacks who had served in the Union army. But when the proposition was defeated by whites who objected to enfranchising any Negroes, the paper altered its stand and became a fierce and steady advocate of voting rights for all people of color. They "must stand or fall together," the *Tribune* insisted. Another New Orleans mulatto agreed, telling Reid that "now we see that our future is indissolubly bound up with that of the negro race in this country; and we have resolved to make common cause, and rise or fall with them. We have no rights which we can reckon safe while the same are denied to the fieldhands on the sugar plantations." Thus in many respects most people of color found themselves in the same boat, fighting together against racial discrimination, and common interest as well as common blood created unity throughout the remainder of the nineteenth century.[5]

That the elite perceived a common interest with the masses in the outcome of certain political issues did not mean that African-American society had become uniform or that it had become entirely unified. It never had been a classless society, and variations in the elements of African and European-American culture resulted in distinctive groupings of African Americans. A complex social organization based on exclusive groupings continued to stratify the population after emancipation, very much as in the dominant society around it. Even the political issues in which so many people from different backgrounds had a common interest failed to gloss over class and cultural divisions. The widest gulf was between the elite, which included light-skinned mulattoes who had been born free, and the poor, oppressed black freedmen. Social groupings formed not only on the basis of skin color, however; upwardly mobile black businessmen and professionals joined the elite. Nor was it based entirely on relative financial condition; some members of the elite enjoyed only modest wealth, even by African-American standards. The determining factors in defining

5. Leon F. Litwack, *Been in the Storm So Long: The Aftermath of Slavery* (New York, 1979), 513–14; Ted Tunnell, "Free Negroes and the Freedmen: Black Politics in New Orleans During the Civil War," *Southern Studies: An Interdisciplinary Journal of the South,* XIX (Spring, 1980), 5–28; Howard N. Rabinowitz, *Race Relations in the Urban South, 1865–1890* (New York, 1978), 226–54; Joel Williamson, *After Slavery: The Negro in South Carolina During Reconstruction, 1865–1877* (Chapel Hill, 1965), 314; New Orleans *Tribune,* February 19, 1869; Reid, *After the War,* 244, 318; Willard B. Gatewood, *Aristocrats of Color: The Black Elite, 1880–1920* (Bloomington, 1990), 68.

these two groups were their social organizations, their manners, and their attitudes. Freedmen's Bureau agent John W. De Forest observed that African Americans in Greenville, South Carolina, "formed distinct cliques of society." Mulattoes, he said, were "anxious to distinguish themselves from the pure Africans," which they often did by haughtily refusing to associate with black folk. The lower classes did not exclude the elite from their social organizations but were, according to De Forest, "sore under the superiority thus asserted." Members of the different social groups within the black community maintained their system of classes, "separate and distinct in manners, habits and customs."[6]

During Reconstruction and the years that followed, the mulatto-dominated elite combined more and more with blacks from the ranks of teachers, ministers, lawyers, and physicians to form an expanded aristocracy with pretensions to leadership within the black community. As the historian Willard Gatewood has pointed out, the "aristocracy of color" held firm to the hope that racial equality would ultimately come to America and that oppression would end, but they also regarded themselves as the best of the race, and "they expected to be in the vanguard of those realizing these objectives." These persons and their families were educated, relatively prosperous, and, above all, genteel. Color still mattered in determining status, but increasingly it was their manners that set the elite apart from the masses.[7]

They remained in their own social organizations. They formed their own churches, such as the Wentworth Street Methodist Episcopal Church in Charleston, which was what an observer called "some of the wealthiest colored families," including the Westons and the Sasportases. A large percentage of aristocrats were Congregationalists and Presbyterians, though the highest percentage belonged to the Protestant Episcopal church. They joined it, as the Episcopal clergyman and historian George Freeman Bragg explained, "to get as far as possible from the ordinary Negro." St. Mark's Episcopal Church in Charleston had a reputation for being the most exclusive and color-conscious church in the South, and it included "the flower of the city"—families like the Dereefs, the Greggs, and the Kinlocks. Members of the lower classes were clearly not welcome in their

---

6. John W. DeForest, *A Union Officer in the Reconstruction*, ed. James H. Croushore and David Morris Potter (New Haven, 1948), 124; D. Augustus Straker, *The New South Investigated* (Detroit, 1888), 81; Thomas Holt, *Black over White: Negro Political Leadership in South Carolina During Reconstruction* (Urbana, 1977), 59.

7. Gatewood, *Aristocrats of Color*, 45, 49, 69–95.

churches, as Ed Barber, a light-colored African American, discovered. "When I was trampin' 'round Charleston, dere was a church dere called St. Mark, dat all de society folks of my color went to. No black nigger welcome dere, they told me. Thinkin' as how I was bright 'nough to git in, I up and goes dere one Sunday. Ah, how they did carry on, bow and scrape and ape de white folks. . . . I was uncomfortable all de time though, 'cause they was too 'hifalootin' in de ways, in de singin', and all sorts of carryin' ons." It was important to the elite to maintain a considerable social distance between themselves and the masses of freedmen. Leaders of St. James AME Church in New Orleans were so proud of its upper-crust membership that they withdrew from the congregation and founded Central Congregational Church rather than submit to a degrading denominational order that freedmen be admitted as regular members. Where social classes were mixed together in the same church, informal but rigid separation often occurred, as in a church in Tougaloo, Mississippi, where the mulatto women students from Tougaloo College refused to sit with ordinary people from the town.[8]

In contrast to the wretched misery that characterized the lives of most blacks, the elite lived in nice houses, wore fine clothes, threw fancy balls, and formed militia clubs, musical bands, and literary and debate societies. Their culture was derived from white society; it was materialistic and Victorian, and it represented the standard against which they expected that they and all blacks would be judged. Many of them, both men and women, were educated in schools and colleges operated by white churches and were taught the same value system that permeated respectable white society. Combined with a bourgeois self-consciousness, the culture of the black elite clearly delineated the contours of a distinct subcommunity. The self-indulgent activities of the aristocracy, at a time when racial discrimination was hardening and white violence intensifying, drew attention to the walls of class that divided the elite from what they termed the "submerged masses."[9]

8. Willard B. Gatewood, Jr., "Aristocrats of Color South and North: The Black Elite, 1880–1920," *Journal of Southern History*, LIV (1988), 3–20; *Christian Recorder*, September 8, 1866; New York *Age*, June 13, 1907; Litwack, *Been in the Storm So Long*, 467; Lucille Hutton, "This Is a Grand Work: A History of Central Congregational Church" (Typescript in Central Congregational Church Records, Amistad Research Center, Tulane University), 1–3; Neil R. McMillen, *Dark Journey: Black Mississippians in the Age of Jim Crow* (Urbana, 1989), 20.

9. John W. Blassingame, "Before the Ghetto: The Making of the Black Community in Savannah, Georgia, 1865–1880," *Journal of Social History*, VI (1973), 463–88; Gatewood, *Aristocrats of Color*, 22, 49.

The money the elite spent on maintaining its social position led to the criticism that it was self-indulgent and insensitive to the needs of economically hard-pressed black folk. The charge was correct to a point. The elite certainly did spend vast sums on fine homes and furnishings, clothes, and pleasure in general. Moreover, in Memphis, members of the elite showed a marked lack of interest in church benevolent societies that assisted the poor freedmen. But the aristocracy did feel a sense of responsibility for the advancement of common people, a kind of *noblesse oblige;* consequently, upper-class churches in many cities provided welfare services for the poor.[10]

The elite also felt obligated to teach the masses proper manners. Members of the black aristocracy had well-defined ideas about personal conduct that included notions about proper behavior in public gatherings such as church services. Church attendance was not as important to them as it was to the lower classes. That is not to suggest that they were any less pious but that they had other social outlets and were not dependent on the Christian gospel for their sense of self-worth. For them, church attendance was largely a social responsibility, and they sometimes seemed more concerned about how people behaved in church than about the theological or spiritual content of the service. They placed great stress on the Victorian values of self-restraint, grace, and dignity, the attributes of polite society, as personified by the northern missionaries who organized the church after the Civil War. A columnist for the New Orleans *Tribune* showed his appreciation for those conventional values when he wrote about the missionaries' personal conduct, which he thought was always "correct" and "gentlemanly." The aristocrats put themselves forward as exemplars for the common folk to follow. They believed that they could instruct ordinary people by setting examples of good behavior. The wife of Henry H. Proctor, pastor of Atlanta's First Congregational Church, believed that the upper class symbolized "a prophecy of the possibilities of the race."[11]

While instructing by example, the elite reproached the common folk for their "heathenish" mode of worship. They were repelled by the ap-

10. Armstead L. Robinson, "Plans Dat Comed from God: Institution Building and the Emergence of Black Leadership in Reconstruction Memphis," in *Toward a New South? Studies in Post–Civil War Southern Communities,* ed. Orville Vernon Burton and Robert C. McMath, Jr. (Westport, 1982), 91–96; Williamson, *New People,* 82–87; Gatewood, *Aristocrats of Color,* 39, 49–50, 76.

11. Gatewood, *Aristocrats of Color,* 22–29, 291–92; New Orleans *Tribune,* March 28, 1865.

parent ignorance, emotionalism, and intemperance in folk religion, what AME bishop Daniel A. Payne believed was "the essence of religion" to most ordinary blacks. One educated woman, for example, was "disgusted with bad grammar and worse pronunciation, and their horrible absurdities." To the well-bred, emotionalism and allied behavior were not "necessary adjuncts to piety." They did not reveal depth of conviction, but rather something far more visceral. They were characteristics bred by slavery; they exemplified the dehumanizing effect of slavery and were to be avoided by free and respectable people. A writer for the Colored Methodist Episcopal church's *Christian Index* ascribed to slavery such behavior as "peculiarly moving mourns, sighs, and shouts" and condemned them as inappropriate among a free people. Francis Grimké, a prominent Presbyterian cleric and pastor of an elite Washington, D.C., congregation, concluded that "where emotion prevails, the underlying conception of religion will be false, pernicious, and degrading." Other spokesmen for respectability and refinement reflected what was in the back of the minds of most whites when he pointed out that whites deemed emotionalism to be symptomatic of inferiority rather than a result of slavery's harsh oppressiveness and that poor and uneducated folk provided whites with a pretext for denigrating all blacks by behaving in ways that confirmed racial stereotypes.[12]

African-American folk culture was criticized by many in the black elite community, who called for reform. Church leaders were in the forefront of active reformers. The movement started with the missionaries who journeyed into the South hopefully, though naïvely, intending to teach the freedmen the beliefs and practices of their middle-class society. In addition to a standard Protestant theology, they bore values that stressed self-restraint and Victorian standards of morality. They regarded the freedmen as intemperate, superstitious, and immoral, but they blamed man, not God, for those disabilities. These characteristics were the consequences of slavery's deprivations and its degradation of the slaves' character; they were not the marks of racial inferiority, as whites claimed. In hoping to reform the freedmen's scarred character and religious practices, the missionaries failed to understand that slave religion

12. Daniel A. Payne, *Recollections of Seventy Years* (Nashville, 1888), 254; Litwack, *Been in the Storm So Long*, 458; William Wells Brown, *My Southern Home: or, The South and Its People* (Boston, 1880), 197; David M. Tucker, *Black Pastors and Leaders: Memphis, 1816–1972* (Memphis, 1975), 22–23; Francis J. Grimké, *The Afro-American Pulpit in Relation to Race Elevation* (Washington, D.C., 1893), 5; New York *Globe*, August 18, 1883.

and patterns of worship constituted a unified and coherent system of beliefs that reflected the slaves' African-American experiences and contributed to their sense of community and of themselves. They compounded their misunderstanding by failing to appreciate the strength of the freedmen's commitment to their religious system. The missionaries' expectations rested on a few widely held but very questionable assumptions. One was that a vast majority of the former slaves had no religious faith whatsoever but clung instead to exotic superstitions, "which belonged to the fetish worship of savage Africa" and could easily be dispelled by Christian education. Another was that the former slaves were calling out—in a "Macedonian cry"—for help to turn their superstitions into a solid Christian faith and their weird customs and wild behavior into the sober deportment of respectable citizens.[13]

Despite their misapprehensions, the missionaries' expectations were not altogether unrealistic. Insofar as their religious experiences in antebellum times had corresponded to orthodox doctrine, the freedmen were receptive to the missionaries and responded warmly to the ideas they preached. Many slaves had been members of their masters' churches or had been encouraged—even compelled—to observe white church services. In many instances, they had been catechized by whites, and their own worship services had been supervised by whites. Being under scrutiny had bred resentment in some cases but had had the opposite effect in others. But regardless of how it happened, large numbers of slaves had already come into contact with the beliefs and practices of respectable whites and had generally accepted them as models for their own. A case in point was Cato Carter, an Alabama slave who had been permitted to choose between attending a white church or a slave church on his master's plantation. He preferred the white one because, he later testified, the slave exhorter was illiterate. He had preached from an open Bible, but Carter claimed he "couldn't read a line no more than a sheep could." That was enough to turn him away from the slave congregation. Such people eagerly followed the leadership of the northern missionaries.[14]

13. G. W. Nichols, "Six Weeks in Florida," *Harper's New Monthly Magazine,* XLI (1870), 663; *Christian Recorder,* November 21, 1863.

14. John B. Boles, "Slaves in Biracial Protestant Churches," in *Varieties of Southern Religious Experience,* ed. Samuel S. Hill (Baton Rouge, 1988), 95–114; Charles S. Johnson, *The Shadow of the Plantation* (Chicago, 1934), 152; Levi J. Coppin, *Unwritten History* (Philadelphia, 1919; rpr. New York, 1968), 105; George P. Rawick, ed., *Texas Narratives* (Westport, 1972), 206, Vol. IV of Rawick, ed., *The American Slave: A Composite Autobi-*

Despite attempts to inculcate the freedmen with the values and manners of middle-class society, slave culture, with its echoes of African antecedents, remained the foundation of the African-American community in the postwar South. The traditions forged in the heat of cotton fields and rice paddies and engraved with the sorrows and delights of the slave quarters continued to command the people's loyalty. In their lifelong struggle against the oppressive forces of slavery, their "soul," or inner strength, had helped them not only to survive but also to achieve and sustain a highly developed sense of personal well-being, a transcendent purpose, and a community spirit. They came to freedom not dehumanized and demoralized, beckoning northern missionaries to save them, but richly endowed with a confidence and self-respect that made them almost defiant against race or class condescension.[15]

Northern whites were largely responsible for creating the impression that the freedmen were demoralized. Although white testimony in the form of travel accounts, personal letters, and government reports broadcast that impression, there were some whites whose vision penetrated black society and who were able to see how their culture had given African Americans the ability to endure suffering and resist despondency and to understand that the freedmen's moral fiber was strong and vigorous. Thomas Wentworth Higginson, a Massachusetts abolitionist who commanded a black regiment during the Civil War, came to the South bearing the typical northern white's mental picture of slaves as immoral, lethargic, and depraved. Like most abolitionists, he had believed that slavery prevented blacks from developing a sense of moral responsibility by rendering them dependent and irresponsible. He expected to find the freedmen unproductive and purposeless, but after spending considerable time observing them both in and out of the military camps, Higginson began to see that they had survived their enslavement with a strong moral character. He had anticipated their courage; "the only real surprise . . . was in finding them so little demoralized."[16]

The slaves' religion had aided them greatly in resisting demoraliza-

---

ography, 19 vols.; Emiline Wright to Edward P. Smith, April 1, 1869, in American Missionary Association Archives, Amistad Research Center (hereinafter cited as AMA Archives).

15. Albert Raboteau, *Slave Religion: The "Invisible Institution" in the Antebellum South* (New York, 1978), 317–21.

16. Thomas Wentworth Higginson, *Army Life in a Black Regiment* (Boston, 1870), 189.

tion. Drinking up the spirit of God, Higginson observed, "they can endure anything." Unable to relate in a positive way to the external world around them, as Lawrence W. Levine has explained, "they extended the boundaries of their restrictive universe backward until it fused with the world of the Old Testament, and upward until it became one with the world beyond." Christian slaves identified with the Israelites whose liberation the prophets had predicted. Their hero was Moses. They often compared their masters to the Egyptian pharaohs. Slavery had invested whites with preponderant earthly power over them, but it did not engender much respect for white people or their values. Frederick Douglass articulated the contempt for the Christianity of southern whites that was common among slaves. In his autobiography, he referred to the "corrupt, slaveholding, woman-whipping, cradle-plundering, partial and hypocritical Christianity of this land." And in much the same way that their religious ideas had met the slaves' need for security, status, and a feeling of community, their beliefs supported them as they moved forward into an era of rapidly expanding opportunities and new challenges after emancipation. Their beliefs infused the freedmen with confidence. Emancipation was more than a political act; it was the fulfillment of divine prophecy. Freedom justified black people's faith and affirmed their place in the sacred cosmos. According to a hymn sung by many former slaves, it was clear who God's people were.

> Lo! Jehova's trumpet sounding
> Sweeps the blast from sea to sea!
> Hallelujah in the highest!
> God hath set his people free![17]

Most of the time the freedmen ignored the reformers, but occasionally they were emphatic in their resistance to efforts to alter their religious beliefs and practices, even when it was relatively prosperous and educated fellow African Americans who were trying to reform them. Al-

17. Higginson, *Army Life*, 41; Lawrence W. Levine, *Black Culture and Black Consciousness: Afro-American Folk Thought from Slavery to Freedom* (New York, 1977), 32–33; Timothy Smith, "Slavery and Theology: The Emergence of Black Christian Consciousness in Nineteenth-Century America," *Church History*, XLI (1972), 497–512; Linda Brent, *Incidents in the Life of a Slave Girl*, ed. Lydia M. Child (1861; rpr. New York, 1973), 10; Frederick Douglass, *Narrative of the Life of Frederick Douglass: An American Slave, Written by Himself* (1845; rpr. Cambridge, Mass., 1960), 153; New Orleans *Tribune*, March 24, 1865.

though they took pride in the accomplishments of black individuals and welcomed those who were willing to help them, they resented those—including the missionaries—who tried to lord it over them with an affected superiority. Bishop Daniel A. Payne of the AME church, who derided African-American folk culture, complained that in Maryland he had been "strongly censured" by blacks because of his "efforts to change the mode of worship or modify the extravagances indulged in by the people." It is hard to know what he meant by "strongly censured," but he may have been fortunate because local blacks could be mighty hard on missionaries. Blacks in Austin, Texas, reportedly threatened to lynch an AME missionary whom they found offensive.[18]

As the sobering realization that they were at odds with most black Christians on a number of points of doctrine and liturgy settled in on the missionaries, they complained that the former slaves were incorrigible. Jonathan Gibbs, a Presbyterian missionary who worked in South Carolina and Florida, noted that many black people remained unregenerate despite efforts to elevate their beliefs. In 1873 he wrote that they "still preach and pray, sing and shout all night long in defiance of health, sound sense, or other considerations supposed to influence a reasonable person." C. B. Martin, a black Baptist missionary in Texas, examined fifty-two churches and reached a similar conclusion. They were in a "prosperous spiritual condition," he reported, but "very indifferent or inferior in regard to the orthodox[y] of the Missionary Baptist Church."[19]

The feature of folk worship that most aroused the interest of outsiders was its emotional exuberance. William Wells Brown, a former slave and abolitionist spokesman, noted the "shouting, loud 'amen,' and the most boisterous noise in prayer" that characterized many churches. Visitors, both black and white, usually took the animation of people engaged in religious ceremonies as a sign of moral and intellectual weakness. But displays of intense emotion were the responses of religious people, whose illiteracy had forced them to devise largely nonintellectual modes of expression, and their religion certainly gave them cause for highly emo-

18. DeForest, *Union Officer in the Reconstruction*, 125; Payne, *Recollections of Seventy Years*, 254; Hightower T. Kealing, *History of African Methodism in Texas* (Waco, 1885), 26–35.

19. Joe M. Richardson, *The Negro in the Reconstruction of Florida, 1865–1877* (Tallahassee, 1965), 89; Colored Baptist Association of Louisiana and Texas, *Minutes of the Eighth Annual Session of the Colored Baptist Association of Louisiana and Texas . . . 1876* (Marshall, Tex., 1876), 7; Payne, *Recollections of Seventy Years*, 254.

tional behavior. For the masses of Christians, religious worship was an extremely powerful and exhilarating experience in which they communed with God. As had been true for their African ancestors, folk worship brought them into contact with the spirit world, an experience that was understandably joyous and exciting in comparison to the drabness of their daily lives. The emotional power of worship services, conveyed by the mesmerizing sermons of the preacher, the singing, dancing, and hand-clapping of the congregation, and the ecstatic behavior of individuals "getting the spirit" was highly contagious. Ironically, even many of the critical witnesses were involuntarily drawn into the electric atmosphere of the black church service. Carry Vaughan, a northern Baptist teacher and missionary, mingled with blacks near New Orleans and heard them sing and shout praises. She reported that "one who has never heard regular plantation melodies cannot picture the manner in which they would sing, 'Oh, run, sinner, run; I've got religion—in the promised land.' " Others, perhaps less tolerant of black culture, remained unmoved and voiced disgust at what they heard and saw, but all of them noted the high level of enthusiasm and emotional intensity that was characteristic of black folk religion.[20]

The goal of worship was to unite God and man. Despite man's sinful nature, a forgiving God was disposed toward his redemption if only man would take the initiative in seeking it. This tenet was fundamental to the theology of black evangelical Protestant congregations and unified the folk churches of all denominations. As Lucretia Alexander, a former slave, put it, in the early years of freedom "you couldn't tell the difference between Baptists and Methodists. . . . They was all Christians." The concept of redemption was transformed into rituals of experience, the most important of which was conversion, the climax of the individual's progression from sinner to child of God. It was a requirement of membership in evangelical churches, and congregations examined petitioners to verify that a spiritual rebirth had actually occurred before they were permitted to join the congregation. Benny Dillard of Georgia remembered that "when somebody wanted to jine our church us 'zamined 'em, and if us didn't think dey was done ready to be tuk in the church, dey was told to wait and pray 'til dey had done seed the light." Conversion was a fundamental principle in white Protestant Christianity also, of course, but it

---

20. Brown, *My Southern Home,* 193; *Home Mission Monthly,* I (May, 1878), 15; Payne, *Recollections of Seventy Years,* 254.

assumed a distinctly African-American form among southern blacks. In the first stage of the ritual, sinners entered a state of awareness of their sinfulness and separation from the sacred cosmos. They repented of past sins and sought atonement and a reintegration with the spirit world. People who were in that state of awareness were referred to as "mourners." They had not yet gone through an experience that might be taken as a positive sign of God's forgiveness. Mourners were not eligible for church membership, but they were certainly welcome at worship services. Indeed, most churches encouraged them to attend by providing a mourner's bench where they might seek "the light." [21]

The conversion experience bore some resemblance to West African beliefs and customs. The experience commenced when God or his surrogates, commonly thought of as angels, touched or spoke to the mourner in a fashion similar to the direct personal contact with the gods of the African spirit world felt by their ancestors. In both African and African-American cultures, the boundaries between the spirit and living worlds were indistinct. Living persons could not cross into the spirit world, but spirits frequently entered the realm of the living, and with direct and sometimes dramatic impact. The drama of the African-American conversion experience reached its climax in those encounters. The first contact with the spirit world was so overpowering that it often remained vivid many years later in the memories of converted Christians. A man named William was putting a roof on his house one day when suddenly he heard God beckoning to him. "O William! O William! O William!" the voice echoed. The conversion experience marked a transition in a person's life, from sinner to a born-again Christian. The converted individual became a new person, not just in a spiritual sense but in the physical being as well. It was a rite of passage every bit as meaningful as those that had occurred for aeons among the tribes of West Africa. A former slave named Morte recalled having heard a voice say to him: "Fear not, my little one, for behold! I come to bring you a message of truth." While he prayed, "an angel came and touched me and I looked new. I looked at my hands and they were new; I looked at my feet and they were new." The message that the people received through such encounters was that they ought to change the way they lived their lives and begin seeking atonement for their sins. It was a message dressed in the language of evangelical Protestant Christianity, that man was sinful and only through spiritual or symbolic death and rebirth could he achieve redemption, but the idea of death and resurrection was common among West Africans. Also, among some West African tribes, individuals who were possessed by a god and became devotees of that god changed their identities, speaking a foreign language and going by a new name. Villagers who called them by their original names and thus betrayed their identity were punished. Slaves had melded Christian ideas with such African religious traditions many generations before in formulating their own religious beliefs, and they were still a central part of a distinctive African-American culture at the close of the nineteenth century.[22]

After the initial awareness of a disunion with the sacred cosmos, or the spirit world, the mourner became a seeker of God's forgiveness. Even though seekers anticipated further contact with heavenly spirits in order to achieve redemption, they usually reported being startled by the suddenness of such encounters and feeling both profound fear and soaring joy when they occurred. They responded to the intense emotional stimulation of the conversion experience in physical ways, by lapsing into trancelike behavior, uncontrollable and body-wrenching contortions, singing, and dancing. During her tour of Virginia in the late 1870s, Mary Allan-Olney witnessed a young woman undergoing conversion. The seeker suddenly burst into wild singing and shouting that was "presently mixed with whoops and shrieks." Then she kicked and struggled violently and threw herself about. Whites like Allan-Olney often exaggerated their accounts of black folk religion to denigrate it, but the behavior she described was commonly associated with the conversion experience, as the testimony of blacks themselves makes evident. One woman recalled many years later that her conversion experience was both unexpected and immobilizing. "I was in my house alone and I declare unto you when His power struck me I died. I fell out on the floor flat on my back. I could neither speak nor move for my tongue stuck to the roof of my mouth; my jaws were locked and my limbs were stiff."[23]

22. Geoffrey Parrinder, *African Traditional Religion* (London, 1954), 70–94, 90–100, 102–103; Rawick, ed., *God Struck Me Dead* (Westport, 1972), 4, 8, Vol XIX of Rawick, ed., *American Slave;* Margaret Washington Creel, "Gullah Attitudes Toward Life and Death," in *Africanisms in American Culture,* ed. Joseph E. Holloway (Bloomington, 1990), 69–97.

23. Mary Allan-Olney, *The New Virginians* (2 vols.; London, 1880), II, 234–62; Rawick, ed., *God Struck Me Dead,* 20.

The intense emotional stimulation of spiritual conversion induced visions in many converts. Visions were a means of communication between deities and living persons; black folk had visions often and took them very seriously. Prominent and recurring in the visions that were associated with conversion was the image of Hell, typically visualized as a huge fiery pit. In the visions, the seeker's inner soul, a "man in a man," was led by one of God's angels to the edge of the pit. Being suspended over it symbolized the mourning condition; falling into it represented the eternal damnation awaiting the unrepentant sinner. One woman saw herself perched on the very brink of Hell: "I was on a little something that was swinging back and forth and it looked as if I must surely fall at any minute." A man saw himself "in two bodies, a little body in an old body." He described his vision in graphic detail: "My body was dangling over hell and destruction. A voice said to me, 'my little one, I have cleansed you of all iniquity. By grace you are saved and it is not yourself but the gift of God. Weep not, for you are a new child. Abide in me and you need never fear.' I looked in the distance and saw the rejoicing and singing." Before the seeker plunged headlong into the abyss, an angel would rescue him or her, and the vision would conclude.[24]

Visions were vivid realizations of images that were locked in the imagination, and they reveal much about the people's perceptions of the world. One person recalled that in his vision he "looked away to the east and saw Jesus." It was common in African-American conversion visions for seekers to look in that direction and see Heaven, God, and a host of angels of deliverance. "I looked to the east and there, near by, was a little path. I followed this and came to the top of the hill. It was so pretty and level. I looked to the east and saw a beautiful field with golden wheat and sheep eating." Another seeker suddenly experienced the sensation of being at Hell's gate. He gazed into the pit and saw Satan, surrounded by tormented souls and with chains locked around his chest and legs. Praying for deliverance, this seeker turned toward the east and saw the "Gospel Train" coming to his rescue.[25]

In many societies the east holds religious significance. It is not inconceivable that African Americans borrowed the symbolic importance of the east from Western religious ideology, perhaps the premillennial notion that Christ would return to earth from the east to commence the

24. Rawick, ed., *God Struck Me Dead*, 42, 48.
25. *Ibid.*, 20, 29, 36.

thousand years of his rule. It also may have been a carryover from the primordial human respect for the east as the direction of the daily rising of the sun, suggesting that the references to the east in African-American conversion experiences were rooted in African experiences and traditions. But the African connection was more than just a continuation of the beliefs of agricultural and prescientific societies. Africa was located east of where African Americans were, and although most African Americans regarded America as their homeland, they acknowledged Africa as their ancestral birthplace and, perhaps through the unconscious memory of culture, as the residence of ancestor spirits. Furthermore, many African societies practiced a ritual of facing east during prayer, and some people believed that their ancestors originated in the east and in that direction were located the spirits of the West African sacred cosmos. African-American praying and making offerings to those spirits may have outlasted the meaningfulness of an archaic religion. Vestiges of African customs or an awareness of Africa as an ancestral homeland may also have been evident in the burial practice among southern blacks of laying bodies on an east-west axis with the feet oriented toward the east. In any event, the African-American sacred cosmos did possess directional properties, and east was the habitation of benevolent spirits.[26]

Although black conversion experiences suggest a cultural continuity with Africa, the concept of conversion was based on the Christian principle of the sinner's spiritual death and rebirth as a new person whose faith in God would lead to redemption. Even here, though, there was a parallel with the West African idea of death and resurrection. Phrases like "God struck me dead" or "I was killed dead by the power of God" were common expressions of what people believed occurred to the sinner. A woman remembered a voice admonishing her, "You got to die and can't live." The new convert was filled with love, not only for God but for fellow human beings as well, and was thus qualitatively better than the old one. The change could be seen in both attitude and behavior. One convert believed that more people should become religious "because they live bet-

26. Eugene D. Genovese, *Roll, Jordan, Roll: The World the Slaves Made* (New York, 1972), 272–73; John S. Mbiti, *African Religions and Philosophies* (New York, 1969), 61, 63, 65, 150; R. S. Rattray, *The Tribes of the Ashanti Hinterland* (2 vols.; Oxford, 1932); Terry G. Jordan, "The Roses So Red and the Lilies So Fair: Southern Folk Cemeteries in Texas," *Southwestern Historical Quarterly,* LXXXIII (1980), 227–58; Parrinder, *African Traditional Religion,* 58; Newbell Niles Puckett, *Folk Beliefs of Southern Negroes* (New York, 1968), 93–94; Creel, "Gullah Attitudes Toward Life and Death," 90.

ter and they love people more." For black folk, living better meant avoiding wrongdoing. Converts gave up smoking, drinking liquor, and gambling and adjusted their overall attitude toward the people around them. They became more loving. "Never had I felt such a love before," one man testified. "I just looked like I loved everything and everybody. I went to work that day shouting and happy." Ideally, the behavior modification that the conversion experience induced was permanent, and often in reality it was long term in duration.[27]

Spiritual conversion was expected to occur in a religious setting, for example, at the mourner's bench in church. For William Black of Marshall County, Mississippi, that was precisely where it happened. "I went to the moaners bench and fell into a trance," Black recalled as he reminisced about his conversion. But because it was a prolonged process that could extend over a period of many months or even years, conversion could occur at almost any time and under nearly any conceivable circumstance. The experience did not depend on external stimulation; therefore, it happened in the unlikeliest places and most incongruous situations, as when William heard God's voice while repairing the roof of his house. Another person remembered that the first time he heard a voice speak to him "it scared me because I wasn't thinking about God or his works." Another man first heard the voice when he was working in a cotton field. Still another had just stopped dancing when he began to think about God and heard a voice speaking to him. Sometimes remorse would strike when the sin was near at hand. "I and three or four others were gambling. I had the dice in my hands. A voice spoke to me and it spoke three times." The man could not ignore the voice; it drew closer and closer, louder and louder. "It said, 'Have you ever thought where you will spend eternity?' " The man "got sorrowful and sad and slipped out of the room and prayed." He determined then and there to follow the Lord. "I saw Him through the eye of faith and heard His voice through the spiritual ear until the heart understood." [28]

The sinner's conversion sometimes took a long time to complete. One man remembered that his conversion experience began when he was a little boy during slavery. His mother had been sold away from him, and he grieved deeply for her. "One evening I was going through the woods

27. Rawick, ed., *Kentucky Narratives* (Westport, 1972), 11, Vol XVI of Rawick, ed., *American Slave;* Rawick, ed., *God Struck Me Dead,* 41–46; Herbert Gutman, *The Black Family in Slavery and Freedom, 1750–1925* (New York, 1976), 71–73.

28. Rawick, ed., *God Struck Me Dead,* 7, 11, 16, 28.

to get the cows. I was walking along thinking about mama and crying. Then a voice spoke to me and said, 'Blessed art thou. An obedient child shall live out the fullness of his days.' I got scared because I did not know who it was that spoke or what he meant. But from this time on I thought more about God and my soul and started to praying as best I knew." He continued to pray and to seek an understanding of God until he was a grown man. Likewise, a woman finally was converted and joined the church "after nearly ten years of experience." [29]

Seekers required time and solitude to reflect on their condition. A teacher on St. Helena Island received a note from a pupil named Caesar saying: "I am not in school today. I guess you might know the reason. I am trying to join the church and I don't want to develop my brain to so much things at a time." In seeking conversion, people often enjoyed the support and cooperation of friends, relatives, employers, and teachers. Men and women received leaves of absence from their jobs, and school-children were excused from class. But absenteeism caused by celebrations and religious experiences annoyed some employers. Revivals were the high time for spiritual conversions, and churchgoers often spent long hours during the workweek attending worship services, disrupting many of the routines of their daily lives. On the David Barrow plantation in Georgia, August was revival time, and all work ceased as the people shifted their attention to worship and salvation. They slaughtered hogs, lambs, and chickens to feed the body while the minister fed the soul with the gospel of Christ, and "for three or four days they do little else, but preach, sing, and eat." During a revival on Benjamin Montgomery's plantation in Mississippi, his daughter Virginia complained that "the hands [were] all broken down having to attend church every night." This was particularly troublesome in the cities, where domestic and other laborers were expected to be on the job on a regular basis and where employers complained the most about disruptions and absenteeism.[30]

The elite usually exhibited less overt manifestation of a mystical experience associated with conversion than did the common folk. In the nonevangelical churches spiritual conversion was not a part of the doctrine. Although in these churches blacks were few in number, they repre-

---

29. *Ibid.*, 61.

30. Rossa B. Cooley, *School Acres: An Adventure in Rural Education* (New Haven, 1930), 151–54; "A Georgia Plantation," *Scribners Monthly*, XXI (1880), 835; Janet Sharp Hermann, *The Pursuit of a Dream* (New York, 1981), 189; Howard N. Rabinowitz, *Race Relations in the Urban South, 1865–1890* (New York, 1978), 209.

sented large proportions of the wealthy and well educated. Yet many members of the upper classes belonged to Baptist and Methodist churches, and conversion was doubtless as profound an experience for them as it was for plain folk. But their responses to emotional stimulation were constrained by their self-consciousness and their sensitivity to the image they projected to others, especially to whites. Conversion for them was a mostly private experience, with little ritual except for the testimony they gave to their congregations to justify church membership. During their worship services, higher-class blacks often became very emotional. Indeed, emotionalism is in the nature of humanity, and evangelical Christianity was a powerful stimulus. For the elite churchgoers, the difference between acceptable and offensive emotional display was largely a matter of degree. But they also possessed an arrogance that allowed them to justify their own rapturous responses to religious excitement while rejecting the delirious celebrations of former slaves. In 1866 a writer for the AME *Christian Recorder* criticized the excessive exuberance of the folk conversion experiences, but he did not condemn all demonstrative behavior. If such behavior came from "natural" causes such as fear or grief, it was acceptable because it was not controllable. If it were the result of supernatural power, "the immediate agency of the Holy Ghost," it did not require control. Indeed, emotionalism that was divinely inspired "is not only worthy of tolerance, but of praise." But the writer regarded the emotional display that frequently accompanied conversion of black folk as "*unnatural* and *unsupernatural*." It was "the counterfeit of Pentecostal power." But even under the influence of "supernatural power," the upper classes believed in and usually practiced considerable self-restraint. In his memoirs, Bishop Daniel A. Payne described his own conversion in a way that he hoped would be instructive as well as inspirational. At the age of thirteen, after praying earnestly for his salvation, he was converted without the slightest hint of a wild, emotional response. "Here I too gave him my whole heart, and instantly felt that peace which passeth all understanding and that joy which is unspeakable and full of glory." Thus, for the upper classes, whom William E. B. Du Bois described as "placidly religious," conversion might come at any time, at any place, and under virtually any circumstance, as it did for poor black folk, but it usually came relatively quietly.[31]

31. W. E. B. Du Bois, *Dusk of Dawn: An Essay Toward an Autobiography of a Race Concept* (New York, 1940), 17; Gatewood, "Aristocrats of Color," 13–14.

Unfortunately, the power of the conversion experience did not guarantee permanent improvement in individual behavior. Every convert was capable of relapsing into sinfulness or "backsliding." Since the initial conversion often occurred during early adolescence, there were abundant opportunities to return to sinful ways. Moreover, black folk took a fairly casual attitude toward backsliding. The sins of wrongdoing, against which ministers preached, were the transgressions of life that many black folk, especially males, relished, and they slipped into and out of bad behavior in a recurring cycle. "I was a great musician," one man recalled, "and at times after I had spent seasons at fasting and praying, I would get tired of it and go back to the ways of the world." Religious people trusted God's redemptive power and his inexhaustible forgiveness, and they believed in their own salvation. According to Paul Radin, blacks rationalized backsliding and continued to enjoy the worldly pleasures of life even after they were converted: "Since, after all, what they desired was status, when they had attained it, even if it was only an inward one, they could safely indulge in backsliding and sin, and yet not run too great a danger of personal disintegration." The sinner could always rededicate himself to Christ. Of course, some did not and were penalized by expulsion from the church. According to some elite blacks, the frequency of backsliding among the masses was testimony to the frailty of their character and the weakness of their faith.[32]

Many activities took place within the confines of the church, but religious worship was the primary one. Indeed, worship was the high point of an ordinary week for many people, and they eagerly anticipated it. Ministers conducted services as frequently as they could. Three services each Sunday were the norm in the urban and small-town churches. Atlanta's Friendship Baptist Church held as many as two or three worship services each weekday as well. Captain Samuel Sloan of the United States Army, stationed in Texas at the end of the Civil War, found the churches flourishing, judged by the frequency with which the congregations gathered. In cities and towns everywhere, church meetings began in the morning, often at sunrise. Afternoon services followed, and there were usually evening services too. Not uncommonly, the evening meetings turned into endless affairs that stretched deep into the night. William Wells Brown

32. George P. Rawick, ed., *Mississippi Narratives* (Westport, 1977), Pt. 1, p. 145, Vol. VI in Rawick, ed., *The American Slave: A Composite Autobiography, Supplement, Series 1,* 12 vols.; Rawick, ed., *God Struck Me Dead,* viii, 7; *Christian Recorder,* April 21, 1866.

attended a Methodist service in Nashville and noted that "the meeting was kept up till a late hour." Occasionally evening services aroused the neighbors who lived within hearing distance of the churches, disturbing their sleep and intruding on otherwise peaceful evenings and evoking angry complaints. Not every church kept late hours. Carry Vaughan attended a service among a large Baptist congregation in New Orleans, "but not till late, as the custom is." In addition to the Sunday services, there were meetings on other evenings of the week, most typically on Wednesdays.[33]

In the hinterlands, early and frequent services were not always possible. There were fewer churches in the country than in towns and cities. And for rural people, living scattered about and with only poor roads providing access to churches, getting to services could be difficult. A sometimes greater problem in the rural areas was the limited availability of preachers. In many places there were fewer regular preachers than there were congregations, and weekly preaching was the exception rather than the rule. As late as the turn of the century, according to one report, no more than one black congregation in twelve enjoyed weekly preaching. Regular preaching no more than twice a month was common, and once every four weeks was not unheard-of. Within the Methodist denominations such situations were rationalized by the circuit system, but in many other black congregations the relative shortage of preachers meant that the people went an indefinite period of time without listening to a regular minister.[34]

When regular ministers were not scheduled to preach, or when it was inconvenient for the congregants to travel to the main church, they made use of exhorters or assistant preachers who conducted services in adjunct meetinghouses. James Lynch reported "several small branches" connected to a Methodist church in Augusta, Georgia, in 1865. On the islands off the South Carolina and Georgia coasts, the people still called these praise houses, as they had during slavery. The number of praise

33. Samuel Sloan to Asst. Adj. Gen., September 30, 1866, in Records of the Superintendent of Education for the State of Texas, 1866, U.S. Bureau of Refugees, Freedmen, and Abandoned Lands, Record Group 105, National Archives (hereinafter cited as Freedmen's Bureau Records); New York *Freeman*, November 6, 1866, January 8, 1887; Rabinowitz, *Race Relations in the Urban South*, 206–209; Brown, *My Southern Home*, 192; *Home Mission Monthly*, I (May, 1878), 15.

34. Johnson, *Shadow of the Plantation*, 13; William E. B. Du Bois, ed., *The Negro Church: Report of a Social Study Made Under the Direction of Atlanta University* (Atlanta, 1903), 122.

houses associated with any one church varied, but in some cases the networks were extensive. Perhaps an extreme example, but one that suggests the full dimensions that were possible under the praise house system, was the First African Baptist Church of Savannah, which at one time had fourteen praise houses associated with it. The advantage of the praise house for rural folk was that it was convenient, and, as a northern schoolteacher in South Carolina explained, "the people can drop in as familiarly as they do at home." [35]

Praise meetings, or "shouts" as the people had called them ever since the days of slavery, occurred as many as two or three times each week and on Sundays when no licensed or ordained preachers were scheduled to preach. As they had among the slaves, shouts incorporated the African traditions of the ring dance, hand-clapping, and leaping with evangelical Christian revival meetings. The shouts were ordinarily less formal than worship services in many of the urban churches, which were presided over by educated ministers, and not as tightly organized, but they could have a far more powerful impact on worshipers. Thomas Wentworth Higginson witnessed prayer meetings among the freedmen of South Carolina during the Civil War, conducted in an African-style hut filled with worshipers "singing at the top of their voice, in one of their quaint, monotonous, endless, negro-Methodist chants." In the background was "a regular drumming of the feet and clapping of the hands, like castanets." As the excitement spread among the worshipers, "a circle forms, winding monotonously round someone in the center; some 'heel and toe' tumultuously, others merely tremble and stagger on, others stoop and rise, others whirl, others caper sideways, all keep steadily circling like dervishes." Shouts were not an exclusively rural phenomenon, and the migration of African Americans from the early days of slavery through the nineteenth century took them to virtually every part of the country. Worshipers in the Avery Chapel AME Church in Memphis held shouts that lasted into the wee hours of the morning, with singing, hand-clapping, and the traditional African-American ring dance that a white observer called a "wild, heathenish jig." Daniel A. Payne encountered the shout in Balti-

35. Reid, *After the War*, 101; *Christian Recorder*, July 8, 1865; Isaac Brinckerhoff, "Thirty Years Among Freedmen, Beaufort, S. Carolina, St. Augustine, Florida, Savannah, Georgia, 1862–1894" (MS in American Baptist Historical Society, Rochester, New York); Emanuel K. Love, *A History of the First African Baptist Church of Savannah from Its Organization, January 20th, 1788, to July 1st, 1888* (Savannah, 1888), 149; Cooley, *School Acres*, 148–51.

more. He was shocked by its power and condemned it, as most educated clergy did, but he had to admit that it was an established part of the worship services of the masses. Sir George Campbell, a British traveler, also witnessed a shout and became locked in the grip of its fervor. James Weldon Johnson, an exceptionally talented wordsmith, recalled shouts from his Florida boyhood and was powerless to put their overwhelming force into conventional language. The shout's strength came from the fact that it permitted people to engage in sacred rituals that aroused and satisfied them. Those rituals featured natural, uninhibited singing and dancing more than prayer and preaching. Rossa B. Cooley, a Yankee schoolmarm who taught in South Carolina's Penn School, wrote that "in our praise houses is found the simplest, the most real form of the Christian religion I have ever seen." [36]

The ring dance was the central feature of the shout. Dancing was not an accepted activity in traditional European-American Protestant ceremony, but African Americans often performed sacred dances. Harriet Beecher Stowe described a dance performed by the worshipers in a Tallahassee church in 1867: "There was a double file of men and women moving and singing and shaking hands and curtseying, all in the most exact time and with the most solemn gravity." In the ring dance, the worshipers cleared the center of the meetinghouse of benches and chairs, then, while some of the people took seats and began singing, the others formed a ring in the center of the floor and began moving in a counterclockwise direction. The performance of the traditional ring dance varied in different localities, but its basic elements were common among African Americans. Exhibiting his usual contempt for the traditions of folk culture, Daniel Payne described the ring dance as he saw it performed. The dancers "formed a ring, and with coats off, sung, clapped their hands and stamped their feet in a most ridiculous and heathenish way." After a while the dancers retired in favor of those who had been singing. By alternating their roles, the congregants were able to keep up the ring dance for several hours. The architecture of some of the newer churches, with pews and benches fastened to the floor, no doubt affected the people's ability to

36. Higginson, *Army Life*, 13; Reid, *After the War*, 101; Sir George Campbell, *White and Black: The Outcome of a Visit to the United States* (New York, 1879), 329; Tucker, *Black Pastors and Leaders*, 21; Payne, *Recollections of Seventy Years*, 253–54; James Weldon Johnson, *God's Trombones* (New York, 1927), 5, 10; James Weldon Johnson, *Along This Way: The Autobiography of James Weldon Johnson* (1933; rpr. New York, 1973), 22; Cooley, *School Acres*, 148–51.

perform the ring dance as they or their ancestors had done it, but standing, clapping, and moving around inside the church all continued to be elements of the worship service and may have been remnants of the traditional ring dance.[37]

The atmosphere surrounding black worship services varied widely according to the composition of the congregation and the kind of service. Opinion differed between white and black commentators over whether the prevailing mood was one of happiness or sadness. Whites who attended black services, especially folk services, tended to report an air of profound somberness pervading the congregation. Philip A. Bruce perceived a contrast between the mood of blacks in church and their normal cheerful temperament. He wrote of the typical black worshiper that "although he is very cheerful in his social instincts and bright in his temper, his religious spirit . . . is more lugubrious than that of the most austere and embittered Puritan." Mary Allan-Olney wrote that by the conclusion of the service people were swaying back and forth and moaning "as if every man and woman was suffering from a distressing toothache." Some blacks recorded similar impressions. Mary White Ovington, the civil rights leader, heard a black congregation in Alabama sing with what she described as "the sorrow of the slaves." It was, she wrote, a "hopeless sorrow that lingers in this generation." [38]

Certainly the frustrations, the poverty, and the intense hostility of whites that mounted through the end of the nineteenth century gave cause for sadness. But African Americans had always found great joy in life, despite its dreariness and brutal oppressions, and the life-affirming quality of their religion is evident in the images of black worship that emerge from most black sources. The prevailing mood was joyous despite the presence of many negative images. Bleak visions of Hell and the specter of Satan haunted the service, and the misery and torment that awaited the unrepentant sinner informed many sermons. Henry M. Turner wrote after visiting a church on Roanoke Island in 1865 that "Hell fire, brimstone, damnation, black smoke, hot lead, etc., appeared to be presented

37. Richardson, *Negro in the Reconstruction of Florida*, 88; Payne, *Recollections of Seventy Years*, 253–54; Tucker, *Black Pastors and Leaders*, 21–22; Robert L. Hall, "African Religious Retentions in Florida," in *Africanisms in American Culture*, ed. Holloway, 110.

38. Philip A. Bruce, *The Plantation Negro as Freedman: Observations on His Character, Condition, and Prospects in Virginia* (New York, 1889), 95; Allan-Olney, *New Virginians*, II, 258; Mary White Ovington, *The Walls Came Tumbling Down* (New York, 1946), 71.

by the speaker as man's incentive to serve God while the milder and yet more powerful message of Jesus was thoughtlessly passed by." But the triumph of life over death usually resonated through the worship service, and sermons generally ended on an uplifting note. The worship service was filled with excitement and with singing, dancing, and fellowship. Such activities were bound to affect worshipers in ways suggested if not described in detail by a humorous rhyme that blacks living along the Brazos River in Texas repeated:

> White folks go to chu'ch
> He nevuh crack a smile.
> Nigguh go to chu'ch,
> You heah 'im laff a mile.

A tendency to dwell on the glories of Heaven and the happiness of another world is understandable, but it should not be mistaken for otherworldly escapism. Their thoughts about Heaven and the joys of salvation provided them with a context for relating the facts of their everyday lives. Black folk had the capacity to integrate the "other" spirit world into their own "real" world so that the joys of one became the delights of the other. In the midst of lives scarred by deprivation, humiliation, and oppression, pleasant thoughts provided black folk with encouragement and perseverance in dealing with the exigencies of their daily lives, as well as many enjoyable moments.[39]

Music contributed immensely to the excitement and the happiness of black worship services. "The music of Negro religion," William E. B. Du Bois wrote in *The Souls of Black Folk,* "despite caricature and defilement, still remains one of the most original and beautiful expressions of human life and longing yet born on American soil." The slave spiritual remained an important part of black sacred music long after emancipation. The plaintive melodies and expressive lyrics that had carried both secular and religious messages among the slaves could be heard in many rural churches. Indeed, they were conspicuous features of religious worship in the Sea Islands well into the twentieth century and were studied by anthropologists and folklorists. But they were performed in other regions of the South as well. Mary White Ovington heard them in rural Alabama as late as the turn of the century, "as they were originally sung, primitive

---

39. *Christian Recorder,* July 1, 1865; J. Mason Brewer, ed., *The Word on the Brazos: Negro Preacher Tales from the Brazos Bottoms of Texas* (Austin, 1853), 12.

music, great group singing." Artists and intellectuals such as James Weldon Johnson and, later on after the turn of the century, Paul Robeson continued to cultivate them and keep them alive. And so did groups like the famous Fisk University Jubilee Singers.[40]

Although the spiritual was the very soul of slave music, or perhaps because it was so closely identified with the slave past, it began to give way after emancipation to the standard denominational hymn embellished by choirs and instrumental music, especially in the elite churches. Missionaries brought denominational hymns with them into the postbellum South, and they changed the character of African-American sacred music. As the form changed, singing often became more stilted and less emotive and spontaneous than it had been before. Some of the dynamic quality of the slave spiritual was lost in the standard hymn. Charlotte Forten, a northern black teacher who participated in the Port Royal experiment, was pessimistic in her assessment of the hymn's impact on African-American religious development. She wrote that she and her colleagues saw crowds of freedmen singing "not their own beautiful hymns, I am sorry to say. I do fear these will be superseded by ours, which are poor in comparison, and which they do not sing well at all." Joseph B. Earnest, a student of black life in Virginia, noted shortly after the turn of the century that the hymns "interest the black worshippers but do not delight them." It was a considerable leap from interest to delight, and the people's lack of delight in their religious worship was disconcerting to at least one minister. Thomas Fuller argued that when the people could no longer sing freely, many stopped attending church.[41]

The new mode of hymn-singing was not as well suited to some congregations as it was to others, and some had to strain to perform the hymns as they were intended. Initially, people were handicapped by their inability to read songs out of a hymnal or by their churches' failure to secure

40. William E. B. Du Bois, *The Souls of Black Folk: Essays and Sketches* (Chicago, 1909), 140; Sterling Brown, "Negro Folk Expression: Spirituals, Seculars, Ballads and Work Songs," in *The Making of Black America*, ed. August Meier and Elliot Rudwick (2 vols.; New York, 1971), II, 209–14; Guy B. Johnson, *Folk Culture on St. Helena Island, South Carolina* (Chapel Hill, 1930), 63–130; Benjamin E. Mays, *The Negro's God as Reflected in His Literature* (1938; rpr. New York, 1968), 19–30; Ovington, *Walls Came Tumbling Down,* 71.

41. Ray Allen Billington, ed., *The Journal of Charlotte Forten Grimké* (New York, 1953), 183; Joseph B. Earnest, *The Religious Development of the Negro in Virginia* (Charlottesville, 1914), 152; Thomas O. Fuller, *History of the Negro Baptists of Tennessee* (Memphis, 1936), 231–32.

sufficient hymnals for each member of the congregation. Those difficulties were eased somewhat as the people committed the words and the tunes to memory and adapted the call-response technique they had always employed to hymns. This technique was an ancient method of singing hymns that went back in America to the time of the Puritans and to Africa as well, and it worked particularly well among the poor, illiterate congregations of the rural South. The song leaders committed verses to memory, choosing appropriate ones for each service according to the message of the sermon. During the service, they set the pitch of the song and then lined out the verses two by two. The congregation followed, setting the words to music.[42]

Choirs and instrumental music were important in the worship service too, especially in the larger urban churches of more affluent people and even in some of the smaller churches. Choirs were sources of both church and community pride, and, according to Bishop Daniel Payne, a good choir could be "a powerful and efficient auxiliary to the pulpit." R. A. Hall, an AME missionary, found no choir among the Methodists of Cumberland, Maryland, when he arrived there at the close of the Civil War. He impressed on the congregation the importance of having one and of learning how to read music. By his own account, he was successful, and he boasted that "now I have one of the best choirs in this part of Maryland." Payne promoted instrumental music along with choirs and stated his belief that "there is not a church of ours in any of the great cities of the republic that can afford to buy an instrument which is without one; and there are but few towns or villages where our Connection exists that are without an instrument to accompany their choir." But pianos and other musical instruments were expensive, and most congregations could not afford them and made do with the sound of the human voice as they anticipated the preacher's sermon.[43]

After a time of singing and other preliminaries that put worshipers in the right mood, the preacher took his position behind the pulpit. The preacher would call on someone from the congregation to pray, and a brother or a sister would say: "Lord Help. Lord make me what I orter be, I wants to be a Christian, Lord I believe, Lord pour down the Holy Ghost." Sermons varied considerably in content and length. Charles But-

42. Lillie B. Chace Wyman, "Colored Churches and Schools in the South," *New England Magazine,* III (February, 1891), 787–88; Mary Ames, *From a New England Woman's Diary in Dixie* (Springfield, Mass., 1906), 80–82.
43. Payne, *Recollections of Seventy Years,* 237; *Christian Recorder,* July 26, 1865.

lington of Warrensburg, Missouri, recalled that there was "very little preaching, mostly praying and singing." In other churches, the sermon was the feature of the worship service. But in most cases, it transmitted the ideological substance and to a large extent the emotional stimulation of the regular church service. Everything that preceded it served to set the scene or to create the right atmosphere. Edward King visited Richmond's First African Baptist Church during his southern tour in the early 1870s and looked "over a vast congregation of blacks listening with tearful and rapt attention to the emotional discourse of their preacher, or singing wild hymns as they are read out, line by line, by the deacon." Sermons, particularly in the churches of the common folk, were laden with imagery and a rich assortment of parables. They were frequently based on Old Testament texts, contained references to Moses and the liberation of the Israelites—a favorite story even after emancipation—and the unquestioning faith of Abraham, sooner or later got around to the punishment awaiting unrepentant sinners, and concluded with the promise of redemption and thrilling descriptions of Heaven. The American Missionary Association's William G. Kephart wrote from Alabama in 1864 that the freedmen there were most familiar with the part of the Bible that contained the story of the deliverance of the Israelites. "Moses is their *ideal* of all that is high, and noble, and perfect in man. I think they have been accustomed to regard Christ not so much in the light of a *spiritual* Deliverer, as that of a second Moses who would eventually lead *them* out of their prison-house of bondage." Deliverance still had political relevance even after emancipation. The freedmen used the story of Moses leading his people out of Egypt to celebrate their own freedom. As time went on, it gave hope to those burdened by hardship and the oppression of Jim Crow. The metaphor for deliverance was "climbin' Jacob's ladder" into Heaven. Charley White, who lived in east Texas, recalled the first sermon he ever heard and the images it contained.

Old man Jerry Mays was the preacher. He talked about Heaven and how everybody [ought] to figure on going there. Said the roads was all gold, and nobody wouldn't have to tote no heavy burden. He said Jesus was already up there, helping God fix the place up nice for us. Then he told how it was down in Hell, with flames kicking up all around, and how the devil was always sticking everybody with a pitchfork. He got the people to humming and moaning till it made my stomach feel shivery. He told them to confess to God about all the devilment they'd been in, and come on down and be baptized and let the water wash their sins away, so they couldn't end up down in hell.

A man from Mississippi remembered that "de preachers 'ud exhort us dat was chillen 'o Israel in de wilderness an' de Lawd done sont us to take dis lan' o' milk an' honey."[44]

Some preachers specialized in particular sermons, repeating them often and occasionally achieving considerable reputations through their skill at exciting audiences. Perhaps the most famous of the old-time preachers was John Jasper, who gained fame as the pastor of Richmond's Sixth Mount Zion Baptist Church. His sermon "De Sun Do Move" attracted large numbers of whites as well as thousands of blacks and drew attention to him and other former slave preachers. The sermon was a celebration of the power of God, manifested when he halted the sun's progress across the heavens and allowed Joshua time to assault the fortified city of Jericho, and of the literal and unvarying truth of the Scriptures. The sermon received notoriety because of Jasper's conclusion that since God had stopped the movement of the sun, its normal condition must be one of motion around the earth. Both condescending whites and embarrassed blacks ridiculed Jasper and his sermon, but it drew thousands of listeners to his church, who were profoundly moved by the powerful appeal of his delivery and by his sermon's rousing message.[45]

African-American folk sermons became part of the public domain. Preachers borrowed freely from each other's sermons, modifying them to suit their own personalities and language skills. A sermon that many preachers delivered in various forms was the "Train Sermon." Its subject was the "Black Diamond Express, running between here and Hell, making thirteen stops and arriving in Hell ahead of time." Still another one, based on judgment day and aimed at arousing sinners and moving them to repent of their misdeeds and seek God's forgiveness before it was too

44. George P. Rawick, ed., *Missouri Narratives* (Westport, 1977), 157, Vol. II in Rawick, ed., *American Slave, Supplement, Series 1;* Edward King, *The Southern States of North America: A Record of Journeys in Louisiana, Texas, the Indian Territory, Missouri, Arkansas, Mississippi, Alabama, Georgia, Florida, South Carolina, North Carolina, Kentucky, Tennessee, Virginia, West Virginia, and Maryland* (London, 1875), 630; W. G. Kephart to Lewis Tappan, May 9, 1864, in AMA Archives; Charley C. White, *No Quittin' Sense* (Austin, 1969), 4; Rawick, ed., *Mississippi Narratives* (Westport, 1972), 41–42, Vol. VII in Rawick, ed., *American Slave.*

45. William E. Hatcher, *John Jasper: The Unmatched Negro Philosopher and Preacher* (New York, 1908), chaps. 12–15.

late, was translated into verse by James Weldon Johnson, one stanza of which read:

> Sinner, Oh, sinner
> Where will you stand
> In that great day when God's a-going to rain down fire.

Another was "Dry Bones," based on Ezekiel's encounter with the scattered bones of a human skeleton that miraculously became reconstituted, symbolizing the death of the sinner and his rebirth as a Christian. Still another widely used sermon was called "The Eagle Stirs Her Nest," referring to how mother eagles stir their young from the nest to teach them to fly. Many of these sermons originated in the slave experience, but they remained relevant after emancipation and could be heard in African-American churches during the civil rights struggle a century later.[46]

Although ministers often preached about the wages of sin, their sermons—at least those of the great number of uneducated preachers—were not notably didactic in the way many sermons in white churches were. No more than they reflected purely Western Christian ceremony and theology did the churches of plain black folk exactly mirror the value system commonly associated with white middle-class America. It was not, after all, the church's purpose to support a social system that exploited and oppressed its members. Until emancipation, the Christian gospel, as slaves had understood it, taught them to resist the domination of their white masters and to accept their own humanity. Christian doctrine as conveyed to them by the slaveholding regime had contained a code of conduct, which slaves had seen for the control mechanism it was and had rejected. Even after slavery, although the political context of their lives had changed dramatically, the religion of the masses continued to focus on the spiritual rewards of redemption and the glories of Heaven rather than the regulation of behavior. Poor and oppressed people wanted to feel good about themselves and needed help in sustaining their resistance to continued oppression; they neither needed nor wanted to hear of their worthlessness. Their preachers and the totality of the worship service were oriented toward their spiritual uplift, both in sacred and psychological senses. The conduct of poor folk in church, which many, particularly white, evangelical ministers denounced as immoral or as contributing to immorality and a disordered character, was accepted by the

46. Johnson, *God's Trombones*, 1–2; Keith D. Miller, *Voice of Deliverance: The Language of Martin Luther King, Jr., and Its Sources* (New York, 1992), 23–28.

people and their preachers as altogether normal. Dancing, for example, an activity that Anglo-American society considered profane if done in church and that some clergymen—especially Baptists—proscribed even outside of church because they believed it led to immorality, was seen in African-American society as both sacred and profane. Many black ministers condemned dancing of any kind, but sacred dances, such as the ring dance, were integral parts of African-American folk worship, and many churches, especially poor Baptist ones, nurtured it. The ecstatic behavior that many outsiders viewed as disgraceful was perfectly normal and acceptable to most lower-class black worshipers. Many blacks regarded their religion and their forms of worship as superior to whites'. Because the thrust of their religion was toward love and humanity, rather than toward a justification of prejudice and oppression, it was more legitimate than white Christianity. Black folks' ridicule of white Christianity was evident in a popular saying that contradicted an oft-repeated white assertion that black worship was largely emotional with little Christian substance. "De Nigguh's long on religion," the epigram went, "and short on Christ'ainty." [47]

The excitement and spirituality that electrified folk church services seemed to many outsiders to lack any positive practicality, leading them to suggest that black folk did not connect religious enthusiasm with moral uprightness. Enoch K. Miller of the American Missionary Association lamented that "religion and practice are with them two separate matters. One of them will make the loudest professions of religion and will yet be guilty of the most unblushing violations of the law." Whitelaw Reid, after attending a worship service, wondered what, if any, effect it had on the people's daily lives. "The prayer was simple, full of repetition, abounding in Scripture language, not always appropriately used; and, on the whole, I was in doubt whether either speaker or congregation understood all of it." He had no doubt about their sincerity or devotion, but, he mused, "it seemed to be mainly emotional, rather than intellectual, and might therefore, well give rise to inquiries as to what effect this abounding religion had on the matter of stealing sweet-potatoes, or taking care of their wives and children, during the week." Philip A. Bruce, whose image of African Americans was shaped by negative racial stereotypes, later wrote that the religion of rural blacks at the turn of the century was "a code of belief, and not a code of morals." [48]

47. J. Mason Brewer, ed., *American Negro Folklore* (Chicago, 1968), 111.
48. Smith, "Slavery and Theology," 497–512; Reid, *After the War*, 106; Bruce, *Plantation Negro as a Freedman*, 99.

But the churches did encase a system of practical morality. Missionaries, especially those who had college or seminary training, expressed concern about the morals of the South's former slave population, mainly about the vices that prevailed among the refugees and immigrants in the towns and cities. When Henry M. Turner arrived in Smithville, North Carolina, in 1865, he reported that there were "not more than fifty pious persons in the town." Many more frequented the local saloons, and the reason, he believed, was that during slavery no one had cared for the slaves' moral conscience. Although the uneducated black preachers bore a reputation, often deserved, for moral frailty, there is no reason to doubt that most of them also preached against sins like drunkenness, violent assault, and adultery. John Jasper, who both smoked tobacco and kept liquor in his home, and drank whenever he felt like it, was described as "unpitying in his castigation of vice." Most of the time, rightly or wrongly, the clergy blamed immoral behavior on slavery, but as the number of town and city churches multiplied toward the end of the century and social problems such as alcoholism, crime, and the decay of family cohesion that accompanied urbanization became more acute, the churches concentrated more and more on how freedom affected the behavior of their congregants. Church leaders still laid the blame on the lingering effects of slavery. Soon after the turn of the century, Hightower T. Kealing, an educator and African Methodist layman from Texas, wrote that the most damning thing about slavery had been that "it did not teach the meaning of home, purity, and providence." [49]

Clergymen generally condemned behavior that damaged individual health or threatened the security of the family. Drinking, smoking, gambling, dishonesty, and sexual impropriety were common targets. The urban churches actively supported prohibition movements. The North Carolina Baptist State Convention, which, like most state organizations, represented the views of prominent ministers, recommended that its pastors deliver sermons on temperance regularly and frequently so as to "impress the necessity of total abstinence among our people." The members of the women's auxiliary state convention of Alabama resolved not to serve their children eggnogs or toddies. In his history of the AME Zion church, published in 1895, Bishop James W. Hood stressed the church's commitment to total abstinence from the consumption of liquor. Church leaders in Virginia told Baptists in that state that although some men

49. *Christian Recorder*, March 4, 1865; Hatcher, *John Jasper*, 18, 106; Booker T. Washington *et al.*, *The Negro Problem: A Series of Articles by Representative Negroes of To-Day* (1903; rpr. New York, 1969), 173–74.

would steal chickens from a darkened hennery and others would rob banks, none was worse "than the man who will not pay back an honest debt."[50]

Regardless of content, denomination, or the social class of the congregation, most ministers in the independent black churches delivered their sermons in the rousing style typical of Protestant evangelicalism. The mode was extemporaneous and full of gusto, embellished with vivid imagery. Preachers endeavored to make connections between contemporary topics and Old Testament lessons about liberation and the power and justice of God. James Lynch, hardly an uneducated backwoods preacher, delivered a funeral sermon shortly after Abraham Lincoln's assassination in the African Methodist Church in Mitchelville, South Carolina. He compared Lincoln to Moses leading his people safely through the wilderness to the banks of the Jordan River. Then, departing from the Scriptures, he painted a metaphorical word picture of John Wilkes Booth, depicting him as the spirit of rebellion, "creeping, creeping up the back stairs" to strike one final blow for slavery and disunion. According to Jane B. Smith, a northern teacher who heard the sermon, the congregation's reaction was powerful. "Here the feelings of his excited audience were wrought to such a pitch, that it was impossible to hear him above their sobs, groans, and shouts." Successful preachers' greatest assets were their language skills—including the use of the dialect of the common people—and their feel for the rhythms that evoked bodily responses. John Jasper was a master at preaching in the dialect of the poor folk who made up his congregation. William Hatcher, a white minister who knew him and heard him preach on several occasions, said of him: "No man could handle a crowd with more consummate tact than he. He was the king of hearts and could sway throngs as the wind shakes the trees." He could read, and he could speak grammatically, but he always fell into dialect when he preached. "But," according to Hatcher, "the wonder of his speaking was his practical independence of language. When he became thoroughly impassioned and his face lit with the orator's glory, he seemed to mount above the bondage of words: his feet, his eyes, indeed every feature of his outer being became to him a new language. If he used

50. Baptist State Convention of North Carolina, *Minutes of the Sixteenth Annual Meeting of the Baptist State Convention of North Carolina . . . 1882* (Raleigh, 1883), 6; Alabama Women's Baptist State Convention, *Minutes of the Women's Baptist State Convention, Ninth Annual Session . . . [1894]* (Montgomery, 1895), 8; New York *Freeman*, April 24, 1886; Rabinowitz, *Race Relations in the Urban South*, 219.

words, you did not notice it. You were simply entranced and borne along on the mountain-tide of his passion." Fancifulness, action, and excitement were among the qualities of a good sermon. For those who could not arouse the strong feelings and deep emotions of the people and enable them to "get the spirit," failure was inevitable and often abject. During his very first sermon, a Tennessee preacher, no doubt trained to appreciate the virtues of a tightly reasoned sermon and to avoid the evils inherent in emotional preaching, and probably suffering from stage fright, discovered the deadening effect that a sober presentation might have on a congregation. In the middle of an uninspiring sermon, he gave up when his congregation failed to respond; he "died dead" and was unable to finish. "I couldn't so much as call the name of the Lord." There is no record of his subsequent career, or even whether he remained in the ministry, but if he succeeded in the future he doubtless gave up the prepared sermon in favor of preaching "de word" as he felt it in his heart and as most congregations wanted to hear him deliver it. Among black folk, preachers like Lynch were renowned for their efforts. John Jasper was certainly one of the best, as was Charles T. Walker of Augusta, Georgia, known as the "black Spurgeon." The people, of course, knew what good preaching was and where to find it. During a visit to Virginia in the early 1870s, journalist and traveler Edward King asked a black man for directions to a particular church he knew of near Petersburg. The man was accommodating, but he advised King to go to another church if he wanted to hear good preaching.[51]

Singing, prayer, and, most of all, the preacher's sermon were intended to prompt audiences to fancy God's heavenly domain and the assortment of angels and spirits that inhabited it. The mostly illiterate masses of black folk perceived the abstractions of the spirit world in the terms of their language and personal experiences. As in most West African religions, African-American deities were anthropomorphic. Their conceptions of the spirit world show a continuity from the religious beliefs of their African ancestors through the ideology of their slave parents and grandparents to their own late nineteenth- and early twentieth-century formulations. A former slave in the 1930s stated his belief that "all o'us when us dies is sperrits." After death, "Us jus' hovers 'round in de sky a-

51. *Freedmen's Record*, I (June, 1865), 98 (September, 1865), 144; Hatcher, *John Jasper*, 95–96; Clifton H. Johnson, ed., *God Struck Me Dead: Religious Conversion Experiences and Autobiographies of Ex-Slaves* (Philadelphia, 1969), 23; King, *Southern States*, 583.

ridin' on de clouds." The African-American belief in ghosts also exemplified their perception of the spirit world. The concept of ghosts (in Africa, the restless spirits of deceased relatives who had not been given a proper burial and who haunt the living to torment them) was not identical to African traditional beliefs but was close enough to suggest continuity. The belief in ghosts was not explicitly taught in most African-American churches, but parents taught it to their children, and over many generations it was a definite part of African-American folk religion. At least some preachers believed in ghosts so, to an extent, they were associated with church worship. Anderson Edwards, a Baptist who had been "preachin' the Gospel and farmin' since slavery times," told an interviewer in the 1930s, "I 'lieve in that hant [ghost] business yet." Spirits, especially the spirits of ancestors, were able to return to earth and visit relatives, and black folk frequently commented on their experiences with them, being visited by them, hearing them speak, and seeing them move about. Encounters with spirits and ghosts were usually fearful, but they seldom brought bad fortune.[52]

Heaven and Hell were the dual centers of the African-American sacred world. Heaven awaited the repentant sinner. It was God's residence but also a place pervaded by happiness and beauty, where the living would ultimately be reunited with departed loved ones. The rewards of Heaven were not easily obtained, as one black Christian explained: "I started traveling and came to a steep mountain. He [God] told me to climb and I said, 'Lord, that mountain is too steep and I can't climb.' The next thing I know I was at the top." God's reward to the faithful was indeed pleasing. "When I saw myself again I was sailing along in a little snow-white chariot and the prettiest singing I ever heard seemed to fill the air." Another individual imagined what it would be like to meet God and to see deceased friends and relatives again. "After some time I came to heaven. I saw God sitting in a large armchair, his head up and looking into space. He neither moved nor spoke. He wore a full armor, and across his chest was a breast-protector that shone as if it was made of bars of gold. My mother was standing there, and she showed me my two brothers who had died. I looked around and saw hosts of angels around two long tables, and they were shouting and clapping their hands." Many

52. Rawick, ed., *Mississippi Narratives*, 15; Rawick, ed., *Texas Narratives* (Westport, 1972), 6, Vol. IV in Rawick, ed., *American Slave*; George P. Rawick, ed., *Texas Narratives* (Westport, 1979), 16–17, Vol. V in Rawick, ed., *The American Slave: A Composite Autobiography, Supplement, Series 2,* 10 vols.

black folk regarded Heaven as a place where they would enjoy all the material things that had been denied them in the living world. In the words of the narrator of a black folktale the image is clear: "Mos' white folks jes' wants de same thing dey done hab while dey's livin' when dey gits up to heabun, but de nigguh, he don' relish de same thing he done hab on urf—he wants everything cep'n what he done hab down heah." Such were the prospects, derived from African-American traditions, the imaginations of black folk, and their interpretations of the Bible, magnified by the force of a fiery sermon that excited the emotions of the people to the extent that they could not keep from shouting, clapping their hands, and dancing. It was an atmosphere of profound joy and celebration, a celebration of life and the redeeming power of God.[53]

Although church services among the masses appeared to be unstructured and disorganized and their success in fulfilling the purpose of religious worship depended entirely on "the spirit," in reality they followed a common, well-established, and distinctive pattern. The physical and verbal responses to emotional stimulation were not coincidental to the fundamental design of the African-American worship service but rather were fully integrated into the ritual. Most people regarded worship as a failure if their emotions were not aroused. Hightower T. Kealing wrote, "It may be remarked, that a shadow of suspicion rested upon the sincerity of . . . anyone who did not heartily and frequently indulge in shouting." The purpose of the black worship service was to draw the congregants toward the sacred world, and black folk judged the service on its success in transporting them. It was successful if it put them in touch with the spirit world, or, as was often said, got them "in the spirit." It was necessary for the preacher and the people in the congregation to work together. The service was a concert with both preacher and congregation participating. The high level of emotional sensitivity and the responsiveness of one stimulated the same feelings and behavior in the other. The physical activity that appeared to be spontaneous was in fact a component of an established ritual. Grunts, groans, and loud "amens" were not so much interruptions of the sermons as they were embellishments that preachers not only tolerated but actively solicited and anticipated. They were elements in the dialogue between preacher and communicant. The narrator of a folktale explained how it worked: "Some sistuhs in de

53. Johnson, ed., *God Struck Me Dead*, 59–60, 91–92, 109–10, 145–46; Brewer, ed., *Word on the Brazos*, 86.

chu'ch meck de preachuh rail pow'ful in de pulpit by doin' what dey calls 'talkin' back to 'im.' Ah mean by dat, when a preachuh put ovuh a good lick again' de Devul, dey say, 'Preach de Word, son!' or, 'You sho' is tellin' de truf now.' Dis he'p de preachuh to git right wid his preachin', so he lack for de sistuhs to talk back to 'im." [54]

Elite urban congregations tended to be more restrained than most poor rural congregations in their worship services. Many, but certainly not all, middle- and upper-class blacks not only criticized the emotionalism of folk churches but scrupulously avoided effusiveness themselves. J. D. Taylor, a prominent Virginia Baptist preacher, boasted to a reporter for the southern Baptist *Religious Herald* that the "senseless whooping and hollering" were fast disappearing from church. Francis Grimké, the respected Presbyterian clergyman and pastor of the elite Fifteenth Street Presbyterian Church in Washington, explained that the minister's injection of emotionalism into the service only when he "gets away from the earth and from the practical, everyday duties of life" and moved "somewhere near the pearly gates" demonstrated the irrelevance of folk worship. Elite congregations sang hymns from standard denominational hymnals, listened to sermons that ministers delivered more articulately and unemotionally than the preachers in folk churches, and behaved with considerable self-restraint. The atmosphere was, as a visitor to Grimké's church phrased it, that of "serious but restrained worship." Many Baptist and Methodist congregations of middle-class blacks who were upwardly mobile exhibited the same qualities. The *Christian Index* described the Collins Chapel CME church of Memphis, a congregation of schoolteachers, postal workers, and other middle-class blacks, as the "most refined and quiet large city congregation in the city." [55]

The decorum of some middle-class and most upper-class churches often impressed white visitors. O. M. Dorman of the AMA visited a church in St. Augustine, Florida, shortly after the Civil War and noticed that members of the congregation were not "noisy, as they are in many places." Lillie Chace Wyman, after touring the South, noted that the congregation in a church she attended at all times fulfilled its part of the worship service with "due decorum and proper subordination to the min-

54. Kealing, *History of African Methodism in Texas,* 37; Brewer, ed., *Word on the Brazos,* 19, 85.

55. Rabinowitz, *Race Relations in the Urban South,* 207–208; *Religious Herald,* July 10, 1889; Francis J. Grimké, *The Afro-American Pulpit in Relation to Race Elevation* (Washington, D.C., 1893), 5; New York *Globe,* January 20, 1883.

ister's role." A white newspaper correspondent discovered that Richmond's First African Church "is not, as I suspected it might be, a mob. It is thoroughly organized. . . . The discipline is strict." Another white reporter noted of Atlanta's Third Baptist Church that "the quietness and attention of the congregation was a source of general remark."[56]

In some cases, however, as William Wells Brown discovered to his chagrin, the worship services of even the most "refined congregations" bore the imprint of African-American culture. After attending services at the prosperous St. Paul's AME Church in Nashville, he complained that "four or five sisters becoming exhausted, had fallen upon the floor and lay there, or had been removed by their friends." He also visited the First Colored Baptist Church. The pastor was Nelson G. Merry, one of the leaders among Baptists in the state and "President for Life" of the General State Convention of Tennessee, who held a piece of paper in his hand and claimed that it was a list of all the deeds of a person awaiting judgment after death.

> For fully ten minutes the preacher walked the pulpit, repeating in a loud, incoherent manner, "And the angel will read from this letter." This created the wildest excitement, and not less than ten or fifteen were shouting in different parts of the house, while four or five were going from seat to seat shaking hands with the occupants of the pews. "Let dat angel come right down now an' read dat letter," shouted a Sister, at the top of her voice. This was the signal for loud exclamations from various parts of the house. "Yes, yes, I want's to hear the letter." "Come, Jesus, come or send an angel to read the letter." "Lord, send us the power."[57]

Besides the regular worship services, various special activities took place in local churches. One of them was the baptismal sacrament, a particularly dramatic and exciting ritual marking a major event in the lives of Christians. Baptism symbolized the death of the sinner and his resurrection and was a prerequisite to church membership. It was a far more dramatic part of the ceremony in Baptist churches than in others because Baptists practiced total immersion of the candidates. African Methodist missionaries occasionally baptized persons by "ducking"; however, that was only a concession to individual preference by flexible ministers and

---

56. Richardson, *Negro in the Reconstruction of Florida*, 92; Wyman, "Colored Churches and Schools in the South," 787–88; Taylor, *Negro in Virginia*, 187; Rabinowitz, *Race Relations in the Urban South*, 207.

57. Brown, *My Southern Home*, 191–93.

not a part of the denomination's doctrine. "I was buried in de water lak de Savior. I's a real Baptis'," commented one Mississippi convert. In the larger urban churches, particularly toward the close of the century, clergymen administered the sacrament in baptisteries constructed within the church building, but for many rural people, townsfolk, and even city dwellers baptism meant a dip in the turbid water of a nearby river or creek. The baptismal sacrament had been an important event on the slave plantations before the war, as Albert Raboteau has noted: "Accompanied by song, shouting, and ecstatic behavior, baptism—especially for Baptists—was perhaps the most dramatic ritual in the slave's religious life." He described some of the ceremony that encapsulated the baptism: "Dressed in white robes and attended by the 'brothers and sisters,' the candidates proceeded 'amidst singing and praises' to the local pond or creek, symbol of the river Jordan, where, according to Baptist practice, each was 'ducked' by the preacher. Sometimes the newly regenerate came up from the baptismal waters shouting for joy at being made new in the Lord." A Georgia former slave recalled that crowds of people flocked to the church when there was a baptism: "Dey dammed up de crick on Sadday so as it would be deep enough on Sunday. . . . At dem baptizin's dere was all sorts of shoutin', and dey would sing *Roll, Jordan, Roll, De Livin' Waters,* and *Lord, I'se Comin' Home.*" The baptisms of many slaves and of black folk following emancipation were consistent with prevailing evangelical Christian customs, but they may also, as Melville Herskovitz and Sterling Stuckey have suggested, have contained vague echoes of the purification rites and ceremonies honoring the water gods of the Yoruba, Ashanti, and Dahomeans of West Africa.[58]

The candidates for baptism sometimes met the preachers and other members of their congregations before the first light of day to prepare for the event. Singing joyfully, the parishioners and initiates wound their way to the baptismal site, candidates draped in white gowns and spectators carrying picnic baskets. Once they arrived at the place, witnesses took up their positions along the bank while the deacons plumbed the water's depth. The service began when the minister stepped down into the stream. He read from the Scriptures, offered prayer, and lectured the can-

---

58. Raboteau, *Slave Religion,* 226–28; Rawick, ed., *Mississippi Narratives,* 15, *Georgia Narratives,* Pt. 3, pp. 252–53, *Florida Narratives* (Westport, 1972), 245, Vol. XVII, *Texas Narratives* (Westport, 1972), Pt. 1, p. 228, Vol. IV, *South Carolina Narratives* (Westport, 1972), Pt. 3, p. 19, Vol. III, all in Rawick, ed., *American Slave;* Melville Herskovitz, *The Myth of the Negro Past* (New York, 1958), 232–34; Sterling Stuckey, *Slave Culture: Nationalist Theory and the Foundations of Black America* (New York, 1987), 34–37.

didates on the meaning and responsibilities of baptism. Those who received the sacrament then entered the water, where they were laid back beneath the surface. Emerging seconds later as reborn Christians, they were greeted by friends and relatives. The ordinary baptismal service was somber in tone, and the effect on both participants and witnesses was especially powerful when it was conducted at dawn and "the red glow of the sunrise made the scene one of peculiar glory." Black folk had a knack for making even the most serious events joyous happenings, and shouts of happiness usually met the resurrected Christians as they emerged from the water. The baptism was usually followed by a picnic.[59]

Another special event that was associated with the churches was the revival, or "protracted meeting." Evangelical revival meetings ordinarily occurred in the fall, after crops had been harvested and people had a little more time on their hands. The revivals began on Sunday and continued for several days, sometimes lasting for weeks. Methodist revivals followed the pattern of the traditional camp meeting. Church leaders tried to conduct revivals away from the church, typically in some nearby retreat. "What was the Feast of Tabernacles," Henry M. Turner once asked, "but camp meetings, where men, women, and children left their houses and tented seven days in the woods, reading the law, weeping, rejoicing, offering sacrifices, thanksgiving, and worshipping God." Revivals were special services intended to convert both sinners and seekers. They were often interdenominational, with Baptist and Methodist ministers participating together. At a revival in Raleigh, North Carolina, in 1866, described as "a revival come down from God out of heaven," a Methodist preacher and a Baptist clergyman joined together to arouse the spiritual fervor of the people and to seek the conversion of sinners. "We called for sinners to come to Christ, and, with little effort on our part, they came flocking to the altar of prayer, to the number of thirty-six." The Methodist minister reported an increase in the number of seekers also, to nearly ninety. "We have had conversions every night. Some are those who, we are told, have been seeking for several months and years." A camp meeting near Jacksonville, Florida, in 1875 ran on for eleven days and, according to reports, yielded more than one hundred converts.[60]

---

59. Rawick, ed., *South Carolina Narratives*, Pt. 3, pp. 108–10, *Alabama Narratives* (Westport, 1977), 55, Vol. I in Rawick, ed., *American Slave, Supplement, Series 1;* Cooley, *School Acres*, 154; Rabinowitz, *Race Relations in the Urban South*, 209–10.

60. For a description of the evangelical revival as it developed during the first half of the nineteenth century see Dickson D. Bruce, *And They All Sang Hallelujah: Plain-Folk Camp-Meeting Religion, 1800–1845* (Knoxville, 1974). Rawick, ed., *Missouri Narratives,*

Not all the events that occurred during revival meetings could correctly be described as "rejoicing in the Lord." Critics of revivals and camp meetings complained that they evoked too much "abnormal excitement." The editor of the *Christian Recorder* stated the opinion, "derived from the facts, that in some instances our revivals are not wisely conducted." One preacher condemned camp meetings as excuses for frolicking and vice. Others complained of the extravagance of revivals. A Baltimore Methodist asserted that "we spend more money for pic-nics, excursions, big Sunday pic-nics, held all summer under the name of camp-meetings . . . than would be needed to run all our schools."[61]

The excesses that no doubt occurred in camp meetings and that church leaders and others often complained about were common but not typical of revivals. Most revivals and camp meetings, like ordinary church services, were filled with the "spirit" and excitement, but that was the life-affirming nature of African-American worship and in no way exemplified any disrespect for God. Many commentators noted the orderliness of the gatherings, even an air of reverence. One newspaper reporter who attended a camp meeting near Pensacola was impressed by the sobriety and the "orderly deportment of the people," although there was a barroom in the same park as the church gathering. Henry Turner defended the revivals despite the evils that he acknowledged were associated with them. He reasoned that although not everything at the gatherings was strictly spiritual, the evils were nothing when compared to those that bedeviled the neighborhoods outside of the church.[62]

Weddings also took place in the churches. Slave marriages had not been formally recognized legally or by the church. Slave couples had formed unions, many of which were strong and enduring despite the many strains the slave system had placed on them. For many slaves, however, especially Christians, the sanctification of matrimonial ties was an important element in their marriages. They wanted whites to recognize and acknowledge not only the holiness of matrimony but its permanence as well. Many masters accommodated their slaves to the extent of conducting formal wedding ceremonies for them or having them performed by ministers and sometimes allowing elaborately festive celebrations to

175; New York *Age,* October 6, November 10, 1888; *Christian Recorder,* May 5, 1866; *A.M.E. Church Review,* IV (January, 1886), 208.

    61. *Christian Recorder,* April 21, 1866; New York *Age,* October 6, 1888; *A.M.E. Church Review,* IV (January, 1886), 208.

    62. New York *Age,* October 6, November 10, 1888.

mark the occasion. Many slaves preferred to have black preachers marry them, and they often engaged in a ceremony called "jumping the broomstick," during which the couple joined hands and jumped, sometimes backward, over a broomstick that friends or relatives held parallel to the ground. But regardless of who sanctioned the marriages, they were never legal or inviolable; the slave owner could dissolve them by selling one or the other of the partners. After emancipation the situation changed dramatically. The Freedmen's Bureau and many state governments legalized slave unions, requiring that men and women who were living together be formally married and proclaiming that slave marriages were legal and binding. The freedmen often sought to solemnize their marriage unions in religious ceremonies, either because they distrusted proclamations or because they wanted the satisfaction of pledging their troth "till death do us part." In a church in Russell County, Alabama, in 1865, twenty-six couples were married on a single occasion although they had lived together for many years and the Alabama constitutional convention declared them legally married. The northern missionaries, who stressed the importance of the family to the moral fiber of society and had legal authority to marry former slave couples, performed many weddings in the period immediately after freedom. Their reports referred to the large number of marriages that they performed. The regular ministry performed marriages in the period afterward.[63]

Death ended the life span, and the funeral to send the deceased into the afterlife was still another regular service that was performed in church. African-American burial and funeral customs were distinctive, as Martha Colquitt's story indicates. Her mother died in Georgia about two years after the Civil War. Sometime later she recalled that a "jackleg colored preacher talked at the funeral." Her use of the term *jackleg*, which referred to an itinerant, uneducated preacher, implies that he was not a regular minister. There probably was no minister in the immediate vicinity of where she and her mother resided. Such a situation would not have been unusual, nor was it extraordinary for a preacher to deliver the funeral sermon sometime after the deceased had been buried. Weeks and sometimes months usually separated funeral sermons from the actual burial of the body.[64]

63. Genovese, *Roll, Jordan, Roll*, 475–81; Peter Kolchin, *First Freedom: The Responses of Alabama's Blacks to Emancipation and Reconstruction* (Westport, 1972), 59–63.

64. Rawick, ed., *Georgia Narratives*, 245.

In the antebellum South, slaves had not always been able to obtain permission from their masters to conduct their own funeral services. And even when the regime granted them permission, there was not always a minister around to preach the funeral sermon until some months after the burial. In those cases, preachers sometimes sermonized for more than one dead slave at a time. As is true of so many other aspects of African-American culture, there is considerable evidence suggesting a linkage between slave burial and funeral practices and the customs of West Africans. For example, not only did African practice call for extending the activity surrounding the funeral over a period of many weeks, but it also involved a great feast for the mourners, both kin and other members of the village. Slaves followed a similar pattern in their burial and funeral practices. Circumstances dictated a quick burial of the body; decay began immediately in the heat and humidity of the South. But slaves seemed deliberately to delay conducting the funeral rite, in which the deceased was praised and prayed over to provide a proper send-off into the spirit world. Likewise, slaves made the funeral an occasion for celebration that included singing and feasting. In their funerals as in any other aspect of their lives, slaves celebrated the triumph of life. Instead of a wake, the slave funeral took on the character of a festival. Eugene D. Genovese quotes a white man who commented on slave funerals: "Their funerals formerly gave them great satisfaction, and it was customary here to furnish the relations of the deceased with bacon, spirit, flour, sugar and butter, with which a grand entertainment, in their way, was got up. We were once amused by a hearty fellow requesting his mistress to let him have his funeral during his lifetime, when it would do him some good. The waggish request was granted; and I venture to say there was never a funeral, the subject of which enjoyed it so much." And as West Africans usually did, slaves frequently placed broken earthenware on the grave as an offering to the spirit of the dead.[65]

Whether African-American funerals were the result of practical considerations in the slave experience or a custom whose roots extended back to the burial practices of West Africa, they carried over into the postemancipation period. Mary Wright of Gracey, Kentucky, later recalled that on at least one plantation where she resided funeral services were held annually on the fourth Sunday in August. On that day, prob-

65. Geoffrey Parrinder, *West African Religion: A Study of the Beliefs and Practices of Akan, Ewe, Yoruba, Ibo, and Kindred Peoples* (New York, 1969), 106–12; Raboteau, *Slave Religion*, 230–31; Genovese, *Roll, Jordan, Roll*, 194–202, 315.

ably at the conclusion of the regular worship services, "all the colored folks would take a basket dinner ter de church en each family dat had buried a nigger would pay de preacher ter preach the sermon foh dat darkie dat died." The separation of burials from funeral sermons had become customary rather than just expedient by the end of the century because even in cities, where churches and preachers were readily available, funerals sometimes followed burials by as much as a year. Other burial customs, such as placing objects on top of graves and laying bodies along an east-west axis, also existed into the twentieth century.[66]

In between the spiritual rebirth of the Christian and physical death was a lifetime of pleasure and pain. Local churches were complex institutions through which people met a variety of community needs. Church leaders accepted responsibility for caring for people in both spiritual and nonspiritual ways. Because the freedmen possessed few social institutions, their churches had to provide services that in the white communities were offered by specialized organizations. Even in urban settings and toward the turn of the century, when an array of secular institutions dotted the social landscape, the church remained the focal point of the community.

Local congregations supported a great many activities through which they aimed to improve the quality of life within the community, or at least to make it more endurable. Parishioners, mainly women, visited the inmates of jails and hospitals to comfort them; gave food and clothing to the indigent; provided pensions to superannuated ministers and the widows of deceased clergymen; and founded hospitals, orphanages, and nursing homes. Large urban congregations often performed all of those tasks, and nearly every congregation regardless of size maintained some ongoing program of benevolence. A study conducted by Atlanta University students in 1897 showed that sixty-five churches in a sample of seventy-nine recorded expenditures for charity.[67]

66. Rawick, ed., *Kentucky Narratives,* 65; *Home Mission Monthly,* I (May, 1878), 15; Creel, "Gullah Attitudes Toward Life and Death," 87–91; Hall, "African Religious Retentions in Florida," 111–14.

67. Kathleen C. Berkeley, "'Colored Ladies Also Contributed': Black Women's Activities from Benevolence to Social Welfare, 1866–1896," in *The Web of Southern Social Relations: Women, Family, and Education,* ed. Walter J. Fraser, Jr., R. Frank Saunders, Jr., and Jon L. Wakelyn (Athens, Ga., 1985), 181–203; Evelyn Brooks, "The Women's Movement in the Black Baptist Church, 1880–1920" (Ph.D. dissertation, University of Rochester, 1984), 109–14; Johnson, *Shadow of the Plantation,* 39; Wesley J. Gaines, *African Methodism in the South: Or, Twenty-Five Years of Freedom* (Atlanta, 1890), 81–82; Ray Stannard

Partly an outgrowth of the Christian doctrine of brotherhood and partly of the nurturing role of African-American women, the welfare function was the logical outcome of ministerial paternalism. Charley White, a preacher in the east Texas town of Jacksonville, worried that with winter setting in and folks becoming cold and hungry "lots of children warn't gonna have nothing for Christmas." He called on several local businessmen to make contributions to a Christmas fund and received substantial amounts of food and clothing for the children and their families. He remembered a white man once telling him: "Reverend White, I wish I could afford to give you more. You're doing more for Jacksonville than any other preacher I knowd." [68]

Many urban churches aided the poor and the helpless by sponsoring or affiliating with benevolent societies. In 1865 the Benevolent Daughters of Zion in Natchez, an AME affiliate, raised and spent $825 in support of the poor and for a burial fund. Those were the primary functions of a similar society operated in conjunction with St. James Protestant Episcopal Church in Baltimore, but in addition, "its regular meetings proved 'a forum' where all things which concerned the advancement of the racial group were discussed." From the 1890s through the turn of the century, Atlanta's First Congregational Church, under the leadership of Henry H. Proctor, had numerous associated women's and men's societies that provided a day nursery, kindergarten, gymnasium, school of music, employment bureau, and Bible school. These are just a few examples of the services hundreds of churches throughout the South, urban and rural, gave the members of their communities. [69]

The black urban communities expanded and matured during the second half of the nineteenth century, begetting a large number and a wide range of social institutions. Despite their continuing sensitivity to the welfare needs of the people generally, and especially the poor and infirm, however, the churches by the turn of the century did not always rank as the most important community service agencies. Because their members were generally poor, they often had little money to spend on charity. Dur-

---

Baker, *Following the Color Line: American Negro Citizenship in the Progressive Era* (2nd ed.; New York, 1964), 51; Atlanta University Conference, *Some Efforts of American Negroes for Their Own Social Betterment* (Atlanta, 1898), 10.

68. White, *No Quittin' Sense*, 157–67.

69. *Christian Recorder*, February 10, 1866; George F. Bragg, *History of the Afro-American Group of the Episcopal Church* (Baltimore, 1922), 97.

ing the entire year of 1912, the collections of the women's auxiliary group of New Zion Baptist Church in North Carolina amounted to only $41.86. In 1898 sixty-five churches each spent an average of $137 for charitable purposes. At the same time, ninety-two fraternal societies, including the Odd Fellows, Masons, True Reformers, Good Samaritans, Sons of Israel, Knights of Pythias, and Knights of Tabor, spent an average of $151. Though twelve churches in Petersburg disbursed $900 for charity, an average of $75 per church, twenty-two benevolent societies spent $2,177, or an average of $98.95 each, on sick benefits alone. Moreover, charity had to compete with other activities for portions of local church budgets. Construction of buildings, educational enterprises, and missionary activities took funds away from charity. Twenty-seven of seventy-nine churches examined by Atlanta University students in 1897 contributed in excess of $100 annually in benevolence, but only five of them devoted more than 15 percent of their annual expenditures to it.[70]

Church welfare programs helped more people than the benevolent societies did, even though they dispensed less money. Churches were especially beneficial to the poor who lived in the countryside, where benevolent societies were nonexistent. The benevolent societies were generally exclusive, middle- and upper-class organizations that required substantial investment for membership and frequently aided only their own members. In one sample, sixty-five churches reported charitable expenditures in 1897 that aided 1,422 persons while ninety-two secret and benevolent societies gave succor to 612.[71]

Local congregations also aided education by disseminating public information. This was a particularly valuable service because of the scarcity and limited circulation of black newspapers and the continued high rate of black illiteracy. Charles Dudley Warner recalled that during a worship service he visited in Virginia, "it occupied the minister a long time to give out notices of the week, and there was not an evening or afternoon that had not its meetings, its literary or social gathering, its picnic or fair for the benefit of the church, its Dorcas society, or some occasion of religious sociability." Literary and debate societies were often associated with churches, and they too served as important disseminators of public

70. Cedar Grove Baptist Association (North Carolina), *Minutes of the Forty-fifth Annual Session of the Cedar Grove Missionary Baptist Association . . . 1912* (Raleigh, 1912), 21; Atlanta University Conference, *Some Efforts of American Negroes*, 6–18.

71. Atlanta University Conference, *Some Efforts of American Negroes*, 10, 17.

knowledge. The Bethel Literary and Historical Society of Washington, the most famous of these, was associated with the Metropolitan AME Church. Public figures realized that the churches were important media of communication and made good use of them in broadcasting their views. Whitefield McKinlay, a Washington businessman and an associate of Booker T. Washington, suggested in a letter to a friend that the best way to bring matters before the people was through their churches. Washington himself, although often harsh in his criticism of the churches (especially the folk churches), had no qualms about using them to deliver his messages to the people; indeed, he devoted his very first Sabbath in Tuskegee to the town's churches, explaining to the congregations his plans for a training school for black youth.[72]

The churches also presented people with recreational opportunities. It was part of Baptist and Methodist dogma to discourage profane dancing, gambling, and baseball, but church leaders recognized that diversion was important to poor, hardworking people. Worship itself, with its singing and shouting, was an amusement of sorts, and meeting friends and exchanging pleasantries were essential parts of the Sunday morning worship services. Members of congregations frequently enjoyed picnics in the afternoon following services. They also had picnics after baptisms, meetings of associations and conferences, and funerals. Sir George Campbell discovered that a Baptist convention usually called for a celebration. "The people attend in large numbers, the women especially, in their best clothes." He found the whole scene "very pleasing and cheerful." A feature of the Alabama Flint River Association meeting in 1885 was a free dinner spread from ample picnic baskets before hungry and happy church members.[73]

Church leaders often organized outings for members of the congregation during the summer. "The excursion season is upon us in full," trumpeted the New York *Freeman,* calling attention to one of the highlights of the summer season for congregations of virtually every denomination. Typical excursions included short train or boat rides to nearby beaches or parks for picnics, games, and social interaction. An announcement in

72. Charles Dudley Warner, *On Horseback: A Tour in Virginia, North Carolina, and Tennessee* (Boston, 1889), 7–10; Whitefield McKinlay to T. McCants Stewart, October 5, 1922, in Whitefield McKinlay Papers, Carter G. Woodson Collection, Manuscripts Division, Library of Congress.

73. Rawick, ed., *Kentucky Narratives,* 65; Campbell, *White and Black,* 343; Huntsville *Gazette,* October 3, 1885.

the Huntsville *Gazette* advertised an excursion organized by a Colored Methodist Episcopal church: "Everyone should enjoy some pleasure, and a trip to the pretty little town of Florence is a good way to pass a day pleasantly." The price of the trip was $1.75. In the summer of 1885, the Birmingham AME Sunday school sponsored a union picnic with other churches to have a "grand time." Norfolk's Bank Street Baptist Church organized an excursion to Richmond in 1888, and several whites went along. A black journalist reported that "coaches reserved for them [the whites] were done away with of their own accord, and the whites occupied each and every car in company with the colored people, and everybody was satisfied."[74]

Concerts, children's music recitals, fairs, carnivals, and magic lantern shows filled the winter months. The Christmas season was an especially festive time in the churches. One year the adult members of the Ebenezer Baptist Church in Richmond packed a large boat full of gifts and then distributed them to excited children on Christmas Day. Churches also provided meeting places for recreational activities other than their own. Culture lovers in Norfolk planned concerts in the Bank Street Church because there was no other place in the city "except the Church where any genteel people can go." Raising money to finance the construction of buildings and to liquidate debts was another reason for social events. August 1, 1886, was Grand Rally Day for Norfolk's Bank Street Church. The object was to generate enough funds to begin construction of a new building. Women in the church organized several clubs and competed to see who could bring in the most money. Ladies Delight presented the church with $16.50, May Club raised $12.16, and Ladies Union Number 2 contributed $30.00. Another group printed a history of the church, whose original building had been erected by Presbyterians in 1802. Copies of the history and pictures of the old building sold for $1.00. A month later, the church organized a second Grand Rally Day during which members solicited more money for the building program. They finally raised sufficient funds to enable church officials to issue an order to begin construction. Other churches used rallies, excursions, rummage sales, lectures, and concerts to raise revenue to finance construction projects, and when they found themselves facing a mortgage note they went through the procedure again. The same week that the Bank Street Church

74. Huntsville *Gazette*, July 22, 1882, June 13, 1885; New York *Freeman*, June 27, 1885, August 27, 1888.

moved into its new building, it had a spelling bee and another Grand Rally to raise money to pay off its new debt.[75]

Congregations that over time achieved financial prosperity—and some that did not—eventually acquired buildings of more substantial proportions than those they had occupied immediately after emancipation. In 1885 the St. Philip Street Baptist Church in Montgomery, Alabama, began raising money for a new building, which a writer for a local newspaper said "promises to be a model of beauty." That same year an AME congregation in Birmingham commenced work on "an elegant brick church" at an initial cost of $7,000. The Metropolitan AME Church in Washington was the pride of the denomination. One of the finest structures owned by blacks, it was designed by the famous architect John Renwick. By the end of the century, impressive church edifices dominated virtually all of the major black population centers and were sources of great pride and enjoyment for the people.[76]

But church building sometimes led to extravagances that the people could ill afford. Large buildings were constructed when smaller ones would have sufficed and would have cost less. The seating capacity of church buildings significantly surpassed the number of communicants. In 1890, for example, the number of communicants in all-black organizations was 2,673,977, and the seating capacity of churches was 6,800,035. Thus the seating capacity exceeded the need by 254 percent. In 1906 the seating capacity was 10,481,738 when the membership stood at 3,685,097, or 284 percent greater than was needed. A newspaper correspondent complained about a $15,000 Gothic building for a church in Washington and asked if church building was being overdone, considering "the vast debts that are fastened upon the shoulders of the new and struggling people already burdened with cares and responsibilities of maintaining households, clothing and educating children, and other expenses growing out of a dignified life and the domesticities."[77]

The indebtedness congregations took on for construction was indeed a burden, especially for small rural churches soon after emancipation. In 1867 Thomas Allen, a Baptist minister, wrote to General Oliver O. How-

75. New York *Freeman*, October 24, 1885, September 10, 1887, August 27, 1888; *Christian Recorder*, February 10, March 10, 1866; Huntsville *Gazette*, July 22, 1882; New York *Globe*, May 12, 1883.

76. Huntsville *Gazette*, September 12, 19, 1885.

77. *Census of Religious Bodies: 1906* (2 vols.; Washington, D.C., 1910), I, 139, 141; New York *Freeman*, November 14, 1885.

ard of the Freedmen's Bureau that his congregation owed $250 on its building. It had been constructed and financed by local whites. The congregation could not meet the mortgage payment. "We cannot rase the money till next year *if* then, and the fact is the church will be taken from us . . . if I can not get the money." Henry M. Turner wrote to the superintendent of education in Georgia of another case involving a church struggling desperately against a crushing debt: "I would remark that the people are very poor and I cannot see how they can possibly pay this debt." He explained bitterly that the church's white creditors were trying to force its sale. "These poor people have worked hard to get their church and school built. And now to have it sold for half its value, from them, is really discouraging." By the turn of the century, overall church indebtedness was actually fairly small in relation to the value of church property, a reported total of $5,005,905 on a valuation of $56,636,159, or 8.8 percent. The average debt per organization, however, was $556, and that was 29 percent of the average property valuation of each congregation.[78]

The range of church buildings and styles of worship among congregations during the decades following emancipation indicate much more than merely differences in social and economic conditions among members of an otherwise homogeneous society. It suggests the continued existence of a culturally segmented black society. The differences between the folk churches of antebellum slaves and the denominational churches of northern blacks were striking and produced tension within the merging black communities of the postwar period. The freedmen easily accommodated the denominational organizations, particularly in church polity, but they did not forsake their traditional beliefs. The common people were often criticized for being superstitious and excessively emotional, but they remained mostly unmoved by their detractors. In their perceptions of the spirit world and in their religious ceremonies, postwar southern blacks revealed deep cleavages along social and cultural lines. Gradually, as more blacks became educated and achieved higher social status, they adopted the values of a middle-class society, and their churches changed. Their meetings became more restrained, and their church buildings took on a more substantial and more prosperous appearance. But the vestiges of the slave experience that melded traditions from Africa and America did not disappear, nor did the tension between

78. Thomas Allen to Oliver O. Howard, February 8, 1867, Henry M. Turner to G. L. Eberhart, March 6, 1867, in Records of the Superintendent of Education for the State of Georgia, Freedmen's Bureau Records; *Census of Religious Bodies: 1906*, I, 142–43.

the folk churches and the higher-status congregations. Despite the differences that divided the community and its churches, the common needs of the people, a sense of mutual responsibility, and a commitment to self-help kept the churches in the center of African-American life, both in small towns and rural areas and in the urban population centers. As W. E. B. Du Bois observed, "The church became the center of economic activity as well as of amusement, education and social intercourse." No other single institution was of greater overall importance to black people.[79]

79. W. E. B. Du Bois, ed., *Economic Co-operation Among Negro Americans*, Atlanta University Publications, No. 12 (Atlanta, 1907), 24.

7

The Preachers

In July, 1867, Enoch K. Miller, an American Missionary Association minister who was frustrated by local preachers' opposition to his missionary work, wrote from Napoleon, Arkansas, that there was a class of men who exercised great influence among the freedmen and monopolized their attention: "I refer to their preachers." A few years later T. Thomas Fortune, writing from an altogether different perspective, made a similar observation: "No class of men wield more influence, for good or evil, among Afro-Americans than the preachers." And at the turn of the century, William E. B. Du Bois wrote in *Souls of Black Folk,* "The Preacher is the most unique personality developed by the Negro on American soil." All three of these commentators acknowledged not only the great power that black preachers wielded in the religious affairs of black men and women but also their role in shaping the people's social and political relationships. Through the immediate postemancipation period, preachers were almost universally esteemed by the freed and the freeborn population alike and were recognized as the social and political leaders of the black community. They were the only group of leaders who crossed the lines between the political, religious, and social realms and who represented the status and economic elites on one hand and the masses of poor and illiterate freedmen on the other. But as both Miller and Fortune implied, the preachers had their critics, and by the close of the century the voices of dissatisfaction reverberated through the black community, emanating from women within the churches and especially from the educated and economically well-to-do members of the upper classes who were asserting their leadership of the race.[1]

1. Enoch K. Miller to William M. Colby, July 31, 1867, in Records of the Superintendent of Education for the State of Arkansas, U.S. Bureau of Refugees, Freedmen, and Abandoned Lands, Record Group 105, National Archives (hereinafter cited as Freedmen's Bureau Records); New York *Age,* September 6, 1890.

Despite the dependence on their masters imposed by slavery and the slaves' inability to control any part of their external lives, the bondsmen had produced their own leaders. Among these were their preachers. The profile and the functions of leaders among slaves differed somewhat from those in a free society, primarily because ultimate authority in the slave system rested in the hands of the white masters. As chattel, the slaves were unable to acquire wealth, education, and high status, qualities that the larger American society valued and that both whites and blacks attributed to leaders. Furthermore, nobody could relieve the slaves of their burden of work, or protect them from punishment, or secure better housing or food or clothing for them if doing so was at variance with the master's will. Leaders among the slaves usually had to accommodate the needs of the slaves with the indomitable will of the masters. The role of the preachers on plantations was thus very difficult. Though often illiterate and frequently subservient to their masters, they were popular and influential among plantation slaves. They enjoyed status not so much because of their relationship with the plantation's power structure as because of their relationship with the power structure of the spiritual world. Their main purpose was to make their people feel good about themselves in spite of the cruel realities of their lives and about their prospects for salvation at some time in the future.[2]

After emancipation, the former slaves naturally looked to the preachers—both the old slave preachers and the northern missionaries—for guidance in spiritual matters, but they also looked to them for help in dealing with the manifold problems and challenges that confronted them. The preachers were not always well-equipped to assist the freed people, but there were few others to whom the freedmen could turn or who could relate to them and their needs in ways that produced confidence. Commentators reported frequently on the preachers and noted their vital role in helping the freedmen adjust to their new lives. A report to the American Baptist Home Mission Society in 1866 explained that preachers were "a class of men who . . . have won the confidence, love, and respect of their people." Another observer noted that "within his own parish he is practically priest and pope." The scope of the preachers' influence stretched far beyond the pulpit and the congregation. Du Bois described the powerful political role of the black preacher as "a leader, a politician,

2. Eugene D. Genovese, "Black Plantation Preachers in the Slave South," *Louisiana Studies,* 11 (1972), 188–214; Albert J. Raboteau, *Slave Religion: The "Invisible Institution" in the Antebellum South* (New York, 1978), 231–39.

an orator, a 'boss,' an intriguer, and idealist." Episcopal bishop John F. Young compared black preachers to the chiefs of primitive tribes, implying a joining of political and religious functions similar to that among the native people of West Africa. Other contemporaries and later historians have echoed and amplified that characterization, suggesting that the role of the preacher in African-American society, mediating between two worlds and combining spiritual and political leadership, followed a pattern carried over from traditional West African societies. In the postwar period, the preachers looked after the freed people's welfare, helping to build an institutional infrastructure that provided a variety of social services ranging from education to burial insurance. The preachers' all-encompassing role gave them visibility and high status in many communities. To the British traveler Sir George Campbell preachers appeared to be a "sort of Christian Brahmins." [3]

John Jasper's career illustrates the evolution of the position of the preacher from slavery into postwar black society and how former slave preachers retained the support of many freedmen by responding to their needs in ways they could appreciate, although they antagonized the growing number of educated and prosperous southern blacks who did not understand at all. Born a slave in Fluvanna County, Virginia, Jasper grew up around tobacco and worked in a tobacco factory in Richmond as a stemmer. He felt the power of God strike him one day while pulling the stems off of tobacco leaves and was converted to Christianity. He felt not only the transforming power of the Holy Spirit but a call to preach God's word to the people as well. He became a member of the First African Baptist Church, one of the few regular black congregations in the antebellum South. It was under the pastoral care of a white minister, Robert Ryland, but Jasper wanted to preach, and he did, although apparently not to that congregation. He earned a widespread reputation for his

3. American Baptist Home Mission Society, "Report of the Thirty-fourth Annual Meeting of the Executive Board," in *Thirty-fourth Annual Report of the American Baptist Home Mission Society . . . 1866* (New York, 1866), 17; New York *Globe*, November 24, 1883; William E. B. Du Bois, *The Souls of Black Folk: Essays and Sketches* (Chicago, 1909), 190; Joe M. Richardson, *The Negro in the Reconstruction of Florida, 1865–1877* (Tallahassee, 1965), 94; Sterling Stuckey, *Slave Culture: Nationalist Theory and the Foundations of Black America* (New York, 1987), 255; Sir George Campbell, *White and Black: The Outcome of a Visit to the United States* (New York, 1879), 344; Armstead L. Robinson, "Plans Dat Comed from God: Institution Building and the Emergence of Black Leadership in Reconstruction Memphis," in *Toward a New South? Studies in Post–Civil War Southern Communities,* ed. Orville Vernon Burton and Robert C. McMath, Jr. (Westport, 1982), 71–102.

funeral sermons. Slaves from neighboring plantations often requested that he be allowed to preside over their funeral services. Through these sermons he gained fame as a preacher to slave audiences. During the Civil War, he preached to wounded soldiers in Richmond hospitals. When freedom finally came, he was about fifty years old, thrust on his own, and with a family but no job and no church to preach to. He found work making bricks and set about building a church of his own among the freedmen. Nine people initially gathered on a small island in the middle of the James River and formed his first congregation. The tiny group worshiped for a while in a house on the island or in a deserted stable, it is not clear which, but the number of worshipers grew, and eventually they purchased from a Presbyterian church a building located in a growing black neighborhood on the north side of the city. This group became the Sixth Mount Zion Baptist Church. The congregation, numbering in the hundreds, outgrew that building, and they and Jasper soon constructed a new one. Ultimately, the church's membership reached two thousand.

According to William E. Hatcher, who knew Jasper and visited his church from time to time, he did not change his preaching style much after emancipation. Continuing in the same manner that had made him popular among slaves, he drew his texts from the Old Testament, created vivid word pictures, and spoke simply and in the dialect of the freedmen. Educated blacks scoffed at both the substance and the style of his sermons, but that did not seem to bother him or his congregation. Indeed, the people came in droves to hear him preach. Nor did his attitude toward whites change very much. In Hatcher's view, Jasper's warm and kindly "allusions to his old master were in keeping with his kindly and conciliatory tone in all that he had to say about the white people after the emancipation of the slaves." There is no record of his sermons taking on an overtly political character or of his being involved in political activity. His fame and his role in the black community of Richmond was as a gospel preacher. At the time of his death, at the age of eighty-nine, he enjoyed the love of his congregation but bore the ridicule of educated blacks for his folksy way of preaching to his people.[4]

Morris Henderson, another Baptist preacher, emerged from the shadows of slavery very much as Jasper had done to become a member of the leadership elite in post–Civil War Memphis. He was born in Virginia in

4. William E. Hatcher, *John Jasper: The Unmatched Negro Philosopher and Preacher* (London, 1908), 23–29, 38, 58–62, 74, 94–105.

1802 and brought by his master to Shelby County at the age of forty-seven. Dark in color, short in stature, and unable to read or write, Henderson preached to blacks under close white supervision until freedom came to him and the other slaves in the county early in 1865. He then led his followers out of the white-controlled Baptist church and formed an independent congregation in a brush arbor. With the assistance of the women of the church, Henderson made a down payment on a building site on Beale Street, and the congregation erected a wood-frame building. The membership of Beale Street Baptist Church multiplied and soon reached several hundred. Active in Reconstruction politics, organizing programs to feed and educate the thousands of freedmen from the surrounding countryside who swarmed into Memphis looking for work, and launching plans to build a fine new church, Henderson was one of the most visible and influential people in the city's black community, and his church, with its twenty-five hundred members, was the largest black church in the city. There were so many members that worshipers were asked to attend only one of the three regular Sunday services so as to make room for all who wanted to attend. After involving himself in political activity during the first few years of freedom, Henderson closed the church to political meetings in 1872, no doubt, as the *Daily Appeal* noted, winning "for him the respect and confidence of the white people." When he died in 1877, five thousand people came to celebrate his life. The *Daily Avalanche* reported that he "has for years been the most influential man of his race in the city of Memphis." It claimed that people "who possessed a hundred times more education looked up to the little man with reverence and respect. On the sincerity of his religion, in the good common sense with which Nature had endowed him, he commanded the esteem of all who met him." [5]

Apart from the religious symbolism inherent in the ministry as an emblem of individual faith, it was a very popular occupation among the freedmen. It was one of the few that were accessible to blacks, and it offered high status, two very important considerations for people trying to advance upward from slavery. In the years following emancipation, preachers were probably the most numerous of all black professionals. It is impossible to know exactly how many there were because preaching was frequently not a full-time occupation, especially in the early years of

5. David M. Tucker, *Black Pastors and Leaders: Memphis, 1819–1972* (Memphis, 1975), 8–14; Robinson, "Plans Dat Comed from God," 73–75, 92.

freedom. The precise number of people who worked on farms or in other jobs during most of the week and preached to congregations on Sunday probably cannot be gleaned from regular census reports. By the turn of the century, however, when censuses of religious organizations began to record such data, the number was considerable. The black church in 1906 had 31,624 ordained ministers. That was 231 more ministers than reported congregations. Most of those ministers, 17,117 in all, were Baptists. The AME church had 6,200 ministers, the AME Zion had slightly over 3,000, and the CME church had almost 2,700. And in addition to ordained ministers, there were countless numbers of licentiates, exhorters, and informal preachers who were not included in those enumerations. In addition, there were in the neighborhood of 400 Presbyterian ministers (counting those in the Colored Cumberland Presbyterian church and the Afro-American Presbyterian Synod), and several small sects reported another 563 ministers. The Catholic church, which stubbornly resisted the creation of an African-American clergy, ordained only 5 black priests between 1866 and 1900. This was far less than the Episcopal church, which had been more liberal than the Catholics in admitting blacks to the ministry. Early in the twentieth century there were 178 black Episcopal ministers, 99 of whom were in charge of southern churches.[6]

The churches' central position in community life combined with a strong desire on the part of blacks to have preachers of their own race in their pulpits, and the high status that preachers generally enjoyed, especially in rural society, led many to aspire to the ministry from the time they were youngsters. As young boys, both Booker T. Washington and Paul Laurence Dunbar were drawn to the ministry, although neither was ever ordained and both later became outspoken critics of the clergy. Charley White, who grew up in the piney woods of east Texas during the 1880s, played preacher the way later generations of children acted out their fantasies by playing everything from soldiers to astronauts. His playmates acted as members of White's congregation, and he preached earnestly and frequently to them. The youthful Wesley J. Gaines preached many funeral sermons for birds, dogs, and barnyard animals that died on

6. *Census of Religious Bodies: 1906* (2 vols.; Washington, D.C., 1909), I, 146; Andrew E. Murray, *Presbyterians and the Negro—A History* (Philadelphia, 1966), 150–51; Stephen J. Ochs, *Desegregating the Altar: The Josephites and the Struggle for Black Priests, 1871–1960* (Baton Rouge, 1990), 36–38; George F. Bragg, *History of the Afro-American Group of the Episcopal Church* (Baltimore, 1922), 285–92.

the farm. The dreams and aspirations of many of these young boys were fulfilled owing to the great number of congregations scattered across the South and the demand from black folk for preachers.[7]

The church accepted virtually any candidate who asked to be licensed. Requirements for entering the ministry varied from one denomination and regional ordaining authority to another, but the universal and usually the sufficient prerequisite was a call from God to preach the gospel. There was no common understanding, however, of what precisely constituted a call, although among freedmen it included a mystical spiritual experience akin to the conversion experience. One old preacher recalled that the first impulse he had after his conversion experience was to go out and preach God's word. Not long afterward he preached his first sermon. The call came to many others in very much the same way. Booker T. Washington wrote that "usually the 'call' came when the individual was sitting upon the floor as if struck by a bullet, and would lie there for hours, speechless and motionless."[8]

Whether the call was true or spurious mattered both to the individual and to a congregation that might receive him as their preacher and spiritual leader, but there was no absolute, objective evaluation that could be made of it. In one sense, the individual himself was the only one who knew for certain that God had called him to preach. The more dramatic the circumstances surrounding it, the more persuasive he might be in trying to prove to others that it was genuine. But ultimately, it was for the congregation to decide by whether they hired him to preach. Emanuel K. Love, the Georgia Baptist and pastor of Savannah's First African Church, attempted to define a true call and its manifestations: "When the candidate has a desire, of which I'll repeat, he is the judge, and the church finds him qualified by moral character, and other requirements, among them the ability to teach, where the church can approve him as a good man and capable of instructing men in the way of salvation, and the judgment of

7. John L. Bell, "Baptists and the Negro in North Carolina During Reconstruction," *North Carolina Historical Review,* XLII (1965), 403; Louis R. Harlan, *Booker T. Washington: The Making of a Black Leader, 1865–1910* (New York, 1972), 62–80; Benjamin E. Mays, *The Negro's God as Reflected in His Literature* (1938; rpr. New York, 1968), 134; Charley C. White, *No Quittin' Sense* (Austin, 1969), 3–5; *A.M.E. Church Review,* V (October, 1888), 69–71; New York *Age,* November 29, 1890.

8. Clifton H. Johnson, ed., *God Struck Me Dead: Religious Conversion Experiences and Autobiographies of Ex-Slaves* (Philadelphia, 1969), 74; Booker T. Washington, *Up from Slavery: An Autobiography* (Garden City, 1949), 81–83.

the church and his convictions of duty coincide, I think that may be regarded as a call to the ministry." [9]

Along with having been called by God to preach the gospel, preachers
were expected to exhibit moral uprightness, familiarity with the Scriptures, and knowledge of denominational doctrine that epitomized the
evangelical standard of Christian behavior. Sins of sexual impropriety
and drunkenness were among the un-Christian behaviors church authorities most commonly guarded against, and although other offenses carried sanctions, these were the ones that were most often cited in the criteria for ordination and for defrocking a minister. Ordaining agencies set
down specific standards against which they measured candidates' qualifications. Cedar Grove Baptist Association in North Carolina, for example, ruled that "no minister dealing in ardent spirits or malt liquors,
or having an interest in any firm, saloon, groggery or jug tavern, traffick-
ing in alcoholic drinks, shall be recognized by this Association." Being
educated was not always a prerequisite for entering the ministry, nor was
it indicative of how successful a person might be in the profession, but
more and more toward the close of the nineteenth century church authorities and laypeople in the congregations demanded an educated ministry.
One former slave, who many years later talked about how he had come
to be a preacher, said that he could not remember exactly but felt that he
"had been ordained of god to preach the gospel even though I couldn't
read and write." But the Cedar Grove Association, like most other regional organizations among Baptists and Methodists, established modest
though surprisingly high standards that reflected the people's appreciation for education and an educated ministry. "No candidate shall be ordained to the ministry within our bounds," the association resolved, "unless he is competent of mastering the English correctly, and also have a
complete knowledge of mathematics." [10]

The effectiveness of procedures for screening candidates was under-
mined by the congregational polity of most black churches and, particu-

9. Emanuel K. Love, *A History of the First African Baptist Church of Savannah from
Its Organization, January 20th, 1788, to July 1st, 1888* (Savannah, 1888), 239–45.

10. Johnson, ed., *God Struck Me Dead*, 84–85; Cedar Grove Missionary Baptist Association (North Carolina), *Minutes of the Eighth Annual Session of the Cedar Grove Missionary Baptist Association . . . 1875* (Raleigh, 1875), 13–17; Berean Valley Baptist Association (Virginia), *Minutes of the Fourteenth Annual Session of the Berean Valley Baptist
Association . . . 1896* (Washington, D.C., n.d.), 9.

larly during the years immediately after emancipation, the compelling demand for black ministers. Given the poor educational backgrounds of most freedmen, strict enforcement of educational standards would have been too exclusionary to allow adequate numbers of blacks into the ministry. In attempting to weigh the importance of setting high standards against the need for ordained ministers, the more practical consideration of having ministers in the pulpits prevailed over the ideal of a learned and articulate clergy. Many ordaining agencies wanted to set high educational standards but usually ordained all but the most woefully deficient candidates who came before them and hoped for the best. When the Missouri Annual Conference of the AME church met in New Orleans in 1865, a committee on admissions and orders reported that one group of men was "considerably deficient" in studies prescribed by the church discipline, but the committee candidly confessed that the church's need for ordained ministers surpassed its desire for a learned clergy. Candidates who promised to pursue theological studies often received ordination. The examination committee of the Northern Neck Baptist Association of Virginia instructed one person to attend school and prepare himself more fully for the work but nevertheless recommended his immediate ordination.[11]

Even though educational attainments were stated requirements for ordination and the people in the congregations had a high regard for education, black folk did not always consider education a qualification for preachers. Many preachers concurred in that opinion. As one minister put it, preachers were "called by God" and not "made by education." The prophets and Jesus' disciples, another minister argued, came to their work with a sense of mission and not as an intellectual pursuit. There was nothing "stated or inferred in the Bible, nor suggested by reason to cause one to conclude that the Almighty has ever changed His method of bringing into service those who are to proclaim and to interpret His word." Many freedmen did not respond to the scholarly discourses that some ministers passed off as sermons. More than a few people thought too much education actually detracted from good preaching. Even late in the century, when there were significant numbers of educated clergymen in the South, sermons were marked by emotional rather than intellectual

11. Charles S. Smith, *A History of the African Methodist Episcopal Church* (1922; rpr. New York, 1968), 935; Northern Neck Baptist Association (Virginia), *Minutes of the Twentieth Annual Session of the Northern Neck Baptist Association . . . 1897* (Washington, D.C., 1897), 13–14.

stimulation and congregations judged their preachers by their ability to get them "in the spirit." [12]

The level of education in the black community between emancipation and the end of the century and the people's attitude about an educated clergy were reflected in the educational attainments of black preachers. Most of the first generation of freedmen preachers were uneducated— even in scriptural principles—and only marginally literate. An officer of the Methodist Freedmen's Aid Society later recalled that hundreds of men who could not read had received ordination as ministers. He had seen one preacher who was supposedly reading from a hymnal but was holding it upside down. James Redpath, a white newspaperman, found a "majority of them illiterate." Isaac Brinckerhoff, a northern teacher who worked among the freedmen in South Carolina, Georgia, and Florida during the 1860s, noted in his journal that many preachers in the rural districts scarcely possessed "the first rudiments of knowledge." Even by the end of the nineteenth century, many ministers were barely literate and mostly uneducated in standard denominational doctrine, as William E. B. Du Bois and his Atlanta University students discovered in their study of black churches. [13]

By no means, though, were all black preachers entirely—or even largely—uneducated or illiterate. The image of an ignorant exhorter reflects only one facet of the black clergy. The missionaries who came into the South at the close of the Civil War were generally well-trained and often college-educated. The seminaries and ministers' institutes that northern denominations and black churches established provided training for students who hoped to enter or were already practicing the ministry. By the close of the nineteenth century, thousands of students had received significant formal theological instruction. An observer at that

12. Lillie B. Chace Wyman, "Colored Churches and Schools in the South," *New England Magazine,* III (February, 1891), 786; Levi J. Coppin, *Unwritten History* (1919; rpr. New York, 1968), 211–12; William E. B. Du Bois, ed., *The Negro Church: Report of a Social Study Made Under the Direction of Atlanta University* (Atlanta, 1903), 84–85; Charles S. Johnson, *The Shadow of the Plantation* (Chicago, 1934), 157.

13. Alexander Crummell, Sermon No. 32 (MS in Schomburg Collection, New York Public Library); James Redpath, "Special Report to M. Pleiance, Secretary of State of the Republic of Hayti, October 1, 1861" (MS in Manuscripts Division, Library of Congress); Isaac W. Brinckerhoff, "Thirty Years Among Freedmen: Mission Work Among the Freedmen, Beaufort, S. Carolina, St. Augustine, Florida, Savannah, Georgia, 1862–1894" (MS in American Baptist Historical Society, Rochester, New York); Du Bois, ed., *Negro Church,* 58–59.

time noted that "forty years ago the minister who could read was the exception; now the exception is the one who cannot." [14]

The formal theological training that black ministers received was limited and rudimentary. Hosts of ministerial students were unable to gain the maximum benefit from their school or seminary experiences because they failed to complete the courses or had to work at tiring jobs to earn the cost of room, board, and tuition. A serious handicap in many instances was the student's utter lack of preparation for collegiate or seminary instruction. One northern teacher reported to the American Baptist Home Mission Society in 1868 that "when they commence study they are as ignorant of the world outside of the very narrow circle in which they have moved, as if they had but lately arrived from the moon." For those who did possess both the willingness and the ability to learn, the training they received was often restricted by the inadequacies of the faculties and the facilities of the schools they attended. Not all of the schools were poor, but many were. [15]

Yet many congregations, especially in Presbyterian and Episcopal churches, placed great value on learning and demanded and got ministers who had impressive academic credentials. William H. Franklin, for example, a Presbyterian minister, was the son of a brickmason in Knoxville and received an elementary education before the Civil War. Afterward he attended Knoxville College, a Presbyterian school, and then a Presbyterian seminary before entering the ministry in Rogersville, Tennessee, where he distinguished himself and became esteemed as a minister and a teacher. Jonathan Gibbs was born in the North and received his ordination from Presbyterian authorities before the Civil War. He attended Dartmouth College and Princeton Seminary and came to South Carolina and Florida as a missionary during Reconstruction. The most outstanding Presbyterian minister of the period was Francis J. Grimké, the mulatto son of a white Charleston father and a slave mother, who attended Lincoln University and graduated from Princeton in 1878. Alexander Crummell, another college-educated minister, attended Beriah Green's Oneida Institute in the 1830s, a school widely known for nurturing antislavery convictions and for educating blacks. After leaving Oneida,

14. Du Bois, ed., *Negro Church*, 96, 122–23.

15. *A.M.E. Church Review,* V (January, 1889), 325–26; American Baptist Home Mission Society, *Thirty-sixth Annual Report of the American Baptist Home Mission Society . . . 1868* (New York, 1868), 11; Ray Stannard Baker, *Following the Color Line: American Negro Citizenship in the Progressive Era* (2nd ed.; New York, 1964), 53.

Crummell was denied admission to the General Theological Seminary of the Protestant Episcopal church because of his race. Nevertheless, he was ordained and appointed to a pastorate. Continually frustrated and often humiliated by racial bigotry both inside and outside of the church, he left the United States and continued his formal education in England, receiving a degree from Cambridge University in 1853. After successfully ministering to blacks in Africa, Crummell returned to the United States in 1871 and became rector of St. Luke's Protestant Episcopal Church in Washington.[16]

Congregations of educated Baptists and Methodists demanded and got educated ministers. William H. McAlpine, an Alabama Baptist, had learned to read and write from his master's children during slavery, was a pupil at a freedmen's school after emancipation, and then attended Talladega College. He became a missionary in Alabama and president of the Alabama Baptist State Convention. He also was a major fund-raiser for Selma University, which the state convention founded and operated, and served on the board of trustees of Lincoln Normal University in Marion, Alabama. J. Francis Robinson was another respected Baptist minister. Early in 1871, T. Thomas Fortune paused in Charlottesville during a trip through the South and took note of Robinson, who was then pastor of Mt. Zion Baptist Church. Fortune was surprised by the universal respect the people accorded him "and the heroic manner in which they held up his hands in the important and necessary religious and educational work he is doing." Born in Winchester, Virginia, in 1862, Robinson attended private and public schools after the war until he was twelve years old, when he moved to New York with his mother. When he was a few weeks short of graduating from a public grammar school there, his mother's illness forced him to quit school and take a job. Shortly after reaching the age of sixteen, Robinson, then a member of a Methodist Episcopal congregation, obtained a license to preach and entered Centenary Biblical Institute, later Morgan College, in Baltimore. Upon completing the theological course, he was assigned to a church in Norwich, New York. Sometime later he forsook the Methodist church and joined the Baptist ministry in Charlottesville. Fortune described him as "an exceedingly progressive young man, an earnest minister, a successful financier, and an effective organizer." Also prominent among the educated clergy were

16. New York *Freeman*, May 23, 1885; Richardson, *Negro in the Reconstruction of Florida*, 154; Du Bois, *Souls of Black Folk*, 215–27; Wilson Jeremiah Moses, *Alexander Crummell: A Study of Civilization and Discontent* (New York, 1989), 11–195.

Daniel A. Payne, Richard H. Cain, James Lynch, Hiram Revels, Henry M. Turner, Levi J. Coppin, Reverdy Ransom, Benjamin T. Tanner, Charles H. Phillips, Charles Pearce, and Anthony Binga. A white teacher who attended the Florida Annual Conference of the AME church in 1874 noted that "many of the delegates were educated men, and all were interested in education." By the turn of the century, most black ministers probably fell in between the categories of illiterate country preachers and the still fairly small group of college-educated and seminary-trained clerics. The type which one of Du Bois' Atlanta University students found to be prevalent in Atlanta was common in the small towns and cities of the New South: "They are not usually highly educated men, although they are by no means illiterate." [17]

The rising level of education among the clergy reflected the deepening social class divisions within the black community. The better-educated ministers were usually very critical of the emotionalism that appealed so strongly to the uneducated masses and attempted to reform their profession. Those clergymen were keenly aware of the images that their less sophisticated colleagues implanted or reinforced in the minds of prejudiced whites. They wanted blacks to make the best possible impression on whites, especially those who criticized blacks and challenged the principle of racial equality on the basis of white superiority. Accordingly, they vigorously agitated for higher levels of learning for preachers. "The indispensable need of ministerial education can't be too much emphasized," one minister mused. Preachers whose congregations included members of the young, educated black elite were particularly vulnerable to pressure to alter their style or vacate the pulpit. Thomas Fuller believed that advances in education among blacks would put many of the older generation of preachers in jeopardy. The "ministers of today must be educated," he insisted, "or they will be forced from their pulpits by the rising pews." In some cities ministers formed societies to inculcate greater respect for high educational standards among members of their profession. [18]

Not only the educational but also the moral standards of black

17. Justus N. Brown to E. M. Cravath, October 20, 1870, in American Missionary Association Archives, Amistad Research Center, Tulane University; New York *Age*, April 18, 1891; Richardson, *Negro in the Reconstruction of Florida*, 93; Du Bois, ed., *Negro Church*, 79.

18. Du Bois, ed., *Negro Church*, 229–49; Love, *History of the First African Baptist Church*, 249, 273–74; Thomas O. Fuller, *History of the Negro Baptists of Tennessee* (Memphis, 1936), 236.

preachers were being challenged by elite blacks by the close of the nineteenth century. Laypeople often criticized the folk ministry. There always were unflattering rumors and stories about individual preachers. Regardless of their truth, they caused the ministry to suffer suspicion and ridicule. The names of preachers occasionally found their way onto the rolls of jailed criminals, although serious transgressions such as larceny or acts of violence do not appear to have been frequent. The moral frailties of black preachers usually took the form of less damnable vices. Most preachers were common people who were neither more nor less upright than their congregants; very often black ministers reflected the values of their neighbors. "The black preacher," Alexander Crummell explained, "is the creation of the people." Black folk were remarkably tolerant of their preachers' behavior. Few labored under illusions about the moral character of their preachers. They imposed higher standards of conduct on them than they did on themselves but did not always expect those standards to be met. This realistic outlook is revealed in a folktale in which the narrator explains: "They ain't no different from nobody else. They mouth is cut cross ways ain't it? Well, long as you don't see no man wid they mouth cut up and down, you know they'll lie jus' like de rest of us." Those who disapproved of a preacher's conduct could do little to change it. They might dismiss him from their church, but there was no way of preventing him from preaching to anybody who wanted to hear him.[19]

What otherwise was virtually an open door to the ministry was generally closed fast against women. The laity was predominantly female, but the pulpit was almost exclusively a male domain. Females enjoyed power and high status in African-American society, but the basis for both was familial and domestic. Some professions were open to women, particularly teaching, and women were prominent in the supernatural realm of magic and conjuring, but the Christian ministry was largely closed to them. The men's protectiveness of their territory was evident in the asser-

19. Zora Neale Hurston, *Mules and Men: Negro Folktales and Voodoo Practices in the South* (1935; rpr. New York, 1970), 37–38; Cedar Grove Missionary Baptist Association, *Minutes of the Eighteenth Annual Session of the Cedar Grove Missionary Baptist Association . . . 1885* (Danville, Va., 1885), 12–13; Baptist State Convention of North Carolina, *Minutes of the Sixteenth Annual Session of the Baptist State Convention of North Carolina . . . 1882* (Raleigh, 1883), 16; Northern Neck Baptist Association, *Minutes of the Twentieth Annual Session of the Northern Neck Baptist Association . . . 1897*, 8; *Christian Recorder*, September 3, 1864; Crummell, Sermon No. 32.

tion of one minister that God had made woman "to be a help meet for man, but not his head." He believed that "she was never made or created to be his High Priest and Ruler in the Church of God." Thomas Fuller, a Tennessee minister, wrote that although no church program could succeed without the women's acquiescence and assistance, their proper role was auxiliary to that of male leaders. "The Baptists of Tennessee and in the South do not take kindly to women preaching," he stated. The field for women was "large enough for the exercise of all their gifts and powers" without their becoming involved in areas already the province of men. Not all women accepted their assigned position in the church organization. One Alabama woman, noting that the ministers did not do much to help in community service work, told the Baptist state convention that "it is no more our duty to help them than it is theirs to help us." And a female teacher in Memphis complained that it was strange that men should "suffer women to do all the drudgery work, plow, plant, cultivate and gather the crop, draw water and split rails," but when it came to mental or spiritual work they acted as if "women had all the muscular strength and they had all the brains and thinking power." A few women did enter the regular ministry, including Sarah Hughes, an educated mulatto whom Bishop Henry M. Turner of the AME church ordained in 1886, and as missionaries both at home and abroad, they carried the gospel to large numbers of Christians and pagans alike. But as a rule women exercised their considerable power in the church from the pew and from their auxiliary organizations.[20]

Women seldom challenged male ministers for positions in the pulpit, but if they accepted their auxiliary status without too much complaint they were not timid about expressing their opinions about how the preachers led the churches. They knew full well that the churches—and the preachers—depended heavily on them and the money they raised for support, and that dependence gave them considerable leverage in influencing church policy. Many educated women believed that uneducated preachers with their pie-in-the-sky sermons were doing very little to help

20. J. P. Campbell, "The Ordination of Women: What Authority for It," *A.M.E. Church Review,* II (April, 1886), 351–54; Wesley J. Gaines, *African Methodism in the South: or, Twenty-Five Years of Freedom* (Atlanta, 1890), 65–66; Evelyn Brooks, "The Women's Movement in the Black Baptist Church, 1880–1920" (Ph.D. dissertation, University of Rochester, 1984), 99–100, 109–10; Fuller, *Negro Baptists of Tennessee,* 238–39; Virginia W. Broughton, "Woman's Work," *National Baptist Magazine,* I (January, 1894), 34.

their people. Indeed, the worst of them were exploiting the people with constant demands for money and were living off them like shameless parasites. They complained about preachers who were not keen on social service. In the years after emancipation, especially as the black urban population increased in size, women became concerned about the problems of poverty, disease, and demoralization that afflicted the people. Relating the conditions of life to spiritual salvation, an idea that was gaining popularity in urban Christianity during the latter part of the nineteenth century and was known as the Social Gospel, many church women registered their impatience with the "otherworldliness" and backwardness of the uneducated ministry. Many women in the church agreed with Nannie M. Burroughs, who headed the Baptists' National Training School for women, when she criticized those who preached "too much Heaven and too little practical Christian living." Some of the more vocal and radical women charged the ministry with sexism by refusing to support training institutes and scholarships for women and girls, programs aimed at enriching their lives. "But our churches find a way to help the men who want to go away to study theology or medicine." [21]

The ministers, educated and unlettered alike, regarded preaching as their primary function but not the only one. When Elias C. Morris, president of the National Baptist Convention, told his fellow Baptists that "ministers are expected to stand for the people in nearly every avenue of life," he was not exaggerating. The older generation of preachers followed the model of the paternalistic master in their relationships with their congregations. Their lack of education and the poverty of their followers severely limited their ability to give material help, but along with communicating their faith and delivering rousing sermons they coached their congregants in everything from relating to God to coping with the mundane minutia of daily life. As a Baptist clergyman told the South Carolina state convention, the preacher must know "the best remedy for teething infants—and preachers generally have much experience on this line; he must be a horse doctor, weather prophet, must attend the living, bury the dead, tell the farmers when to plant, act as bondsman for all his people; in short, he must know as nearly as possible everything under the sun as it is possible for the human mind to know." If he was successful, he commanded the complete loyalty of his congregation and became its

21. Brooks, "Women's Movement in the Black Baptist Church," 98–101, 216–17, 294–95.

patriarch. T. Thomas Fortune remarked in 1883 that "to speak in damaging terms of one of our ministers, even when he is guilty of the offense charged, is to arouse his congregation to a frenzy." Indeed, he added, preachers frequently enjoyed their congregations' support regardless of their behavior.[22]

But a preacher could not behave arrogantly or arbitrarily and get away with it. Black folk knew how to suffer external oppression, but they had no tolerance for tyrants among their preachers. "The people like to have a large voice in all their religious affairs," commented one observer. "Takin' it all and all," explained John Harris, a Georgia Baptist preacher, "you're only at a church as long as you'n the members agree on everything. Just let something come up in the church where the pastor don't see things just the way all his members wants him to, and right then they'll throw him out for sho, before he know's what's happenin'." The respect and allegiance that most preachers enjoyed grew out of the love and mutual support the evangelical church promoted among members of the community of true believers. Successful preachers carefully cultivated their congregations for sympathy and support, emphasizing the necessity for clergy and laity to help one another live in accordance with God's law. The career of Emanuel K. Love, a Baptist minister in Savannah, serves as an example of how successful preachers plotted their course so as to gain the confidence of their congregations. Love resigned his position as a representative of the American Baptist Publication Society in 1885 to accept a call to the pastorate of the First African Baptist Church in Savannah. On his arrival there, he set about placing himself firmly in control of the congregation. He instructed them that the first thing they must do was trust him. "For in order that we may follow one we must first have faith in such an one." The second requirement was that they love him, "for there will be times when you will be called upon to bear very much with your leader, and if you don't love him you can't bear the burdens that may be put upon you." The third commandment was that they obey him, "for the good book informs you that obedience is better than sacrifice." At the same time, Love warned the congregation that they must not be

22. National Baptist Convention, *Journal of the Twenty-first Annual Session of the National Baptist Convention . . . 1901* (Nashville, 1901), 26–28; *Christian Recorder*, March 4, 1865; Baptist Educational Missionary and Sunday School Convention (South Carolina), *Minutes of the Seventeenth Anniversary of the Educational, Missionary and Sunday School Convention of the Colored Baptists of South Carolina . . . 1893* (Columbia, 1893), 57; New York *Globe*, June 30, 1883.

disrespectful, critical, or complaining. They should commend him when he preached a good sermon, and when he did not preach well, they should not complain but instead help him to do better the next time. Maybe not all preachers were so explicit in stating what they expected from their congregations, and certainly not all of them succeeded in getting it, but the good ones did. The bonds that were formed between preacher and congregation were the strongest ones outside of the family that existed within the black community, and one must believe they were far stronger than typically existed within the white churches.[23]

The generation of freedmen in the postwar black community respected, loved, and often venerated their preachers, but it was a rare preacher who went totally unscathed by criticism. The stress that black clergymen placed on raising money from their congregations often caused them to appear avaricious, conniving, and self-serving and to gain reputations for taking advantage of their congregations. The people may have loved them, but they had to keep watch on them too. "Everything," Francis Grimké noted, "seems to be arranged with reference to the collection. The great objective point seems to be to reach the pocketbooks of the people." Black folk seemed to be less offended by the antics of their preachers, real or legendary. They saw their preachers as fallible human beings and accepted them as such. The preacher's foolishness was the subject of many jokes, or "lies," told by black folk. The tone of these tales suggests not only that the people could be critical of their preachers but also that they did not always take their preachers as seriously as the preachers sometimes took themselves. According to one folktale, the "haid deacon of de Mt. Zion Baptis' Chu'ch up at Rocky Hill" had a son named John, "de black sheep of de family, de baby boy." John usually became offensive when his father entertained the local preacher for a Sunday chicken dinner. The reason for John's attitude was that the preacher "lack de same paa't of de chicken dat li'l John lack, an' he tuck de drumsticks offen de platter an' put 'em on his plate." Presently the hot-tempered boy shouted: "Ah done tole y'all Ah'm gittin tiahed of dese damn preachuhs eaten' up mah paa't of de chicken." When on one occasion the preacher encountered John alone he asked where the boy had been. John replied that he had been in Hell, where his father had told him

23. New York *Age*, September 15, October 27, 1888; Campbell, *White and Black*, 344; George P. Rawick, ed., *Georgia Narratives* (Westport, 1977), Pt. 1, p. 294, Vol. III of Rawick, ed., *The American Slave: A Composite Autobiography, Supplement, Series 1*, 12 vols.; Love, *History of the First African Baptist Church*, 94–96.

he was bound if he did not stop being disrespectful to the preacher. "Well, how is things down dere?" the preacher inquired. "Jes' lack dey is heah," John answered, "so many damn preachuhs 'roun de fiah till you cain't git to hit." [24]

As public servants, ministers needed community support. A successful preacher was one who could raise money for church buildings and activities as well as for his own salary and accommodations. The AME *Christian Recorder* suggested that clergymen who experienced difficulty with fund-raising should endeavor to get the congregation "spiritually alive," in other words, work on their emotions until they were responsive to a persuasive appeal. Finances might take care of themselves, but "we do say that the burden of church financiering will be immeasurably lightened." Bishop Jabez P. Campbell's secret was not to permit the fervor of converts to grow cold, "for they do better at this time than any other." [25]

Preachers' salaries varied widely depending on individual congregations' ability to pay and the preachers' ability to elicit contributions. By the end of the nineteenth century in rural and small-town churches, especially those that recognized and accepted a professional ministry, salaries generally ranged from $250 to $350 per year, averaging $316 for CME, $315 for AME, $313 for AME Zion, and $227 for Baptist clergymen. Two preachers in Farmville, Virginia, however, received $480 and $600 respectively in 1898. Both were young members of the progressive element of the clergy that stressed education and were graduates of theological schools. In about 1900, a black minister in Sandy Spring, Maryland, who was pastor of three churches, one of them some distance from the other two, received a combined income of $600. In cities and larger towns average salaries were somewhat higher. According to census figures, urban salaries averaged $835 for AME ministers, $698 for AME Zion, $605 for Baptist, and $350 for CME ministers. By comparison, the average white minister earned about $1,000. Those figures provide a

24. Huntsville *Gazette*, April 14, 1883; Charles Dudley Warner, *On Horseback: A Tour in Virginia, North Carolina, and Tennessee* (Boston, 1889), 9–10; Wyman, "Colored Churches and Schools in the South," 788; Francis J. Grimké, *The Afro-American Pulpit in Relation to Race Elevation* (Washington, D.C., 1893), 7; Hurston, *Mules and Men*, 37–38; J. Mason Brewer, ed., *The Word on the Brazos: Negro Preacher Tales from the Brazos River Bottoms of Texas* (Austin, 1953), 92.

25. *Christian Recorder*, July 20, 1899; Edward W. Lampton, *Digest of Rulings and Decisions of the Bishops of the African Methodist Episcopal Church from 1847 to 1907* (Washington, D.C., 1907), 254.

good indication not only of the earnings of urban ministers but also of the relative wealth of congregations in those denominations. Individual salaries, however, did not always conform to those averages. Some urban ministers earned far less while some, especially Episcopalian and Presbyterian ministers and Methodist hierarchs, received annual salaries of up to $1,500. Preachers in denominations or sects that did not believe in a professional ministry received no income at all. Most ministers who supported themselves outside of the pulpit were farmers; others worked as laborers or teachers or at some other occupation. John Harris rented a farm and worked at other odd jobs to supplement his farm and ministerial income. His congregation did not like his working outside of the church, which evidently created a problem. "My members never wanted me to keep no other job," he told an interviewer, "but just to preach for 'em and visit 'round 'mongst the disabled members." But Harris had a family to support and rent to pay, and he did not trust his church income. "I needed my daily wages too bad to depend on a church salary." Consequently, "I worked every day when I was pastorin' churches." [26]

Preachers often endured considerable hardships in fulfilling their ministerial duties. The poor went hungry, and itinerants spent nights in uncomfortable places. Circuit riders covered hundreds of miles each month, preaching to different congregations each Sunday. Ministers sometimes experienced great difficulty in obtaining their salaries, small as they were. Bishop Jabez P. Campbell of the AME church told the General Conference in 1880 that some preachers and their families had endured much suffering because of unpaid salaries. An officer of the Cedar Grove Baptist Association of North Carolina maintained that a church must never "promise more than it is able to pay" but should always pay "what it promises promptly, timely and uncomplainingly." According to the "law of Christ," a preacher "shall have a proper return from those whom he serves." The pastor required to labor without food, clothing, or a place to shelter himself and his family could "neither preach nor discharge any of the claims" of his office. In 1902 a minister in Thomas County, Geor-

26. *Census of Religious Bodies: 1906*, I, 94–97; W. E. B. Du Bois, "The Negroes of Farmville, Virginia: A Social Study," *Bulletin of the Department of Labor*, III (January, 1898), 16–17; William Taylor Thom, "The Negroes of Sandy Spring, Maryland: A Social Study," *Bulletin of the Department of Labor*, VI (January, 1901), 72; Rawick, ed., *Georgia Narratives*, 276–304.

gia, charged that 75 percent of the churches there were in debt to their former preachers.[27]

During the troublesome years that followed the Civil War, preachers who took part in political activities sometimes suffered reprisals from angry whites. Conservative whites used intimidation to discourage black political leaders from organizing Union League and Republican party groups and from voting and campaigning for public office, and preachers were not exempted from such treatment. More than one preacher was attacked or felt the threat of bodily injury or was arrested by white authorities, and more than one church was set afire by night riders. Even after the collapse of the Republican state governments in the South, many black preachers who challenged white supremacy found themselves in mortal danger.[28]

Attacks on black preachers did not come only from whites. Ministers, though supposedly men of peace and goodwill, occasionally became the objects of bitter animosity within their own communities, as an incident reported in a church in 1890 illustrates. There were several aspirants for a vacant pastorate. One of the candidates, favored by the women of the congregation but strongly opposed by some of the men, had to hide because of threats made against him. Charley White, an east Texas minister, once attempted to escort from his church a woman who had come inside in an inebriated condition and inappropriately dressed. The woman suddenly drew a knife on him and threatened to stab him if he did not leave her alone. On another occasion a drunken husband threatened to shoot up White's church if the man's wife did not come out of the building immediately. She walked out and thus averted a possible disaster, but the threat of violence was so great that another female church member offered her services as White's armed bodyguard. Thomas Fuller, writing in 1938 about earlier events, told of three ministers who had been shot to

27. North Mississippi Conference (AME), *Journal of the Thirtieth Session of the North Mississippi Annual Conference of the A.M.E. Church . . . 1906* (Jackson, 1906), 8; Hightower T. Kealing, *History of African Methodism in Texas* (Waco, 1885), 36–37; Smith, *History of the African Methodist Episcopal Church*, 129; Cedar Grove Missionary Baptist Association, *Minutes of the Eighth Annual Session of the Cedar Grove Missionary Baptist Association . . . 1875* (Raleigh, 1875), 17; *ibid., 1889* (Raleigh, 1889), 10; Du Bois, ed., *Negro Church*, 60.

28. Peter Kolchin, *First Freedom: The Response of Alabama's Blacks to Emancipation and Reconstruction* (Westport, 1972), 121; Edmund L. Drago, *Black Politicians and Reconstruction in Georgia: A Splendid Failure* (Baton Rouge, 1982), 164–71.

death in Memphis during the previous quarter-century, one who was ambushed on his way home, another attacked while he was inside his church at the end of a service, and the third killed as he visited people in the neighborhood. For some preachers the rewards of their calling were indeed hard-earned.[29]

By the close of the nineteenth century the status of the preacher was showing signs of decline. It was a development that the American Baptist Home Mission Society had predicted in 1866, when it concluded that "if we devote ourselves to educating the youth, neglecting the education of their preachers, we elevate the youth to an intellectual plane from which they shall look down upon the meager attainments of their present religious leaders." The ministers greatly influenced the attitudes of the people. The Chicago *Defender* described ministers as occupying positions of "moral, spiritual and, in a sense, the social leadership of the Race. They have the ear of the people even more than a newspaper, for they reach a multitude of people who neither read nor think." But in 1903 Du Bois noted that "the old leaders of Negro opinion . . . are being replaced by new." The old preachers did not command the respect they once elicited, and the younger ones did not enjoy the loyalty the old generation had had because they were not patriarchal figures.[30]

The increasingly frequent criticisms directed at the ministry also explained the change in preachers' status. The generation of educated blacks who had grown up since the Civil War refused to accept the old preachers, whom they regarded as superstitious and backward, as leaders. The critics were not irreligious; they were disgusted by the emotionalism, ignorance, and occasional moral lapses of the churches' old leaders. They preferred ministers who "did not indulge in moaning, running

29. Washington *Bee,* November 8, 1890; White, *No Quittin' Sense,* 149–51; Thomas O. Fuller, *The Story of the Church Life Among Negroes in Memphis, Tennessee, for Students and Workers, 1900–1938* (Memphis, 1938), 16.

30. F. M. Gaebel to G. L. Eberhart, May 25, 1867, in Freedmen's Bureau Records; Washington *Bee,* November 2, 1889; Benjamin P. Mays and Joseph W. Nicholson, *The Negro's Church* (New York, 1933), 50–51; Robert T. Kerlin, ed., *The Voice of the Negro, 1919* (New York, 1968), 176; Du Bois, *Souls of Black Folk,* 80; *Census of Religious Bodies: 1906,* I, 91–92; *Christian Recorder,* October 15, 1870; Emma Lou Thornbrough, *T. Thomas Fortune: Militant Journalist* (Chicago, 1972), 25, 56; Benjamin E. Mays, *The Negro's God as Reflected in His Literature* (1938; rpr. New York, 1968), 128–55; New York *Freeman,* June 25, 1887, February 9, 1889; Ida B. Wells, *Crusade for Justice: The Autobiography of Ida B. Wells* (Chicago, 1970), 22; New York *Age,* September 6, November 29, 1890.

around the sanctuary, and condemning all religious denominations but their own." They wanted preachers who would address contemporary social problems as well as the hereafter. T. Thomas Fortune demanded that ministers "preach less about the hell beyond the Jordan and more about the one, ever present, on this side of the river." He advised them to "make religion attractive. Let Daniel remain in the lion's den, and tell us about the sins of gamblers, stock jobbers, thieves in the temple; you will find plenty of Biblical philosophy to back you up." Ida B. Wells, one of the new generation of blacks who were intensely anxious to improve the condition of the race, condemned the black ministry's failure to provide "practical talks" and guidance in worldly matters. The poet Paul Laurence Dunbar, who once aspired to the ministry, wrote disparagingly:

> I am no priest of crooks nor creeds,
> For human wants and human needs
> Are more to me than prophets' deeds;
> And human tears and human cares
> Affect me more than human prayers.
>
> Go, cease your wail, lugubrious saint;
> You fret high Heaven with your plaint,
> Is this the "Christian's Joy" you paint?
> Is this the Christian's boasted bliss?
> Avails your faith no more than this?
>
> Take up your arms, come out with me,
> Let Heaven alone; humanity
> Needs more and Heaven less from thee,
> With pity for mankind look 'round
> Help them rise—and Heaven is found.

Booker T. Washington, who understood the influence of the churches among black folk as fully as anyone and who, as a race leader, worked closely with the churches and church leaders, could not have agreed more with Dunbar's sentiments. Washington thought the ministry not only irrelevant but also unfit mentally and morally to lead the people. In a widely quoted article that appeared in the New York *Christian Union* in 1890, he asserted that "three-fourths of the Baptist ministers and two-thirds of the Methodist are unfit, either mentally or morally, or both, to preach the Gospel to any one or to attempt to lead any one. . . . There is no use mincing matters. Every bishop, every presiding elder, every leading man who comes into contact with the ministry knows exactly what we are talking about." The critics also blamed church indebtedness and the slow economic advancement of African Americans on ministers. "It is a lamentable fact," Fortune wrote, "that our churches are always head and ears in debt, and if a pastor happens to come to a church and finds it free from debt, he is unhappy until he gets his church ten, fifteen, or twenty thousand dollars in debt." That was an exaggeration. The average indebtedness was only a few hundred dollars, and three-quarters of the churches reported no debt on their property. But it was a powerful accusation that revealed the impression that many people in the community had of the preachers, an attitude manifested in a folk rhyme: "Preacher in de pulpit preachin' mighty well; But when he gits the money yo' ken go to hell." [31]

Washington and the other detractors drew a mixed response from the preachers to the criticisms directed at them. Some ministers defended themselves and their profession. The Eufaula Baptist Association in Alabama announced a boycott of Tuskegee Institute in reaction to Washington's article, and the Alabama state convention declared that his allegations regarding the ministers' fitness to preach had been "made at the expense of the truth." Yet Daniel A. Payne was probably closer to the truth than the Alabama Baptists when he agreed in an open letter to Washington that the clergy did not measure up to the standards imposed by the educated and upwardly mobile segment of the black community. He averred that "in regard to the moral qualifications of the Methodist and Baptist ministers, so far as I have seen and known them by personal contact, I believe that you have not overstated, but rather understated the facts. I say, emphatically, in the presence of the great Head of the Church, that not more than one-third of the ministers, Baptist or Methodist, in the South are morally and intellectually qualified." Francis Grimké too was disturbed by the number of clergymen who were "ignorant men— men who can scarcely do more than read and write. Some of them can hardly do that." [32]

31. New York Age, February 9, 1889, July 10, 1891; Mays, Negro's God, 134; New York Globe, May 12, 1883; New York Freeman, June 25, 1887; Ida B. Wells, Crusade for Justice: The Autobiography of Ida B. Wells (Chicago, 1970), 22; Census of Religious Bodies: 1906, I, 143; J. Mason Brewer, ed., American Negro Folklore (Chicago, 1968), 336.

32. New York Age, November 29, December 6, 1890; Alabama Baptist State Convention, Proceedings of the Twenty-third Annual Session of the Alabama Baptist State Convention . . . 1890 (Montgomery, 1890), 21; Grimké, Afro-American Pulpit, 4; Love, History of the First African Baptist Church, 274; George W. Clinton, "The Pulpit and the School Room," A.M.E. Church Review, V (April, 1889), 395; Wesley J. Gaines, The Negro and the White Man (Philadelphia, 1897), 129–30; Christian Recorder, October 15, 1870.

The rising volume of criticism directed at ministers thrust the churches into deep and serious division over the proper character of the ministry and the need for reforms. Frederick Douglass, one of the churches' leading antagonists, had said as early as 1883 that the younger generation "demand an educated, chaste, and upright ministry.... These old-fashioned preachers minister to passion, decry the intellect, and induce contentment in ignorance and stupidity, and are hence a hindrance to progress." Charles Tanner, the son of Methodist bishop Benjamin T. Tanner, wrote in the New York *Age* in 1888, "We are ... divided into two classes religiously, the old church folks and the model church. Yet we worship in the same church." A little Baptist church in Palatka, Florida, exemplified the situation that Tanner alluded to. In 1888 some of the younger members claimed that the pastor, who had been at his post almost twenty years, was not keeping pace with the intellectual progress of the race and was thus incapable of providing effective leadership. The older element maintained that because the preacher had guided the church through many hard times and the construction of a new building he should be allowed to remain in the pulpit for as long as he wished. After the insurgents lost an election on the question, they withdrew and established a new church. It was perhaps a wish to avoid such a division that prompted Levi Thornton, a Baptist minister, to make a poignant appeal to the younger members of the First African Baptist Church of Savannah to be patient with the old preachers: "Deal tenderly with them, you men. Do not run over them because you are educated, young and strong. Notwithstanding their superstition, the people are living in them." [33]

The churches depended on the people for their existence, and the spirit of the people truly lived in the preachers. The old-time preachers and their style of ministry were still well liked by many churchgoing blacks at the close of the nineteenth century. There was truth in the statement that "the church which does not have its shouting, the church which does not measure the abilities of a preacher by the 'rousement of his sermons, and indeed does not tacitly demand of its minister the shout-producing discourse, is an exception to the rule." Education, however, was lifting some ministers "out of sympathy" with their congregations, and as people ac-

33. Frederick Douglass, "The Condition of the Negro," in *The Life and Writings of Frederick Douglass*, ed. Philip S. Foner (4 vols; New York, 1950–58), IV, 405–406; New York *Age*, June 30, October 20, 1888; Love, *History of the First African Baptist Church*, 238.

quired education and respectability they became less tolerant of the older generation of emotional preachers. Perhaps the traditional preacher was a dubious leader, but he, as well as the younger generation of ministers, "fairly represented those whom they lead." [34]

34. Du Bois, ed., *Negro Church,* 58, 64; New York *Globe,* November 20, 1883; Richardson, *Negro in the Reconstruction of Florida,* 91; Johnson, *Shadow of the Plantation,* 170–79.

Epilogue: Looking into the Twentieth Century

The turn of the century marked the beginning of a new era in the growth and internal development of the black community and a new chapter in the history of the black church. Several changes had become visible in the black population since the coming of freedom. One was the isolation of black society from the mainstream of American life. Any lingering hopes spawned by the idealism of Reconstruction that race would not be a determining factor in building a new South evaporated with the proscriptions of Jim Crow. Blacks were clearly on their own, and they would have to make their way on their own resources. Another was that the second generation since emancipation, better educated than the freedmen and forming a larger middle and upper class, had become the leaders, breadwinners, and homemakers of the black community. The level of literacy, which had been only about 5 percent in the slave population, stood at about 70 percent by the end of the century, and economic progress could be measured in the steadily increasing numbers of businessmen, professionals, skilled industrial laborers, and landowners among the ranks of southern blacks. Also, a population that historically had been overwhelmingly southern and rural was migrating in considerable numbers to the towns and cities of the South and by World War I would flood into the industrial cities of the North. The urban migration placed many strains on black people, separating them from their rural roots and, particularly in the South, encumbering them with an oppressive burden of segregation, sharpening social differences, and fragmenting social institutions. The influx of blacks into the cities also increased the racial tension that periodically exploded into lynchings and race riots. But despite the intense hostility that southern blacks encountered in their contacts with the white world, they had worked ever since emancipation to raise themselves up out of the desolation of slavery and build autonomous and relatively secure lives for themselves. The large number of

333

schools and colleges offering education to black students, coupled with hard work and an enormous amount of determination and perseverance, had produced the "talented tenth" that William E. B. Du Bois regarded as essential to continued race progress. A solid middle class of shopkeepers and skilled workers had achieved respectability and a measure of economic security by the beginning of the new century.[1]

These changes carried important implications for the church and its leaders, particularly the old, unlettered preachers. Intellectuals and well-to-do business and professional people, as well as middle-class individuals struggling for respectability, increasingly evinced an intolerance of the older generation of preachers who had for so long been leaders in their communities but now symbolized the past rather than the future. They were embarrassed by the clergy's lack of education and by the uncontrolled emotionalism that often substituted for a solid scriptural exegesis in Sunday sermons. And their business sense was offended by the preachers' seeming obsession with raising money to build grand new churches that were monuments to their ministries and to their extraordinary skills as organizers and promoters but far exceeded the needs and means of their congregations. Some of the most damning criticisms came from inside the church, from the increasing number of educated ministers, from members of the large, urban, "high-toned" congregations, and from denominational leaders. "The average Negro preacher is a curse to his race," exclaimed Bishop Henry M. Turner. Another commentator stated the opinion that ministers "seem to have the idea that their only mission in life outside of making a loud noise in church service is to raise money for themselves." Even the church as an institution came under censure. A conference of scholars, businessmen, and professionals meeting under the auspices of Atlanta University in 1903 concluded that the church needed "cleansing, reviving, and inspiring." Another conference a decade later reached a similar conclusion: "The majority of Negro churches remain . . . financial institutions catering to a doubtful round of semi-social activities." By the turn of the century, the church had clearly lost much of its status in black society.[2]

1. U.S. Bureau of the Census, *Negro Population in the United States, 1790–1915* (Washington, D.C., 1918), 35, 405.

2. John Dittmer, *Black Georgia in the Progressive Era, 1900–1920* (Urbana, 1977), 51–52; William E. B. Du Bois, ed., *The Negro Church: Report of a Social Study Made Under the Direction of Atlanta University* (Atlanta, 1903), 208; William E. B. Du Bois and A. G. Gill, eds., *Manners and Morals Among Negro Americans,* Atlanta University Publications No. 18 (Atlanta, 1913), 7, 110.

Interdenominational rivalry and bickering among the leaders of the larger organizations further discredited the church in the eyes of many blacks. The Methodists continued to talk about a union, but instead of doing anything they complained about one another, and they overbuilt churches in an attempt to enhance their standing in the community. Dissension within the National Baptist Convention tore at the organization's seams and led to expressions of disgust from outside the church over the petty jealousies and senseless squabbling that kept it in a state of turmoil and were an embarrassment to the race. The convention's founders had intended to foster unity and coordinated effort among Baptists by forming a national organization, but bitter personal rivalries and disagreements over convention policy kept the denomination from marshaling its considerable resources and focusing them on race advancement. A major controversy arose over the way the corresponding secretary of the National Baptist Publishing Board, Richard H. Boyd of Texas, conducted its business. A successful businessman, Boyd had made the publishing operation profitable, but he had offended some leading figures in the process. He ran the board as if it were his personal enterprise, was criticized for not contributing generously enough to the financing of other convention programs, refused to make the board's account books available for audit, and avoided paying off a mortgage that his wife held against some of the board's property. He alienated the supporters of convention president Elias C. Morris in 1910, when he tried to engineer the election of Charles T. Walker of Georgia as leader of the organization. Morris was reelected. His legal adviser, Wilford H. Smith, who was also Booker T. Washington's attorney, convinced Morris that incorporating the organization would enable the leadership to direct the affairs of the boards and gain control of their property. Moreover, "in the event of a split in the Convention, or the want of harmony," the convention would stand a much better chance of maintaining its integrity against separationists if it were incorporated. Opponents of incorporation feared that it would concentrate too much power in a few hands and create a denominational oligarchy.[3]

When the convention held its annual meeting in Chicago in September, 1915, several contending forces threatened to tear it apart, including progressive and conservative elements vying to influence the direction of the church as well as those on both sides of the incorporation issue. On the first day, a messenger from Georgia complained that churches were

3. Lewis G. Jordan, *Negro Baptist History, U.S.A., 1750–1930* (Nashville, 1930), 129–31, 250–51.

becoming too "up to date" in providing billiard tables to attract members. A heated debate followed during which another messenger moved to accept a charter of incorporation. The debate deteriorated into a near riot as people turned over chairs and clamored to be heard, and in the excitement several messengers came near to exchanging punches. When it became apparent to Morris that the opponents of incorporation were in the majority, he attempted to adjourn the session. While those who favored incorporation sang their closing hymns, some of their opponents elected their own slate of officers. For several days the two factions wrestled for control of the convention. The Morris group finally won a court order barring the opposition faction from the meeting hall. Led by Boyd, delegates mostly from Arkansas and Texas repaired to a local church and organized the National Baptist Convention of America.[4]

The raucous Chicago meeting fractured the largest of the black church organizations and deepened an already significant erosion of popular support for church leaders. Leaders both inside and outside the church had dreaded such a display because it reinforced white prejudices against the entire race. Referring to the participants in the convention's disturbance as "a bunch of greasy disorganizers," the Chicago *Defender* angrily prophesied that the meeting would go down "as one of the most disgraceful, and, to the mind of the layman, disgusting affairs that was ever pulled off in Chicago."[5]

When it lost standing within the community, the church faced powerful challenges to its political leadership in the midst of mounting racial discrimination. The church came to be seen more and more as a social rather than a political institution. The developing ideology of accommodationism permeated the black South, including the church, and made militant protest not an option in response to discrimination. The absence of expressions of outrage at intensified racial discrimination and violence was evidence of the church's increasingly apolitical stance. The church had never been in the forefront of militant radicalism, even during slavery. The Gospel of Deliverance that filled the slaves' church had been more subversive than confrontational. Its greatest contribution to antislavery resistance had been to instill in Christian slaves a faith in providential justice, which had encouraged them to resist the system by outlasting it. The church had been messianic only as it stressed the parallel

4. Chicago *Defender*, September 18, 1915; Washington *Bee*, September 18, 1915.
5. Chicago *Defender*, September 18, 1915.

between God's directing Moses to lead the Jews out of their bondage and the surety that he would see that they were delivered from enslavement. With the notable exception of Nat Turner, it had inspired no frontal assaults against the slave regime. After emancipation, churchmen, although very active politically, generally took an accommodating position on issues that related to race advancement because they believed that by loving their enemies they could make most of them their friends, and God's justice and their own hard work would take care of everything else. Despite the frustrations of Reconstruction and the rising power of Judge Lynch and Jim Crow, few people had felt betrayed by their faith. By the end of the nineteenth century, they had made significant progress on several fronts. For an ever-growing portion of the population, the new Moses was Booker T. Washington and the gospel was his pragmatic message of accommodation, self-help, and racial separation. From his headquarters in Tuskegee, Alabama, Washington preached the message of salvation through hard work, frugality, the development of the skills of self-reliance, and acceptance of racial separation and political disfranchisement. He argued in public that political activity and racial integration were secondary in importance to learning how to become successful businessmen, farmers, and homemakers. Acceptance by a bourgeois society would come when black peasants and unskilled laborers joined the ranks of the bourgeoisie. These middle-class values took root in black society, permeated the church, and made it even more conservative and accommodationist.

In the past, some elements within the church had protested against discrimination, and a few leaders, most visibly Henry M. Turner, assumed the demeanor of Christian warriors. After his expulsion from the Georgia legislature, Turner had used his position in the church and the Old Testament principle of retributive justice to wage a holy war against white racism, and he did it from deep within the crucible of the South, not from a more secure base in the North. Southern newspapers, he wrote, had teemed with slander against him, accusing him of almost every crime imaginable. "I have been arrested and tried on some of the wildest charges and most groundless accusations ever distilled from the laboratory of hell. Witnesses have been paid as high as four thousand dollars to swear me into the penitentiary; white preachers have sworn that I tried to get up insurrections . . . a crime punishable with death; and all such deviltry has been resorted to for the purpose of breaking me down, and with all they have not hurt a hair of my head." Turner finally turned his back on America and led the campaign for emigration to Africa, but he refused to turn his cheek in submission to racism. By the beginning of the century, the back-to-Africa movement had failed for lack of support, but Turner continued to demand an immediate and complete end to racial discrimination. He was no friend of the Tuskegee group that supported Booker T. Washington or of their accommodationist platform. Washington, for his part, spoke disdainfully of Turner, in private referring to him as "a silly, senile old man." When Turner died in 1915, the same year as Washington, other southern churchmen such as William Jefferson White, editor of the *Georgia Baptist,* demanded radical change in social and political affairs, but there was no one who possessed Turner's charisma or enjoyed his visibility. Other radical clerics such as the AME's Reverdy Ransom were based in the North.[6]

Many other ministers expressed opposition to discrimination and lynchings, but they usually did so circumspectly. In attempting to defend their self-respect and that of their congregations, they searched for some ground on which they could stand in Christian brotherhood with whites. The Alabama Baptist State Convention, for example, "emphatically" condemned discrimination in railroad accommodations, and a Florida Baptist, responding to whites' assertion that the violent attacks against blacks were a justifiable punishment for the crime of rape, said that "lynching is worse entail for a generation to leave posterity than raping." But such protestations were usually muted or dressed in assurances that blacks did not desire social intimacy. "We have never urged social equality as a prerequisite to Negro greatness," Emanuel K. Love insisted. "We think it rather [more] damaging than helpful to the race." Faith in God was still paramount in the church's response to discrimination. As one minister put it, "God's operations may be slow in the incipience, but the triumph is sure and not distant." Wesley J. Gaines instructed his followers to be patient, explaining that "when by the slow but potent process" of education "we shall be qualified for the best and most intelligent citizenship, then he will assert himself with power, and contribute his share in controlling and shaping the legislation of the country."[7]

6. Carter G. Woodson, *The History of the Negro Church* (Washington, D.C., 1972), 211; Dittmer, *Black Georgia,* 180; Washington to Abraham Grant, Tuskegee, Alabama, January 3, 1908, in Carter G. Woodson Collection, Manuscript Division, Library of Congress.

7. John Michael Matthews, "The Dilemma of Negro Leadership in the New South: The Case of the Negro Young People's Congress of 1902," *South Atlantic Quarterly,* LXXIII

The muted political protest that emanated from the church during the dark days around the turn of the century and the highly emotional and spiritual quality of black folk religion lure one to conclude that the institution acquiesced in the hardening policies of discrimination and oppression and then encouraged the congregations to concentrate on developing their personal respectability or to escape from their hardships into the intoxication of an otherworldly doctrine. To arrive at such a judgment, however, one has to discount the theme of protest that runs clearly and powerfully, albeit subtly, through the history of the popular denominations, the uplifting effect of African-American religion and black nationalism as they existed within the church, and the community support services that the church provided and that helped black citizens overcome the array of obstacles that whites erected against their progress. After emancipation, the leaders of the independent churches vigorously promoted the interests of the race and criticized any person or group that discriminated against blacks or, like the Colored Methodist Episcopal church, acquiesced in it. During Reconstruction, the church and its leaders refused to give up the rights they attached to freedom. At great peril, the churches organized and conducted Republican party meetings, encouraged their members to vote, took the leading role in representing the freedmen in government, and tried to make the best deals they could in necessary coalitions with whites.[8]

Most ministers adopted more conservative strategies than Henry Turner did in dealing with the political issues of the time, but that is not to say that their goals were any less ambitious because they understood and accepted the reality of overwhelming and violent white power. Turner acknowledged that it would be suicidal for blacks to dare whites to use their power against them. When, from the relative security of his Phila-

---

(1974), 130–43; (Alabama) Colored Baptist State Convention, *Minutes of the Sixteenth Annual Session of the Colored Baptist State Convention . . . 1883* (Montgomery, 1883), 15; *National Baptist Magazine*, I (January, 1894), 6–11; Emanuel K. Love, *A History of the First African Baptist Church of Savannah from Its Organization, January 20th, 1788, to July 1st, 1888* (Savannah, 1888), 207, 321; Ray Stannard Baker, *Following the Color Line: American Negro Citizenship in the Progressive Era* (2nd ed.; New York, 1964), 20; *A.M.E. Church Review*, V (July, 1888), 46; Wesley J. Gaines, *The Negro and the White Man* (Philadelphia, 1897), 175.

8. August Meier, *Negro Thought in America, 1880–1915* (Ann Arbor, 1963), 218–24; I. A. Newby, *Black Carolinians: A History of Blacks in South Carolina from 1895 to 1968* (Columbia, 1973), 146–50; Dittmer, *Black Georgia*, 167.

delphia office, Benjamin T. Tanner advised southern blacks to remain in
the South and struggle for their rights, Turner lashed out, stressing the
risks in being black and being too assertive or militant. "Oh what a brave
man he is," Turner replied. "Would to God we had him here just long
enough to teach us that lesson by example. I think the buzzards would
have a good bait the next day." In Mississippi, and probably elsewhere,
blacks accepted the reality of a literacy test for voting, but some suggested trying to subvert it by a campaign in which the churches and Sunday schools would participate in teaching people to be literate enough to
qualify to vote. The mass churches also actively encouraged people to
escape oppression and find economic opportunity by migrating to the
industrial cities of the North.[9]

Historically, the independent churches had stood as symbols of most
southern blacks' desire to be separate from whites, an aspiration that derived from their feeling that they were better Christians than whites. The
white churches were blighted by racism. During slavery, they had offered
a rationalization for the slave system; since emancipation, they had practiced racial discrimination inside their sanctuaries and accepted it outside. The white churches denied the brotherhood of man and ignored the
fact that while on earth Christ had chosen to live among the masses. In a
message to the Convention of Colored Men in Louisville in 1883, Frederick Douglass remarked that not even white churchgoers, who "profess
to follow the despised Nazarene . . . have yet conquered this feeling of
color madness." The New York *Age* proclaimed that "there is enough
color prejudice in the white churches of the United States to eternally
damn the whole of them." Editor T. Thomas Fortune protested that
whites who attended black church services were not segregated or otherwise humiliated as blacks were in white churches. Black congregations
seemed to go out of their way to be hospitable to whites. "We have noticed," he said, "especially in the South, that when a white man or woman
visits a colored church all the church authorities break their necks in an
effort to find such a white person the very best and most prominent seats
in the church." Church officials echoed those assertions. According to the
Christian Recorder, the Christian religion of whites was merely "organized hypocrisy." T. McCants Stewart, a lawyer and an AME minister,
drew a clear distinction between African-American religion and white

9. *Christian Recorder,* January 14, 1875; Neil R. McMillen, *Dark Journey: Black
Mississippians in the Age of Jim Crow* (Urbana, 1989), 53–54.

Christianity when he said that it was "hard for a Negro, under certain conditions, to be a Christian. It is not easy for him to believe in humanity. Christianity is an institution which belongs almost exclusively to the whites." Benjamin T. Tanner pointed out that it had been an immoral caste system in the white church that had driven Richard Allen and his followers out and led them to found the African Methodist Episcopal church one hundred years before. "A century quite has passed away, and . . . the *status quo* can scarcely be said to have changed a hair's breadth." Thus "the necessity for independent colored church organizations still exists." It may be argued that separatism kept blacks isolated from the progress that was taking place in the country during the nineteenth century, but that view has been nurtured by the protests of the modern civil rights movement and does not reflect the situation that most southern blacks faced at the turn of the century. Integration was not a realistic goal in turn-of-the-century race relations; the most likely alternatives to voluntary separatism, as Howard N. Rabinowitz has observed, were either forced segregation or total exclusion from jobs, decent housing, and social institutions.[10]

Forced segregation was a reality in the Presbyterian Church in the United States of America, the northern Presbyterian church, after the turn of the century. A union of the PCUSA and the Cumberland Presbyterian church in 1905 signaled the northern church's acceptance of the Cumberland church's policy of strict racial separation. Francis J. Grimké, the outstanding pastor of Washington's elite and mostly black Fifteenth Street Presbyterian Church, saw the merger as a denial of inherent racial equality. Writing to a white clergyman who supported the union, he said that whites were an enigma; they said one thing and did another: "Sometimes you seem very religious, especially when you are talking about Home Missions, and Foreign Missions, and about the advancement of the Master's Kingdom in general; but when it comes to the concrete test of your religion, as seen in your dealings with the vexed race question in this

---

10. *Christian Recorder,* June 3, 1865, November 16, 1876; Philip S. Foner, ed., *The Life and Writings of Frederick Douglass* (5 vols.; New York, 1950–58), IV, 379–80; New York *Freeman,* November 20, 1886, August 20, 1887, June 28, 1890; William E. B. Du Bois, "Religion in the South," in *The Negro in the South: His Economic Progress in Relation to His Moral and Religious Development,* ed. Booker T. Washington and W. E. B. Du Bois (Philadelphia, 1907), 175–77; Washington *Bee,* May 21, 1892; *A.M.E. Church Review,* II (July, 1885), 87–88; Howard N. Rabinowitz, *Race Relations in the Urban South, 1865–1890* (New York, 1978), 329–39.

country, you seem to be nothing but a set of hypocrites, utterly destitute of the spirit of Christ." Despite Grimké's protests, the church proceeded to segregate its black congregations.[11]

Operating in a milieu of materialism and the values of market capitalism, the independent black churches represented black enterprise. The business aspects of the churches, their property holdings, and their very size helped blacks to develop confidence in their ability to make their own way in a competitive world. The churches were the largest and most powerful institution in the black community. By 1890 they owned property worth $26.6 million. Those buildings, most of which were meeting-houses, increased in value to $56.6 million by 1906. The National Baptist Convention's publishing board owned facilities that were worth $100,000 by 1900. And between 1896 and 1900 African Methodists raised $1.7 million for general church operations. The National Baptist Convention was the largest black organization in the world. In 1901 its president, Elias C. Morris, told the organization that "ownership and control of our institutions serves to inspire the great Baptist family and to give substantial standing among other religious bodies." It also demonstrated the race's competence in managing its own affairs, helped to promote the spirit and the skills of self-reliance, and set "an example worthy of immulation [sic] of unborn generations." During the Zion Methodists' centennial celebration, Booker T. Washington noted that "one hundred years in the life of a religious body born in poverty, in the midnight of bondage, amidst the throes and groans of slavery . . . furnishes an occasion for supreme thanksgiving and congratulations."[12]

The church's popularity and its ability to respond effectively to the people's many needs are evident in its growth throughout a period of mounting intimidation from without and criticism from within the black community. Even though the church could not protect its followers from white oppression, it could lessen some of the consequences, and thus it

---

11. Francis J. Grimké to Howard Agnew Johnson, January 9, 1905, in *The Works of Francis J. Grimké*, ed. Carter G. Woodson (4 vols.; Washington, D.C., 1942), IV, 94.

12. *Census of Religious Bodies: 1916* (2 vols.; Washington, D.C., 1919), I, 134; National Baptist Convention, *Journal of the Twenty-first Annual Session of the National Baptist Convention . . . 1901* (Nashville, 1901), 94–96; Victoria E. Matthews, ed., *Black Belt Diamonds: Gems from the Speeches, Addresses, and Talks to Students of Booker T. Washington* (New York, 1929), 29–30; W. E. B. Du Bois, ed., *The Negro Church: Report of a Social Study Made Under the Direction of Atlanta University* (Atlanta, 1903), 114, 127.

remained a valuable institution. It was probably because whites would not be diverted from the course of discrimination and segregation that black people sought refuge in their churches. The number of church members grew from 2.6 million to 3.6 million between 1890 and 1906, an increase of nearly 38 percent. The National Baptist Convention was the biggest gainer with 2.2 million communicants, up by almost 68 percent. In 1906 it claimed 61 percent of all black church members. The African Methodist Episcopal church remained the largest independent Methodist organization and grew by 9 percent from 1890 to 1906. It reported 494,777 communicants in 1906, or 13.4 percent of all black churchgoers. The AME Zion church had 5 percent of the membership of black church organizations in 1906, but its 184,542 communicants represented a remarkable decrease of 47 percent from 1890. Some Zion Methodists probably moved to the Methodist Episcopal church, which reported an increase of 62,302 black communicants in 1906 over 1890, a total of 308,551 communicants. Others left to join holiness and pentecostal churches. The Colored Methodist Episcopal church reported 172,996 communicants in 1906, an increase of almost 34 percent and 4.7 percent of all the churchgoers in the independent black organizations. The Colored Cumberland Presbyterian church reported 18,066 communicants in 1906, only 0.5 percent of all black communicants but a gain of 39 percent over 1890, reflecting the expansion of the middle and upper classes that it attracted. Congregationalists made up 0.3 percent of the total, but their 11,960 communicants were 73 percent more than in 1890, further indication of the growth of the black upper classes. The Roman Catholic church reported 38,235 black parishioners in 1906, 1 percent of the total and a 163 percent increase over 1890.[13]

In its willingness to embrace the poor of all races, the Catholic church may have come closest to being nondiscriminatory of all the Christian churches. It had tried to proselytize blacks, presenting itself as a universal church devoid of racism. In a sermon on the race problem in 1890, Cardinal John Ireland stressed the fundamental equality of all people and implied a condemnation of social segregation, something most whites insisted on and a majority of blacks probably accepted. "No hall, no parlor

13. These figures are for the country as a whole, but because the northern migration had only just begun in 1906, they provide a fairly clear picture of the distribution of church members in the South (*Census of Religious Bodies: 1906* [2 vols.; Washington, D.C., 1910], I, 139).

is worthy of existence where a man is excluded or driven to a corner because of his color," he said. Another Catholic clergyman told his Washington, D.C., congregation that "every and any man is welcomed to the citizenship of this Free country." These words fell soothingly on the ears of many black listeners and caused them to speak favorably of the church. Frederick Douglass remarked that the church "welcomes to its altars and communion men of all races and colors." T. Thomas Fortune told his readers that "in all of her sanctuaries every one knows that all, rich and poor, high and low, are on equal footing." Black folk were receptive too. One Arkansas Baptist thought that "if those Catholics could get control there would be a good time all over the world. The Catholics are good folks." But the Roman church never succeeded in drawing many blacks into its sanctuaries outside of areas such as Louisiana, where it was established in the local culture, and its resistance to a black priesthood contributed greatly to that failure.[14]

The churches continued to provide an outlet for the emotions of common folk and some relief from the tedium, humiliation, and deprivation that blighted their lives. Beyond the escape from daily toil, the churches promised salvation and justice. The African Americans' religion promised rewards for faithfulness and upright behavior; it instilled a positive approach to life, a worldview that enabled black folk to endure tribulation and to realize personal fulfillment and community cohesion. Many years after he was emancipated, a Mississippi former slave expressed a sentiment that many other blacks embraced: "I'se gwine a-go right 'long an keep a-trustin' de good Lawd an' I knows ever'thing gwine a-come out all right." It is easy to read submissiveness into such an attitude, but the vast majority of blacks were not Sambos, and their churches did not provide them with mere opiates. To look upon African-American religion as "otherworldly" as opposed to "thisworldly" imposes a far greater separation of the two worlds than black folk generally made. Theirs was a holistic and integrated worldview, not just in a spiritual sense but in social organization as well. God was on their side. Justice, like freedom, would ultimately prevail in this world and in the next. Confidence that everything would work out all right in the end provided them with the strength to resist their mistreatment at the hands of whites. They were God's chil-

14. Washington *Bee,* May 17, 1890, December 5, 1891; New York *Globe,* December 1, 1883; Arna Bontemps, *100 Years of Negro Freedom* (New York, 1961), 119; George P. Rawick, ed., *Arkansas Narratives* (Westport, 1972), 177, Vol. VIII in Rawick, ed., *The American Slave: A Composite Autobiography,* 19 vols.

dren, and the white supremacist was a wretched sinner doomed to suffer the wages of sin.[15]

Life was worth living even though survival sometimes required tipping one's hat, muttering "yassah boss," and resenting every minute of it. As a popular verse suggested, they deserved more than whites were willing to give, but they would take whatever they could get.

> Our fadder, wich art in heaben
> White man owe me leben an' pay me seben;
> Dy kingdom come—Dy will be done;
> Ef I hadn't tuck dat, I wouldn't git none.

The belief in ultimate justice, however, did not dissolve feelings of anger or the desire for vengeance, as was captured in one black man's ironic prayer for a white minister: "Lawd, gib him de eye ob de eagle, dat he may spy out sin afar off, weave his hands to the gospel plow, tie his tongue to de limbs ob truth, nail his ear to the South Pole. Bow his head away down between his knees, and his knees way down in some lonesome dark and narrow valley where prayer is much wanted to be made. 'Noint him wid de kerosene oil of salvation and set him on fire." But in the end there would be justice for all. "All must be well," in the words of a hymn,

> Though we pass through tribulations,
> All must be well.
> Ours is such a full salvation,
> All is well.

This was not a strategy of escapism but one for living and making the most of a bad situation. The churches provided blacks with a reason for living and a basis for psychic survival, despite the necessity for adopting a self-deprecating mode of coping with a world full of white power.[16]

As the Baptist and Methodist churches became more conservative, with expanding bourgeois values, their services and congregations looked and sounded more and more like the Presbyterian, Congregational, and Episcopal churches of the black aristocracy. Black folk felt increasingly

15. Rawick, ed., *Mississippi Narratives* (Westport, 1972), 17, Vol. VII in Rawick, ed., *American Slave.*

16. New York *Age,* October 12, 1889; Levi Jenkins Coppin, *Unwritten History* (Philadelphia, 1919), 53–54; Thomas O. Fuller, *The Story of the Church Life Among Negroes in Memphis, Tennessee, for Students and Workers, 1900–1938* (Memphis, 1938), 1; J. Mason Brewer, ed., *American Negro Folklore* (Chicago, 1968), 140, 336; Lewis Tucker Record Book (MS in Carter G. Woodson Collection, Manuscripts Division, Library of Congress).

uncomfortable in these churches, especially those in the cities, both in the South and elsewhere, where rural people were migrating in search of higher-paying jobs and better lives. Not only did the upper-crust congregants make them feel unwelcome, but the more sedate pattern of worship and more intellectual ministers failed to provide the excitement and sense of community that their rural folk churches did. The Holy Spirit, manifested in possession and expressed in shouting, clapping, and dancing, and the vivid images of man's ascent to heaven were harder to find in the high-toned churches of upwardly mobile people and even in the Baptist and Methodist congregations of plain folk. The latter began to lose their appeal to poor, uneducated people, who looked in growing numbers to the new holiness, pentecostal, and spiritual movements for the religious experiences that would elevate their lives.

The holiness movement within American Protestantism in the late nineteenth century came in response to the evangelical denominations' drift away from the emotional excitement of the Great Awakening revivalism that began in the eighteenth century and continued into the early nineteenth century. As Baptist and Methodist churches in the cities became more affluent through the industrialization of the American economy, they began to reflect a more materialistic value system and a more restrained form of worship. Emotional excitement, shouts and praises from the congregation, and trances and other physical responses to the stimulation of the service were not consistent with the values of a materialistic, bourgeois society and were discouraged in favor of more controlled, dispassionate, and undemonstrative behavior. The Social Gospel, which directed the churches' attention to the growing problems of urban slums, was further indication that the mainstream denominations were placing greater emphasis on the material aspects of the environment as a factor in salvation and less importance on sanctification and the outward manifestations of the baptism of the Spirit. Social Gospelers argued that the transforming power of God was not always greater than the corrupting influence of poverty, lack of education, and despair. The holiness movement reflected a theological resistance to the drift in Protestant Christianity and an attempt to keep the Awakening alive. It incorporated a high level of emotional excitement, an ascetic doctrine that substituted the reward of spiritual salvation for material success and earthly pleasures, and a strictly literal interpretation of the Bible. Its adherents placed great value on the sanctification, or "holiness" in attitude and behavior, that was manifested in old-time revivalist religion. As they always had been, they were mostly poor and illiterate people with few prospects for social and economic advancement.[17]

The Great Awakening revivals of the eighteenth and nineteenth centuries had brought large numbers of African-American slaves to Christianity by allowing them to retain many African religious traditions. In turn, the holiness movement appealed to lower-class blacks who languished in the backwater of the early twentieth-century South and were alienated by the theological conservatism that was overtaking the black church by allowing them to retain their African-American folk religion. Several holiness and charismatic sects arose within black society. They had limited appeal to rural blacks, whose Baptist and Methodist churches continued to encase traditional African-American theology and ceremony, but they played an ever more important role in the lives of the growing numbers of urban blacks during the twentieth century. Several of these groups bore the label "Church of God." Among them was the Church of God in Christ, founded in 1895 in Lexington, Mississippi, by C. H. Mason. In 1905 E. D. Brown of Redemption, Arkansas, founded the Free Christian Zion Church of Christ. It took in mainly Methodists who protested financial assessments by the church to pay the salaries of clergymen. Brown himself had been an AME Zion missionary.[18]

A variety of charismatic sects emerged at the dawn of the new century. There had been millenarian activity among southern blacks before, although seldom and without significant long-term effects. In 1889, for example, a white man by the name of Jacob Orth, also known as Dupont Bell, appeared in heavily black Liberty County, along the Georgia coast, claiming to be the Messiah. He convinced as many as a thousand blacks that the world as they knew it was coming to an end and a thousand years of holiness on earth would soon commence. He predicted that the end would come on August 16. A series of natural disasters, including a major earthquake, floods, fires, and a person being struck by lightning convinced them that Bell was genuine and ignited what has been called a "Christ Craze." The events were taken to be signs from God. Economic strains associated with the decline of the rice industry, mounting violence

17. Frederick Dale Bruner, *A Theology of the Holy Spirit* (London, 1970), 19–149; Vinson Synan, *The Holiness-Pentecostal Movement in the United States* (Grand Rapids, 1971), 165–84; Henry F. May, *Protestant Churches in Industrial America* (New York, 1949), 91–265.

18. *Census of Religious Bodies: 1936* (2 vols.; Washington, D.C., 1941), II, 441–48; *Census of Religious Bodies: 1916*, II, 290.

and exclusion that were elements in the assertion of white supremacy and that disabled established leaders, and the strength of traditional African-American religious beliefs all combined to make Bell and his message seem credible. The opposition of local clergymen prevented the millenarian gospel from entering the mainstream of local black churches, and so they adhered to him. He gathered his audiences in revival meetings of the sort they were accustomed to and preached in the exciting, highly emotional style they preferred. When he was arrested, convicted of lunacy, and committed to the state asylum in Milledgeville, one of his followers, a black man named Edward James, became the group's leader. Reports of sexual misconduct and murder associated with the craze, combined with the social and economic disruption caused by a large number of people refusing to work or to carry on their daily routines, led to James's arrest. When August 16 came and passed without the world coming to an end, the movement collapsed.[19]

The Christ craze showed that blacks were vulnerable to charismatic religious figures, and at various times in the twentieth century such persons built large followings. Some charismatic sects bore the name Church of the Living God. The largest of these was the Church of the Living God, Christian Workers for Friendship, established at Wrightsville, Arkansas, by a Baptist named William Christian. The group placed great value on divine revelations by Christian, who was its "chief." Among its beliefs was that Christ was black. Its offshoots included the Church of the Living God, General Assembly, organized in 1902, with headquarters in Waco, Texas, and the Church of Christ in God. Still another charismatic sect that arose in 1892 was the Church of God, Saints of Christ, founded by William S. Crowdy, an employee of the Santa Fe railroad. Crowdy reportedly had a vision of God calling him to lead his people to the true religion and making him a prophet. Crowdy went to Lawrence, Kansas, and organized a church. The sect believed that Africans were descended from the ten lost tribes of Israel. Its catechism, published in a pamphlet entitled *Seven Keys*, outlined a doctrine that included observance of the Jewish calendar and feast days, keeping the Jewish Sabbath, and use of

---

19. Thomas F. Armstrong, "The Christ Craze of 1889: A Millennial Response to Economic and Social Change," in *Toward a New South? Studies in Post–Civil War Southern Communities,* ed. Orville Vernon Burton and Robert C. McMath, Jr. (Westport, 1982), 223–45.

Hebrew names. The prophet was thought to be in direct communication with God and transmitted the gospel to his followers.[20]

One of the most significant turn-of-the-century black religious figures was William Joseph Seymour, a founder of pentecostalism. He was born in Centerville, Louisiana, in 1870 and raised amid poverty and the intensifying racism of the post-Reconstruction South. He became a Methodist after moving from Louisiana to Indianapolis, and when he moved from there to Cincinnati, he came under the influence of Martin Wells Knapp, a white evangelist, who, like Seymour and many other lower-class blacks and whites, was concerned about the absence of holiness in the mainline evangelical churches. Seymour, who had a background of African-American religion, found Knapp's fervent preaching and strong belief in the power of God to take possession of the human soul and through it heal the sick and disabled deeply satisfying. He was also attracted by Knapp's apparently unconditional acceptance of him as a black man. He joined an interracial group called the Evening Light Saints, which avowed the entire sanctification of believers, as the apostles of Christ had been infused with the Holy Spirit on the day of pentecost. They believed that sanctification was more than personal or spiritual holiness but had social or community manifestations as well. Seymour thought those beliefs, the presence of women in the pulpit, and interracial worship signified the pentecostal movement's commitment to equality and justice in a multiracial society.

After answering a divine call to preach the gospel and being ordained by the Evening Light Saints, Seymour returned to the South, settling first in Houston, Texas, and then Jackson, Mississippi. He became exposed to the idea, put forth by Charles Fox Parham, a holiness minister, that the power of God, the baptism of the Spirit, could cause a person to speak in a foreign language. In many West African religions, devotees of a god or a spirit would speak in a foreign tongue. This element attracted Seymour to Parham's Bible institute in Houston and became a tenet of the gospel he preached. He moved to Los Angeles, where he founded a congregation and preached the pentecostal gospel to both whites and blacks, and from Seymour's mission the pentecostals fanned out across the country.[21]

20. *Census of Religious Bodies: 1916,* II, 204–205, 217–18; Elmer T. Clark, *The Small Sects in America* (New York, 1949), 120–21.

21. Iain MacRobert, *The Black Roots and White Racism of Early Pentecostalism in the USA* (New York, 1988), 37–59.

Like the holiness and pentecostal churches, congregations of black spiritualists flourished early in the twentieth-century urban environment and appealed primarily to lower-class people. All of those sects, and indeed the black church generally, represent African Americans' response to their lowly status in American society. The spiritualist churches were set apart from the others, however, by their emphasis on spiritual means of obtaining material goods, power, and prestige, all of which were denied to lower-class blacks, rather than compensation for not having them. Although its origins are obscure, the movement seems to have been a product of the migration of rural southern blacks to the urban South and North before World War I. It grew out of the frustration and disillusionment of people seeking the Promised Land of prosperity and serenity but finding instead mostly hardship, detachment from family and friends, and white hatred. Unable to find material or spiritual fulfillment in the mainstream churches, they combined the threads of African spiritualism that were present in African-American Protestant Christianity with the polytheism of Catholicism and such mystical African traditions as voodoo into a powerful and popular sect. That merging of the spiritual and the material provides a loop that connects twentieth-century urban African-American culture with its seventeenth- and eighteenth-century rural antecedents. The storefront church, as opposed to the praise house and the traditional church building, also marks the close of an era in the development of the black church and the beginning of another.[22]

The holiness, pentecostal, charismatic, and spiritualist sects claimed approximately thirty thousand black adherents in 1916, a relatively small number. Almost 95 percent of the black church's communicants were members of Baptist and Methodist organizations. The new churches failed to attract much support from rural blacks because their doctrine and liturgy did not differ much from the beliefs and practices found in rural Baptist and Methodist churches. The people were suspicious of the new sects because in at least some parts of the South the "sanctified folks" were believed to be responsible for spells being placed on people. But when southern blacks migrated to urban areas, these groups gained substantially in importance and paved the way for such later charismatic figures as Father Divine and Daddy Grace. The Baptist and Methodist churches continued to predominate even though there were, including the

22. Hans Baer, *The Black Spiritual Movement: A Religious Response to Racism* (Knoxville, 1984), 3–42.

holiness, pentecostal, spiritual, and a host of splinter Methodist bodies, a total of nineteen independent black denominations at the beginning of the century.[23]

The church contributed immeasurably to the transformation of African Americans from slaves to free people. Throughout the half-century that followed emancipation, it led and supported the development of black community life. It showed remarkable vitality as it spread across the South, drawing in people for fellowship, mutual aid, and the powerful message of salvation. Its presence and influence in black communities were so overwhelming that black social organization took on an almost one-dimensional quality. The third of a century that followed emancipation was a pioneering period for black Americans and for institutions like the church. By the twentieth century, black society had become much more complex; it confronted challenges and generated new expectations. New institutions and leaders emerged, but when the civil rights movement began to gain momentum in the 1950s and the people gathered for the great push toward real liberation, it was the church that provided the driving force, and the Reverend Martin Luther King, Jr., and the Southern Christian Leadership Conference emerged as the front-line leaders in that phase of the march from slavery to freedom.

23. Charley C. White, *No Quittin' Sense* (Austin, 1969), 120.

Index